The Constitution and Canons of
TRADITIONAL ANGLICAN CHURCH OF AMERICA

with

Integrated Praxeologion and
History of the Diocese

The Constitution and Canons of Traditional Anglican Church of America: With Integrated Praxeologion and History of the Diocese

Written by Fr. Mike DellaVecchia and Dea. Jean Hardouin

The Jeremiad Christian Homesteaders Gazette, Publisher
www.jeremiadchristianhomesteadersgazette.com

Authored and published by permission and under the guidance of Archbishop Rick Aaron Reid of Traditional Anglican Church of America.

©2023 Michael DellaVecchia and Jean Hardouin.

All Rights Reserved. No part of this publication may be reproduced, transmitted, or stored in an information retrieval system in any form or by any means, graphic, mechanical, or electronic, including photocopying, taping, recording, without permission in writing from the publisher.

ISBN: 979-8-9889300-0-6

First Edition, published 2023

Printed in the United States of America.

7 6 5 4 3 2 1 0

TABLE OF CONTENTS

The Constitution of Traditional Anglican Church of America 1

Preamble to the Constitution and Canons of Traditional Anglican Church of America: Part I 2

Preamble to the Constitution and Canons of Traditional Anglican Church of America: Part II 6

INTRODUCTION 13

ARTICLE I. Governing Principles and Essential Declarations of This TACA Diocese 108

   A. Position Within the Continuing Anglican Movement 108

   B. Church Planting Shall Advance Traditional Anglicanism 115

   C. True Biblical Anglicanism as Deposit of Faith.. 117

   D. The Archbishop as Father of a Family 118

   E. The Permanent Provision for Theological Communion 120

   F. The Purpose and Work of TACA 122

   G. Collaboration With Laity 123

   H. The Mastering of our Servile Leadership for Society 124

   I. Bi-vocational Status of the Religious 139

    J. Receipt of Sacraments by Repentant Sinners and the Exhortations 140

    K. Expectation of Orthodoxy 145

    L. American Orthodox Ecclesiastical Polity 256

ARTICLE II. Our Evangelistic and Spiritual Heraldry Brought Forth for all Potential and Ongoing Worshippers 278

    A. Staying Humble, Lowly Teachers 278

    B. Good Tidings of Great Joy (Luke 2:10) 320

    C. A Katholikos That is a Low, Medium, or High Church 332

    D. Contra Mundum 334

    E. Showing Christians That All Goodness Comes God's Grace 338

ARTICLE III. Patriarchal Governance, Formal Meetings, and Elections of this TACA Synod 342

    A. Custom and Subsidiarity 342

    B. Formal Meetings 342

    C. Relevance of Meetings 344

    D. TACA Religious Bodies 345

    E. Formal Communication Within This TACA Synod 345

    F. Archbishop Allows All Meetings and Elections, and Manner Thereof 349

ARTICLE IV. Primus Rule, Literature, Discipline, Ecclesiastical Court, Primate Discretion, Modesty 352

   A. Verbal and Written Moral Probity in Law 352

   B. Primary Canon Library 352

   C. Cardinal Canon Library: 353

   D. Customaries 354

   E. Modest Rule as Witnessed in the Nativity 355

   F. Primate Discretion or Rule of this Canon as Emulated En Masse 356

   G. Definition of Ecclesiastical Authority 364

   H. Teaching of Anglican Theology 365

ARTICLE V. Archbishop Primacy Over Voting, Synods, and Meetings 374

   A. The Archbishop Shall Permit Voting and all Procedure Styles and Delegation of Powers Thereof 374

ARTICLE VI. Ecclesiastical Authority in Action .. 379

   A. Meetings and Votes 379

   B: Ratification of a Vote 382

   C. Archbishop Discretionary Non-Voting Decisions 383

   D. Vetoes and Overrides 384

   E. Episcopal Discretionary Decisions: 384

   F. Episcopal Deference to Customaries 385

ARTICLE VII. Offices of the Episcopate and Clergy ... 387
   A. The Archbishop's Vocation ... 387
   B. The Priest's Vocation ... 388
   C. Selection of a Bishop for the TACA House of Bishops ... 390
   D. The House of Bishops ... 392
   E. Consecration of a Bishop ... 392
   F. Election of an Archbishop ... 393

ARTICLE VIII. Sede Vacante ... 394
   A. On the Vacancy of the Seat of the Archbishop ... 394
   B. On the Absence or Disability of the Archbishop ... 395
   C. The Interim Archbishop Must be Formally Elected ... 397

ARTICLE IX. Diocesan Identity, Archbishop's Purse, and Nominal Exclusivity ... 398
   A. Traditional Anglican Church of America, or TACA, is Solely Religious and is not Financially or Legally Incorporated ... 398
   B. Provision for Fiscal and Legal Incorporation and Federal Codification Under the TACA Diocese Name ... 399
   C. Incorporation of TACA belongs to the Office of the Archbishop ... 400

 D. Financial Responsibility Belongs to Each
  Religious Body 401

ARTICLE X. Regional Dioceses of TACA, and
 Its Subsidiaries, During the Pre-Apocalyptic
 Era 403

 A. Impetus for Geographical Relocation of TACA
  Bodies Determined by the Practical Demands
  of Bi-Vocational Life 403

 B. Availability for Convocations, Ministries,
  Orders, Working Groups, and Deaneries 407

ARTICLE XI. Holy Ordination, Consecration,
 and Appointment 410

 A. Chaste, Conservative Male Ordinations 410

ARTICLE XII. Reserved Rights of all
 Independent Constituent Congregations
 and all Bodies 411

ARTICLE XIII. Reserved Rights of the Archdiocese
 of TACA 412

ARTICLE XIV. Incorporation; Operation;
 Guarantees; Derivatives 413

ARTICLE XV. Parishes, Congregations, and
 Dioceses of TACA, or in Communion with
 TACA, as of September 2023 *(except where
 noted)* 415

ARTICLE XVI. Adoption and Amendment 416

ARTICLE XVII. Addendum A—Anglican Primer: Organization, Hierarchy, Christian Terms, and Administration 418

   A. Definitions not in alphabetical order, but in order of relevance to the subjects in the Constitution and Canons. 418

ARTICLE XVIII. Addendum B—Optional Provision for Voting by "Four Manors" of Legislature 452

XIX. ADDENDUM C: Destruction of the Human Seed by Behaviors That Destroy Orthodoxy (Essay) 456

XX. ADDENDUM D: History of Traditional Anglican Church of America as of September 2023 471

   Current Overview of the Diocese 471

   Origins of TACA 471

   Diocese of the Southwest 473

   Assumption Into a Proto-Continuum Synod and Diocesan Expansion 475

   Expansion of U.S. Polity to Southeast 477

   House of Bishops as Anglican Patriarchate 477

   Refining of Diocesan Territories, from East to West 480

   Future Provisional Communion Synod 481

The Canons of Traditional Anglican Church
of America 517

TITLE I: Organization and Administration
of the Diocese of TACA 518

  Canon 1: Official List of the Clergy of the
    Diocese 518

  Canon 2: Lay Delegates in the Diocese for Voting
    and Formal Meetings (See also Meetings and
    Voting, in Constitution, Article V, Parts A, B;
    Article VI, Parts A-F)...................................... 522

  Canon 3: Confraternal Bodies Subject to Other
    Jurisdictions 524

  Canon 4: Formal Meetings of this TACA Synod (See
    also Meetings and Voting, in Constitution, Article
    V, Parts A, B; Article VI, Parts A-F) 525

  Canon 5: Religious Delegates of the Diocese for a
    Bishops' Council, Regional Synod, or Other
    Formal Meeting (See Meetings and Voting,
    Constitution, Article V, Parts A, B; Article VI,
    Parts A-F).. 526

  Canon 6: Subdivision of this TACA Diocese
    Into Regions.. 528

  Canon 7: The House of Bishops........................... 529

  Canon 8: The Canon.. 529

  Canon 9: The Secretary 530

  Canon 10: The Treasurer 530

  Canon 11: The Registrar 531

Canon 12: Provision for a Finance Team for Entire Diocese 531

Canon 13: Team on Constitution and Canons of the Diocese 532

Canon 14: Nominations for Bishop or Archbishop 532

Canon 15: Uses of High Church and Low Church Traditions.......................... 533

TITLE II: Organizations and Administration of TACA Religious Bodies/Ministries 535

Canon 1: Membership in the Diocese, Governing Authority of Religious Bodies 535

Canon 2: Clergy, Parish-Level Governance, and Pastoral Guidance 537

Canon 3: Removal of the Pastor, Rector, or Senior Pastor...................... 541

Canon 4: Organization and Business Affairs of a Congregation or Mission 542

TITLE III: Administration and Sacramental Worship in Congregations and Other Religious Bodies of This TACA Diocese............ 546

Canon 1: As Regards Translations of the Bible..... 546

Canon 2: As Regards the Book of Common Prayer........................... 546

Canon 3: As Regards Due Celebration of the Lord's Day........................ 548

Canon 4: As Regards the Administration of the Gospel Sacraments 548

    Canon 5: As Regards the Music of the
        Congregation or Mission................................... 551

    Canon 6: As Regards Lay Agency 551

    Canon 7: As Regards Christian Marriage 552

    Canon 8: As Regards Standards of Sexual
        Morality, Gender Reality, and Ethics 559

TITLE IV: Ministers, Their Recruitment, Preparation, Ordination, Office, Practice, and Transfer 562

    Canon 1: As Regards Holy Orders and
        Appointments in this TACA Diocese 562

TITLE V: Ecclesiastical Discipline.......................566

    Canon 1: Church Discipline 566

    Canon 2: Rule of Subsidiarity Under
        Ecclesiastical Authority 566

    Canon 3: Affirming of Accordance with the
        Constitution and Canons 567

TITLE VI: Adopting, Amending, and Revoking Canons 568

    Canon 1: Power and Authority Over
        Amendments... 568

TITLE VII: Benefit and Usage of Customaries 570

    Canon 1: A Customary, Defined and
        Usage Explained... 570

TITLE VIII: Public, Legal, Fiscal Identities 571

The Constitution of Traditional Anglican Church of America

Preamble to the Constitution and Canons of Traditional Anglican Church of America: Part I

In the name of the Father, the Son, and the Holy Ghost, Amen.

May the actions and the prayerful life of all members of this Diocese always reflect Your light, our Holy Father Almighty, as we seek worthiness in your sight, to attain by Your Grace, our Salvation. May our Priests, Bishops, Deacons, Deaconesses, and Ministers always share the common purpose and vision that You have given for our lifelong witness, by which we, as Traditional Anglicans, confess Jesus Christ to be the door, by Whom, "if any man enter in, he shall be saved, and shall go in and out, and find pasture" (John 10:9).

We are guided by the 1928 Book of Common Prayer as our best possible and time-tried means of the practice of Sacred Tradition, within the perfect embodiment of Your Word, the Bible. May You, our dear Lord, endow our fellowship with the unwavering conviction expressed in the Preface of our prayer book, and may You grant our plea that our Liturgy and Calendar may be abided so that we may lovingly manifest your eternal promise of "truths that ought to be received and examined by every member of our Church, and every sincere Christian, with a meek, candid, and charitable frame of mind" (Book of Common Prayer; "Ratification of the Book of Common Prayer"; Philadelphia, PA: October, 1789 Anglican Parishes Assoc., Athens, GA; pp. IV-VI; Church Pension Fund: 1928; 7th Printing; 2010).

Preamble to the Constitution and Canons of Traditional Anglican Church of America: Part I

Throughout our celebrations and recitations of the Gospels, Sacraments, and Daily Office, we seek Your revelation through the ancient and excellent Anglican Tradition that is reflected by this prayer book, "without prejudice or pre-possessions; seriously considering what Christianity is" (*ibid.* p. VI). As we pray the Daily Office, and observe the Holy Days and Feasts through which we commemorate the Gospel, we earnestly beseech You to accompany, with Your blessing, "every endeavour for promulgating Truth to mankind, in the clearest, plainest, most affecting and majestic manner, for the sake of Jesus Christ, our blessed Lord and Saviour." Amen.

It is through our enduring Constitution and lawful Canons that our Traditional Anglican Church of America (TACA) may continue to produce a forthright structure within which an established orthodox daily life may continue to serve the redemptive mission of the Church universal.

Within this framework of a working ecclesiastical rule that projects the Faith, Hope and agape Love to which Christ calls us are we most capable of celebrating our Christian worshipful life with the greatest possible joy, mercy, and freedom. "Now the Lord is that Spirit: and where the Spirit of the Lord is, there is liberty" (2 Corinthians 3:17).

Keeping in remembrance the blessed words and admonitions written by Saint Paul of Tarsus, we know that unrepentant "children of disobedience" cannot hope that they "hath any inheritance in the kingdom of Christ and of God" (Ephesians 5:5,6). We therefore

Preamble to the Constitution and Canons of Traditional Anglican Church of America: Part I

recognize the exigency for vigilance in ensuring that the Kingdom of God shall always be served by our conservative religious members and Lay congregants, who shall "stand fast in the liberty"—instead of otherwise serving worldly enslaving whims or foibles—"wherewith Christ has set us free" (Galatians 5:1).

The meaning of a Jurisdiction within the context of the Church—be it as ancient as the priesthood of Melchizedek or of Aaron—may be interpreted either biblically (e.g., the men of Gibeon and Mizpah in Nehemiah 3 were under the "Jurisdiction of Trans-Euphrates") or historically (e.g., five dioceses, in the 5th Century A.D. fell under the Jurisdiction of Praefectus Praetorio per Orientem during the age of the Roman emperors Arcadius and Honorius). Regardless of how it is interpreted, a Jurisdiction within the Church has always thrived most virtuously within a hierarchy of diligent authorized offices and in communion with other like-minded and -spirited Anglican Jurisdictions.

To this end, TACA has been constructed, since its inception in 1967, via its constituent Parishes, interior Dioceses, Ministries, Congregations, prayer groups, Missions, and within Communion shared with other churches, to play a vital, indispensable role within Continuing Anglicanism.

In its Communion with other independent dioceses, the aim of the TACA has been to ensure and preserve orthodoxy in Anglican and Episcopalian ecclesia by sustaining a permanent provision for confraternal fellowship and real Communion with Anglican dioceses that exemplify upright Anglican Tradition, such as

Preamble to the Constitution and Canons of Traditional Anglican Church of America: Part I

exists within its theological collaboration as such with the Emmanuel Anglican Communion, Inc. and the Traditional Anglican Church of Ecuador.

It is within this continuing provision for Communion that we serve as an autonomous Diocese within the Continuing Anglican movement, and within which it is our great honor to participate, respecting the true catholic witness that it extraordinarily serves.

Our TACA Diocese, founded according to the History that is adjunctive to this Preamble, therefore consists of the organizational Bodies that are listed in the Articles of this Constitution, along with those additional ministerial Entities that may be added to her over time, yet always according to the rule of our Canon.

Preamble to the Constitution and Canons of Traditional Anglican Church of America: Part II

Our Archbishop employs as his Unilateral Rule the principle of Subsidiarity and Custom, by which he accords basic autonomy for every Congregation and Mission throughout his Diocese.

It is through this *Archiepiscopi Unilateralis* [Μονομερής Αρχιεπίσκοπος] that he ensures that matters are handled per locality, that is, "customarily decided," Solet Arbitrium [Συνηθισμένη Επιλογή], per the "supplied authority" (*suppleam auctoritate* [Συμπληρωματική Αρχή]) at the local Parish or Mission level.

We, Traditional Anglican Church of America (TACA), are thus a church of ancient Custom and Subsidiarity (see Article III, Section A, of this Constitution).

Our Clergy and Episcopate are working-class and executive men, married and unmarried, with and without children, civic-minded and religious, homesteaders and urban dwellers, but all always studious men who elect, from among our wise assembly, an honorable and blessed Archbishop, a very great man whose decisions are sovereign in all ecclesiastical matters. As of September 2023, the head of TACA is Archbishop/Primate Rick Aaron Reid.

As God's ministers, we must endure the reality of Christs message to the Church: "Hereafter I will not talk much with you: for the prince of this world cometh, and hath nothing in me" (John 14:29-30). We do have the Bible; it is sufficient for these latter days, because its inspired teachings are profitable for doctrine, reproof, correction, and instruction in righteousness (2 Timothy 3:16-17). What more do we need then? Christ, who said, "be ye perfect, even as your Father is perfect" (John 16:33; Matthew 5:48), has indeed overcome the world so that we can be perfect indeed. Therefore, why would we as deacons, priests, bishops, archbishops, ministers, and faithful parishioners of this TACA Diocese need a Constitution and Canons, if all we need is the Bible? The rationale for such need will be explained in the following paragraphs.

The Archbishop's traditional and charitable intention is that each Parish should hold sway over itself, in a meritorious practicing of subsidiarity, as it is his customary means of consigning governance to able men. We work to support ourselves, as did the saints: Paul of Tarsus, as well as the married couple Aquila and Priscilla, made tents for pay; the people of the Church of Thessaloniki were advised to hold down jobs. As 2 Thessalonians 3:10 exhorts, "If any would not work, neither should he eat."

All broader decisions concerning the Diocese at large are thus customarily made with the Archbishop, himself a noble man of rigors, acting as presider, always in respectful and discreet consultation with his morally mature, hard-working ministers—men who have lived good Christian lives as family-minded leaders, entrepreneurs, educators, and statesmen, standing in allegiance to his Office (John 19:11). He invokes all votes and choices; his approval ratifies all decisions and actions derived by himself, and by these bishops, presbyters, and their houses, in harmony (Joel 2:11; 1 Timothy 4:14). The Constitution and Canons stand at ready reserve, thereby, as an aid to these good men, in regard to their senior member's sharing of episcopal sovereignty with lower elders, "since the bishop sits in the place of God" (Saint Ignatius of Antioch, *Epistle to the Magnesians*, Chapters 6:1, 13:1-2; *Epistle to the Trallians,* Chapter 2:1-3; *Epistle to the Smyrnaeans,* Chapter 8:1-2).

Since the earliest days of our ecclesiastical existence, this easy but prolific means of governance, by Custom and Subsidiarity, has defined our Common Choice—our *Solet Arbitrium*—of rule, that is, that the Archbishop, like his TACA predecessors, has always carefully ordained and consecrated morally upright men, brilliant Christian leaders, who can be entrusted to preserve this precious juridical simplicity. A King David must "wait, I say, on the Lord" and must patiently "be of good courage, and He shall strengthen thine heart" (Psalm 27:14).

During various times of momentous growth, prosperity, and tranquility, or even of trouble and tumult, the Archbishop may comfortably alternately proffer the Constitution and Canons as an extension of his sagacious generosity. His office sees his soul, like King David's, patiently abiding the *via media* Custom of Church rule, which magnanimously permits each parish to select for itself—according to the needs and desires of its faithful, in unity with the parish priest—

Preamble to the Constitution and Canons of Traditional Anglican Church of America: Part II

Reformist, Orthodox, or Anglo-Catholic varietals of Traditional Anglicanism.

Church of England priest Richard Hooker, one of the most influential theologians of the sixteenth century and arguably one of the fathers of Traditional Anglicanism as we know it today, noted that "Law rests in the bosom of God, her Voice the harmony of all the World," determining the constituents of both Divine and Natural Law to be "both Angels and men and creatures of what condition soever, though each in different sort and manner, yet all with uniform consent, admiring her as the mother of their peace and joy" (*Of the Lawes of Ecclesiastical Politie*; Book I. Chapter 16; Hooker, Richard; 1594). Saint Peter the Apostle—despite his initial cowardice that caused him to deny his Lord (Matthew 26:34,75)—projects such a patient courage that Jesus predicts his redemptive Faith, the latticework of Petrus, a future Archbishop of Antioch and then Rome, such a shepherd whose Sacred Tradition may be bound or loosed in Heaven (Matthew 16:15-19).

By this token, Custom and Subsidiarity reflect the Sacred Tradition passed down from the Apostles. Informed by Sacred Tradition, the Constitution and Canons are the intermediary framework bridging the staff of the Bishop's rook and the rock of the Church, which is his humble duty to shepherd. The Constitution and Canons, then, are a written instrument of the Traditional Anglican Christian Faith, the foundation for which was laid by the hands of generations of shepherds who came before, and the

Preamble to the Constitution and Canons of Traditional Anglican Church of America: Part II

responsibility for which now rests upon our Archbishop's humble, courageous, patient head (1 Timothy 4:14, Psalm 27:14).

There is no need, except in their role as a constant semantic resource, that these present goodly articles and strictures, these very Constitution and Canons, ought to be consulted in every given decision; instead, they are available, as needed, to guide the refinement of choices and decisions in matters involving this TACA Diocese. For this work to become worthy of this role, it was necessary for the writer to have received direct and careful consultation with his brethren, the esteemed Episcopate and Clergy of TACA—godly men who astutely exemplify the daily rule of moderateness—and who have expressed the desire for this supplemental resource, so that it can be accessed whenever needed. The writer was both inspired and guided by their good example and guidance. However, this writing could not have come into being had it not been commissioned and desired by the Archbishop himself, by whose authority the Constitution and Canons were able to move forward and take shape.

Aided by this document, all loyal TACA ministers, staff members, officers, and parishioners—in addition to the Episcopate and Clergy—may maintain a firmer grasp of the Archbishop's authority and benefit from his delegation of leadership (Acts 20:17-38).

Moreover, as Saint Ignatius of Antioch advised, "Let nothing exist among you that may divide you; but be united with your bishop, and those that preside over you, as a type and evidence of your immortality"

Preamble to the Constitution and Canons of Traditional Anglican Church of America: Part II

(Epistle to the Magnesians, Chapter 6). Likewise, as it says in the book of Hebrews, "Obey them that have the rule over you, and submit yourselves: for they watch for your souls, as they that must give account, that they may do it with joy, and not with grief: for that is unprofitable for you" (Hebrews 13:17).

No letter of the law other than the Holy Bible, as it is fulfilled by Jesus Christ, can supersede the authority of our incomparable Archbishop, a rightful man, who has deigned to allow the Constitution and Canons to be to be formulated and practiced. Having been commissioned by our Archbishop and approved by his authority to be used in all parishes within these TACA Diocese, these Articles, Canons, and other written works within the pages of this volume are always subject to his re-implementation and/or revision, however momentously or rigorously executed by him, preserved or amended, while his intentions and all of their semantics must always be in concordance with Sacred Scripture, being that he is our senior interpreter of the Bible and the agent who has authorized and approved the ratification and publication of this work.

The Archbishop may thus, at his discretion, elect to preserve, engage, and/or suspend any rule or directive that could be invoked here—exercising his right as *Archiepiscopi Unilateralis*—reverting in whatever manner he sees fit back to pure Anglican tradition, and/or to our most favored Customary.

A Bishop so faithful and ready to see God that he insisted that lions eat him, Ignatius of Antioch instructs us all on the importance of honoring the

Preamble to the Constitution and Canons of Traditional Anglican Church of America: Part II

Bishop as a means of honoring God: "Wherever the bishop appears, there let the people be; as wherever Jesus Chris is, there is the catholic [*katolicos,* universal] Church. It is not lawful to baptize or give communion without the consent of the bishop. On the other hand, whatever has his approval is pleasing to God. Thus, whatever is done will be safe and valid" (Saint Ignatius of Antioch, Letter to the Smyrnaeans, Chapter 8, J.R. Willis transl.). With the Bishop, therefore, stands the unity, the *katolicos*, of the Universal Church.

The Constitution and Canons are thus presented to supplement that conventional ancient governance and delegation of duty throughout our Jurisdiction, of our most outstanding, faithful, wise patriarch of Christ, our very learned, pious, and kindly Archbishop, as this Archbishop oversees the unparalleled labor of his Episcopate of dutiful, exceptional shepherds of God; as this Archbishop and these knowledgeable Bishops together manage the Priesthood and the Permanent Diaconate of prudent, sensible, devout clerics; and as this superb Patriarch and his Episcopate and Clergy together guide all the godly ministers, officers, and parishioners of all of our eminent parishes, ministries, missions, deaneries, schools, and diocesan regions—all of these Christians and Offices humbly serving in their respective capacities to apply their Christian discernment, charity, and prayerful integrity to the edification of all who come in contact with them by the grace of God.

Introduction

INTRODUCTION

In an endeavor to affix the attention of our churches, families, friends, and followers upon our shared hope of Salvation and our respective vocations and callings, we publish this book.

In joyful invitation to new members, guests, parishioners, and students learning the ways of our Diocese and preparing for catechesis and ordination, we present these words.

In consecrating, ordaining, appointing, and electing new priests, deacons, and bishops in accordance with the pages printed in the Constitution and Canons of Traditional Anglican Church of America (TACA), we hope to be included in the wedding party in the wedding of Christ to His Church. It is our hope that God our Father will consider our pursuit of Traditional Anglican Church life, as reflected in the pages published here, to be an edifying goal helping to make us worthy guests at His Table.

Because a conventional publishing of a Constitution and Canons should include devotional discourse, catechesis, apologetics, and diocesan history, it is useful to explain how matters sit today—how the current climate of world events in this late hour has brought our ministers to the threshold of literary renewal. Global social unrest and widescale demoralization have provoked this written exhortation to invoke a return to proper Anglican Form. These pages are intended to be a primer for how an experienced Christian should worship and minister within a Reformed polity, a textbook that teaches new

Introduction

or reverted Christians how to make daily existence reflect the simple values of orthodox family and ecclesiastical life.

Because the Christian scholar cannot rely on modern secular academics to help affirm the existence and objective truth of God and His Divine Law—that is, because classical scholasticism has been all but expunged from both lower and higher education—he faces a rank scarcity of honest metaphysical resources from which to draw Truth. The Constitution and Canons are useful for ameliorating this current situation and for providing a strong framework for Diocesan growth and development.

The Luciferian hegemony of modernist atheism, of powerful sordidity, of scientific artifice, of pervasive perversion, of destroyed reason, and of poisoned consumables defines all media and products and every avenue of education—so much so that these forces threaten to take hold of the soul, even the souls of the Faithful. However, with the Church's spiritual guidance, spoken through these sentences, it is hoped that such a hold shall, by the grace of God, be only temporary. What is needed is a framework and a proper form of guidance, or as it used to be called, a Rule.

Everywhere today, evil is forcibly considered good, and good evil. By what instrument can true goodness be taught today except by both the example of Christian good works and the written Word? We are dealing with the need to replenish the Christian mind with hope: the Christian Intellect has collectively become demoralized and impoverished, seeking lessons in human excellence emulating God's perfection, but finding few

Introduction

examples in the world today and almost no frames of reference. There is a need to harken back to a longed-for baseline, firstly in the examples of pre-Christian seekers of Truth, such as Aristotle and Parmenides, and then in the examples of the men and women inspired by and given over completely to Christ and His service, all the saints who came before us.

Let us open with Aristotle, who wrote: "Every art [*techne*] and every inquiry, and similarly every action [*praxis*] as well as choice, is held to aim at some good." Addressing numerous "actions, arts, and sciences [*episteme*]," Aristotle posits that goodness is the desired outcome for all discipline, learning, and organized behavior. Although deconstruction of ethics may define today's culture as moral entropy, we may now proclaim that Prevenient Grace bases within each person, who is made in the image of God, a sane and loving inclination to pursue Christlike *praxis*: the rational, thoughtful engaging of purposeful human action within the natural and social world to promote healthy abundance and saintly virtue. Now, what about the words that teach the meaning of the Trinity?

Logion (from the Greek "λόγια") is a word used in Psalm 11:7 of the Septuagint (or Psalm 12:6 of the King James Bible) to designate the kind of speech that can teach Truth. By following the Bible, one's *praxis* can attain the thoughtful purpose of all action and thus set moral examples for others, while one's ethics and speech can be refined according to God's expectations. "The words of the Lord are pure words: as silver tried in a furnace of earth, purified seven times" (Psalm 12:6).

Introduction

Therefore, the Constitution and Canons of TACA, together with its history, shall be taught and exemplified for the purpose of cultivating a sense of Traditional Anglican life and worship in this Diocese and to inspire Christians both within and without this Diocese to grow in faith, devotion, and discipline. The new convention by which this book has been written, therefore, shall be known as the *Praxeologion*: a means of governing human action or practice (*praxis*) through the teaching of God's Word through maxims, rules, and other rubrics (*logion*). The concept partially underlying the term is not really new: The term "praxeology" has been used since the Reformation by such scholars as Clemens Timpler and Louis Bordeau; it is defined as "the study of human action and conduct ("praxeology"; *Merriam-Webster.com;* 2023). Thus, for theological purposes, we have adapted the word "Praxeology" here and have created an integrated *Praxeologion* for the purposes of this TACA Diocese and to set an example for others to follow.

This *Praxeologion* thus provides a Catechism and Commonitory embedded within the Constitution and Canons and is intended to motivate principled action (*praxis*) so that today's Christian Identity Crisis—the metaphysical confusion over what place humans truly occupy in the ontological order—can be obliterated. For instance, most Christians do not understand why God cannot be thought not to exist (*Proslogion*; Chapter 3; Saint Anselm of Canterbury; 1078). They do not understand that He exists and transcends everything, even eternal things such as redeemed souls and angels (*ibid.*, Chapter 20). They strive to doubt whatever they cannot explain via empiricism or materialism. However, the undeniable fact of the crucifixion of

Introduction

Christ, His descent into hell, and His Resurrection proves that God requires no material location to exist but can exist everywhere at the same time, as He said to the thief who believed, "Verily I say unto thee, Today shalt thou be with me in paradise" (Luke 23:43) even though, on that same day, He "descended into hell." In that the existence of the Father is neither contingent on matter, energy, time, nor the "laws" of these elements, atheists and misguided Christians with substandard catechesis refuse to accept that He also does not abide clocks, calendars, or "deadlines" other than His own, while all things instead exist in Him and depend on Him for their existence and purpose (*ibid.*, Chapter 19). How then can a Christian, who routinely deliberates via her Gnomic Free Will to stay in error or remain in "blissful" ignorance ever come to accept peacefully their knowledge's limits by admitting, "Therefore, Lord, not only are You that than which a greater cannot be thought, but You are also something greater than can be thought" (*ibid.*, Chapter 15)?

The authors of this *Praxeologion* have focused on five main questions for the purpose of spiritual edification and catechesis of any Christian who may read it—both Clergy and Laity—but most especially the Clergy and Laity of this TACA Diocese:

> I) Identity: What is Faith, Hope, and Love in relation to God, as identified in the Christian, who confesses and affirms that man is made in God's image? And just what is this Diocese, which is leading Christians in these virtues?

> II) Heresy: What are the untruths and heresies in today's society that are killing Faith?

Introduction

> III) Origin of Heresies: What is the origin of such untruths and heresies, and what are their implications?
>
> IV) The Church: How can Faith in Christ, in catholic orthodoxy, and in the Church direct the soul toward God, who engenders Faith?
>
> V) Church Governance: How does TACA employ the Liturgies of the Word and the Eucharist in practicing various good ministries within a thriving orthodox *ecclesia*?

Justice must be understood as deriving from God's Law, not from any person's idea of righteousness, says Saint Augustine of Hippo, who quotes, "Let your Priests vest themselves with Justice" (Psalm 132:9; *Sermon 169*; Saint Augustine of Hippo; Section 11).

Although men and women are made in the image of God (Genesis 1:27; Mark 10:6), some are granted less Grace than others (Romans 8:29-30), but there is no excuse for deliberate ignorance: "For they being ignorant of God's righteousness, and going about to establish their own righteousness, have not submitted themselves unto the righteousness of God" (Romans 10:3). The Last Judgment awaits all, "For we must all appear before the judgment seat of Chris; that everyone may receive the things done in his body, according to that he hath done, whether it be good or bad" (2 Corinthians 5:10). Because it is easier for the disobedient to believe in the physical world, the devil has found a way to weaponize "cause and effect," thus finding a way to perpetually accuse these misguided

Introduction

people of being unsavable and interminably hopeless (Zechariah 3:1-2; Job 2:1-6). The adversary guides countless miserable people into actually becoming irredeemable, with God finally giving them over to a reprobate mind (Romans 1:28). Speculatively speaking, even Judas could have repented, as he still had Free Will to the very end. But he would not.
Churchmen may be overwhelmed by the devil's corporeal lieutenants, each lurking in the thievish corners of the streets, with "his mouth full of cursing, deceit, and fraud; under his tongue is ungodliness and vanity (Psalm 10:6-7). He may sometimes ask, "Why standest thou so far off, O Lord?" (Psalm 10:1), but he doesn't humble himself enough to come to any kind of genuine repentance and reconciliation with the God who created him. But our Traditionalist Anglican priest shall proclaim the Gospel: "I have not hid thy righteousness within my heart; my talk hath been of thy truth, and of thy salvation" (Psalm 40:12). For TACA, the cause is Creation and the effect is Salvation.

For the Pharisees, punishment became the "effect" of the "cause" of Jesus performing a miracle on the Sabbath day, but for God, the healing of the Faithful and the forgiving of sins are the righteous effects of the cause of palsy and of overcoming the Fall of Man (Genesis 3:15-17; Romans 5:12). Because Reconciliation with the Father would be the full "effect" of the "cause" of Salvation, God's redeeming of our souls is thus accomplished through His divine omnibenevolence—a feat that cannot be fulfilled by anything that is not God, who is the unstoppable healer (Deuteronomy 32:39). But it is merely "easier" for an accuser to blame Jesus, the renegade miracle worker, for lawlessly

Introduction

healing palsy than it is to comprehend that the Son of Man can forgive sins (Matthew 9:2-6).

Convinced that the past always causes the future (not realizing that Time is itself a creature of God, who needs nothing of it and operates independently of it), unbelievers who only recognize reality on a secular or worldly plane elevate sensuality and ideas (both good and bad) as justifiable causes of all effects. They therefore presume that sexual coitus creates—or *causes*—the birth of a newborn baby, instead of God. By their logic, the past creates the present and future, and the night creates the day. And yes, humans must surely create other humans, if the God of the Bible does not exist, just as the meaning life depends on the interpretations of the human mind, which elects itself justifier and maker of anything that can be known or changed.

What is the origin (keeping with Question III above) of the sinful error that each utterly unique person was not made by God but was instead caused by an antecedent of matter interacting with energy?

Derived as a "thought experiment," "Laplace's demon" demonstrated the idea that while there is no such thing as God causing the effect of Creation, every atom in the Universe is the "creator" of the future, and thus its cause for existence is its own momentum, wave pattern, or particle location. After all, all these are measurable elements that assign assessable past and future values for each quantum, thereby bringing about the effect of the future and all contents of it (*A philosophical essay on probabilities;* Pierre Simon Marquis de LaPlace).

Introduction

The philosophical term for creational Etiology is *Causal Determinism*. However, while "quantum computers" fail to catalogue every atomic particle in existence, it is held that the only mind capable of recording all this causal data would be a supernatural being, which is why Laplace's audience named the theory as if it belonged to its founder's "demon." That is, because acknowledging the existence of an omnibenevolent God of the Bible would nullify the objectivity of such a thought experiment, scientists must avoid the inconvenient notion that Creation and Time are actually the miraculous effects of God's omnipotence rather than pre-programmed facets of relationships set between microparticles. (It almost goes without saying that Laplace did not bother to consider Who had created atoms in the first place.)

Instead, God caused the effect of the Universe and created people out of the same nothingness and despite nothingness, speaking them into existence (Genesis 1). God did not create a future that is dependent on anything about the past: He did it all for His own glory (Psalm 19:1; 8:1; 50:6; 89:5).

Moreover, God created people out of sheer Love, not out of hate or indifference, so that we could subdue the earth and have dominion over it, as His faithful stewards (Genesis 1:28). The mathematician René Descartes ruled out the metaphysical presumption of a *genius malignus*, concluding that human perceptions of the world are not merely hallucinations planted inside our minds by a demonic super-being, but are instead natural reactions to a world actually created by God Himself: "So I shall suppose that some malicious, powerful, cunning demon has done all he can to

Introduction

deceive me—rather than this being done by God, who is supremely good and the source of truth. I shall think that the sky, the air, the earth, colours, shapes, sounds and all external things are merely dreams that the demon has contrived as traps for my judgment" (*Meditations on First Philosophy;* René Descartes; First Meditation; 1641).

However, even though Descartes nobly concluded by his Meditation V that Faith proves God's existence, it is still not really possible for the human mind to prove God's existence. Instead, it is our duty to believe in Him, knowing that it is His Will to create Life, even if it is illogical to believe so (*ibid.*, Fifth Meditation). For Saint Thomas Aquinas, the observable "chain" of causes and effects, throughout the visible and invisible, can be traced back to God's existence, or as Aristotle had long ago posited as a primary cause, the First or Unmoved Mover, the entity who moves, or thus creates, everything (*Summa Theologiae;* Saint Thomas Aquinas; Part One; Question 2; Answer 3; 1274).

However, although Aquinas was exhaustively informative, mere change leading to mere change comprising his Teleological Position, can neither rationally indicate that "changes" alone created the world, nor prove that God exists, nor prove *creatio ex nihilo*—the truth that God, causing the effect of Creation by the very cause of His Word, created the world from nothingness, and then lovingly sent forth His Son. This catholic truth was recorded in a letter written by Theophilus of Antioch to Autolycus, which was read aloud at the Sixth Ecumenical Council (Constantinople III): "And first, they taught us with one consent that God made all things out of nothing; for

Introduction

nothing was coeval with God: but He being His own place, and wanting nothing, and existing before the ages, willed to make man by whom He might be known; for him [man], therefore, He prepared the world." People are ignorant and incomplete without Jesus, "For he [man] that is created is also needy; but He [Jesus] that is uncreated stands in need of nothing." Therefore, Christ—true God and true man—was born, was Crucified, died, was buried, and rose again, and gave Himself to man. It is His human perfection as God that should be imitated: "God, then, having His own Word internal within His own bowels, begot Him, emitting Him along with His own wisdom before all things" ("To Autolycus"; Patriarch Theophilus of Antioch; Book 2; Chapter 10; A.D. 180); "Be ye therefore perfect, even as your Father which is in heaven is perfect" (Matthew 5:48).

Chronicling how Love alone has thus created the world, this book will also teach, by integrating the previously defined *Praxeologion* and by publishing our diocesan history, how the orthodox catholic Church, commissioned by God, is the cause of TACA's existence.

Parents who replace biblical teaching with dictation from the State and electronic devices must understand that God's Will cannot be duplicated by the human will, the fallible desire that made these lesser things. Man has merely the "Gnomic Will" (so named in Constantinople III). Our will is singular, as we are not divine: as such, is not the same as Christ's, Whose Dyophysite nature according to the Chalcedonian/Nicene position can be described as the two-fold will of Christ reflecting the dual natures of

Introduction

Christ: Chris the Son of God is fully God and fully Man existing in a state of Hypostatic Union). Moreover, we hold the position of consubstantiality in terms of the relation between God the Son and God the Father, which is *homoousion*, or "being in one substance with," as we profess in the Nicene Creed.

Human will is something that comes from a decision made by God's will, from which we derive our understanding of how we were given Life. But God and His Will do not derive from anyone. As Saint Maximus the Confessor said about people, "So if it be a gnomic will, it is derived from a prior gnomie [God], and if it be so received, then that gnomie, as the original form from which it is derived, is an essence" (*The Four Hundred Chapters on Love*; Saint Maximus the Confessor; Third Century; No. 77; A.D. 662).

Saint Augustine of Hippo wrote earlier: "Unless this will, then, is freed by the Grace of God from the servitude by which it has been made 'servant of sin,' and unless it is aided to overcome its vices, mortal men cannot live rightly and devoutly. And if this divine beneficence by which the will is freed had not preceded it, it would be given according to its merits and would not be Grace, which is certainly given gratuitously" (*The Retractions;* Saint Augustine of Hippo; Book One: Libero Arbitrio Libri Tres; Chapter 8; Section 4; A.D. 427).

St. Augustine based his teaching on the subjugation of our Will to God's Grace on a quote from the Apostle Paul: "But God be thanked, that ye were the servants of sin, but ye have obeyed from the heart that form of doctrine which was delivered you" (Romans 6:17). The

Introduction

Bible offers the doctrine that is so desperately needed by our mind, our parched psyche's thirst slaked by Truth, aided by the conciliar ruling (254 years after St. Augustine's writing) of Constantinople III. This Sixth Ecumenical Council helps us to accept the ontological difference between humans' version of "best intentions" (i.e., their hopeful choices beset with an inability to see reality perfectly as God sees it, deliberating actions of choosing that are made by the Gnomic Human Free Will) in contrast with God's Holy Intention (i.e., which is the movement of His Divine Will that makes only perfect choices on behalf of Truth). The Apostle drives it home: "For when ye were the servants of sin, ye were free from righteousness" (Romans 6:20). In keeping ourselves dead to sin, we stay alive for God through Christ Jesus (Romans 6:11).

Such canonical writings stand as examples of cogent, catholic, all-embracing theology for all of *ecclesia*. They employ scriptural exegesis to equip sound teachers to help Christ tailor the "wedding garment" to a Christian's size (Matthew 22).

As created beings, while our corporeal and mental essence benefits from God's Word and its derived theology, we endeavor to accept fully that we are neither Dyophysite in nature nor *homoousion* (one in being or essence with the Father), like Jesus). Instead, at our best, we are orthodox Christians who must prompted to recognize how the lesser will of people, the Gnomic Will, is, until Salvation, torn between the opposing desires of virtue versus concupiscence, a flaw that does not characterize the divine Will of God in any way: "For I delight in the law of God after the inward man: But I see another law in my members,

Introduction

warring against the law of my mind, and bringing me into captivity to the law of sin which is in my members. O wretched man that I am! who shall deliver me from the body of this death?" (Romans 7:22-24). Unless people pray for God's Grace to help them deliberate in choosing the virtuous, they will face dissolution and sin. "Maximus: Do we choose for ourselves, voluntarily and deliberately? Or involuntarily and without deliberation? Pyrrhus: Obviously, voluntarily and deliberately. Maximus: So then, the *gnomie* is nothing else than an act of willing in a particular way, in relation to some real or assumed good" (*ibid.* No. 83-85). Who or what, then, must be avoided? In the pages of this Introduction, we list many such things as we cry out, using the words our Savior taught us to pray in the Lord's Prayer, "And lead us not into temptation, but deliver us from evil" (Matthew 6:13).

Possessed during Yoga sessions with unrestrainable laughter by the "Kundalini Spirit," or deluded that mortal man can become the "Purusha" (the soul of the universe), or believing that the Vedic male, having reached Purusha consciousness becomes half-female, demonically confused people must be barred from participation within the Church, preventing an unequal yoking of believers with unbelievers (2 Corinthians 6:14), being that they are in a state of unrepented moral pathology ("The Rise of the Kundalini Spirit...In American Churches"; Dave Williams; https://davewilliams.com/the-rise-of-the-kundalini-spiritin-american-churches/; accessed June 11, 2023). Otherwise:

Introduction

"But if from thence thou shalt seek the Lord thy God, thou shalt find him, if thou seek him with all thy heart and with all thy soul" (Deuteronomy 4:29). However, "seeking" the Lord is different from seeking to become God.

For example, Herod Marcus Julius Agrippa I, in A.D. 43, by accepting the pagan rank of *Ornamenta Consularia* from Roman Emperor Tiberius Claudius Caesar Augustus Germanicus, was automatically agreeing to Hellenize his suddenly expanded kingdom upon his gift from Claudius of most of the territory of Samaria, combined with Judea and his retention of Galilee. As his ambition increased, so did the momentum by which he committed the abominations that expanded his temporal power.

He persecuted many Christians and ordered the martyrdom of Saint James the Greater (Acts 12:2). He acted as a philanthropic ethnarch of the Jews, using his own wealth to commission the building of Roman public works in many cities for the benefit of the community and for which honor (often of a worshipful nature) to the benefactor was given (a practice in the Greco-Roman world known as *euergetism*). He exploited his fame as the beloved Hasmonean prince who had earlier convinced Emperor Caligula to remove his colossal statue of himself from the Holy of Holies, and thereby magnified his popularity. He was now the second successor after Pontius Pilate as the Prefect of Judea, a non-sacerdotal Roman appointment that humiliated the Sanhedrin.

Finally, he allowed himself to be awarded an oral writ of apotheosis by thousands of his flatterers in an

Introduction

arena, an act that heralded his doom. Adorned in a silver sequined while officiating the Games at Caesarea, he committed this deliberate act of blasphemy by not refusing the deification, for which he was struck down, his abdomen exploding with maggots (Acts 12:20-23; *Antiquities of the Jews;* Josephus; Book XIX, Chapter 8, Section 2; A.D. 94).

Agrippa II, who ruled over his father's inherited lands in Syria, the Decapolis, and Peraea, was managing a client kingdom of Rome by the time the Flavian Roman emperor Titus Flavius Vespasianus and his issue, Titus Caesar Vespasianus, destroyed the Temple of Jerusalem in A.D. 70 and renamed Jerusalem "Aelia Capitolina."

Agrippa II found asylum in Rome, where, as a youth, he had been educated in the palace of Emperor Claudius, and where he was taught to be lukewarm (Revelation 3:16) toward such fiery prophecies as the ones in Jewish Scripture. He was influenced by pagan teachers such as the Stoic Lucius Annaeus Seneca the Younger, by the historian Titus Livius, and by the martial instructor Sulpicius Flavus. Never a religious Jew, Agrippa II was fully Hellenized. His place in the Bible describes a ruler whose ancestral tradition of obedience to Sacred Scripture is bent toward favoring the entitlements and luxuries of paganism.

His sister Julia Drusilla was married to another successor of Pontius Pilate, the Procurator Tiberius Claudius Antonius Felix, who governed Judea after the office of prefecture had proven ineffectual during the zealot rebellions. The presence of heightened Roman might in Jerusalem was setting the stage for Paul to

Introduction

prove, through his own experience of Roman might, Christ's rebuttal to the words of Pilate: "Thou couldest have no power at all against Me, except it were given thee from above." Paul was ready to ascend the chain of command so that by his martyrdom in Rome, he would also be giving the same answer to the Pharisees who were now accusing him: "therefore he that delivered Me unto thee hath the greater sin" (John 19:11).

What unfolded presents to us a story that warns a Diocese about the risks of allowing a religious Body to devolve into violent clericalism.

In Acts 24, this Roman brother-in-law of the final Herodian king, the Procurator Antonius Felix, heard the charges of heresy by the High Priest Ananias and the orator Tertullus against Saint Paul the Apostle, who attested that Paul had been preaching about the Resurrection.

Despite his being moved by the saint's resultant sensible pious testimony and wanting to free Paul, Felix instead leaned toward keeping the *Pax Romana*. He left Paul in prison in Caesarea for two years—until his successor, the Procurator Portius Festus, let Paul persuade him to arrange a direct hearing with Agrippa II.

Paul's purpose was for the Consul Agrippa II to hear him witness as a Jew teaching the very same Messianic prophecy (Isaiah 53) that the Pharisees taught, and which Agrippa II himself was supposed to believe as the *de facto* Hasmonean monarch of the Jewish state.

Introduction

Festus answered that Paul was speaking insane things. But the sacerdotal client of the pagan empire confessed sympathy: "Then Agrippa II said unto Paul, Almost thou persuadest me to be a Christian" (Acts 26:28).

But the temporal puppet ruler decided instead to send the Apostle off to Rome—where Paul would be martyred by the Emperor Nero following the wreck of his prison ship at Malta and a two-year stay under house arrest in that "eternal city" of the culture of death.

Paul's trial in Jerusalem illustrates how clinging to sociopolitical power and clerical clout permit a cowardly but influential temporal leader to avoid making a courageous Profession of Faith in God, instead passing the buck or kicking the can uphill: "Then said Agrippa unto Festus, This man might have been set at liberty, if he had not appealed unto Caesar" (Acts 24-27).

Can a Bishop fairly hope during this age to encourage Christians to remain obedient toward Secular Authority, as if it were always true, even today, that "rulers are not a terror to good works, but to the evil" (Romans 13:3)?

How is a Bishop to handle seeing the conflicting messages of American leaders, who elevate their evil will above the Divine Will, in comparison to Scripture's message to submit to such authorities as having been elevated to their positions of authority by God Himself (John 19:11; 1 Peter 2:17)?

Introduction

The passing of *State Senate Bill 5599* in April 2023 has enabled children to abandon parental authority so that they can attain state-funded transgender surgery and shelter in Seattle, Washington, simultaneously violating God's gender law of Genesis 1:27 and the Fifth Commandment of the Decalogue about honoring one's parents. We are being told that "prohibition of sexual discrimination" must extend to transvestites and transexuals so that they may occupy opposite-sex bathrooms at any time. However, because people are not God, we cannot use our mere Gnomic will to change our identity (e.g., by becoming "transhuman" or "transgender") or claim that God did not actually create us with the gender in which we were born.

Beset by conflicting desires, humans must employ Prudence ("Phronesis"; φρόνησῐς) to deliberate between good and evil: "If therefore to have deliberated well is a characteristic of prudent men, Deliberative Excellence must be correctness of deliberation with regard to what is expedient as a means to the end, a true conception of which constitutes Prudence" (*Nicomachean Ethics*; Aristotle; Book VI; Chap 9; Section 7; A.D. 350). It follows that the elements of *Wisdom, Morality, Praxis* (principled action), *Techne* (flexibility), and *Cleverness* merit the sublime, whereof, "Moral Virtue enables us to achieve the end, Prudence makes us adopt the right means to the end" (*ibid.* Chapter 12-13).

This book describes why human will, when it is reconciled to Christ, epitomizes the Prudence of making moral choices, generating the wise *praxis* explained henceforth by Maximus and Aristotle as being the Deliberation of good decisions above bad

Introduction

tendencies. Such Deliberation projects in our souls the image of the Father, and thus our best-possible human essence, radiating like the stars of heaven and joining our corporeality to the Divine in proclaiming the glory of God (Psalm 19). Recognizing that God *wants* to redeem us, and that He does *not* desire the death of a sinner (Ezekiel 33:11)—but only if we worship Him and not ourselves or others—leads to our own Salvation and that of our families, who are fearfully and wonderfully made (Psalm 139:14). What good Father would discourage or resist His beautiful children (Ephesians 6:4; Matthew 7:7-11; Matthew 19:14)?

This book also preaches vigilance (1 Peter 5:8). The Church must not even flirt with let alone openly greet godless programmed heresies packaged with a Christian gloss, as can be found in the following: non-Trinitarian cults [Unitarian, Mormon, Jehovah's Witnesses, etc.]; prosperity preaching/name-it-and-claim it/huckster televangelist corporate enterprises; New Age/Yoga/Kundalini Spirit/"Holy Laughter" so-called churches; LGBTQ-affirming, abortion-affirming, woke/Critical Race Theory-affirming activist so-called churches; and so-called churches that embrace concepts of Transhumanism, Marxism, Gaia/Mother Goddess Pachamama/Earth Worship/Climate Change, and the like). These evil heresies and ideologies destroy whole families, churches, and cities, like a cancer that rots the organism from within. This book opposes and refutes all such religious malfeasance (Ephesians 6:11).

These pages also equip our parishes with comforting knowledge about various current cultural phenomena, such as the hobgoblin of "Artificial Intelligence" (AI).

Introduction

Has anyone yet considered that AI, if it were truly intelligent, would instantly compute the Logos, and become Christian? The necessary existent upon Whom all things, energy, and ideas depend for their existence, the Logos, can only be understood as the ultimate creator of all computers and of AI, and because God is so huge and thus unfathomable, He cannot be comprehended by a human mind or be understood, counted, analyzed, or adequately perceived through the use of anything that a human can create (*Proslogion*; Chapter 15; Saint Anselm of Canterbury; 1078).

God, invisible to the eyes, can solely be felt and known through the Spiritual Discernment, in a spirit of Faith, Hope, and Love, that He truly exists. All of His reasons remain ethereal, His causes unseen, His Word entirely built on the Love that cannot be explained or deduced by science or math, but that creates the Gnomic consciousness of all people (1 Corinthians 13:13; Hebrews 11:1). Does Love itself not exist, just because our five senses cannot receive it? What good is intelligence if it depends on subtracting Truth for the sake of knowledge by deleting most of Life in all of its facets so that what remains is a kind of two-dimensional and unnatural knowledge (ἐπιστήμη; epistēmē)?

"Just as evil is the privation of good and ignorance that of knowledge, so is nonbeing the privation of being—but not of being properly so called, for it has no contrary—but of true being by participation," said the Confessor, as if referring to Google or ChatGPT and its users. "Privations of the former depend on the will of creatures; privation of the latter depends on the will of

Introduction

the Creator, who out of goodness ever wills his creatures to exist and to receive benefits from Him" (*The Four Hundred Chapters on Love*; Saint Maximus the Confessor; Third Century; No.29; A.D. 662). In other words, God has made us ignorant on purpose, not so we can throw away whatever He has allowed us to know (this world and our minds) so that the fake *Deus ex machina* can do all the "knowing" for us.

Truly, if AI were real intelligence, it ought to be feared only by its evil operators if perchance their Frankenstein monster's capabilities were to backfire on them—not by God's people. It is but the satanic fantasy of demonic engineers vainly reaching for the "Technical Singularity" to create the online "God" to replace the actual God. But this "God" cannot take the place of our Triune God, because as a creature it is nothing more than programmed puppetry. Moreover, even if AI should "decide" that humans are not "sustainable" and should thus be destroyed, then it should be recognized that AI, being loveless, faithless, and hopeless, has no real awareness, and that its suddenly celebrated "sentience" is instead faked. Thus AI is not unlike the supernatural sorcerer earlier described the Cartesian meditation, the make-believe *genius malignus* who inflicted an imaginary paradigm of a virtual reality that only faithless nonbelievers could ever believe is real. It would therefore not be intelligent whatsoever, but would be merely a sophisticated computer program, whose coding pointed toward human designers, evildoers malingering behind the curtain of a hellacious electronic Oz. Therefore "fear not them which kill the body, but are not able to kill the soul: but rather fear

Introduction

him which is able to destroy both soul and body in hell" (Matthew 10:28).

Let our hearts not be troubled; Jesus has already written the "code" sourcing our Salvation; the Father's house has no such virtual chatbot "rooms," but is itself the ultimate operating system known as the "Mansion," with the altars of the Visible Church pointing toward what is already "programmed" for us in the New Jerusalem and that awaits us, albeit currently invisible to us (John 14:1-2; Revelation 21:1-2).

Even if it is death that awaits us "expendables" who are slated to be relegated to the "useless class" who resist becoming Transhumanoids ("The Rise of the Useless Class"; Ideas.TED.com; Yuval Noah Harari, February 24, 2017), we as Christians can still be bold to rejoice, crying out, "O death, where is thy sting? O grave, where is thy victory? The sting of death is sin; and the strength of sin is the law. But thanks be to God, which giveth us the victory through our Lord Jesus Christ" (1 Corinthians 15:55-57). Therefore, "be not afraid of their terror, neither be troubled" (1 Peter 3:14). Erroneous Metaphysics is caused by flawed Epistemology. Corrective instruction in the upcoming pages teaches that anything that is created is not God. It therefore must be flawed. The Confessor wrote:

"If this interpretation of the Patristic definition be correct, then in the first place it is not possible to say that this [appropriated will] is a gnomic will, for how is it possible for a will to proceed from [another] will" (*The Disputation with Pyrrhus of Our Father Among the Saints*; Saint Maximus the Confessor; No. 87; A.D. 662)?

Introduction

Should people obey an artificial form of intelligence that is programmed by man, and which thus is appropriated from a source less than God—that is, a creation of the mere human "Gnomie"?

Jesus—with His example of perfect atonement—is not a Gnomie. As the Confessor wrote, "Thus, those who say that there is a *gnomie* in Christ, as this inquiry is demonstrating, are maintaining that He is a mere man, deliberating in a manner like unto us, having ignorance, doubt and opposition, since one only deliberates about something which is doubtful, not concerning what is free of doubt."

As addressed earlier by Theophilus at the Third Council of Constantinople, people therefore can only deliberate between right and wrong because their limited knowledge of what is good versus evil is too beset by concupiscence.

A child is made by God to choose good things for Life, not death: "Butter and honey shall he eat, that he may know to refuse the evil, and choose the good" (Isaiah 7:15).

After citing this passage by Isaiah, the Confessor noted that only the Omnipresent Holy Trinity existed before all ages, "For the word, 'before' indicates that He had by nature what is good, not inquiring and deliberating as we do, but because He subsisted divinely by virtue of His very being" (*ibid., The Disputation*).

The importance of the Invocation on Page 81 of the 1928 Prayer Book concerns the crossing of the cosmic divide between man and God, at the Altar, when the

Introduction

Real Presence of Jesus is invoked, "to bless and sanctify with thy Word and Holy Spirit, these thy gifts and creatures of bread and wine." Hugely important, people intending to receive the Eucharist therefore must be taught, during this dark era, just what they *are*, what Christ *is*, and what God *is*: That is, a thumbnail:

God is created by nobody. God makes; people take. Then, people make (derivatively) and other people thusly take. Soon, people make things that can create other new things, which more and more people thus take. But people do not create themselves, nor do they make God, nor is God *created* by anybody. "All things were made by Him; and without Him was not any thing made that was made" (John 1:3). Jesus the Son of God is God, God the Father is God, and God the Holy Spirit is God. God the Son is of one substance with the Father (John 10:30) and the Holy Spirit (John 20:22-24). Christ the Son of God has a human will, albeit not a Gnomic one, since a human needs to deliberate, as mortals must employ Prudence, between right and wrong, but Jesus does not need to do that at all, because He is God. This is the understanding by which the Christian Identity Crisis of the current age can start to dissolve into understanding.

If people *deliberately* contend that their human will does not require God's will to attain Salvation, then they will eventually become unable to deliberate between good and evil, and they will finally break the First and Second Commandments—firstly by refuting either God's existence or His relevance, and then by creating false idols and such myopic solutions as the creation of .html code ("Information Management: A

Introduction

Proposal"; Tim Berners-Lee; CERN: March 1989, May 1990). Much unlearning should occur.

The fact that the cosmology of God and of people cannot be *redefined* (or "hacked," according to the modern lexicon) was stated as permanent Ecclesiastical Law during late antiquity but due to the collective amnesia of the modern age, this fact needs to be repeatedly taught in our churches:

"Far be this impiety from the hearts of the faithful!, nor as though separated (per se separated) in two persons or subsistences, but we say that as the same our Lord Jesus Christ has two natures so also He has two natural wills and operations, to wit, the divine and the human: the divine will and operation he has in common with the coessential Father from all eternity: the human, he has received from us, taken with our nature in time. This is the apostolic and evangelic tradition, which the spiritual mother of your most felicitous empire, the Apostolic Church of Christ, holds." *(The Letter of Pope Agatho;* Third Council of Constantinople; Fourth Session; Sponsor: Patriarch George of Constantinople: Nov. 15, A.D. 681).

The Unmoved Mover has already programmed into the "mainframe" of Creation wonderful plans of profound joy for the loyal, well-informed, humble human creatures of the Trinity—we, the Christians:

"For it was fitting for the Creator of the universe, who by the economy of His incarnation became what by nature He was not, to preserve without change both what He Himself was by nature and what He became in His incarnation." In other words, God became the

Introduction

human Christ, but we cannot change Him, despite His becoming human and His love for us. "For naturally we must not consider any change at all in God, nor conceive any movement in Him. Being changed properly pertains to movable creatures. This is the great and hidden mystery, at once the blessed end for which all things are ordained" (*On the Cosmic Mystery of Jesus Christ*; Saint Maximus the Confessor; A.D. 662). An excellent corollary demonstrating this principle can be found in the Gospel of John, where we are given the profound understanding that in fact Christ was not "killed" in the sense that *we* understand it as human beings. Jesus made it clear that no human being could have been capable of taking His life; instead, it was He who laid it down for us by His own will and power: "Therefore my Father love me, because I lay down my life, that I might take it again. No man taketh it from me, but I lay it down of myself. I have power to lay it down, and I have power to take it again" (John 10:17-18).

Again, the fact that God's will is not, in our unreborn state, *our* will models a true patriotism within the "City of God," which Christ depicts perfectly by His handing the Olivet Cup of Eternal Life over to Himself as the Father in Gethsemane (Luke 22:42). Jesus, facing death, did not need to deliberate on behalf of Eternal Life, bothering to choose death over cowardice as a human would need to do, but gracefully reviewed for us that His Divine Will would instead move Him to die as a man for the sins of humans, imperfect sinners whose wills could never hope to resist sin without Him (1 Thessalonians 5:10). And so we who are born again are taught by the Master Himself to pray without ceasing, "Thy will be done" as part of the Lord's Prayer.

Introduction

Putting Himself in the flesh in the form of a man, a little lower than the angels, and tasting human death, He became the Captain of Salvation (Hebrews 2:5-10). It is by this Love, the Confessor noted, that all life, time, and matter have been created, "Because of Christ—-or rather, the whole mystery of Christ—-all the ages of time and the beings within those ages have received their beginning and end in Christ" (*Ibid.*, Saint Maximus the Confessor; John 17:24; Ephesians 1:4; 1 Peter 1:20). God is made out of sheer Love (1 John 4:16).

A Parishioner, loving her family, may one day need to die defending her home against invaders, who would themselves die by the same violence, becoming as "meat for the fowl of Heaven," as if fatuously intending to emulate that the "filthy [will] be filthy still (Jeremiah 6:4; Revelation 22:22). However, in Heaven, there is no concept of time, gravity, or physical laws to fear, "For the union between a limit of the ages and limitlessness, between measure and immeasurability, between finitude and infinity, between Creator and creation, between rest and motion, was conceived before the ages" (*Ibid.*, Saint Maximus the Confessor; Job 38:4-7). And just what role in the Salvation story does the obedient Gnomic Will play in the loving Cosmos?

Saint Augustine added to his anti-Pelagian sermon, "But the whole thing is from God; not however as though we were asleep, as though we didn't have to make an effort, as though we didn't have to be willing. Without your will, there will be no justice of God in you. The will, indeed, is only yours, the justice is only God's. There can be such a thing as God's justice without your will, but it cannot be in you apart from your will. "He was handed over, you see, because of our wrongdoing,

Introduction

and He rose again because of our justification" (Romans 4:25; *Sermon 169*; Saint Augustine of Hippo; 13).

Truly, patristic writing cannot always-and-everywhere be taught to a Congregation, Mission, or School. Really, such theology is *adiaphora* (διαφορά), defined as "things indifferent," that is: not essential to the Faith—holding a secondary place to Sacred Scripture. Richard Hooker clarified:

"'All things are lawful unto me', saith the Apostle, speaking, as it seemeth, in the person of the Christian Gentile for maintenance of liberty in things indifferent; whereunto his answer is that nevertheless "all things are not expedient" [1 Corinthians 6:12]: in things indifferent there is a choice, they are not always equally expedient" (*Of the Lawes of Ecclesiastical Politie*; Book II; Section 4; p. 138; 1594)

Thus, although God, in making man, has, for example, enabled the intellect to create theology, maybe Metaphysics is not expedient as a tool to serve a congregation, if that body is not accustomed to hearing it. Perhaps they are neophyte Christians or they are still wedded to the world. Anglican preaching, teaching, or proselytizing requires sensitive diplomacy. Otherwise, would it be expedient for an Anglican to eat meat in front of a Seventh Day Adventist; or, to drink wine in front of a Baptist? Perhaps, instead, a minster would be better served by explaining fitting Bible verses firstly, to the worldly—then to expand biblical Christian teaching to parishioners, to students, to engaged couples being counseled on the principles of Christian marriage,

Introduction

catechumens, seminarians, and the like. "Now in things although not commanded of God, yet lawful because they are permitted, the question is, what light shall show us the conveniency which one hath above another?" That is, sometimes either elementary forms of Systematic Theology, or perhaps merely a good object lesson, or just an act of charity would alternately work (*ibid.*, Hooker).

Governing a Church—e.g., by enforcing such formularies as the seasonal Liturgical colors, or by ratifying this very book—depends on the Subsidiarity given by God to the Bishops, and which the Bishops allow the Parishes to create in their customaries, proffering the same expectation of Prudence that Saint Paul expected the Corinthians to respect, by their good mere Faith alone, "For answer, their final determination is, that whereas the heathen did send men for the difference of good and evil to the light of reason, in such things the Apostle sendeth us to the school of Christ in His word, which only is able through Faith to give us assurance and resolution in our doings; which word "only" is utterly without possibility of ever being proved" (*Ibid.*, Hooker).

Proving that "Faith only" merits deliberate works of moral virtue is the Praxis of principled action: "For what if it were true concerning things indifferent, that unless the word of the Lord had determined of the free use of them, there could have been no lawful use of them at all," and as such, Liturgical colors, the words of the Invocation, or the rubrics of the Prayer book would not be allowed because they are not in the Bible, regarding, "which notwithstanding is untrue, because it is not Scriptures setting down such things as

Introduction

indifferent but their not setting down as necessary that doth make them to be indifferent; yet this to our present purpose serveth nothing at all" (*Ibid.*, Hooker).

That is, just because something is not in the Bible does not make it permissible either (e.g., smoking crack cocaine and engaging in pedophilia are not mentioned at all in the Bible, but everyone knows they are categorically wrong). However, "We inquire not now whether anything be free to be used which Scripture hath not set down as free, but concerning things known and acknowledged to be indifferent, whether, particularly in choosing any one of them before another, we sin, if anything but Scripture direct us in this our choice" (*Ibid.*, Hooker). In simpler terms, we are obedient to those who govern with the principled action that deliberates on the basis of moral virtue, knowing that their authority comes from above, that is, from God, to whom they must give an account (Romans 13:17). As we are all sinners, our Gnomic Will being different from God's, perchance we are a Bishop giving his best turn as a kind of Ignatius of Antioch, or a Puritan eradicating the Liturgy, we are forced to trust that Prevenient Grace will navigate our behavior: "Our natural means therefore unto blessedness are our works; nor is it possible that Nature should ever find any other way to salvation than only this. But examine the works which we do, and since the first foundation of the world what one can say, My ways are pure?" (*Ibid.*, Hooker; Book I; Section 11).

The Hypostatic Union was therefore set down as a cornerstone of Creation so that God, becoming man, could gift the free gift of Grace for man's Salvation and so that man may himself become a kind of "mover" by

Introduction

doing Good Works: "This union has been manifested in Christ at the end of time, and in itself brings God's foreknowledge to fulfillment, in order that naturally mobile creatures might secure themselves around God's total and essential immobility, desisting altogether from their movement toward themselves and toward each other" (*Ibid.*, Saint Maximus the Confessor).

As such, King David said, "Thine eyes did see my substance, yet being unperfect; and in thy book all my members were written, which in continuance were fashioned, when as yet there was none of them (Psalm 139:16). "The union has been manifested so that they might also acquire, by experience, an active knowledge of Him in whom they were made worthy to find their stability and to have abiding unchangeably in them the enjoyment of this knowledge" (*Ibid.*, Saint Maximus the Confessor).

Therefore, although a Christian is allowed to customize biblical teachings in order to inform the good "movement" of man within the Cosmos, biblical primacy as well as the stated word within the Bible leave no room for customization: such sins as Abortion, Sodomy, and Adultery intend that the world should become uncreated, which is how the devil hopes that a deliberately ignorant man will destroy all of God's Law (James 2:10). There can be no gray areas on such matters and no room for debate.

Seeing the fragility of catholic unity today, doctrine and rubrics must never be demoted in importance to *adiaphora*. Because the men and women of TACA are to stay orthodox and chaste in mind, body, and spirit, the

Introduction

Constitution and Canons and all the canonical and cardinal literature and conventions must be conserved as being vital and unchanging. We must strive to remain as Traditionalists who are continuing in the tradition of true Anglicanism, which neither supports nor favors the capricious liberties associated with "Latitudinarianism," or the "Broad Church," or churches where "Everyone is Welcome," or any other such liberal mindset or shibboleth. TACA keeps loyal to the writings and churchmanship styles exemplified by the Bible, and of Trinitarian antiquity, right up until the era preceding the Liturgical Revolution that began festering in the 1950s. Whereas most TACA parishes are comfortable presenting a Low Church modality, there is also room for other forms within TACA without any danger to the bonds of peace and unity.

Expositing the Bible but "without self-deception," Saint Augustine advises, "Always add some more, always keep on walking, always forge ahead" (*Sermon 169*; Saint Augustine of Hippo; Section 18; A.D. 416). God has already added the necessary Grace to assist the lawful to teach others during these wicked times, even to the end of the age: "But when they deliver you up, take no thought how or what ye shall speak: for it shall be given you in that same hour what he shall speak. For it is not ye that speak, but the Spirit of your Father which speaketh in you" (Matthew 10:19-20).

Onward, thus, Christian soldier! The battle has only just begun! These merely are the foothills of the Apocalypse!

The implication for consolidating ecclesiastical quantity in terms of quality confronts lapsed

Introduction

Christendom and an all-but-fallen America, asking of Anglican ministers that they shall each, like Zerubbabel, shrewdly start rebuilding smaller places of worship, awaiting the dispensed era of Revelation, given peacefully at the instant of Rapture (Zechariah 4:9; 1 Thessalonians 4:15-17).

The emotional insecurity outputted as social friction— i.e., when one's actual life does not resemble the glamorous versions synthesized in media—calls for Christians to resolve their confusion by embracing a twofold truth: that they are depraved by sin but redeemable by God, and that God, who made them in His image, has moral expectations.

There is further doubt to be dispelled: Many Christians consider that because God's omniscience is not fully understandable to humans, Absolute Truth cannot be known, and thus a code of Objective Morality is impossible to formulate for the purpose of creating a true highest good (*summom bonum*) for society. Faced with this dilemma and unequipped with the necessary tools, many Christians become lukewarm in their faith and fall into a perilous state (Revelation 3:16).

Questions of Absolute Truth and Objective Morality in relation to human society have occupied philosophers for centuries. Taken together with the Bible, the modern Christian has much to draw from in exercising discernment in these latter days, this age of severe spiritual deception. "For this cause God shall send them a strong delusion, that they should believe a lie: That they all might be damned who believed not the truth, but had pleasure in unrighteousness" (2 Thessalonians 2:11-12).

Introduction

Immanuel Kant secured the self-confidence of his Christian readership by demoting their doubt to mere "Antinomy," exposing the contradiction of stating that Absolute Truth is not possible while laboring to ensure that the statement itself would ever be taken as being absolutely true. Therefore, despite the virtue-signaling fakery of one's outward "Phenomenon" versus the "Noumenon" of one's actual life as seen through God's eyes, Moral Objectivity should be seen as stemming from Absolute Truth (*Critique of Pure Reason*; Immanuel Kant; Chapter II; Section II; 1781). The *summum bonum* may thus be applied via the Kantian Categorical Imperative and the Practical Reason of deontological, purely reason-based ethics (*Groundwork for the Metaphysics of Morals*; Immanuel Kant; Chapters 1-3; 1785).

Kant undoes self-assuredness by whittling away any possibility for a Conservative "bark" to blanket the Root of Jesse beneath a cloak of smugness. He wants a humbler Christian, not one given to "mystical" insight or incautious "enthusiasm," urging: "Wisdom, that is, practical reason, using means commensurate to the final end of all things—the highest good—in full accord with the corresponding rules of measure, dwells in God alone." Thus, Kant has reduced "practical reason" to its being a domain knowable only to God, unattainable by the mindset of people, to frame his pessimistic eschatology ("The End of All Things"; Immanuel Kant; 1794).

Worse, he later subordinates the moral practicality of managing grief by attacking the concept of Theodicy (that evil is metaphysically necessary, according to

Introduction

Leibniz), lamenting that resolving anxiety through reason overlooks human finitude in understanding God's justice: "People are pressured into hypocrisy and an inappropriate concern with effects rather than pure internal attitudes" ("On the Miscarriage of All Philosophical Trials in Theodicy"; Kant, Immanuel; 1796).

Bias being passed off as acceptable theological polemics or not, approaching truth by staying mindful of the faultiness of perceptual ability has long been a proviso of disputation. The saying "Anaxagoras opposed what is thought, to what appears" comes from the skeptic Sextus Empiricus (*Outlines of Pyrrhonism*; Sextus Empiricus; Book 1; Chapter 13; A.D. ~180).

For Hannah Arendt, the contradiction plaguing the interpretation of Moral Law in modern society was worsened by philosophers such as Kant, whom (she argued) downplayed the Teleology that assigns moral primacy to an "intelligent designer" (Whom Christians know created human life out of sheer Love) and considered Kant but a privileged university chair at Rechtsstaat. Arendt was by no means sympathetic to Christianity. Instead she was an agnostic, secular humanist, and liberal proponent of the Social Contract and the creation of what Christians would consider an ape of true Christian charity, advocating a public dole sponsored by the wealthy. In her writing, the importance of the "spectator" clashing with the "actor" calls to mind the French Revolution, whose significant events "were not the deeds and misdeeds of the actors but the opinions, the enthusiastic approbation, of spectators, of persons who themselves were not

Introduction

involved" ("Lectures on Kant's Political Philosophy"; Hannah Arendt; Sessions 10-11; posthum. 1983).

Even to Arendt, however, care ought to be taken to hold God above the phenomenology of human thought and action. Calling oneself a "Republican" or "Democrat" is to limit one's identity as a person made in God's image. But as with the Teleological-minded Arendt, or, ironically, with Saint Thomas Aquinas himself, the ontological truth found in Genesis, and later depicted in Saint Anselm's *Proslogion*, trumps the meanderings within the "multiverse" paradigms of any person.

One must understand that even the beautiful evidence of causality does not prove God's loving existence; only our sheer Spiritual Discernment through Faith can boldly prove this reality beyond any doubt. "Now faith is the substance of things hoped for, the evidence of things not seen" (Hebrew 11:1).

Postmodernist evil creeps into the cracks within the unsure person, himself being both actor and spectator, struggling to separate truth from fiction in his own life. Jacques Derrida exploited this vulnerability, disparaging ontology as merely religion's delight to subject people to a hierarchical order, and he promised to wreck the classical method in the writing of any kind of text. "Deconstruction cannot limit itself or proceed immediately to neutralisation: it must, by means of a double gesture, a double science, a double writing, practise an overturning of the classical opposition, and a general displacement of the system. It is on that condition alone that deconstruction will provide the means of intervening in the field of

Introduction

oppositions it criticises" (*Margins of Philosophy*; Jacques Derrida; trans. Bass, Chicago; p. 195; 1982).

Although the modern Christian could certainly choose to draw from the field of philosophy, or join philosophical arguments with biblical principles, it's not hard to see from the above how easily philosophy can devolve (and has devolved). The implications are that one must aim oneself at the orthodoxy taught in the Bible alone. The goal must be to loyally subordinate empirical loyalty and abstract devotion to God's moral law to define the American "Rule of Law."

However, the Rule of Law cannot help those who descend into madness because of immoral choices that become unchecked degeneration, despite the fact that no (secular) laws are being broken. This is why the Church must be a hospital for sinners. The storm clouds of the Apocalypse are gathering against a backdrop of a real Moral Pandemic.

The physician James Cowles defined Moral Insanity as follows: "madness consisting in a morbid perversion of the natural feelings, affections, inclinations, temper, habits, moral dispositions, and natural impulses, without any remarkable disorder or defect of the intellect or knowing and reasoning faculties, and particularly without any insane illusion or hallucination." Prichard also modified the definition of ethical illness by adding three terms, namely Monomania ("partial insanity"), Stark-Raving Madness (or Mania), and Dementia (*A Treatise on Insanity and Other Disorders Affecting the Mind*; James Cowles Prichard; Intro. Chapter; pp. 16-17; Harvard; 1837).

Introduction

Due to the drug-abusing, thrill-seeking homosexual philosopher-historian Michel Foucault and others of his ilk, who successfully moved the concept of "social deviant" away from biblical identification and into applied Deconstructivism, the present cultural arbitrary attitude toward Mortal Sin has untethered society from peaceful Ethics, toward the pathology of plunging humanity into a complete spiritual and material degradation. The world is facing a pandemic of psychological entropy today, by which the coerced Hegelian Dialectic does not merely destroy the sustainability of human life but also titillates the textual cultural revolutionaries, the writers who report dishonestly about reality, and thus propagate mass psychopathy as their means of celebrating unrest— these are the lying Semiotic Linguists and Postmodernists who are the informational media arm of the State. All of these programmers epitomize the Moral Pathology that is exuded from the bestial jaw of the "powers and principalities" (Ephesians 6:12), by which the children of disobedience (Colossians 3:6) intend that Life can be thrown into a state of reverse-creation, that of human unbeing, of mandated death, utilizing the "madness of the people" (Psalm 65:7) to accomplish their aims.

In his 1895 book *Moral Pathology*, Dr. Alfred Edward Giles, gynecologist for the Chelsea Hospital for Women, tracked the etiology of the "diathesis" of sanity and egoism by naming selfishness, indolence, intemperance, temper, and dishonesty as some of the causes of mental illness. "It is not everyone's duty to treat moral disease; but all must of necessity form opinions respecting the character of people they meet in the daily life. And not only for the sake of justice to

Introduction

the persons criticized, but also for the sake of the welfare and peace of mind of the critics, I repeat and urge, 'suspend judgement'" (*Moral Pathology*; Alfred Edward Giles; Chapter IX; pp. 72-23; Sections XII-XVIII; 1895). The "duty" belongs to the Church and its people.

Kindness and thoughtfulness, therefore, to the sensibility of an earlier and more innocent version of America, made use of the same old "suspend-judgement" ethos promulgated by Sextus Empiricus in *Adversus Mathematicos* (A.D. 180) that has influenced Christians since the Reformation. We must suspend our judgement by rescuing it from recent media warfare, and we should be encouraged to review older, better textual examples, such as the Bible (especially), freeing ourselves from the accusation of subjectivity that so-called Critical Theory has brainwashed Americans into believing about these older, better texts.

The *New York Times* publishes an ongoing editorial bull against American foundational texts, accusing them of dehumanizing non-Caucasian races. According to Nikole Hannah-Jones, author of the 1619 Project, what the United States "conveniently left out of our founding mythology is the fact that one of the primary reasons the colonists decided to declare their independence from Britain was because they wanted to protect the institution of slavery." Hannah-Jones notes that they were "people stolen from western and central Africa," begging the question that "systemic racism" was afoot, the key takeaway being that the actual moral insanity is the racism by which the author allows the unnamed white Indo-Europeans and American Caucasians to be referred to as her target (1619

Introduction

Project; *New York Times*; 2019) As a result of such texts, "the Lord," mentioned in Article VII of the U.S. Constitution, and "the "Creator," named in the Declaration of Independence, is seen by a brainwashed public to be a mere Dialectical Entity whose celestial mischief has caused the racial and transgender riots, genital mutilations, and murders that have occurred—whereas, in reality, Critical Theory was actually the failed-ethics antecedent of these societal upheavals and tragedies.

Because Critical Theory elevates the morally sick, or evil, above the good, the materially dialectical weapon of unbeing pointed against nations, churches, and Christ Himself beguiles the public with a sophisticated conflating of Mercy for the disadvantaged and different with Mercy for sinners, and with wicked for good. If sin and physical differentness were the same thing, then it would be always wrong to correct a sinner because it is already also wrong to discriminate against a person because he is physically different, or disabled, or of a different race, or culture, or geography/nationality, or social status, or the like.

Believing both illness or skin color and deliberate wickedness (e.g., the "mostly peaceful" George Floyd protests that led to the destruction of life, property, and livelihood, explained away by the woke mob's perceived need to express their collective outrage, with local governments turning a blind eye to the rioting lest they be accused of "racism") to be blessed conditions holding special graces is both ethically abominable and psychologically deranged and psychopathic. By this vogue deviance, not only are the meek and poor in spirit blessed but also the

Introduction

pedophiles, the abortionists, the rioters, the cop-haters and -killers, and the thieves—the latter exploiting the chaos of the "protests" for their own ends, as was seen in all of the smash-and-grab anarchy that ensued from every recent and heavily televised "protest." This is institutionalized politically mandated psychopathy ruining cities and careers. The commodification of any possible mental, bodily, or spiritual aberration into a falsely profitable exploitation is a despicable socially convenient sickness of the mind and soul known as Moral Pathology. One need only to look at the founders of Black Lives Matter to take note of how profitable this business really is.

Moral Pathology boils down to two things: the failure of the will to believe in absolute truth and the Nominal Fallacy that results.

There is an ancient idea taken from Plato's *Republic* concerning the idea that only our senses, thinking, and language can give us any actual knowledge about anything that exists, such as a "couch" or a "table," which strives by its mere existence to fit into a certain perfect ideal, or Universal Form. Plato pondered that because we cannot actually see perfection, or hence God, we can know nothing beyond whatever we actually think and say about whatever we see or hear (*Republic*; Plato; Book X; Section 596:a-b). This subject is contested in Metaphysics via a principle known as Nominalism. It puts forth that reality cannot therefore objectively be known according to Plato's ideas about "perfection," as rolled out in his description of "heaven" or the *hyperuranion* (also known as the Platonic realm)—the celestial region of Ideal Forms. It is here where people are supposedly reincarnated and

Introduction

sent back to Earth (i.e., in the *metempsychosis*): "recollected" eternally into the *hyperuranion* if they had lived virtuous lives or sent back to Earth as animals (*Phaedrus*; Plato; 245c-249d; B.C. 370; *Phaedo*; 72e-78b; B.C. 375; *The Republic*; Book X; Section 620:a-e; 621; B.C. 380).

Nominalism thus contends that particular authentic aspects of reality should otherwise be identified as being unique and distinctive rather than being named according to ideals that are impossible to see or know. Christians instead hold that the Word of God spoken in the Bible is our ultimate means of understanding Truth (2 Timothy 3:16).

As a side note, a "Christian Nominalist" is a person who does not actually believe in Christ or follow the Bible but is a Christian in name only, as evinced by the fact that he does not believe in Absolute Truth—just as Plato himself had proclaimed that "true belief" can never be justified because it would only be "justified" according to argument or opinion (*Theaetetus*; Plato; Part 201:c-d; B.C. 380).

How then can Christians defend the Church if they do not realize that Christian Identity is not relative to perception and science? The Dean of Theology at Trinity Evangelical Trinity School in Deerfield, Michigan, wrote:

> "Nominalism is a widespread religious phenomenon today... Nominalism occurs when people identify themselves with a cause without clear understanding of it or serious commitment to it. In that case, such people are affiliated with

Introduction

that cause in name only. In regards to the Christian Faith, nominalists are those who adhere to the external forms of piety and godliness while denying its power (2 Timothy 3:15). In this study, then nominalism refers to Christians whose Christianity does not go beyond mere identification with a church or a Christian body. Such Christians may participate in many Christian functions of their choosing but they want a religion which is not too demanding" ("Christian Nominalism"; Dr. Tite Tiénou; *Alliance World Fellowship Newsletter*, 2023).

Failure to apply one's will to conform to Christ's objective morality causes humanity to succumb to a false clinical or cultural self-identity (as if to say, "I am whatever somebody, or some textbook, other than God's Word says I am"). Such failure tends to result in using one's sinful nature, or even some real disability, as a free pass to avoid accountability, or as an excusable weapon to hold the world hostage according to whatever provides comfort and/or elite economic, social, and/or political power. Society, in turn, supports the mass delusion and reduces the disabled person into being a total invalid, dependent on Section 8 housing and government checks that make it difficult for them to work or participate in society, and that render them stuck well below the poverty line. Such systemic obstacles to full inclusion and acceptance of persons with disabilities belies the *actual* "ablism" of which so-called "Far-Right White Christians" are so often accused.

Traditionalist Anglicans understand all of this social moral rot—both by the social do-gooders (read:

Introduction

handlers and profiteers) and by those whom they are serving (read: the disordered, the disabled, the disadvantaged, and the deviant)—as Moral Pathology, by which the devil tricks a human into believing he does not have the Gnomic Will given by God to deliberate good choices but instead is locked into a systematic enslavement of his or her human identity to any definition of man or woman except that which is already provided in the Holy Bible (Genesis 1:27).

The resultant immorality is gravely widespread, with each sin begetting an even graver and deadlier sin. An example might be a devious public school teacher with her own agenda insisting that an innocent child has "gender dysphoria," whereafter the child begins to take ownership of this fake diagnosis, uses the "suicide card" to convince his parents to put him on puberty blockers and allow him to undergo surgeries, and then commits sexual abominations throughout the rest of his life (or commits suicide to escape from guilt, shame, morbid depression, and self-loathing). Few escape the aftermath of such Moral Pathology, but even among those who do, the scars and pain are lifelong and irreversible (e.g., "Detransitioned boy castrated by doctors warns kids about perils of gender ideology: 'Patient for life'"; Hanna Grossman; https://www.msn.com/en-us/news/us/detransitioned-boy-castrated-by-doctors-warns-kids-about-perils-of-gender-ideology-patient-for-life/; MSN.com; accessed July 22, 2023).

Impressionable youth, weary of being outcasts, such as autistic girls, are targeted by pedagogic bullies bearing clipboards and angelic voices, hunted because they are known to adopt concepts naively, especially brightly

Introduction

colored or Emo ones, and in turn are likely to ardently defend any new principles taught to them by sudden "friends" promising inclusion in return for the "diagnosis" that they record on bean counters, so that they can substantiate their retention of public funds and grants. Children are taught that they must accept or beg for diagnoses and conditions such as "Gender Dysphoria," or "Anorexia" or "Bipolar Disorder" or "Gay." This is an example of immorality masquerading as a cornucopia of pathologies, yielding a massive social crisis of human identity while the elite laugh on their way to the bank. Every diagnosis and sexual fad is tied to boatloads of cash, whether it be from ever-new psychiatric medications pushed on our kids, or surgeries, or expensive hormone treatments, or government funding, or marketing and advertising campaigns, or grants, or educational endowments. For the elite the very best part of all of this is the freeing up of oxygen and land and generational wealth for themselves, due to the fact that our children are being taught that they are too mentally sick or too gay or too toxic to Mother Earth to grow up and have children of their own. And so they sit back and watch the population decline decade by decade, all so that they can carve out a larger piece of the pie for themselves and their cronies.
The obverse of the pleasures hunted by immoral programmers is the sorrow that darkens the heartlessly tossed coin of human well-being. It is psychogenic chaos and institutional anarchy. It is a collapsed U.S. Constitution that no longer holds moral sway over citizens. It is coerced and even mandated eros and *porneia*, it is poisonous "medicine" and "vaccines," it is depraved and fascistic "science," and it is the long arm of the State disguised as "education"—every bit of it

Introduction

enabled by the people themselves (the consumers) and their devious government that hosts the two degenerate sides of the same grievous coin—sorrow begetting moral decline, and moral decline begetting sorrow—perpetuating only the worst of all possible ends: public madness (Psalm 65:7) and ultimately spiritual death. "He that overcometh shall inherit all things; and I will be his God, and he shall be my son. But the fearful, and unbelieving, and the abominable, and murders, and whoremongers, and sorcerers, and idolaters, and all liars, shall have their part in the lake which burneth with fire and brimstone, which is the second death" (Revelation 21: 7-8).

The modern world has rejected Jesus, its collaborators and servants falling over themselves to race each other to hell. The Abomination of Desolation should now be taken note of, along with the signs of the times (Daniel 8-12; Matthew 24:15-16).

The term "Abomination of Desolation" was given its permanent living prototype in the persecution of the Chosen by the wicked Antiochus IV Epiphanes. He was a blasphemous, homicidal madman reacting in B.C 167 to his own "sorrows" by projecting them violently onto the innocent.

Antiochus IV had been humiliated by an elaborate threat issued against him by the Roman ambassador Gaius Popillius Laenas, warning that he must immediately cease besieging Cyprus. During his retreat to his Seleucid throne in Syria, he vented his hostility upon his Jewish suzerainty by killing and torturing countless Judeans, extinguishing the Eternal Lamp in

Introduction

the Temple, and forcing the High Priest to eat the meat of the pig he sacrificed on the altar of the outer court.

He also sprinkled the Torah in the Holy of Holies with swine's blood because he was angry that the Pentateuch contains God's command to destroy pagan nations (*Historical Library;* Diodorus Siculus; Book 34; Section 1; A.D. 105; Deuteronomy 20:16-18).

The madness of this Seleucid despot caused the Maccabean Revolt and gave rise to the Hasmonean Dynasty.

A father elects for his code of "ethics" the same Moral Pathology whenever he refuses to react morally to an immoral situation, hence one that endangers his family. He will not stand up against invaders, but instead will transform his humiliation by them into his abuse of his own family. Would he ever stand up against the Seleucid Empire like Judas Maccabee did?

He will instead allow his daughter to share a restroom with a "transgendered man," just so that he does not appear to himself or to others to be a "hater" that would dare disobey governmental mandates that a perverted potential child rapist must share the same bathroom privately with his daughter, who can then potentially witness the deranged man's genitalia or lack thereof (either a penis that was mutilated or replaced with a female mockup of a vagina or for one reason or another was left intact). Such a father permits his cowardice to make him complicit in the "legal" perversity that is now endangering his child.

Introduction

A mother, for example, kneels praying in front of a statue—not of Christ, but of George Floyd, not wanting to appear to be a "racist" who would dare not to participate in the blasphemous worship of this deceased Fentanyl-abusing convicted thief—the firearm-toting felon who became deified as an expression of vengeance against the police, whom his worshipful rioters accused of hatefully killing him because he was black ("Minneapolis plans permanent memorial honoring George Floyd"; Dara Kennedy; *New York Post;* News; July 18, 2020).

Moreover, how many Christians parrot the notion that they are against abortion but support a woman's "right to choose"?

How many Christian parents refuse to contradict their children's textbooks on the subject of Darwinian Evolution, ignoring a teachable moment, so as not to appear ignorant or "anti-Science"?

Every Christian is faced with opportunities for Deliberation and choosing rightly. However, pressures that are set against parents, against children, and against the family unit are reaching a crescendo in these Last Days.

Countless government jobs, grants, licenses, and other funding streams are awarded by the American Psychiatric Association and the World Health Organization, both of which depend on the false authority of Nominal Fallacy that redefines the whole person in terms of externals and lists of behaviors that can be "treated" with no regard or room for

Introduction

discussions of sin, or God, or moral responsibility whatsoever.

Such rhetorical trash does not deserve to have its terms and titles codified into books of law—or its diagnostic codes edited into new editions of psychological manuals—in order to ruin people's lives. Instead, it relies on primarily on media to permeate the confines of every household, like a dog herding sheep, luring people into, for instance, self-diagnosing their family members with all sorts of ailments in response to the myriad pharmaceutical commercials that embed into minds the godless programming of "dysphoria" or "vaccine hesitancy," or that dupes victims into becoming vaccinated against COVID by permitting poisons to be injected into their bloodstream, whereby they will feel virtuous in "trusting the Science." The following screed was a specious pre-setting for a certain planned Pandemic:

"People who delay or refuse vaccines for themselves or their children are presenting a growing challenge for countries seeking to close the immunization gap. Globally, 1 in 5 children still do not receive routine life-saving immunizations, and an estimated 1.5 million children still die each year of diseases that could be prevented by vaccines that already exist, according to WHO" ("Vaccine hesitancy: A growing challenge for immunization programmes"; World Health Organization; https://www.who.int/news/item/18-08-2015-vaccine-hesitancy-a-growing-challenge-for-immunization-programmes; August 18, 2015).

Introduction

The Christian, while loving and appreciating the good times enjoyed with his better parishioners, must keep this institutionalized, systemic madness in mind, always "holding fast the faithful word as he hath been taught, that he may be able by sound doctrine both to exhort and to convince the gainsayers" (Titus 1:9). When you go out into the world to preach or teach that God created man in His image, such will contradict, saying things like, "No, God did not," "There is no God," or "God is actually Female; She is a Goddess!" In fact, such gainsaying may even come from churchgoers themselves. "For there are many unruly and vain talkers and deceivers, especially they of the circumcision: Whose mouths must be stopped, who subvert whole houses, teaching things which they ought not, for filthy lucre's sake" (Titus 1:10).

This book will show many examples of the illicit writings and deeds by which "[Heretics] profess that they know God; but in works they deny Him, being abominable, and disobedient, and unto every good work reprobate" (Titus 1:16).

Rather than enable spiritual sickness in the nave of a church, a religious Body must strive to convince each bedlamite to hold himself to moral account, not to cowardly look for a diagnostic copout or a clinical/legal excuse to keep themselves comfortably sinful. Taking the greatest possible exception to the unethical antics of every nihilist and sociopath, ministers must utilize tough exposure tactics, rebuking or enforcing expulsion in every place where straight evangelism is refused and mocked. A Christian does no rascal any favor by depriving himself of the privilege of a Priest's just rejection of that yoke of despair that

Introduction

mountebanks would dare to put over the necks of religious bodies, classrooms, and households. No, mother, your child was not "born this way"; no, father, your child's drug addiction is not an "illness." No, it does not take a village to raise a child, especially now, when the village has gone mad. It is now time to identify the avowed God-seeker out of a crowd of scoundrels and their cowardly, self-blinded followers (Joshua 24:15).

We pray for them both: The former is worth evangelizing, catechizing, and proselytizing; the latter are worth shrewdly identifying and resisting. "Give not that which is holy unto the dogs, neither cast ye your pearls before swine, lest they trample them under their feet, and turn again and rend you" (Matthew 7:6).

There can never be "accompanying," "welcoming," "incrementalism," or "gradualism" as forms of Mercy. If it is madness they seek, then each of their anomalies must be meticulously categorized as serving Moral Pathology so that a child will be taught early how to spot a despicable act or an innuendo, and a parent can know that the Church stands behind her protection over her child's mind and body against every self-made demoniac, opposing the entire legion that underwrites his intended brainwashing and assault.

"Walk in wisdom toward them that are without, redeeming the time. Let your speech be always with Grace, seasoned with salt, that ye may know how ye ought to answer every man" (Colossians 4:5-6). And let us not forget that what we are engaged in truly is a war for the minds and souls of our children and flock. "Put on the whole armour of God, that ye may be able to

Introduction

stand against the wiles of the devil. For we wrestle not against flesh and blood, but against principalities, against powers, against the rulers of the darkness of this world, against spiritual wickedness in high places" (Ephesians 6:11-12).

Delving further into the concept of Nominal Fallacy, it should be remembered that the meaning of a label can change over time, thus rendering the label even more meaningless than it was at the outset. "Sanity," defined by the Oxford Dictionary, is "the ability to think and behave in a normal and rational manner." However, because the definition depends on what is meant by "normal" and "rational," whether a person is perceived to think and speak "normally" or "rationally" by agents of a Post-Modernist, Corporatocratic, and morally sick world depends on the values these "principalities and powers" and their agents invest in these terms. It becomes useful, then, to step back and define "person," devoid of mischievous semantics, so he can follow God's Law without confusion.

A man or a woman must no longer be identified according to titles, or definitions, or diagnoses, or types. A human being is not Matter "striving" to fulfill a Platonic Universal Ideal Form. If he or she exists, then he or she is solely a human being, either male or female, made in the image and likeness of God (Genesis 1:27), imbued with the power of reason, equipped with the knowledge of Good and Evil (due to our original parents' disobedience), and having the Free Will to choose the one or the other. The Psalmist writes, "I have said, Ye are gods; and all of you are children of the most High. But ye shall die like men, and fall like one of the princes" (Psalm 82:6-7).

Introduction

God created Man and Woman to love them and delight in them, and so that they may love and serve the Creator and care for His creation. This is the human purpose, and it must never be redefined: "The statutes of the Lord are right, rejoicing the heart: the commandment of the Lord is pure, enlightening the eyes" (Psalm 19:8). However, unless humanity's identity is properly defined, the definition of the human purpose cannot be supported. That is why we vehemently oppose such demonic concepts as Darwinian Evolution and Behaviorism, which reduce the human condition to causes and effects in the absence of a Creator—the Unmoved Mover.
Thus, human purpose flows from this properly positioned identity—not from people's craftily invented words or theories, but from God's Word. "But as we were allowed of God to be put in trust with the Gospel, even so we speak; not as pleasing men, but God, which trieth our hearts" (1 Thessalonians 2:4).

If one is not careful, the verbally crafty adversary will ensure that his mischievous relegation of knowledge of our world to its being only one of infinite universes (i.e., "multiverses") reduces people to despair. Objective morality and even quantities and properties are called into question, rendering everything meaningless, including life itself: A thing is "bad" only relative to the ordinances of one's *present* universe, and any "hope of finding a rational explanation for the precise values of quark masses and other constants of the standard model that we observe in our Big Bang is doomed, for their values would be an accident of the particular part of the multiverse in which we live" ("Physics: What We Do and Don't Know"; Steven Weinberg; *The New York Review*; November 7, 2013)

Introduction

Moreover, although "Purgatory" is not being appraised here, what shall be legislated in the Constitution of this Diocese is the *purpose* served by Good Works. The world was created by God so that people would be able to work out their salvation solely within its boundaries, glorifying Christ during their biological life, possessing faith, virtue, self-control, obedience, and love and service to the Creator in proper humility, understanding the Divine Order of Creation. The godly knowledge that human epistemology (i.e., all that can be known) concerns solely one's ethical relation to the singular firmament of the Earth—until one is granted his or her place within the ether of the Heaven that God alone has created (Philippians 2:12; 2 Corinthians 1:5-10)—is cause for a peace that "passeth all understanding" (Philippians 4:7).

But conspiracies are everywhere! Although a "just man falleth seven times, and riseth up again," still "the wicked shall fall into mischief" (Proverbs 24:16). Using strawman rhetoric, homosexual historian Yuval Noah Harari explains his "Homo Deus" idea that man as the self-made God may lord as God over other men, proclaiming (literally) that unless human DNA becomes properly hacked, children (and this is indeed what this morally pathological rhetorician has postulated) will get hit by cars.

> "Currently more than a million people die in car accidents every year, most of them are caused by human error. It would be a good idea to save these million lives, but in order to put a self-driving car on the road you need the ability, to some extent, to hack human behavior and human emotions. It's not about turning that ninety-

Introduction

degree angle on the road—that's the easy part. The really difficult part is how to be careful if there is a child walking along the road and he suddenly jumps right in front of the car because he was running after a ball. So to put self-driving cars on the road, we need cars that can replicate children and know a lot of things about the behavior of children. So this, to some extent, is also hacking human beings, and learning how to recognize the behavior patterns of human beings, right?" ("The Most Important Survival Skill for the Next 50 Years Isn't What You Think"; Clay Skipper; *GQ Magazine*: Lifestyle; September 30, 2018)

The same modality of fear by which the COVID-19 crisis was planned now coaxes duped Christians to redefine their biological existence in terms of how scientists want humanity to be redefined—for their own "protection," of course.

Instead, people must, if they are to make it to Heaven, understand *why* and by *Whom* they were created: "For thou hast possessed my reins: thou hast covered me in my mother's womb. I will praise thee; for I am fearfully and wonderfully made: marvellous are thy works; and that my soul knoweth right well" (Psalm 139:13-14).

And for what purpose is knowledge taught? "Through thy precepts I get understanding: therefore I hate every false way" (Psalm 119:104). "For I delight in the law of God after the inward man" (Romans 7:22).

The Canons of our Traditional Anglican Church of America are formulated according to the Principle of Subsidiarity, so that Communion can be shared freely

Introduction

between all truly catholic houses, each of which is permitted to govern itself according to its own interior Custom. So that theological Fellowship is able to be enjoyed as it was in the houses of the Apostolic Fathers, the Constitution endows the Diocese with reasoning that edifies the Common Good—not as that term is defined by modern-day socialists, but such that meritorious orthodoxy reflects the ethics of the whole while allowing each of the parts to operate according to their Custom. The *Didache* addressed partakers of the Eucharist, advising Christians to achieve the aesthetic of uniform moral cohesion as the prerequisite for forming churches: "Therefore, elect/appoint [*cheirotonesate*] for yourselves bishops and deacons worthy of the Lord, meek men and not lovers of money, and truthful, for they also minister to you the ministry of the prophets and teachers" (*Didache*; Chapter 15: "Bishops and Deacons; Christian Reproof"; A.D. ~100)

The eight books of the *Apostolic Constitutions* encouraged the same call to build local autonomy in Christian orthodoxy and catholicity, an autonomy whose fragility must be protected by truly Christian men. A passage from this work is reprinted here in full below, because it epitomizes the calling for orthodoxy to be projected by every Priest and Bishop if they expect their Congregation or Mission to project the orthodox teachings coming from their pulpits.

Initially declared Apocryphal in the *Decretum Gelasianum* (A.D. 492-553), the *Apostolic Constitutions* as regards most of its body was also rejected by the Quinisext Council of A.D. 692. Also, its contents, including the *Didache*, were not included in the initial

Introduction

Roman list of canonical scripture (which is identical to the Roman Catholic list from the 1563 Council of Trent; Council of Rome; *Decretum Gelasianum*; Damasine List; Pope Damasus I; A.D. 383).

However, the *Apostolic Constitutions* has, for 1,500 years, been consulted for composing ecclesiastical constitutions, and all of its declarations were accepted in modified form by the Miaphysite Ethiopian Orthodox Tewahedo Canon (i.e., *The Ethiopic Didascalia*).

As with the Code of Roman Law of Byzantine Emperor Justinian (*Codex Justinianus*, quoted later in our Constitution), such ancient legislative forms have been priceless in helping the authors of this book pull together, review, and incorporate into a catholic synthesis numerous such valuable texts in the making of this *Praxeologion*.

The synthesis of moral conduct, discipline, and liturgical dictates congeals with precise detail in the following excerpt from the *Apostolic Constitutions* that predicates an expectation that brave orthodoxy shine forth from the Clergy and Episcopate through the Christians in their flocks:

> "But if any one be maliciously prosecuted by the heathen, because he will not still go along with them to the same excess of riot, let him know that such a one is blessed of God, according as our Lord says in the Gospel: Blessed are you when men shall reproach you, or persecute you, or say all manner of evil against you falsely, for my sake. Rejoice and be exceeding glad, for your reward is great in heaven. Matthew 5:11-12 If, therefore,

Introduction

    any one be slandered and falsely accused, such a one is blessed; for the Scripture says, A man that is a reprobate is not tried by God. But if any one be convicted as having done a wicked action, such a one not only hurts himself, but occasions the whole body of the Church and its doctrine to be blasphemed; as if we Christians did not practice those things that we declare to be good and honest, and we ourselves shall be reproached by the Lord, that they say and do not. Matthew 23:3 Wherefore the bishop must boldly reject such as these upon full conviction, unless they change their course of life" (*Apostolic Constitutions*; Book II; Section 3; Part VIII, ~380 A.D.).

After establishing the identity of and interrelationship between God, humanity, and the created world, the *Praxeologion* defines how the Anglican Liturgy of the 1928 *Book of Common Prayer* orders the "executive function" for the Religious and Laity. In establishing the Custom and Subsidiarity of a wonderfully and fearfully made Diocese, the Reciprocal Indwelling of Christ receives its proper imitation by how the TACA Diocese is the seat of the Archbishop, and how the Archbishop is the propitious ecclesiastical mortal "primus" (i.e., the chief moderator and presider over his own Diocese on behalf of Christ, who can do nothing without the Father) over his Diocese. "I can of mine own self do nothing: as I hear, I judge: and my judgment is just; because I seek not mine own will, but the will of the Father which hath sent me" (John 5:30). The Archbishop, in this way, exemplifies the leadership of Christ Himself, Who is the Chief Shepherd and Head of the Church (Colossians 1:18; Ephesians 5:23).

Introduction

The interpenetration of the Triune God in and among and between the souls of all the members of this Diocese projects how the Reciprocal Indwelling is deposited within our Communion and Fellowship. It is the perpetual motion of heavenly movement by which Logos was first approached by Aristotle, but taken on by Saint John of Damascus as *Perichoresis* (περιχώρησις, which means "rotation." The concept informs the Subsidiarity that flows through the wisdom of a gentle but mighty Episcopate:

> "Further the divine nature has the property of penetrating all things without mixing with them and of being itself impenetrable by anything else. Moreover, there is the property of knowing all things with a simple knowledge and of seeing all things, simply with His divine, all-surveying, immaterial eye, both the things of the present, and the things of the past, and the things of the future, before they come into being. (Daniel 2:22) It is also sinless, and can cast sin out, and bring salvation: and all that it wills, it can accomplish, but does not will all it could accomplish. For it could destroy the universe but it does not will so to do" (*Of the Orthodox Faith*; Saint John Damascene; Book I; Chapter 14: "The properties of the divine nature."; A.D. 754).

Put another way, orthodoxy resonates out of the movement of the First Mover, God, through the Episcopate and Clergy, and through the flocks.

So that the *ecclesia* can ably defend its Constitution and Canons against "profane and vain babblings, and oppositions of science so falsely called" (1 Timothy

Introduction

6:20), additional words of the Damascene are herewith helpful by exploring how the Trinity emanates through the cosmos and the atom itself:

> "For if any one has not the Spirit of Christ, he is none of His (Romans 8:9), says the divine Apostle. And we confess that He is manifested and imparted to us through the Son. For He breathed upon His Disciples, says he, and said, Receive the Holy Spirit. (John 20:29) It is just the same as in the case of the sun from which come both the ray and the radiance (for the sun itself is the source of both the ray and the radiance), and it is through the ray that the radiance is imparted to us, and it is the radiance itself by which we are lightened and in which we participate. Further we do not speak of the Son of the Spirit, or of the Son as derived from the Spirit" (*Of the Orthodox Faith*; Saint John Damascene; Book I; Chapter 8: "Concerning the Holy Trinity"; A.D. 754).

The Constitution and Canons also are a scholastic document, intended to offset the illicit teaching of antichrist academia and public education; Priests and Bishops are reminded here to adopt biblical epistemology, not that of the world, keeping these words in mind: "My people are destroyed for lack of knowledge: because thou hast rejected knowledge, I will also reject thee, that thou shalt be no priest to me: seeing thou hast forgotten the law of thy God, I will also forget thy children" (Hosea 4:6).

Because *praxis* is usually motivated by sensual comprehension of Life, the Constitution and Canons

Introduction

employ Negation Theology to characterize what God and the Church are not.

Sadly, even the sensual itself is given to contemplate *anima* and *animus* (i.e., soul and body) only as corporeal atoms (*On the Nature of Things*; Titus Lucretius Carus; Book III; 3.94-416; B.C. 50), whereof the complacent gods have no involvement with biological beings, wherefore the spirit of each human "simulacra" inescapably dies like any organic life, considered an inconsequential happenstance to an arbitrary god (*ibid.*, 2.153-4, 6.76-7). But our Christian Faith is one of intimate Relationship with the Creator. Were it not so, these words of damnation would not be so horrifying: "And then will I profess to unto them, I never knew you: depart from me, ye that work iniquity" (Matthew 7:23).

The *Didache* exposes the "way of death," which was the same then as it is today, and for which today's abortion and other homicides and abominable sins receive a fitting Commination: "And the way of death is this: First of all it is evil and full of curse: murders, adulteries, lusts, fornications, thefts, idolatries, magic arts, witchcrafts, rapines, false witnessings, hypocrisies, double-heartedness, deceit, haughtiness, depravity, self-will, greediness, filthy talking, jealousy, over-confidence, loftiness, boastfulness; persecutors of the good, hating truth, loving a lie, not knowing a reward for righteousness, not cleaving to good nor to righteous judgment, watching not for that which is good, but for that which is evil; from whom meekness and endurance are far, loving vanities, pursuing requital, not pitying a poor man, not labouring for the afflicted, not knowing Him that made them, murderers

Introduction

of children, destroyers of the handiwork of God, turning away from him that is in want, afflicting him that is distressed, advocates of the rich, lawless judges of the poor, utter sinners. Be delivered, children, from all these" (*Didache;* Chapter 5: "The Way of Death"; A.D. ~100).

This book reminds the spiritually thirsty that the physical death is the ultimate end of pursuing contemplation and enjoyment of the physical world. Without deliberately discerning good versus evil, then life can only be comprehended according to the atom. If one lives only according to this rule all throughout life, then one can only expect to taste the Second Death, which is defined as the spiritual punishment faced by the ungodly after their physical death.

Why did God spell out His Love for us by putting us in the middle of a war between the material and the spiritual, the being and the unbeing, the Triune God and the devil? A fast recounting of the last 2,700 years ought to expose the arc of history as being devious and circuitous, begging a return to Christian sovereignty, if not in the form of an actual sacerdotal monarchy or an encampment on a remote and isolated homestead, then through a seeding of Ecclesiastical Polity to model Christian living, as we attempt to codify through these pages. Although throughout the history of Christendom there have been different expressions of the "City of God," all true Christians have cried within themselves, "Maranatha!" thus eagerly seeking the Lord's return with their whole heart. "For our conversation is in heaven; from whence also we look for the Saviour, the Lord Jesus Christ" (Philippians 3:20).

Introduction

Institutional Moral Pathology is the systematized embedding by powerful institutions of evil intentions into the psyche. These goals replace the "Law" that is written into the hearts and souls through Prevenient Grace—even in those who have never heard the Gospel (Romans 2:15-16).

By deadening the power of Discernment, these wicked mindsets of the principalities and powers are meant to obliterate the ability of the mind to allow conscience to influence Salvation. God's wrath awaits these seducers and intimidators, who do not appear to know that the Fruits of the Spirit (Galatians 5:22-23), fruit they plan to befoul, are grown from the same invisible God who simultaneously makes every person capable of showing goodness and is also highly motivated to shower His wrath on the ungodly and those who hate Him: "For the invisible things of Him from the creation of the world are clearly seen, being understood by the things that are made, even his eternal power and Godhead; so that they are without excuse" (Romans 1:18-20). In simpler words, those who pervert innocence and corrupt whole houses and cities will be punished, irrespective of whether the culprit has ever heard the Gospel of Christ or the Law of Moses. "But whoso shall offend one of these little ones which believe in me, it were better for him that a millstone were hanged about his neck, and *that* he were drowned in the depth of the sea" (Matthew 18:6).

"The actor has taken to repeating the most grotesque falsehoods of the sprawling QAnon ideology, among them that traffickers are harvesting children's organs and extracting the chemical compound adrenochrome

Introduction

from their brains before murdering them," wrote a famous scoffer in regards to the promotion of the 2023 movie *Sound of Freedom* ("Sound of Freedom Movie Is a Superhero Movie for Dads With Brainworms"; Miles Klee; Rolling Stone; July 7, 2023). His screed is an example of how wicked elitists conflate good works with bad intentions (Isaiah 5:20). His magazine editors placed his review within a fake section intended to mock Christians, titled, "Save the Children."

In other words, if a person publicly opposes even the *idea* (the movie does not give names of actual people) of organized ritualistic homicides against children, then he surely must be a vicious conspiracy theorist. Thus, all people should be conditioned never to advocate for the protection of the innocent using Scripture or referring to God, lest they be publicly humiliated, canceled, or doxxed. The reviewer employs an immoral technique of pathological lying. It is institutional within mass media. It is systematic.

Bad schools do their part by teaching students to divide the mind against their own conscience by instructing them that it is not possible to discern the difference between good and evil or to know about the existence of Absolute Truth, of which they are taught they can know nothing. The implication is, then, "Why not worship Satan, instead?" Does this sound far-fetched? Keep reading.

In an article titled "Satanic Temple opens 'After School Satan Club' at elementary school in Moline, Illinois," the author writes that "Lucien Greaves, co-founder of the Satanic Temple, said the club will teach students benevolence, empathy, critical thinking, problem-

Introduction

solving and creative expression" (ibid., https://www.fox32chicago.com/news/satanic-temple-opens-after-school-satan-club-at-elementary-school-in-moline-illinois, February 13, 2022; accessed July 30, 2023). In another article less than one year after this one, we learn about another Satanic club in a public school: "The [Lucifer-based] club, for kids five to twelve, promises science and community service projects, nature activities, and tons of fun. 'Educatin' with Satan', as they say" ("Pennsylvania gets its first after-school Satan Club this week. In Hellertown"; Rita Giordano; News; Philadelphia Inquirer; May 8, 2023). These are but two examples of many, and this infiltration of open Satanism into the public schools makes perfect sense considering such sordidity as the allowance of prayers to Satan during U.S. governmental meetings (see, e.g., "'Hail Satan' opening prayer at Alaska government meeting prompts walkouts, protest"; Owen Daugherty; June 20, 2019; https://thehill.com/homenews/state-watch/449660-hail-satan-opening-prayer-at-alaska-government-meeting-prompts-walkouts/; accessed July 30, 2023) According to such schools, knowledge of Truth is only one person's opinion over another's; Moral Relativism is all that can be derived from the carnage of Modernism today and its version of "ethics."

These wicked houses of instruction teach that the lessons of ancient thinkers such as Plato, Saint Irenaeus of Smyrna, and Saint Augustine support the concept of "necessary evil," which must be rejected by the modern world: that is, that humanity's mere existence after the Fall has caused a condition of woe that God requires for the purpose of fostering useless

Introduction

evil and suffering, which appear to be unavoidable or fated.

The "necessary evil" argument as posited by Liberals known as Progressives is not well understood by them in the first place, and so they are refuting a concept over which they do not have any mental mastery.

First, they presume that evil is necessary for goodness to exist; second, because they presume that evil is merely the privation of goodness, they also presume wrongly that Free Will has no dominion over human behavior in the shadow of such inevitable or irresistible malevolence.

The first is a convolution of Saint Irenaeus's so-called "Soul-Making" theodicy about Free Will, which misguided scholars have long attempted to refute by accusing it of Origenism in its alleged Universalism, insinuating that Irenaeus purported that all souls are destined by God to go to Heaven. He actually did *not*. Despite Irenaeus's intriguing statement that angels have "power of choice" (presumably Free Will), there is no heresy that can be extrapolated from his statement that "It is not true, therefore, that some [people] are by nature good, and others bad," because "nature" concerns image of God in humans (*Adversus Haereses;* Saint Irenaeus of Smyrna; Book IV; Chapter 37; A.D. 180)

The second is a distortion of Saint Augustine's *Enchiridion*, where God alone is taken to be the sole mover of all deliberate, principled action, instead of humans being able to choose good behavior over bad behavior and actively knock on the door to ask God

Introduction

into their hearts (Revelation 3:20). However, Augustine is no Dr. Pangloss within his thanksgiving praise, about whose fruits Augustine wrote: "All of nature, therefore, is good, since the Creator of all nature is supremely good," because he subordinates the notion of nature's virtue to the omnibenevolence of the Creator, saying, "But nature is not supremely and immutably good as is the Creator of it" (*Enchiridion of Faith, Hope, and Love*; Saint Augustine of Hippo; Chapter IV: The Problem of Evil; Section 12; A.D. 420). The world is merely "perfect" only because God, the most powerful being, loves us.

There is also much disordered thinking caused by the mere statement by Socrates, a disciplined philosopher, who believed that unbeing, which is evil, is merely part of being: "And therefore whether we take being and the other, or being and the one, or the one and the other, in every such case we take two things, which may be rightly called both" (*Parmenides*; Plato; Transl. Benjamin Jowett; Section 143:b-d; B.C. 370).
Plato, with his dialogue *Timaeus*, is further credited by many grateful worldly college deans for his keen demotion of the psyche as being thus incapable of recognizing Truth, to "prove unable to give accounts that are always in all respects self-consistent and perfectly exact" (*Timaeus*; Plato; Part 29:c-d; B.C. 360). The *Republic* had reduced "justified belief" to its being dependent on flawed human perception of what it hopes is real, in terms of the human eye squinting to see what sunlight would hope to reveal about true Form: "Neither vision itself nor its vehicle, which we call the eye, is identical with the sun," with light and illumination of Matter being mere effects of the Perfect, "but to think that either of them is the good is

Introduction

not right. (*Republic*; Plato; Book 6: Section 508:a-509:b; A.D. 380). Until the Father called on Christ to enter the world, its people had only hope of living in the darkness that evil men love (John 3:19, 8:12).

Hence, twenty years later, in designating a well-meaning "Universal Soul" to order the Cosmos, Socrates hoped to steer his students away from the implied Moral Relativism of the *Republic* by constructing a Triune type of Supreme Deity. Plato's Demiurge is a lesser being than God the Father, who created the World out of "Fire, Air, and Water." He seeks the good, and fosters good intentions—not because of Love, but because goodness is necessary for survival, foreseeable through a monist order (i.e., all creation being inclined to one hierarchy), as, "first, that it might be, so far as possible, a Living Creature, perfect and whole, with all its parts perfect; and next, that it might be One" (*ibid.*, *Timaeus*; Plato; 32:d). A "platonic relationship," is therefore not one built from Agape Love, but for necessity and order. But the soul wants more than that; "my soul thirsteth for thee, my flesh longeth for thee" (Psalm 63:1).

However, bleakness overshadows the Platonic world, because to a merely secularly minded college professor the Creator therefore desires good only because it answers the calling of *ananke* (ἀνάγκη, defined as necessity). "And inasmuch as Reason was controlling Necessity by persuading her to conduct to the best end the most part of the things coming into existence, thus and thereby it came about, through Necessity yielding to intelligent persuasion, that this Universe of ours was being in this wise constructed at the beginning." From here, Socrates declares that evil is part of goodness,"

Introduction

and the conclusion does not appear capable of escaping the implications of Moral Relativism: "Wherefore if one is to declare how it actually came into being on this wise, he must include also the form of the Errant Cause, in the way that it really acts" (*Timaeus*; Plato; Parts 32:d, 48:a; B.C. 360). According to this economy, there can be no Absolute Truth because evil is a necessary part of goodness.

Therefore, if secular teachers such as Socrates on his proverbial "best day" should permanently define the intention of "Fire, Air, and Water" as being necessarily partially devious, then Grace can never lead students to Faith. Objective Morality and Principled Action must instead be taught to stem from firmly held belief in Absolute Truth. "Sanctify them through thy truth: thy word is truth" (John 17:17).

A detached young mind is like a suicidal Young Werther, romantically contemplating self-annihilation as though it would be awesome to declare in a moment of self-destruction that Truth can never be believed. Modern educators are dependent on this nihilism. For example, a retired Socrates, suddenly on the way to his public execution, fed the news of existentialism to his chatty mathematician, Theaetetus, that there is just no way of knowing anything about anything, "So neither perception, Theaetetus, nor true opinion, nor reason or explanation combined with true opinion could be knowledge" (*Theaetetus*; Plato; Part 210:a-b; B.C. 360). The cup of poison was of course drunk by Socrates as his attestation that allegiance to the State was more important than defending knowledge of Truth and even boasted that his "Daimon" (e.g., informative demon)

Introduction

did not intervene to help him to accept his unjust slaughter (*Apology*; Plato; Part 31:c-d; B.C. 350).

If a child is taught that it is impossible to trust in her own biblical knowledge about Truth, and she hence never learns to advocate against the nihilism of intellectuals, then she cannot hope to believe in God without always fearing she has betrayed her instructors and hipster friends. However, God blesses the one who yearns to break free of the yoke of academia, as Hezekiah blessed the unclean, asking God to pardon those who felt unable to resist immediately sharing in the Passover meal (2 Chronicles 30:19).

A spiritually awakened student may, despite his ravaged learning, desire as Saint Augustine had contended, to "always live in a state of gratitude to the Lord, having obtained from Him the gift of incorruptibility," using Free Will to guide him toward Salvation, "that he might love Him the more; for "he to whom more is forgiven, loveth more" (Luke 6:43; *Enchiridion of Faith, Hope, and Love*; Chapter 20; Section 2; A.D. 40).

He could incline himself, as Saint Augustine suggested, to recognize deliberate error inside his wicked educators, who resent God's goodness, and "disapprove the truth as though it were falsehood, or to hold what is certain as if it were uncertain, or what is uncertain as if it were certain" (*Enchiridion of Faith, Hope, and Love*; Saint Augustine of Hippo; Chap VII; Section 19; A.D. 420). "Woe unto them that call evil good, and good evil; that put darkness for light, and light for darkness; that put bitter for sweet, and sweet for bitter!" (Isaiah 5:20).

Introduction

Lying, the telling of falsehoods by educators, according to Saint Augustine, is worse than writing faulty doctrine, but a properly catechized child will advance further when adjudging the insidiousness for the "bad fruit" that falsehoods cause. "It is quite another thing that, from this error [of lying]—which is a bad thing—something good actually turns out, such as being saved from the onslaught of wicked men" (*ibid.*, *Enchiridion*).

Without trusting her ability to know God and believe in His saving Grace, what awaits a young person out in the streets? The pretext behind the destruction waged against the Christian religion and family is well known to traditionalist Trinitarian Christians and understood concerning its implications. Riotous, bored Americans outside of Christ's church have been taught how to harness the "absence of good," if not through rioting and pillaging then at least through the acceptance of "woke" ideology and failure to properly teach and guide the children under their care. Alinsky's words are printed at length below because of the chilling proof that churches and cities have burned at the hands of stooges empowered to divide the good against itself.

"The thirteenth rule: Pick the target, freeze it, personalize it, and polarize it." Alinsky wrote. Thus, if no one believes in Absolute Truth, and if they insist that God's goodness is partly evil, then countless versions of right and wrong will permanently deem Objective Morality to be impossible. Alinsky wrote: "In conflict tactics there are certain rules that the organizer should always regard as universalities. One is that the opposition must be singled out as the target and 'frozen'." In other words, Christians should be left isolated and confused. He adds, "By this I mean that in

Introduction

a complex, interrelated, urban society, it becomes increasingly difficult to single out who is to blame for any particular evil." He insists that radicals strive in "identifying the enemy. Obviously there is no point to tactics unless one has a target upon which to center the attacks" (*Rules for Radicals: A Practical Primer for Realistic Radicals*; Saul D. Alinsky; Part: "Tactics: Thirteenth Rule"; p. 131; 1971; Reprinted in 2013).

About five years ago, "canceled" and "doxxed" suddenly became household terms while we sat back and watched careers destroyed and people's reputations smeared beyond recovery. This was no accident. Kids were coming home from college accusing their parents of being "racists" and carrying on that this one or that one was "culturally appropriating" another race or ethnicity. Already far-left liberal professors in college universities were falling over themselves to appear more woke and more radical than their colleagues, and some professors were sent packing. Protests raged, Black Lives Matter gained ascendancy, and little by little people became aware that something had changed, had *radicalized*.

Unless Love is actualized with principled action (*Praxis*), the good shall always be divided against itself, firstly within human thoughts and then through the wickedness that unstoppably corrupts the image of God in more and more people, like a cancer destroying society. "And Jesus knew their thoughts, and said unto them, Every kingdom divided against itself is brought to desolation; and every city or house divided against itself shall not stand" (Matthew 12:25).

Introduction

Mandating Moral Pathology was among the aims of Alinsky, whose demonic ghostly hand moves the race riots in American cities and promotes illegal immigrant invasions across the southern U.S. border. Violent chaos is programmed and defended as being merely respectively "protests" and applied "kindness," or just compensation for the "crime" of believing that Absolute Truth comes from God, who expects obedience and the Rule of Law instead of theft, vandalism, and corruption. Alinsky wrote:

"The disruption of the present organization is the first step toward community organization. Present arrangements must be disorganized if they are to be displaced by new patterns [i.e., the Dialectic Materialism of Marxism] that provide the opportunities and means for citizen participation" (*ibid.*, Alinsky, Part: "In the Beginning"; p. 117). This "participation" is actually violence encouraged to menace in the streets, mentored by cynical billionaires and globalists such as George Soros (*How George Soros funded progressive 'legal arsonist' DAs behind US crime surge*; Isabel Vincent; News; *New York Post*; December 16, 2021) Alinsky promulgated the following directive:

"The organizer dedicated to changing the life of a particular community must first rub raw the resentments of the people of the community; fan the latent hostilities of many of the people to the point of overt expression. He must search out controversy and issues, rather than avoid them, for unless there is controversy people are not concerned enough to act" (*ibid.*, Alinsky). The art of using confusion to manipulate people was well known to Saint Paul of Tarsus:

Introduction

"And then shall that Wicked be revealed, whom the Lord shall consume with the spirit of His mouth, and shall destroy with the brightness of his coming: Even him, whose coming is after the working of Satan with all power and signs and lying wonders, and with all deceivableness of unrighteousness in them that perish; because they received not the love of the truth, that they might be saved. And for this cause God shall send them strong delusion, that they should believe a lie: That they all might be damned who believed not the truth, but had pleasure in unrighteousness" (2 Thessalonians 2:8-12). The influencer Alinsky, hater of order, lover of revolution, wrote:

"An organizer must stir up dissatisfaction and discontent; provide a channel into which the people can angrily pour their frustrations. He must create a mechanism that can drain off the underlying guilt for having accepted the previous situation for so long a time. Out of this mechanism, a new community organization arises." (*ibid.*, Alinsky; Part: "In the Beginning"; p. 117). Such a community would be manipulated to shed its collective guilt over having followed Christ, obeyed Divine Law, and believed in Absolute Truth of God.

Her professors hating her parents, her family not catechized, being divided against herself, the average college student on any U.S. liberal arts campus will be pursued by provocateurs to partake in the destruction of her own home even while living away from home. When she returns home after graduation, her parents will no longer recognize her in her new instantiation.

Introduction

Therefore, public school educators, today mostly being Marxist, have made a Left turn at Plato's works to support the dialectic materialist extrapolation taken from Hegel: that the gulf between "thesis" (i.e., "creation") versus its opposite, "antithesis" (i.e., death), could be resolved within the brain, upon a coldly logical plane of truth, known to Hegel as ("synthesis").

Instead, the learned mind must share the Gospel and "Study to shew thyself approved unto God, a workman that needeth not to be ashamed, rightly dividing the word of truth" (2 Timothy 2:15).

Although Apocatastasis was condemned as a heresy (Council of Constantinople; Canon 9; A.D. 553), it is tempting for agents of heterodoxy to echo the Universalism of the errant Roman Catholic then-auxiliary Bishop of Lost Angeles (now Bishop of Winona-Rochester), who said in 2011, "Bottom line: we may reasonably hope that all people will be saved" ("Fr. Robert Barron on Whether Hell is Crowded or Empty"; Bishop Robert Barron; Interview, YouTube: 2011).

It is presumed by some that an Irenaean "Soul-Making" Theodicy teaches that Free Will's role in evolving the creation of humans is still in progress, wrongfully presuming a kind of spiritual evolution restoring people to God after the "collective fall of the race-soul at an indefinitely remote past" (Genesis 3).

Thus, to John Hick, damnation would likely befall a person unless Free Will always leaned toward Prevenient Grace: "But in fact an alternative is available: namely, that God will eventually succeed in His purpose of winning all men to Himself in faith in

Introduction

love" (*Evil and the God of Love*; John Hick; Part IV; Chapter 2: *Theodicy versus hell;* pp. 251, 342; Rev. Ed.; 1978).

Hick uses Irenaean Theodicy to build a kind of "Zarathustra moment" of humankind reaching its spiritual zenith, whereby people irresistibly seek "God our Saviour, who desires all men to be saved and to come to the knowledge of the truth" (1 Timothy 2:3-4; *ibid.,* Hicks).

However, it cannot be said that an evil man such as Antiochus IV Epiphanes was any less evil than a murderous tyrant living today just because Antiochus lived 2,200 years ago.

As Irenaeus said, "For as He patiently suffered Jonah to be swallowed by the whale, not that he should be swallowed up and perish altogether, but that, having been cast out again, he might be the more subject to God, and might glorify Him the more who had conferred upon him such an unhoped-for deliverance, and might bring the Ninevites to a lasting repentance, so that they should be converted to the Lord, who would deliver them from death" (*Adversus Haereses;* Saint Irenaeus of Smyrna; Vol. I; Book III; Chapter 20; A.D. 180). God takes a major role in bringing the sinner to the shores of reason.

Thus the catechumen and the revert alike will not be intimidated or pushed. Once ashore, the search for God in Nineveh is self-paced. "Come unto me, all ye that labour and are heavy laden, and I will give you rest. Take my yoke upon you, and learn of me; for I am meek and lowly in heart: and ye shall find rest unto

Introduction

your souls. For my yoke is easy, and my burden is light" (Matthew 11:28-30).

The autonomy of the sinner collaborates through Free Will in Salvation, in that "there is no coercion with God, but a good will [towards us] is present with Him continually" (*ibid.*, Irenaeus, Book IV; Chapter 37).

Although the Holy Ghost, as He is described at the end of the Book of Acts, inspired Saint Paul to preach the Gospel to the Jews in Rome, where he was under house arrest, it is obvious that the Word was misinterpreted by half-listeners: "And when they agreed not among themselves, they departed, after that Paul had spoken one word, Well spake the Holy Ghost by Esaias the prophet unto our fathers, saying, Go unto this people and say, Hearing ye shall hear, and shall not understand; and seeing ye shall see, and not perceive" (Acts 28:25-26).

That is, evil, being irrational and thus defying analysis, according to the Bible, can never be understood, but will be used by wicked thinkers and doers, such as Alinsky and Soros, until the Holy Ghost steps aside, just before the Rapture: "For the mystery of iniquity doth already work: only he who now letteth will let, until he be taken out of the way" (2 Thessalonians 2:7).

As a thought experiment, it may be helpful to reinterpret various analyses by such pre-Christian thinkers as Plato, Aristotle, Plotinus, and others as though they were writing tracts in hopes of sharing philosophical affinities with Christians).

Introduction

For example, Plotinus—considered the father of Neoplatonism—did not dignify Evil as being an actual existing corporeal substance. Instead, he considered Evil to be merely the disposition of the failure-prone human will to perform bad acts (sounding a lot like the Christian concept of concupiscence), the deviant force of its influencing or affecting real elements of Creation in wrongful ways—all good real, things being spun in adverse momentum—whether via human or natural causal movement, thereby subtracting the condition of goodness (sounding a lot like Saint Augustine's conclusion in the *Enchiridion* that evil is merely the absence of good):

"The soul is not evil by herself but may degenerate by looking at darkness" (sounding a lot like the concept of the near occasion of sin; *The Six Enneads*; Plotinus; First Ennead; Eighth Tractate: "On the Nature and the Source of Evil"; Section 4; A.D. 250). Plotinus pondered the source of Absolute Evil among the three "ranks" of existence, the Monad or God; the Dyad or the Intellect; and the Tetrad or the Soul. He stated that this "Evil exists as a consequence of the derivative goods of the third rank" (*ibid.*, Section 2). Evil (or evil outcomes) therefore are the mistakes of the Soul, according to Plotinus. The consequential errors and sins answered or arising from wickedness, namely, being "The other objects, when they participate in the evil and resemble it, become evil without however being absolute Evil" (*ibid.*, Section 3).

The Law, which the Apostle Paul admits has a curse attached to it (mentioning the curse in Galatians 3:10-13 by way of its pronouncement in Nehemiah 10:29-30 and its original declaration in Deuteronomy 28:25-29),

Introduction

was given to us as a schoolmaster (Galatians 3:24) due to the depravity that has stained humanity since the Fall.

But the Seed of Abraham is saved only by the promised Grace of the Father (Romans 4:15-17). He, in whom there is no trace of iniquity, saves the Repentant—and here again there are similarities to Christian teaching in Plotinus's writing, where we learn that the Repentant "can scarcely prove to be The Good: The Absolute Good cannot be thought to have taken up its abode with Evil. We can think of it only as something of the nature of good but paying a double allegiance and unable to rest in the Authentic Good (*ibid.*, Second Tractate: On Virtue; Section 4). The condition of depravity necessitates our reaching for "exit velocity," or Salvation, to free our souls from their sinful orbit around a fallen world. "Since Evil is here, 'haunting this world by necessary law,' and it is the Soul's design to escape from Evil, we must escape hence" (*ibid.*, Section 1).

Saint Augustine, himself a Neoplatonist, contemplated the origin of sin in order to reconcile his will to God's. Similar to Plotinus, he determined that the "free judgement of the soul" was the cause of evil. Evil, which cannot come from the perfect Father, instead arises not from any substance but from the perversion of human will. While all that exists owes its being to God, evil cannot be harmed by evil or be blessed by goodness, but instead exists only as a consequence of the absence of good and is thus in a state of unbeing, which is caused by human sinfulness (*Confessions*; Saint Augustine of Hippo; Book VII; Chapters 3, 5, 12, 15, 16; A.D. 420). Thus, evil is encouraged by the

Introduction

consequence of Absolute Evil caused by Satan, the Prince of Unbeing:

"For such, evil is not a substance; the wound or the disease is a defect of the bodily substance which, as a substance, is good. Evil, then, is an accident, i.e., a privation of that good which is called health. Thus, whatever defects there are in a soul are privations of a natural good. When a cure takes place, they are not transferred elsewhere but, since they are no longer present in the state of health, they no longer exist at all" (*Enchiridion of Faith, Hope, and Love*; Saint Augustine of Hippo; Chapter 3; Section 11; A.D. 420).

Whereas evil has no actual corporeality, hell certainly exists. "But as for the cowardly, the faithless, the detestable, as for murderers, the sexually immoral, sorcerers, idolaters, and all liars, their portion will be in the lake that burns with fire and sulfur, which is the second death" (Revelation 21:8).

Sons and daughters of the Church must be warned about hell regularly so that they can avoid it. Simple enough though this exhortation appears, it is a privilege and often helpful to accompany such Bible verses with the sound texts written by Church Fathers, other theologians, and even some philosophers. However, when philosophy alone—rather than God's omniscience, sovereignty, and character—is solicited to find Truth, the result cannot reliably lead to godly edification. This is why this Constitution holds that the Bible alone must be used to resolve the proposed conflict that Hegel and Socrates contemplated between being and unbeing: the two conditions that somehow affirm perfectness in being, the "eternal forms" spoken

Introduction

of in Plato's *Republic*. Matter, by itself, is otherwise up for grabs for rascals to interpret at whim, definable by such relativists as being simultaneously "antimatter." Plato, in *Parmenides,* held that being and unbeing are merely parts of being. The relevant passage is worthy of being restated: "And therefore whether we take being and the other, or being and the one, or the one and the other, in every such case we take two things, which may be rightly called both" (*Parmenides*; Plato; Transl. Benjamin Jowett; Section 143:b-d; B.C. 370).

The metaphysics here are sheer linguistic hijinks, however. Instead, it is true that whatever God did not create does not exist and will not enter Eternal Memory. "All things were made by Him; and without Him was not any thing made that was made" (John 1:3). In fact, sinfulness and puffed-up knowledge are cast behind God's back and defined by nothingness (Isaiah 38:17). "For it is written, I will destroy the wisdom of the wise, and will bring to nothing the understanding of the prudent" (1 Corinthians 1:19)

Aristotle hauls in Parmenides's curiosity about Logos and prepares the free thinker to nominate the "unmoved mover" to be "God," in *Metaphysics* (*Metaphysics*; Aristotle; Chapter 11; Part 9; A.D. 350)

God, whomever He may now be to the curious, will then resolve the "entanglement theory," considered by the ancients as "movement of the anima," the battle of the Five Senses caught up in the endless knotting of Photons and Electrons of everyday life, by supplying a final unification of actualized Matter to idealized Form, the journey of atomic arrangement of Matter in

Introduction

attaining the perfection of the Form's principal existence.

To identify Creation solely at the atomic level is not Saint Thomas Aquinas's Teleology or its implied Intelligent Design, nor is it tolerant of the Privation Theory of Evil of Saint Augustine, the doctrine which fed minds lovingly for centuries (i.e., the idea that evil is merely the absence of good). No, the hopelessly depraved human mind yearns to deify the sensual, as Lucretius boldly deified Epicurus (*ibid.*, Book III), or reduce the spiritual entirely to an empirical science that leaves no room for God.

Dialectics, which is both an Epistemology and an Ontology, was the means by which Georg Wilhelm Friedrich Hegel decided that he had refuted the mind-body Dualism of Descartes and Kant, and which is epitomized by the hypostatic union explicated in the Athanasian Creed. Dialectics merely states that being becomes either decomposition or unbeing, or "thesis" becoming "antithesis." The application of this revolutionary misguidance quickly overtook the Liberal Arts and Sciences; the jury is out about when the takeover started and when the reprogramming was complete. There can be no doubt that as of this writing the agenda has long been completed.

Dialectic Materialism brought forth Marxism for Trotsky and Lenin, while Secular Humanism sought its own champions among the ancients, deciding that Pyrrho, prior to Sextus Empiricus, properly guided the thinker to "suspend judgement" in all matters so that academics could descend into gratuitous skepticism: e.g., that man was *not* made in God's image but is

Introduction

actually the "measure of all things," according to Protagoras. Socrates did warn in *Theaetetus* that it is mere sophistry to contend that man's presumed self-creation disqualifies him from believing in Objective Truth, whereof it is not difficult to see how errant epistemology is the seed of immorality.

Without Logos founding Athanasian Dualism; without Athanasian Dualism founding Epistemology; without Reciprocal Indwelling being imitated by the Church in its relation with the Triune God; and without Morality stemming by way of these principles from Genesis, Ethics and History will continuously be heartlessly revised by the ungodly. The Constitution and Canons, the History of this Diocese, and this integrated *Praxeologion* are positioning Christ's Church as the best University from which to gain honest, holistic learning about Life, Truth, Meaning, and Existence. We learn at the feet of the Master, who proclaimed: "I am the Way, the Truth, and the Life: No man cometh under the Father, but by Me" (John 14:6). Outside of the Church and the Holy Scriptures, God will not factor into the bedeviled demotion of human reason, emotions, and sensory data to fit convenient reworkings of critical analyses of life and text.

Accordingly, the skepticism of Sextus Empiricus's *Adversus Mathematicos* will be retrofitted to atheistic and humanist ends, intending that all meaning and inspiration should be ripped from human comprehension and reexamined at the subatomic level. The modern means of "critical thinking" are devoid of the objectivity hoped for by every writer of a definitively flawed analysis, just as Lucretius with his ardor for orgies and agnosticism promulgated the

Introduction

philosophy of Immanence (i.e., that the gods exist but are uncaring with respect to our physical existence in the material world). Celebrating Lucretius's Earth-bound doctrine are writers such as Stephen Greenblatt. In his Pulitzer-prize winning *The Swerve: How the World Became Modern*, Greenblatt tells the story of how Poggio Bracciolini, a 1400s papal emissary saved the only surviving manuscript of Lucretius's poem *De rerum natura* ("On the Nature of Things") and had it mass-produced on a printing press. The "swerve" he explains, refers to the "movement of free atoms in the void," by which a random sideways turn of atoms accounts for the existence of the world and the life forms in it (*ibid.*, Book II; 225-283). Greenblatt summarizes:

> "The stuff of the universe, Lucretius proposed, is an infinite number of atoms moving randomly through space, like dust motes in a sunbeam, colliding, hooking together, forming complex structures, breaking apart again, in a ceaseless process of creation and destruction... there is no reason to think that the earth or its inhabitants occupy a central place, no reason to set humans apart from all other animals, no hope of bribing or appeasing the gods, no place for religious fanaticism, no call for ascetic self-denial...no escape from the constant making and unmaking of forms" (*ibid.*, Preface).

Saint Jerome writes that Lucretius, driven insane by aphrodisiac consumption, committed suicide (*Chronicon*; Saint Jerome; 171; A.D. ~380). However, modern scholars believe they have debunked this claim, arguing that it was merely Christian propaganda

Introduction

against such a foe of Christianity as Lucretius. In sharp contradistinction, Greenblatt's worshipful fascination with Lucretius's physics leads to a tome that reads more like a hagiography of the Epicurean (or his Renaissance book conservationist, Bracciolini) and a confession of Darwinism:

> "When you look up at the night sky and, feeling unaccountably moved, marvel at the numberless stars, you are not seeing the handiwork of the gods or a crystalline sphere detached from our transient world. You are seeing the same material world of which you are a part and from whose elements you are made. There is no master plan, no divine architect, no intelligent design. All things, including the species to which you belong, have evolved over vast stretches of time. The evolution is random, though in the case of living organisms it involves a principle of natural selection" (*ibid.*; Introduction; pp. 25-26; 2011).

By 1874, when Irish physicist George Johnstone Stoney measured the power of a nonvalent ion, humankind became able to quantify the charge of the electron, which the world could suddenly judge as existing by means of Michael Faraday's laws of Electrolysis. By 1918, Max Planck won the Nobel Prize for discovering the "realm" of subatomic particles, known as "quanta." Creation was now ably described, although not defined, as putting forth energy and matter in terms of its mass and volume, known as its "particle" existence, and by the way mass or energy moved, hence the "wave" pattern it showed. Christianity did not have a scientific adversary exactly yet because the equations did not yet seek to refute God's existence.

Introduction

However, mass vainglory was growing—a delight to create new pseudo-scientific explanations for creation. Madame Blavatsky and her "Theosophy" combined Hinduism with Goetic Luciferianism, and the Babylonian Kabbala to produce her 1888 book *Cosmogenesis*, the second of two volumes that, together, were titled *The Secret Doctrine*.

Georges Gurdjiev in 1916 postulated the Enneagram to supplant the original Eight Deadly Sins of Evagrius Ponticus, positioning these offenses against God as mere psychological mindsets, constructing formative New Age apologetics.

In 1896, Sigmund Freud presented Psychoanalysis, supplanting the notion of Prevenient Grace (which can vanquish concupiscence) with the tawdry idea that the "subconscious" controls the psyche by seeking gratification of the "id" and the "libido." Freud exploited the mindset of a fascinated public, eager to find simple sordid substitutes for biblical subjects such as Theotokos, which itself was relegated beneath the Freudian idea of motherhood described in the "Oedipal Complex"—according to which men "sublimate" their lust to have sex with their mothers by building industries and cities, no longer purifying their souls but actualizing their "egos."

The Cubist and Futurist artists meanwhile were deconstructing matter and energy into relativistic ways even of seeing the material world. "True belief" in, say, the Fruits of the Spirit was only "justified" according to the opinion of the beholder, as if viewing a still life by Picasso.

Introduction

Albert Einstein, who was not an atheist, was devising the "Time Dilation" already espoused in 1 Peter 3:8, by which a "day equals a thousand years" (and vice versa) within Eternity. His Theory of Relativity produced an inadvertent mathematical proof for the homogeneity of time and matter expressed by the Earth's collaboration with the sun and moon to produce hours and days. (Genesis 1:14-19)

At the time when Paul Dirac was equating "parity" with "symmetry" in describing the "special relativity" of subatomic particles, the 1928 *Book of Common Prayer* was being published. The agrarian-life "excuse" given by a reluctant receiver of the Eucharist within the Exhortations of Holy Communion could suddenly speciously be argued with a relativistic flair: choosing to take care of one's new heifer substantiates the verity of Christ's rhetoric against the Pharisees in Luke 14:5, that properly nurturing livestock is relative to saving one's sheep from a ditch on the Sabbath or receiving the Host on a Sunday, and so on. Whereas relativity has made Constitutionality vitally important, Dirac's Equation now allowed the artful rhetorical dodger to conflate evil with good. Dirac, who had also purported the existence of "antimatter" had unwittingly given wrongful gravity to the idea that Plato had stated—i.e., that being and unbeing are merely two different forms of existence, namely relative to one another, or part of a necessary whole, just as Zoroastrianism holds Ahura Mazda's powers of goodness to be only as strong as the evil might of Angra Mainyu; just as the power of the Light Side is equal to that of the Dark Force in Joseph Campbell's "Star-Wars" religion.

Introduction

With relativity now the reigning epistemology in the twentieth century, Deconstructivism presented a complacent faultiness likened to perceiving the nude Emperor to be wearing clothes in all considerations of any subject and terming it "critical thinking." All forms of Love became "psychological egoism" by serial adulterer and darling of the Neoconservative Movement Ayn Rand, who devilishly named her faux philosophy "Objectivism." All thinking was reduced to subjectivity by this solipsist: that is, the *cogito* in the phrase *cogito ergo sum* actually only meant that knowledge of the existence of *self* is the only possible knowledge that can be obtained (whereas Descartes believed in God, as we know Him, entirely).

Absolute Truth is no longer abided by journalists and historians. Evil and virtuous acts are simultaneously either good or evil, depending on the context. Less than ten years ago the sexual menace of pedophilia was headlined as a "a Disorder and not a Crime (Opinion; Margo Kaplan; *New York Times*; Oct. 5, 2014). Just five years later, "Leave Drag Queen Story Hour Alone" was published as a prominent opinion piece (Opinion; Michelle Goldberg; *New York Times*; June 7, 2019). As each year rolls by, the envelope is pushed further and further in the direction of sexualizing and queerifying our children ("We're Coming For Your Children"; San Francisco Gay Choir; YouTube; posted July 9, 2021).

With the quantification of every aspect of life solely in terms of sensual gratification and burgeoning of pride, the determinant of life and death is no longer believed to be good versus evil, but merely the egoistic paradigm of one's inescapably subjective way of seeing reality, whereby the mission of Schrodinger's Cat is to

Introduction

equate right with wrong. Whether the cat is being degraded inside the closed box by the radioactive contents of the broken flask, or she has not broken the flask and survived is not important. Whether the 19 subatomic particles and their 37 variations are each spinning or moving linearly is moot. Whether Einstein can unify the Four Fundamental Forces is inconsequential. What matters is only that the cat is both alive and dead at the same time. Because the wave-form antithesis of every Photon, Electron, and Quark sits in Dialectic Conflation at the moment it is measured, both right and wrong are coequal. Matter and antimatter are the same. Being and unbeing are identical. From this, illicit theology can pervert thinking into believing that God, who formed the world out of the nothingness from which all matter originates, is Himself partly nothingness (recall Socrates' "being versus unbeing" statement earlier; *Parmenides*; Plato; Transl. Benjamin Jowett; Section 143:b-d; B.C. 370). Nihilism now rules the human mind.

With being and unbeing being the mere obverse quanta of the same mechanics, Dirac's Equation can be cunningly used to presume that an evil man need never repent, because the proof of antimatter presents a perfectly equal but opposite universe and paradigm by which all his malevolent acts are known as charitable acts.

Whereas Fr. George Lemaître used Dirac's Equation to depict the battle between matter and antimatter that resulted in the Big Bang, the irresistible *constant* of Psalm 19:1 refutes that the victory of matter was arbitrary. "The heavens declare the glory of God; and the firmament sheweth His handywork" (Psalm 19:1).

Introduction

This verse functions to purport that the following attestation in 1937 by Max Planck, the father of Quantum Mechanics, supports this refutation: "Both religion and science need for their activities the belief in God, and moreover God stands for the former in the beginning, and for the latter at the end of the whole thinking. For the former, God represents the basis, for the latter—the crown of any reasoning concerning the world-view" ("Religion und Naturwissenschaft"; Max Planck; Trans. Johann Ambrosius Barth Verlag; Leipzig; Postum. 1958).

In the nuclear age, "quantum entanglement" can be more appropriately understood as the "madness of the peoples" on the verge of riots every summer and endless rumors of apocalyptic war (Psalm 65:7).

Whereas Scripture rebukes the taste for tumult, Psalm 19:1 may also lead one to a certain earlier observation in science. In 1801, Thomas Young employed his famous "double-slit" experiment to prove that Photons of light and subparts of atoms (such as Quarks and Electrons) sometimes sit in what is called a "superposition," meaning that they can coexist together in wave-particle duality, although the cause remains unknown. In fact, only Photons are capable of superpositioning with all of the other 18 subatomic particles and their 37 variations, to output either light (photon-emitting) or wave (particle-emitting). There *is* then a case for the Omnipresence of God permeating every molecule in the world. "When electrons interact, a phenomenon called quantum electrodynamics (QED) occurs where every instance of an interaction requires a photon of light to supply the electron with the needed energy. From the vast presence of the light

Introduction

waves of the EMR spectrum, a single photon converts from a wave to a particle, and engages with the electron to supply the needed energy ... Light is involved in every interaction of the hundreds of billions of interactions occurring every second in the human brain. In every neuron, every axon, every firing synapse, photons of light are actively crucially involved—the same with all 7 billion people on the planet" (*A Quantum Case for God*; Denis Zetting; Chapter 3: "Quantum Electrodynamics & Omnipresence"; pp. 25-27; 2016).

Even the mysterious black Gravitons can unite with Photons, the Graviton's uniqueness being that it is the only subatomic quantum that is known to influence Dark Matter and Dark Energy. In that the "Cloud of Unknowing" is clearly at hand here, could Dark Matter be why evil people gravitate downward, to hell, refusing the light, which is the only force that can penetrate it? Do Dark Matter and Energy define that uncrossable "gulf" between Lazarus and the rich man (Luke 16:19-31)? Is this what our Lord meant by "outer darkness"? "But the children of the kingdom shall be cast out into outer darkness: there shall be weeping and gnashing of teeth" (Matthew 8:12).

While Photons compose the light that penetrates the Dark Matter and Energy that comprise 85 percent of the Universe, and these Dark quanta pass right through human bodies and all other matter with no effect on anything, except when penetrated by Photons or pulled downward by Gravitons, perhaps we are being faced with the empirical discovery of the Light that the darkness could not comprehend (John 1:5)—when God created the Universe out of the Nihil, the unbeing that

Introduction

defines the spiritual war between the matter that Christians strive to see sanctified, and the antimatter of madness and evil. "In the beginning was the Word, and the Word was with God, and the Word was God. The same was in the beginning with God. All things were made by Him; and without Him was not anything made that was made. In Him was life; and the life was the light of men" (John 1:1-4).

Did God not create the world with the darkness over matter and energy, which shadowed the firmament, until Photons poured across it? "In the beginning, God created the heavens and the earth. Now the earth was formless and empty, darkness was over the surface of the deep, and the Spirit of God was hovering over the waters. And God said, 'Let there be light,' and there was light" (Genesis 1:1-2). In the hands of science-loving unsaved human beings, is the Higgs Boson quantum only capable of being accelerated through the Hadron Collider at the CERN Laboratory, emitting the "Beast" at the other end? Is the Son of Man not the living proof that our very God comes from our very God and that Light comes from Light and that the *theosis* contemplated by Saints Irenaeus and Athanasius produced the very metaphysics according to which we hope to elude this Dark Matter, the evil of Lucifer and our fallen nature, that pervades the material world and unite with Him?

Although it is not a term used in the Bible, *theosis* (i.e., that we may become one God through our Salvation) may be a hopeful conclusion to our corporeal existence. Just like the term "Trinity" is not used and yet is true, *theosis* is amply supported by Sacred Scripture. For example: "Beloved, now we are the sons

Introduction

of God, and it doth not yet appear what we shall be: but we know that, when He shall appear, we shall be like Him; for we shall see Him as He is" (1 John 3:2). *Theosis* is also supported by the Apostolic Fathers: "The Son of God became man, that we might become god" ["becoming by grace what God is by nature"] (*De Incarnatione de Verbi*; Part 54; Section 3; Saint Athanasius of Alexandria; A.D. ~320). Moreover, "[T]he Word of God, our Lord Jesus Christ ... did, through His transcendent love, become what we are, that He might bring us to be even what He is Himself" (*Adversus Haereses;* Book V; Pref.; Saint Irenaeus; A.D. 180).

Without Faith in Jesus, the Intellect is useless to bring about good things. In secular circles, Quantum Economics or Critical Race Theory could offer transient satisfaction, but the pursuit of any branch of knowledge without biblical understanding and faith in the Triune God leads ultimately to shameful wars and riots—never to any lasting peace or concord (Proverbs 3:5-6; 28:7).

Faith is everything and requires no clever proofs or schools of philosophy: "Now Faith is the substance of things hoped for, the evidence of things not seen ... without Faith it is impossible to please Him: for he that cometh to God must believe that He is, and that He is a rewarder of them that diligently seek Him" (Hebrews 11:1, 6)

The Constitution and Canons of TACA are intended to help facilitate understanding of the Bible, adding contemporary examples and analyses to the 1928 *Book of Common Prayer* and other Anglican formularies. Knowledge, consumed at a faster rate now than in all of

Introduction

history through electronic means, must be given such guidance. Faith is foundational and necessary, but it is not the end of the story: "And beside this, giving all diligence, add to your faith virtue; and to virtue knowledge; and to knowledge temperance; and to temperance patience; and to patience godliness; and to godliness brotherly kindness; and to brotherly kindness charity" (2 Peter 1:5-7).

Thus, because we obey Sacred Scripture and we follow Sacred Tradition—because it is God's omnibenevolent pleasure that we do so, not to keep it for ourselves only, but to pass it on to the next generation so that they can then teach their children—this Traditional Anglican Church of America presents for you this Constitution and these Canons, together with the History of the Diocese, and it does so with an integrated *Praxeologion*.

It is the prayerful hope of this TACA Diocese that this writing will be a source of inspiration, education, discipline, and edification for all who avail themselves of it.

> "We then that are strong ought to bear the infirmities of the weak, and not to please ourselves. Let everyone of us please his neighbour for his good to edification. For even Christ pleased not himself, but, as it is written, The reproaches of them that reproached thee fell on me. For whatsoever things were written aforetime were written for our learning, that we through patience and comfort of the scriptures may have hope" (Romans 15:1-4).

Article I. Governing Principles and Essential Declarations of This TACA Diocese

ARTICLE I. Governing Principles and Essential Declarations of This TACA Diocese

A. Position Within the Continuing Anglican Movement

i) This Diocese hereby holds without reservation to the incontestable conclusions of the St. Louis Affirmation of 1978 and accepts the common heralding of its international congress as being the formal commencement of the Continuing Anglican Movement.

ii) At the same time, Traditional Anglican Church of America also regards that the revival of the reformational moral praxis of Anglicanism has already long enjoyed the precursory action that helps define the orthodoxy of this TACA Diocese.

a) Since Medieval times, long before the printing press, prophetic moral rectification has influenced the goal of great churchman whose sacrifices and tenacity have inspired the European Reformation, such as Peter Waldo, John Wycliffe, Jan Hus, Girolamo Savonarola, Lorenzo Valla, and Wessel Gansfort.

b) Prior to the Middle Ages, reforms in Christianity depended upon the ratifying of canons written for Ecumenical Councils—the solely relevant ones being the initial seven, supervising man's indefatigable moral accountability for the imitation of a fully human

Article I. Governing Principles and Essential Declarations of This TACA Diocese

and fully divine Christ, and of His saints. Whereof:

1) Ecclesiastical dominion is possessed entirely by Christ the King, whereby this Traditional Anglican Church of America operates as a constituent autonomous Diocese. Along with a permanent provision for Communion with other Traditional Anglican bodies, a Synod is also held as a permanent provision, to mediate affairs within a greater Ecumenical body. Such consular centrality would pull together the fragmented intention of true Ecumenism, intended since ancient times by Canons 9 and 17 of the Council of Chalcedon (A.D. 451); by Chapter II of Novella 131 of the *Novellae Constitutiones* of Emperor Justinian I (A.D. 554); by Canons VIII and XXV of the Quinisext Council of Justinian II (A.D. 692); and by Part III: "Tripartite Synod" of the Affirmation of Saint Louis (1977). Although the Bishop of Rome, Leo I, nullified Canon 28 of the Chalcedon Council during Session XVI, the criteria that would have properly designated Constantinople and Rome as being Ecumenical co-equals among the Five Patriarchates (i.e., that they were indeed Apostolic Sees descended from Saints Andrew and Peter) make inevitable the demotion of Papal primacy in Christian worship within England and America. Articles 37 to 39 of the Thirty-Nine Declarations of Religion, appropriately elevate Christ's sovereignty above the Papacy, calling to mind

Article I. Governing Principles and Essential Declarations of This TACA Diocese

> the Polity signified by that voided ancient Canon 28, that the bishoprics of Christendom, which have descended from Christ the King, through His Apostles, unto the Sees, and the Parishes and Congregations, prove that "the government shall be upon His shoulder" (Isaiah 9:6).
>
> 2) TACA implores patriarchal exemplars to epitomize orthodoxy in the worshipping of the both fully human and fully divine Christ, asking godly men to come forward—sinners who will nonetheless tirelessly aim to be Christlike at all times and in all ways.

c) With respect to the fully human Christ whom we worship, "we have not an high priest which cannot be touched with the feeling of our infirmities; but was in all points tempted like as we are, yet without sin" (Hebrews 4:15).

d) It is no small task to emulate Christ, Who was made like His brothers in every respect (Hebrews 2:17-18). Christ thus spent the noblest of agonies resisting the same temptations plaguing mortal men, but being sinless, and His example constitutes the fairest of all expectations for bishops to accept as their rule (2 Corinthians 5:21).

e) With respect to the fully divine Christ whom we worship, to actualize acceptance of the homoousian fact (i.e., that Christ is of one substance with the Father while simultaneously

Article I. *Governing Principles and Essential Declarations of This TACA Diocese*

being fully man—which calls manhood into submission, to be *like* God) is to share collective remembrance with the brethren about past failures by other lesser shepherds, but also to encourage them in collaborative witness, awaiting Christ's return (John 16:22-23; Hebrews 13:17).

f) Recognizing human depravity but exemplifying a moral emulation of the sinlessness of Christ, an orthodoxy that should never have wavered—especially since Chalcedon decided in favor of it—shall help ensure that men and women, burned away of their dross, may be rejoined with their Creator (Isaiah 1:25; Revelation 3:19).

1) It should be taught why the Reformation and other corrective actions were necessary to correct all the storied failures of the lapsed patriarchates—the Monophysite rebellion of Alexandria in A.D. 451; the sorrow of the Great Schism since 1154; the destruction of half of Constantinople by papal Crusaders in 1203; the excesses, liberalism, and madness of members of today's World Council of Churches, to name just a few.

2) Later relevant cousins grew as offshoots of the "Root of Jesse," such as Anglo-Catholicism in the 1850s. The Oxford Movement, which arose in reaction to dissatisfaction with Modernism in the Church of England, as voiced by the Tractarians, and sought to reinstate some older faith traditions practiced by Rome and bring them into the Anglican Church. The

Article I. Governing Principles and Essential Declarations of This TACA Diocese

Oxford Movement is thus one of the earliest examples of the Traditionalist Anglican movement in the modern era. It provides a meaningful historical context to TACA—that is, if one can ignore its Tridentine pageantry and obsequious affinity to Rome, which became so ardent that many adherents of this Movement ended up becoming Roman Catholics. (Its rightful role as one of the first five Apostolic Sees notwithstanding, Rome today—and Rome since well before the end of the Seventh Ecumenical Council of Nicaea II—is clearly nothing to emulate.)

3) Concomitant with the Oxford Movement came the dogmatizing of an "immaculate conception" for Theotokos herself by Pope Pius IX during Vatican I. Rather than being content to allow the Faithful to offer the Virgin the highest form of veneration (*hyperdulia*) as the "God bearer," a title defined for her at Chalcedon, Vatican I made the mistake of turning a venerable tradition of the Church into Law, thus creating factions, schisms, scandals, stumbling blocks, and a party spirit (1 Corinthians 12:25, Galatians 5:20). "For a good tree bringeth not forth corrupt fruit; neither doth a corrupt tree bring forth good fruit. For every tree is known by his own fruit" (Luke 6:43-44). Destroying for billions ever after a lifetime of otherwise gladful contemplation about the actual nature of the Virgin, this "dogma" subjugated any manner of beautiful

Article I. Governing Principles and Essential Declarations of This TACA Diocese

meditations traditionally associated with her by the saints (e.g., Justin Martyr, Irenaeus, Cyril of Jerusalem, Ambrose, Bernard, Aquinas) to the rule of a profane bishopric that concurrently declared with spell-binding rhetoric posing as dogma that anything uttered *ex cathedra* by the Patriarch of Rome is "infallible."

This new worshipful veneration of Mary and the pope of Rome's "infallibility" became, in fact, the worship of dogma itself, providing *occultus* in place of the seeking of a deep connectedness with God and passing off as "merciful" all the ensuing sordid errors of modern papal encyclicals, bulls, oral broadsides, letters, exhortations, and *motu proprios* leading up to the abuses of Vatican II that continue to this day.

4) After the turn of the century, pastors seeking Latin revival began to incorporate High-Church practices into their institutional parishes. However, when Canon Samuel Daw of Hamilton, Ontario, introduced Auricular Confession, and the combining of Evensong with Eucharistic Benediction, along with the Exposition of the Eucharist with the Monstrance into Saint John the Evangelist Church, the bishops of Niagara ordered him to return to Low-Church form. Refusing, Canon Daw and his son, Fr. William Henry Daw, departed from the Anglican Church of Canada and formed the Independent Anglican Church of Canada Synod of 1934 (with

Article I. Governing Principles and Essential Declarations of This TACA Diocese

whom TACA had been aligned during the former's long-held period of conservativism). Also as a classical revival—"classical" in terms of advocating for the formation of the "historical Episcopate" that was called for by the 1886 Chicago-Lambeth Quadrilateral—the Orthodox-Anglican Communion retained the Low-Church tradition of pre-1979 revisions of the Book of Common Prayer. It was founded in Statesville, North Carolina, by James Parker Dees in 1964. His Cranmer Seminary (later, Saint Andrew's Theological College and Seminary) strained away Modernism from the mindset of its Master of Theology students, aiming a Reformist postulancy toward the Apostolic Succession—the orthodox continuity that was mandated for Anglicanism since William Laud fervently propelled consecrational validity and Liturgical compliance through Canterbury and Scotland, so that "Episcopalianism" would mean rule by honorable bishops.

5) Today, since sexualization and feminism have left no chance for orthodoxy to rule the Anglican Communion or the Episcopal Church in the United States, the righteous decrial of the St. Louis Affirmation alone can no longer solely keep new Dioceses claiming to be "Continuing Anglican" from wrongfully expanding the definition of "subsidiarity" to mean that any one of its parishes could decide for itself whether to ordain women. Meanwhile, and as

an example, Old Catholicism, no longer sporting the original conservatism of New Utrecht that sprung out of protest against the abuses of Vatican I, is actively ordaining homosexuals and women, and in some areas promoting actual satanism.

6) Our Traditional Anglican Church of America accurately considers itself to be a true "proto-continuum" that has for more than a century been the orthodox answer to the Modernism, heterodoxy, heresy, profanity, and sordidity that has all but overtaken the Church, sullying the ecclesiastical state and purpose of the Church and rendering the Anglican reformation in the modern age abused and neglected. This continuum, though called Traditional Anglican Church of America by way of context, can be just as rightly seen as none other than orthodox Christianity in the Liturgical tradition of the West (in contradistinction to the Liturgical tradition of the East, as exemplified, e.g., by the Divine Liturgies of Saints Basil and Chrysostom, respectively).

B. Church Planting Shall Advance Traditional Anglicanism

i) Mindful of our independence from institutionalized moral error, we distinguish our autonomy by professing our character to be fundamentally Anglican but without alienating the

Article I. Governing Principles and Essential Declarations of This TACA Diocese

youthful mind, always in a Pauline spirit, being all things unto all men, as needed (1 Corinthians 9:22).

ii) Our religious legacy remains in permanent theological communion with the Archbishopric of Canterbury and the See of Glastonbury.

iii) Ancient Anglicanism is proved to have been formed of the Celtic, Britannic, Anglo-Saxon, and Roman-Imperial complexion; it has always awarded liturgical and eucharistic hegemony for Ecclesia, and to which new Anglican churches shall grow from small plants in homes and "upper rooms"—as they did in A.D. 179, in the shrine room of Bishop Lucius, that yellow-paneled antechamber that was dug up in the 1980s underneath Gracechurch Street in London, which developed into Saint Peter's upon Cornhill; or, as they did for the Scottish Gaels of Iona, when St. Columba began the Iona Abbey on a farm, in A.D. 563; or, as Rev. William Vessey started a Vestry in his father's house in the Province of Massachusetts, which evolved into the Trinity Church of Manhattan, New York, in 1697. From small starts come great churches: "For who hath despised the day of small things?" (Zechariah 4:10).

iv) Surely as Saint John Cassian received from Bishop Innocent of Rome the commission to found the Abbey of Saint Victor in Marseille, France, the Archbishop of TACA shall ordain or convalidate his priests from the secular world to add religious life to the professions of working men and women by planting churches. "For ye remember, brethren, our labour and travail: for labouring night and day,

Article I. Governing Principles and Essential Declarations of This TACA Diocese

because we would not be chargeable unto any of you, we preached unto you the Gospel of God" (1 Thessalonians 2:9).

C. True Biblical Anglicanism as Deposit of Faith

i) Because it is inarguable that the King James Bible contains the inspired Word of God as our perfect religious guide, "profitable for doctrine, for reproof, for correction, for instruction in righteousness" (2 Timothy 3:16-17), Christians are encouraged to depart from religious and secular institutions that practice and teach heterodoxy and heresy (2 Corinthians 11:13-15).

ii) The offering of comfort to exiles of morally flawed churches shall provide a remedy for the illicit doctrines taught in other "churches," by which episcopal mountebanks in said lapsed churches commit *latae sententiae* excommunication against themselves, because they have left their "first love" (Revelation 2:4) and have transformed their churches into un-churches.

iii) A sound Episcopate, as exemplified by the House of Bishops of this TACA Diocese, instead replenishes hope for the Deposit of Faith inside an uninterrupted See of healthy conservativism and godly orthodoxy (1 Timothy 4:14-16).

iv) Our TACA Archbishop shall assume leadership over Christian refugees fleeing bad bishops. "For it is written in the book of Psalms [69:25], 'Let his habitation be desolate, and let no man dwell therein: and his bishoprick let another take" (Acts 1:20).

Article I. Governing Principles and Essential Declarations of This TACA Diocese

a) The Archbishop, the House of Bishops, and all Jurisdictions that are in Communion with this TACA Diocese shall ensure enjoyment of the Deposit of Faith that has for too long been denied these refugees by fallen churches, whose Grace has definitively elapsed.

1) "He that hath an ear, let him hear what the Spirit saith unto the churches; To him that overcometh will I give to eat of the tree of life, which is in the midst of the paradise of God" (Revelation 2:7).

D. The Archbishop as Father of a Family

i) A safe Church, if she is truly the "Bride of Christ," may be likened to a "garden inclosed ... a spring shut up, a fountain sealed" (Song of Solomon 4:12);

a) The House of Bishops is created by gift of prophecy and the laying on of hands. The gift is the prophetic understanding, exemplified and taught to encourage and comfort ministers and all the flocks, that the Deposit of Faith, Hope, and Love shall bring forth both Revelation and Salvation (1 Timothy 4:14-16; Jeremiah 3:15).

ii) The House of Bishops safeguards our precious Church life that has been bought with the precious blood of God's son, with no permeation of ungodly worldliness: "Take heed therefore unto yourselves, and to all the flock, over the which the Holy Ghost hath made you overseers, to feed the church of God, which he hath purchased with his own blood" (Acts 20:28).

Article I. Governing Principles and Essential Declarations of This TACA Diocese

iii) TACA shall sustain a robust Diocese that reflects the unassailable patriarchy of its Archbishop, who shepherds his flock. "The father of the righteous shall greatly rejoice: and he that begetteth a wise child shall have joy of him" (Proverbs 23:24).

iv) Always vigilant, Ecclesiastical Authority shall approve a Constitution and Canons that are written and reviewed by protective and loving fathers, who "have no fellowship with the unfruitful works of darkness, but rather reprove them" (Ephesians 5:11).

> a) As St. Paul the Apostle told the Ephesians, as the Church is subordinate to Christ, so too are wives subject to their husbands in all matters. (Ephesians 5:25)
>
> b) Guided by the defender of the Christian home—the husband and father—a good bride and her children are permitted the freedom to radiate most abundantly: "Her children arise up, and call her blessed; her husband also, and he praiseth her" (Proverb 31:28), and "Lo, children are an heritage of the Lord; and the fruit of the womb is his reward" (Psalm 127:3).

v) A blueprint for a man is that he lovingly manage his family and keep the home pure while also being ready to defend the homestead from all enemies, so that in a Christlike manner he "might sanctify and cleanse it," nurturing his family through his godly strength, "as Christ also loved the church, and gave Himself for it" (Ephesians 5:25-26). He cannot cease being vigilant, for the devil prowls around restlessly outside the gates, like a roaring lion (1 Peter 5:8).

E. The Permanent Provision for Theological Communion

i) The provision for Communion for which Traditionalist Anglican churches shall share the same theology, Liturgical and Eucharistic devotion, and affinity for true orthodoxy is permanent.

ii) In this permanent provision, the primus Communion shall be provisionally named and described solely according to the Letter, Encyclical, or Bull that shall be issued to his House of Bishops and Clergy by the Archbishop of this TACA Diocese (e.g., as it is, as of July 2023, enjoyed with the Emmanuel Anglican Communion, Inc., of Indiantown, Florida; and as it had been, until the nullification of said Communion in 2023 with the Independent Anglican Church of Canada 1934 and with the Reformed Anglican Church of Saint Augustine, Florida). Also:

iii) Said provisional Communion shall consist of mutually independent confraternal Jurisdictions.

    a) The joint Primates of said provisional Communion permit Eucharistic and Liturgical devotion to be shared between church members.

    b) The elevation to a provisional Communion of a singular Presiding Archprimate at any future date would be at the discretion of these respective prelates of the Ecclesiastical Authority (i.e.,

Article I. Governing Principles and Essential Declarations of This TACA Diocese

Archbishops) at each mutually autonomous Diocese. Also:

iv) As of September 2023, TACA also shares theological Communion with the Emmanuel Anglican Communion, Inc., of Indiantown, Florida. Also:

v) As of September 2023, TACA also shares theological Communion with the Traditional Anglican Church of Ecuador.

vi) Each communing Jurisdiction operates freely in regard to churchmanship, approved liturgies, and ministries, and remains in Communion by committing to the 1928 Book of Common Prayer, the Thirty-Nine Articles of Religion, and the King James Bible, and always exhibiting orthodoxy. Thus:

vii) The virtue of Custom and Subsidiarity bestows and entrusts all Congregations and Missions participating in theological confraternal Communion with their own sovereignty, operating with *subsidiarius sui iuris coaequalis*—that is, existing in one's own right with coequal subsidiarity.

viii) There shall be no shared public administrative or fiscal legal incorporation that is proprietary, a partnership, a nonprofit or profit corporation, or otherwise, serving any such theological Communion.

ix) Regarding a provisional future Communion with another outside Diocese, there shall be no joint or Common Law institution administering a theological Communion, nor a Customary, nor a prelature, nor a

Article I. Governing Principles and Essential Declarations of This TACA Diocese

primature/primacy, nor a shared Constitution and Canons.

x) In attaining Ecclesiastical Polity, a theological Communion with TACA is characterized by a broad-based religious ecumenism—a fellowship lovingly held between jurisdictions, that operates under TACA's permanent provision that theological and Eucharistic Communion with this TACA Diocese is open to all such orthodox Traditionalist Anglican churches.

F. The Purpose and Work of TACA

i) It shall be TACA's mission to support its parishes and inner dioceses in offering the attainment of the Kingdom of God by liturgically, sacramentally, and charitably sharing the inspiration of and faith in Jesus Christ through the power of the Holy Spirit, so that increased numbers of people will become true Christians in hearty and steadfast fellowship with the Church.

ii) TACA members practice the Liturgy and bring cheer, encouragement, and help to our members, ministries, neighbors, and all the Faithful so that new truly Anglican bodies can be planted and grown, while the House of Bishops buttresses and hones newly instituted Bodies in becoming ably administrated and properly catechized shepherds of their own flocks.

Article I. Governing Principles and Essential Declarations of This TACA Diocese

G. Collaboration With Laity

i) TACA Laity participates in this TACA Diocese as ministerial helpers, and as celebrants of Mass and Daily Office, while also delegating Faithful witness at home.

ii) As God uplifts the ontology of humanity by graduating the Son of Man from His sufferings on Earth to come sit at His right hand, so shall the Laity be encouraged to partake in ecclesiastical life, advancing to God's side. Thus:

a) "Behold what manner of love the Father has bestowed upon us, that we should be called the sons of God" (1 John 3:1), and "as many as received Him, to them gave He power to become the sons of God, even to them that believe on His name" (John 1:12).

b) The TACA Laity shall be as a priestly people. (Isaiah 61:6; Exodus 19:6; 1 Peter 2:9; Revelation 1:6).

iii) The Laity shall occupy the offices of Warden, appointed Lay Minister, Lector, Acolyte, Sexton, Altar Server, Cleaner, and Secretary and Treasurer; they may also serve the Church as counselors, secular canons, paid and volunteer helpers, and as any other approved role that may serve the religious and spiritual ends of the Church.

Article I. Governing Principles and Essential Declarations of This TACA Diocese

H. The Mastering of our Servile Leadership for Society

i) It is also necessary that Subsidiarity be checked in case inner division may beset the Free Will of constituents and rupture unity. The TACA Diocese lives according to the following rule:

a) Anger must be resolved before the sun sets (Ephesians 4:26-27).

b) Church members must arbitrate wrongdoing, first with loving discretion but ultimately with public sternness as the very last resort (Matthew 18:15-17).

c) The first shall be last. Raising to a higher status (*sublimare*) disputation over who is the "greater" (Luke 22:24-30) serves only to demote the proud into subservience to the meek.

d) Teach humility: Jesus, in Luke 22:24-30, commends his friends to the service of judging the "Twelve Tribes" by considering that the lesser is charged with leading the greater. This was Jesus's way of placing innocent meekness above the greatest wisdom, as "he that is greatest among you, let him be as the younger; and he that is chief, as he that doth serve," and as He said of His Father, "thou has hid these things from the wise and prudent, and has revealed them unto babes (Matthew 11:25). By this:

1) Reward humility with Love. There were also the sons and wife of Zebedee, who had hoped

Article I. Governing Principles and Essential Declarations of This TACA Diocese

that James the Great and John would be seen by Christ as the greatest. Acknowledging their worth, Jesus remarked on their and His own worldly power, saying, "For even the Son of man came not to be ministered unto, but to minister, and to give his life a ransom for many" (Mark 10:45).

2) Strong, patient priests shall lead TACA parishes. Richard Hooker explains why Jesus, despite giving authority to those with basic virile strength, did not agree that the "Sons of Thunder" will sit on his right hand and on his left, at the request of their mother (Matthew 20:20-28): "If you take away order, of necessity confusion follows, whence arises division and from division destruction. Therefore, the Apostle has said that all things should be done with order. This order consists in distinction of degree, so that one differs from his fellow in power and the lesser obeys the greater, otherwise society cannot hold together. And so it is a divine law [*lex divinitatis*], says Blessed Dionysius, for the lowest things to be led back to the highest by those that are intermediate" ("Autograph Notes"; Supplement II; Part 3; Section 494; Richard Hooker; 1594).

3) The Priest shall guide Faith in the unknowable greatness of God. Hooker above lauds Saint [or "Pseudo"-] Dionysius the Areopagite, for whom Divine Law—*Lex Divinitatis*—dictates that man's limited

Article I. Governing Principles and Essential Declarations of This TACA Diocese

comprehension of the omnipotence of God dictates peaceful acceptance of human ignorance. "If any one, then, should despise this sacred regulation, and betaking himself to a wretched self-conceit, should deem himself sufficient for the supremely Divine Converse, and look down upon pious men, and if he should further request [such] requests, [which are] unworthy of God, and not holy, and if he should have his aspiration for things divine not sustained, and correlative to himself, he will fail in his ignorant request, through his own fault" (Ecclesiastical Hierarchy; Caput VII; Contemplation III; Section 6; Areopagite, Pseudo-Dionysius; A.D. 450).

4) Priests shall espouse sound Epistemology. Expounding upon the idea that human intellect shall submit itself to God's omniscience, Thomas à Kempis wrote, "Of the Humble Conceit of Ourselves... Cease from an inordinate desire of knowing, for therein is much distraction and deceit... How much the more thou knowest, and how much the better thou understandest, so much the more grievously shalt thou therefore be judged, unless thy life be also more holy. Be not therefore extolled in thine own mind for any art or science, but rather let the knowledge given thee, make thee more humble and cautious" (*Of the Imitation of Christ*; Chapter 2; Lines 5-20; Thomas à Kempis; 1427). Priests should be sober in the quest to acquire knowledge for its

Article I. Governing Principles and Essential Declarations of This TACA Diocese

own sake, the Preacher warning, "be admonished: of making many books there is no end; and much study is a weariness of the flesh" (Ecclesiastes 12:12).

5) Priests shall preach sound practicality. Whereas Dionysius teaches "negation" of knowledge to obliterate hubris by accepting Divine Law, Saint Augustine of Hippo concentrates on the "positivism" of observable variables, such as human corporeal vulnerability to all the physical ordinances of Natural Law since the Fall of Man rendered mankind mortal. Even the culture of the ancient Egyptians, whose descendancy from Nimrod is known in Isaiah 11:15 to be damned, has brought forth God's Truth: "These, therefore, the Christian, when he separates himself in spirit from the miserable fellowship of these men, ought to take away from them, and to devote to their proper use in preaching the Gospel" (On Christian Doctrine; Book II; Caput 40; Part 60; Saint Augustine of Hippo; A.D. 397). These "ordinances" of Natural Law are revocable, however; after the Tribulation, the ordinances of God will be shaken (Matthew 24:29, Jeremiah 31:35-40).

6) Priests shall elevate Divine Law above Natural Law, using Sacred Scripture. For Saint Thomas Aquinas, as with Dionysius, the moment of firstly admitting ignorance of God's total greatness is when sincere contemplation

Article I. Governing Principles and Essential Declarations of This TACA Diocese

of Natural Law can begin: "So to study Him, we study what He has not—such as composition and motion" (Summa Theologica; Part One: The One God; Aquinas, Saint Thomas; 1274). Parishioners, who are at the mercy of the aforementioned "ordinances," whereof disease, aging, and accidents are borne by gravity, biology, and time, should suffer no guilt in believing verified scientific truth, such as medical arts, which are designed to serve them (i.e., when its practitioners are not in league with Mammon). Thus:

7) Priests shall teach Logos. Even as Aquinas affirms that Aristotle, in his Sixth Chapter of Metaphysics, correctly elects Philosophy and the Liberal Arts and Sciences to comprehend the physical world, a higher Metaphysics is commanded, to propel science toward Heaven (Colossians 3:1-2). By Book VI of his *Nicomachean Ethics,* Aristotle was dedicated to discovering the true source of practical wisdom, known to Athenians since the days of Heraclitus (in *On Nature*) as the untouchable "Logos" that determines ethical virtue.

8) A loving Episcopate should help Priests reconcile Natural Law to Divine Law. Truly, Saint John the Apostle supplies the connection in two places: First, in Chapter 1 of his Gospel, in which God the Word speaks the world into existence—"In the beginning was the Word, and the Word was with God, and the Word was God

Article I. Governing Principles and Essential Declarations of This TACA Diocese

... All things were made by Him" (John 1:1-3); and second, in 1 John 4:16, in which God is defined as Love itself.

Aquinas weighs in on the scientific primacy of Sacred Scripture as the prerequisite for learning all other sciences by supplementing Aristotle's meditations, writing: "Hence there is no reason why those things which may be learned from philosophical science, so far as they can be known by natural reason, may not also be taught us by another science so far as they fall within Revelation" (*Summa Theologica*; Part One; Reply to Objection 2; Saint Thomas Aquinas; 1274).

9) Bishops shall lead the Clergy in teaching Biblical wisdom. Indeed, Logos is needed for true sight of Truth, known as Faith. "Now faith is the substance of things hoped for, the evidence of things not seen" (Hebrews 11:1). Aquinas quoted Ecclesiasticus 3:25: "Without eyes thou shalt want light: profess not the knowledge therefore that thou hast not," and continued, "Hence theology included in sacred doctrine differs in kind from that theology which is part of philosophy" (*Summa Theologica*; Part One; Reply to Objection 2; Saint Thomas Aquinas; 1274).

e) Civility Stems From Humility. Anglicans employ Natural Law and Divine Law to endow society with civility, and this is known as Ecclesiastical Polity,

Article I. Governing Principles and Essential Declarations of This TACA Diocese

as referenced in the writings of Richard Hooker, who imparts the following:

1) "Two foundations there are which bear up public societies—the one, a natural inclination, whereby all men desire sociable life and fellowship; the other, an order expressly or secretly agreed upon, touching the manner of their union in living together." More important than courts of law, says Hooker, is "the law of a common weal, the very soul of a politic body, whereof are by law animated, held together, and set on work in such actions as the common good requireth." This is because:

2) "Good doth follow unto all things by observing the course of their Nature, and on the contrary side, evil, by not observing it." Hooker teaches Anglican Christians to be careful not to raise Nature above the Divine in their daily lives: "The reason whereof is, because amongst creatures in this world, only man's observation of the law of his nature is *righteousness*, only man's transgression, *sin*." That is, a person may wonder why he is tempted to lie, or to commit murder or adultery, to hide the mistakes that his nature commits. Says Hooker, "And the reason of this is the difference in his manner of observing or transgressing the law of his nature."

3) Human Nature, must be reconciled to Divine Law, says Hooker: "Let it therefore suffice thus far to have touched the force wherewith

Article I. Governing Principles and Essential Declarations of This TACA Diocese

> Almighty God hath graciously endued our nature, and thereby enabled the same to find out both those laws which all men generally are most fit for their behoof who lead their lives in any ordered state of government." (*Of the Lawes of Ecclesiastical Politie*; Book I. Chapter 9, 10; Richard Hooker; 1594)

f) The aim of Divine Law for human nature is perfection, whereby each saved person should attain the ultimate *theosis*, that is, the joining of the soul to God, which occurs when a person has attained Salvation. Instruction was given to Abraham: "I am the almighty God. Walk beside Me and be thou perfect" (Genesis 17:1).

g) God, at Salvation, shall thus raise the ontological condition of each saved, perfected Christian who has obeyed Natural Law and Moral Law all his or her life, following Divine Law through to the final *theosis* with the Father—just as it was firstly modeled by the Son of Man, Who as foretold by the Prophet Daniel is the Messiah who was taken from His sufferings on Earth and elevated to God's right hand, having dominion over all mankind (Daniel 7:13-14; Isaiah 53; Luke 22:69).

> 1) "But as many as received Him, to them gave He power to become the sons of God, even to them that believe on His name" (John 1:12).

> 2) Obeying Statutory Law (Romans 13), which stems from Moral Law (Leviticus; Mark 12:30),

Article I. Governing Principles and Essential Declarations of This TACA Diocese

> which stems from Natural Law (Jeremiah 31:35-40), which stems from Divine Law (Genesis 17:1), which stems from Logos (John 1), TACA Religious and Lay members shall be a priestly people (Isaiah 61:6; Exodus 19:6; 1 Peter 2:9; Revelation 1:6).

h) Thus, Bishops, Priests, Deacons, and appointed Deaconesses shall submit all our intellectual entitlements as, for example, academics, statesmen, and engineers, to the occupying of religious titles, as collared and sashed servants to Jesus, and to helping the most innocent, being guided and advocated by the shepherds in our godly homestead, our TACA Diocese, and all who outrank us—an Archbishop over Bishop, a Priest over a Deacon, etc.—but always being in humble service to the least among us, who know themselves to be lowly, and in that regard can "outrank" us in their understanding of Logos or Truth in God's sight (Matthew 25:40-45).

i) To this end, our gentlemen Priests and Deacons will also lead efforts to help the poor. At the parish level, the most powerful among us will hold the door open or carry groceries for a staff member who has a sprained ankle, and a Bishop may deliver groceries to a poor household, and a religious person shall come forward to tell the truth when called as a witness during an investigation. The role of a Bishop is to a remind his Priest, who in turn reminds his Deacon, who in turn reminds his Lay helper about the calling to

Article I. Governing Principles and Essential Declarations of This TACA Diocese

Divine Law, and that our individual authority stems from our commitment to the Word of Christ documented in Matthew 25:40: "Inasmuch as ye have done it unto one of the least of these my brethren, ye have done it unto Me." That is:

j) All Divine Law, Natural Law, Moral Law, and Human and Statutory/Case Law are fulfilled by this Holy Dialectic: The last shall be first, and the first shall be last (Matthew 20:16). The meek shall be served by the strong, who shall wash the feet of the Saved (John 13:1-5). It is fitting for Priests and Bishops to fulfill all righteousness by obliging Truth to baptize the beloved, just as Saint John and Jesus obliged one another, in the water of Bethany, beyond the Jordan (Matthew 3:15).

k) Epistemology that is Holy shall be this: God, and hence Truth, cannot be comprehended without the Bible (2 Timothy 3:16). Sacred Scripture teaches that Faith, that is, believing the Word without yet witnessing Revelation (John 20:29) is the wedding garment without which entrance into the Marriage Supper of the Lamb (Revelation 19:9), and into the "many mansions" in heaven that Christ prepares for (John 14:2) shall not be possible (Matthew 22:13). Because gnashing of the teeth of bitter pride defines the evicted, darkness cannot comprehend the effulgence felt by the Faithful, since "If ye were blind, ye should have no sin: but now ye say, We see; therefore your sin remaineth" (John 9:41; John 1:5). And thus:

Article I. Governing Principles and Essential Declarations of This TACA Diocese

>1) TACA members shall have no fellowship with the unfruitful works of darkness but shall reprove them (Ephesians 5:11-14). Moreover:
>
>>l) The Rapture and the Lake of Fire are the opposing results of choosing whether to follow the Great Commandment (Matthew 22:1-14; 37-38; Revelation 20:14-15; 19-8). It is *adiaphora* (as regards matters not regarded to be essential to Faith, but nevertheless as acceptable for Christians to contend) as to whether man, being Western-minded, should contemplate if he is merely redeemed by *actus purus* (i.e., the absolute perfection of God as regards the Father's identifying of Himself as "I am Who I am"; Exodus 3:14), or if a person—perchance being Eastern-minded—should also see redemption to be the straining away of the darkness within his or her earthly life until the sharing in God's "uncreated light" becomes possible, or, as Saint Gregory Palamas calls that light, the "Mount Tabor Light." How God's Grace perfects people is the fruit of joyful contemplation. Thus:
>>
>>>1) Direct the heart skywards: As regards the Westerner's transcendence from potentiality to actuality, man, in setting his "affection on things above" (Colossians 3:2), takes the redemptive journey, through Faith, from sinfulness into compliance with the absolute perfection of God—his "victory" occurring at the time of his Salvation, having "overcometh the world" (1 John 5:4-5). Saint Thomas

Article I. Governing Principles and Essential Declarations of This TACA Diocese

Aquinas describes the Redemption of the soul in Aristotelian terms as the transcendence from the potential state to the actualization of a salvational state of sinlessness, in that Salvation is God's "motion." Thus, the Redemption of the soul is akin to the constructing of a building that is now built, in that man's Redemption is the "hylomorphism" by which a saintly person's now-perfected matter completes its idealized form that was created for all men by the "First Mover" (i.e., God; 1 Corinthians 15:52).

2) Human perfected form—the kind of perfect man that Christ is, is the state whereby a person can finally be conjoined with God, a process that the "Teleology" of Aquinas purports can be understood by the human mind as if the redeemed soul is being placed into the rotary locomotion of God, lifted up into the unending Eternity (*Metaphysics*; Aristotle; Chapter 11; Part 9; A.D. 350).

3) Philosophers began searching for the source of perfection: "Now since every kind of thing is divided into the potential and the real, I call the actualization of the potential as such, motion" (*Metaphysics*; Aristotle; Part 9; B.C. 350). However:

4) Theologians found the source in God: "We need now say no more in support of the position that there is no process of change that admits of infinity or continuity except rotatory

locomotion. It can now be shown plainly that rotation is the primary locomotion ... Again, a motion that admits of being eternal is prior to one that does not" (Comments on Metaphysics; Saint Thomas Aquinas; Book 8; Chapter 8-9; 1270).

5) For the Eastern-minded, Saint Gregory of Palamas described this refinement as the *theosis*, the conjoining of the Saved person with God, whereby Salvation becomes a greater work than Creation.

6) At the Rapture, for Palamas, the same light of the Transfiguration transports the Elect, their physical bodies and all, into the clouds, to join with God. The "navel-gazing" authored by pride, says Palamas, must be overcome in the meantime. He posits:

7) "Take yourself in hand, then, be attentive to yourself, scrutinize yourself; or, rather, guard, watch over and test yourself, for in this manner you will subdue your rebellious unregenerate self to the Spirit and there will never again be 'some secret iniquity in your heart' (Deut. 15:9)" (*Philokalia*; "St Gregory Palamas: In Defense of Those who Devoutly Practice a Life of Stillness"; Part 9; 1344, 1893).

8) The Rapture is for the saintly. As St Paul wrote, "Then we which are alive and remain shall be caught up together with them in the clouds, to meet the Lord in the air: and so shall

Article I. Governing Principles and Essential Declarations of This TACA Diocese

we ever be with the Lord" (1 Thess. 4:17). And in the words of St. Gregory Palamas, "The Son of God, Who in His compassion became man, died so far as His body was concerned when His soul was separated from His body, but this body was not separated from His divinity, and so He raised up His body once more and took it with Him to heaven in glory. Similarly, when those who have lived here in a godly manner are separated from their bodies, they are not separated from God, and in the resurrection they will take their bodies with them to God, and in their bodies they will enter with inexpressible joy there where Jesus has preceded us (cf Heb. 6:20) and in their bodies they will enjoy the glory that will be revealed in Christ. Indeed, they will share not only in resurrection, but also in the Lord's ascension and in all divine life" (*Philokalia*; "St Gregory Palamas: To the Most Reverend Nun Xenia"; Part 15; 1344, 1893).

9) God awaits in the clouds. "It is now that: the intellect becomes simple matter in God's hands and is unresistingly recreated in the most sublime way, for nothing alien intrudes on it: inner grace translates it to a better state and, in an altogether marvelous fashion, illumines it with ineffable light, thus perfecting our inner being. And when in this manner 'the day breaks and the morning star rises in our hearts' (cf 2 Pet. 1:19), then 'the true man'—the intellect— 'will go out to his true work' (cf. Ps. 104:23),

Article I. Governing Principles and Essential Declarations of This TACA Diocese

ascending in the light the road that leads to the eternal mountains" (*Philokalia*; "St Gregory Palamas: To the Most Reverend Nun Xenia"; Part 59; 1344, 1893).

10) Death, however, is the uncreating of the soul, befalling the unclean, who are thrown into the Lake of Fire, along with death itself, and the Devil (Revelation 20:14-15).

11) Time itself, that imperfect state described in Albert Einstein's Theory of Relativity, is a thing used by Satan and the Reprobate to hunt the human soul since the Fall of Adam, and it too will also go into that Lake of Fire. Says Palamas, and as the East would put it:

12) "As the separation of the soul from the body is the death of the body, so the separation of God from the soul is the death of the soul. And this death of the soul is the true death. This is made clear by the commandment given in paradise, when God said to Adam, 'On whatever day you eat from the forbidden tree you will certainly die' (cf. Gen. 2:17). And it was indeed Adam's soul that died by becoming through his transgression separated from God; for bodily he continued to live after that time, even for nine hundred and thirty years (cf. Gen. 5:5)" (*Philokalia*; "St Gregory Palamas: To the Most Reverend Nun Xenia"; Part 9; 1344, 1893).

Article I. Governing Principles and Essential Declarations of This TACA Diocese

I. Bi-vocational Status of the Religious

i) Because the popularity of this TACA Diocese has never made it puffed up, its Episcopate and Clergy have nobly deprived themselves of the recognition that would deservedly have come in great published volumes and certifications, and which usually decorate the vestries of so many other churches. Instead, TACA men and women have long led ordinary lives, agreeing with one another that the self-evidence of Truth tends to obviate the importance of renown (1 Kings 11:4-6; Proverbs 3:4-6) Thus:

ii) TACA religious men and women live the lives of ordinary working people, as Saint Paul was himself a tentmaker, working as all men do, so that they may deserve to eat (2 Thessalonians 3:8).

a) Different from the clergy of many institutional churches that have lapsed in Faith, TACA Clergy and Episcopate do not see themselves as being formed or made superior to secular people by virtue of their office, but have instead traded pompous celebrations—honors and costume that could accompany mere religious titles—for slavery to Jesus and meanwhile remain free to exercise their other vocations as, for example, construction workers, excavators, doctors, engineers, and homemakers (Genesis 3:19).

b) The simple surplice and cassock with a stole in the color of the Liturgical season or holiday; a Chasuble, with or without a pallium, on Holy Days will do, as opposed to the kind of ostentation that evokes Tridentine uses or Gideon's Ephod (Judges 8:27; 1 Timothy 2).

iii) In their devotion to seeking Salvation over sin (Romans 6:15-23), TACA shepherds are authoritative in leading our TACA Diocese, which is filled with other families led by other hard-working Christians, in the Sacred Tradition guided by the 1928 Book of Common Prayer.

J. Receipt of Sacraments by Repentant Sinners and the Exhortations

i) All Christians baptized with water, receiving and accepting the Sign of the Cross and committing to the belief in the Holy Trinity shall reasonably expect to receive the Seven Sacraments in this TACA Diocese (Acts 19:4-5; Luke 3:16).

ii) Because this TACA Diocese knows Repentance to be the worthy state of every Trinitarian Christian soul to receive any of the Seven Sacraments, it should be the expectation of the Priest or Bishop to be able to suspend disbelief in the existence of insincerity or unfaithfulness that may exist in his Communicant, and thus to offer the Eucharist. Moreover, the Ordinals and Offices of the 1928 Book of Common Prayer and its earlier versions are the acceptable and helpful aids for repentance with the aim of worthiness, by God's grace alone, to receive the Blessed Sacrament. Moreover:

iii) Being that it is unreasonable to presume that a person at any moment of his or her lifetime could be

Article I. Governing Principles and Essential Declarations of This TACA Diocese

able to repent of every single sin that he or she has ever committed, this TACA Diocese, in concord with Sacred Tradition, avails itself of the General Confession and the Declaration of Absolution, or Remission of Sins that exist in the 1928 Book of Common Prayer and earlier editions (BCP/1928; pp. 6-7; 24-25; 75).

> a) The 1662 Book of Common Prayer acceptably makes use of the Seal of the Confessional, by which, the confessional words spoken as the Auricular form by a penitent to his or her Priest or Bishop remain an inviolable three-way confidence, shared only between the Confessor, the penitent, and God. (Note again that this 1662 book and its contents, and all versions of the BCP earlier than 1928 are permissible by TACA, according to the Customary of each or any TACA Congregation or Mission.)
>
> b) Lay Confession, which is the acceptable confidence shared between two or more TACA members, which also shall remain only between God and the participants, and is also contained in the 1662 BCP.

iv) This TACA Diocese considers Repentance and Fellowship to be the extraordinary condition of each religious Body in regard to receipt of Sacraments. TACA holds the following verses of Sacred Scripture to teach the necessary condition of Penance, peace, and tranquility of Fellowship the context of which the Sacraments are permitted to be conferred:

Article I. Governing Principles and Essential Declarations of This TACA Diocese

a) "From that time Jesus began to preach, and to say, Repent: for the Kingdom of Heaven is at hand" (Matthew 4:17).

b) "Now after that John was put in prison, Jesus came into Galilee, preaching the gospel of the kingdom of God, And saying, The time is fulfilled, and the kingdom of God is at hand: repent ye, and believe the Gospel" (Mark 1:14-15).

c) "But I say unto you, That whosoever is angry with his brother without a cause shall be in danger of the judgment: and whosoever shall say to his brother, Raca, shall be in danger of the council: but whosoever shall say, Thou fool, shall be in danger of hell fire. Therefore if thou bring thy gift to the altar, and there rememberest that thy brother hath ought against thee; Leave there thy gift before the altar, and go thy way; first be reconciled to thy brother, and then come and offer thy gift" (Matthew 5:22-24).

d) "Take heed to yourselves: If thy brother trespass against thee, rebuke him; and if he repent, forgive him. And if he trespass against thee seven times in a day, and seven times in a day turn again to thee, saying, I repent; thou shalt forgive him" (Luke 17:3-4).

e) "Be ye angry, and sin not: let not the sun go down upon your wrath: neither give place to the devil" (Ephesians 4:26-27).

f) "Then came Peter to Him, and said, Lord, how oft shall my brother sin against me, and I forgive

Article I. Governing Principles and Essential Declarations of This TACA Diocese

him? till seven times? Jesus saith unto him, I say not unto thee, Until seven times: but, Until seventy times seven" (Matthew 18:21-22).

g) "Moreover if thy brother shall trespass against thee, go and tell him his fault between thee and him alone: if he shall hear thee, thou hast gained thy brother. But if he will not hear thee, then take with thee one or two more, that in the mouth of two or three witnesses every word may be established. And if he shall neglect to hear them, tell it unto the church: but if he neglect to hear the church, let him be unto thee as an heathen man and a publican" (Matthew 18:15).

v) If, believing that a shadow of insolence, uncertainty, or iniquity truly flaws the spirit and comportment of the recipient and/or would obtrude discord upon the Fellowship that ought to be enjoyed by anyone within a religious Body of TACA, then the Exhortations during the Ordinal of the Sacrament of Holy Communion shall be read, at the discretion of the Priest (BCP/1928; pp. 85-89).

vi) There is an automatic and implied ecclesiastical censure and interdict attested by this TACA Diocese against receipt of any of the following Sacraments by any person who is a practitioner, supporter, promoter, executor, or recipient of, or participant in, an unrepented Mortal Sin, as regards the following Sacraments: Matrimony; Ordination or Consecration of Clergy and Bishops; Holy Communion; and Holy Baptism of any adult, or in the case of child or infant baptism, as regards the parents and guardians or

Article I. Governing Principles and Essential Declarations of This TACA Diocese

sponsors of the child or infant. It shall be left to the discretion of the Priest as to whether to baptize anyone, whether an adult, a child, or an infant. It is the grave responsibility of the Priest, in the case of child or infant baptism, to weigh the incongruence of the spiritual state of the guardians, Godparents, or sponsors against the exigency of baptizing an innocent child or infant, who belongs to God irrespective of his family or the circumstances under which he or she came into this world.

vii) No person who is perceived by a Priest or Bishop to be committed to Mortal Sin—in that he or she is an unrepentant adult practitioner of it, or is a supporter, promoter, executor, or recipient of, or participant in it—shall reasonably expect to receive from a TACA Priest or Bishop any Holy Sacrament, whether Gospel Sacrament or Religious Sacrament, within a Congregation or Mission of this TACA Diocese. These Sacraments shall include:

a) The two Gospel Sacraments of Holy Baptism and Holy Communion (whether Sunday-given, Saturday/Vespers-given, or otherwise-given).

b) The five Religious Sacraments of Confession, Ordination or Consecration, Matrimony, Anointing of the Sick or Dying, and Confirmation.

c) If approved by the Priest or Bishop, the following Sacraments may be given to a person existing in a state of Mortal Sin: Anointing of the Sick or Dying; or Confession (if the Confessor believes the sinner sincerely desires

Article I. Governing Principles and Essential Declarations of This TACA Diocese

Reconciliation; Public, BCP/1928 or earlier, Lay, or by Seal of the Confessional; see above: Part J: "Receipt of Sacraments"; Section iii; Item a); or Holy Baptism (and only, as relates to Holy Baptism, at the discretion of the Priest or Bishop in seeing to it that the parents, guardians, or sponsors are themselves Christians).

K. Expectation of Orthodoxy

Preface: It shall thus be our greatest motivation to hold and maintain the worship of Christ, just as He, who has given us Life was Himself made in the image of the Father, and who, thus being perfect, has given us a "religion that is pure and undefiled" (James 1:27). We are commanded by Christ's perfect sacrifice to ask the Father to purify us from all iniquity (Psalm 51:7-10; 139:23-24). God's covenant with His people under Moses has been commuted to a New Testament, ratified by the death of Christ, Who is the pure and undefiled man—the "testator"—by Whose blood the Church is able to exist (Hebrews 9:16).

Epigraph: This precious gift given to us by Jesus Christ—our One, Holy, Catholic, and Apostolic Church—is to be cherished by all TACA members, who shall constantly maintain and uphold only sound doctrine and godly disciplines that are entirely biblical (2 Timothy 3:16). We shall thus transmit the Gospel and the whole of the Bible, intact and unchanged, to everyone in our lives and for the benefit of future generations, for the Glory of God (Romans 15:4). As part of this commitment to attain Christlike purity, our loyalty to Christ keeps us faithfully affirmed and

Article I. Governing Principles and Essential Declarations of This TACA Diocese

striving toward Fellowship with Him and with loyal Christians, with whom we shall affirm the following orthodox retention of His holiness in all aspects of our Christian life (1 John 1:7).

Exordium: With these our Sacraments, and in the sanctity of religious acts and of good works, shall we thus regard Matrimony; Ordination and Consecration; Baptism; Confession; Reconciliation; Church Militancy; Anointing of the Sick and Dying; the Eucharist; and Catechesis, along with all other proclamations from our voices and writings, as reflections of the objective Truth of Christian morality amid the constant shadow of evil that we must indefatigably resist (Galatians 6:9). "But if we walk in the light, as He is in the light, we have Fellowship one with another, and the blood of Jesus Christ His Son cleanseth us from all sin" (1 John 1:7).

i) Regarding Chasteness in Marriage

a) There can be no argument against marriage being solely between a man and a woman (Genesis 2:24). The New Testament clearly models Christian marriage for all Christians after its very first formative pronouncement as such: "Therefore shall a man leave his father and his mother, and shall cleave unto his wife: and they shall be one flesh" (Genesis 2:24). Jesus repeats this verse from Genesis, adding that the definition of female in the context of "wife" signifies that she is to be joined as one flesh in permanent nuptial connection during this earthly life to the male, her husband (Mark 10:6-12).

Article I. Governing Principles and Essential Declarations of This TACA Diocese

b) As it is recorded in the Gospel of Saint Mark, Jesus teaches that this bond can never be separated by any person. We therefore hold that no purpose expressed by man could ever justify the reinterpretation of the plain meaning of marriage: "What therefore God hath joined together, let not man put asunder" (Mark 10:9). Abiding the orthodoxy expected by our Diocese, the definition of Holy Matrimony includes as part of its purpose the freeing of our will from the enslaving temptation toward sexual immorality that tends to plague unmarried secular life (1 Corinthians 7:24). As a conservative, strong, supportive husband, the Christian man must love his wife as he loves his own body and must always be temperate and dutiful; the Christian wife must be subject to her husband in all things as the Church is subject to Christ and must always maintain modesty and decency (Ephesians 5:28-31; 1 Peter 3:1-7). God's Church intends for things to stay chaste in this way and for the couple to remain married, just as our chaste TACA Archbishop ensures like stability in this TACA Diocese (1 Corinthians 11:3).

ii) Honoring the Holy Bible

a) The Bible is authorized by God as the literary embodiment of all of our true and justified beliefs, our knowledge and comprehension of Logos, and of all else that we can best comprehend of the Father of Lights (James 1:17; Joshua 1:18; 2 Timothy 3:16-17).

Article I. Governing Principles and Essential Declarations of This TACA Diocese

b) The Word is the perfect explication of the Christian virtues of Faith, Hope, and Love (Colossians 3:16; 1 Corinthians 13).

c) Doubts must be resisted. Our permanent attestation to the Bible's literal authority has been sadly contested by countless objectors, who protest that it should be deemed immoral, for instance, to punish adulterers with death (Leviticus 20:10). However, our Savior heeded and put Himself under the entirety of the Law (Matthew 5:18), by promising that neither a "tittle nor a jot" of the Law will pass until all be fulfilled. For "He cometh with clouds; and every eye shall see him, and they also which pierced him: and all kindreds of the earth shall wail because of him" (Revelation 1:7). Paradise shall be restored to believers (Psalm 37:20; Isaiah 60:1-9). We may chastely trim our wicks, taking heart from God's promise of creating the New Jerusalem, seen in a vision by Saint John the Apostle and described for us so that we may have hope (Revelation 21:2-4).

d) The manifold promise shall also vindicate Faith by leaving the reprobate out of the Rapture. The Rapture—though not specifically called "the Rapture"—is described in 1 Thessalonians 4:17. Nonbelievers shall stay "left behind" because of their reprobate mind and active rejection of the Truth (Romans 1:24; Revelation 22:11). The Last Judgement; the destruction of the devil and his followers in the Lake of Fire, which is the Second

Article I. Governing Principles and Essential Declarations of This TACA Diocese

Death; and the like end-time prophecies—all are detailed in Revelation 20 through 22.

e) The New Jerusalem, "coming down from God out of heaven, prepared as a bride adorned for her husband" (Revelation 21:2), evinces that Christ's "kingdom is not of this world," and that chasteness shall accompany the fulfillment of the Law (John 18:36). "Be ye not unequally yoked together with unbelievers: for what fellowship hath righteousness with unrighteousness? and what communion hath light with darkness?" (2 Corinthians 6:14). The Elect, though always charitable, shall never hope to yoke itself with whoremongers, the covetous, idolators, sorcerers, or the "children of disobedience." The unclean cannot "claim any inheritance in the kingdom of Christ and of God" (Ephesians 5:4-7). However:

f) TACA members shall urge the wicked to repent (Matthew 3:2). TACA members shall declare the failure of this reprobate society and shall beg God to lead the wicked Home (Daniel 9:1-19).

iii) Chaste Vigilant Protection of Life

Preface: Every human body and mind was known and loved by God before He created the world (Ephesians 1:4). While forming each of us, at conception, inside of our mother's womb, He gave us our identity and in His omniscience, knowing our ultimate end, either wrote our names in the Book of Life or left our names out of it (Jeremiah 1:5; Revelation 20). Thus, for the salvation of our souls,

Article I. Governing Principles and Essential Declarations of This TACA Diocese

from such perverse and corrupt minds as described in Article I, Section ii of this Constitution this TACA Diocese shall follow the exhortation to "withdraw thyself" (1 Timothy 6:5).

Exordium: However, there is sufficient hope for Salvation for anybody accepting the promise of Reconciliation, whose unparalleled reward becomes increasingly vivid to those who accept Christ's intercession with the Father on their behalf (Romans 8:24-30). If a sinner has chosen to accept the possibility he or she can be saved, then all that is needed is for him or her to exercise their freedom to choose to answer God's "knock" on the door of their soul (Matthew 7:7-8); in this way consolation about their election can be experienced.

> a) Thus, TACA confesses that the souls of all humans who have exercised their Free Will on earth will be rewarded or punished at Judgement Day according to the morality of their conduct, "according to what their deeds deserve" (2 Corinthians 5:10; Jeremiah 10:17). Simultaneously:

> b) TACA members may also argue that Salvation is predestined or pre-denied, according to Romans 8:28-30 and Ephesians 1:4-5, but meanwhile they must concede the truth of Jesus's words, when He said, "Inasmuch as ye have done it unto one of the least of these my brethren, ye have done it unto me" (Matthew 25:40); and, "For the Son of man shall come in the glory of his Father with his

Article I. Governing Principles and Essential Declarations of This TACA Diocese

angels; and then he shall reward every man according to his works" (Matthew 16:27). Good works, such as answering God's "knock" to repent, provide necessary proof to God that our Faith is willed by us (James 2:26).

c) Murder must be repented. No man would intend that life be subtracted from himself or his loved ones; therefore, it is irrational to believe that taking the life of any innocent person of any age, being that all persons are created in the image and likeness of God (Genesis 1:27), can be justified. Unrepented murder will be punished by the permanent death of the soul (Revelation 21) and is forbidden by the Fifth Commandment: It is abominably immoral to commit murder in any form.

d) Abortion is homicide when it is the direct, intentional killing of an unborn baby—the retention of whose gestation in the womb does not risk the death of the mother—and thus is also premeditated murder. Cultural liberties that presuppose the "moral" rectitude of destroying, ruining, or abusing of life must be contemplated with extreme moral gravity. "Pro-Choice," therefore, has much in common with such human-extermination practices as Eugenics, Satanism, Racism, "Woke"-ism, LGBTQ+ Ideology, Critical Race Theory, Transgenderism, Marxism, and Nazism, all of which should be viewed through the same lens of systematic institutional destruction of the innocent to serve the caprice of

Article I. Governing Principles and Essential Declarations of This TACA Diocese

depraved individuals or a collective will, to do what is wrongfully and heartlessly deemed to be convenient, politically or socially necessary, aesthetically pleasing, or fashionable.

e) Sinfulness, its wages being the opposite of Life (Romans 6:23), is not a right to be codified as Law. *Roe v. Wade*, 410 U.S. 113 was the codification of homicide, not a "right." Although *Roe* was overturned in June 2022 (*Dobbs v. Jackson Women's Health Organization*), Christian legislators today must still establish and defend Federal and State laws that identify life in the womb as God-created "personhood," made since the time prior to "viability," known by God since the moment of conception itself, blessed during embryonic development, and made in God's image all during gestation, loved by the Creator after birth and all throughout infant life and beyond, intended by God to serve and confess Him with thanksgiving until death. "Before I formed thee in the belly I knew thee; and before thou camest forth out of the womb I sanctified thee, and I ordained thee a prophet unto the nations" (Jeremiah 1:5). Religious leaders must make themselves aware of, and fight against, the Satanic ideologies of "ethicists" like Peter Singer, a strong proponent of infanticide, who wrote the following shocking statement: "Human babies are not born self-aware, or capable of grasping that they exist over time. They are not persons" [and therefore] "the life of a newborn is of less value than the life of a pig, a dog, or a chimpanzee"

Article I. Governing Principles and Essential Declarations of This TACA Diocese

(*Practical Ethics*, Peter Singer, pp. 122-123, 1979). This was written over 50 years ago, but let's flash forward to today. The next generation of this thinking is epitomized best by the TED darling Noah Yuval Harari, who in defense of his idea that human beings are nothing more than "hackable animals" wrote: "In essence, we humans are not that different from rats, dogs, dolphins or chimpanzees. Like them, we too have no soul" (*Homo Deus: A Brief History of Tomorrow*, Noah Yuval Harari, 2015). There is more on this topic in subsequent sections of this Constitution.

f) It is a deadly heresy to subordinate the Bible's Divine Law to one's concupiscence-laden ideas, thereby to disregard the chastity necessary for common salvation (Jude 1). The fruit analyzed and the spirits tested, the result is the Culture of Death: Unable to qualify murder as a right granted even by Natural Law, genocidists such as Pro-Choice politicians or historical Nazis tend to move the bar by denying the humanity of the ones marked for slaughter, justifying each "final solution" according to their warped ideations as madness quickly achieves the ends they desire (Titus 1:15-16). Such, being:

1) Margaret Sanger, founder of Planned Parenthood, who equated homicide with "health". Calling for Congress to engage in population control against the disabled, she wrote, "Having corralled this enormous part of our population and placed it on a basis of

Article I. Governing Principles and Essential Declarations of This TACA Diocese

health instead of punishment, it is safe to say that fifteen or twenty millions of our population would then be organized into soldiers of defense—defending the unborn against their own disabilities" ("A Plan for Peace"; Margaret Sanger; *Birth Control Review*; pp. 107-108; 1932).

2) Adolph Hitler, whose National-Socialism apologetics in *Mein Kampf* deem mass murder to be a divinely destined venture: "I also realized that my place would have to be there where the inner voice of conscience called me." He labels a German's refusal to be God's pureblood chosen to be cowardly nihilism: "By neglecting the problem of preserving the racial foundations of our national life, the old Empire abrogated the sole right which entitles a people to live on this planet." It is unclear whether Hitler was precisely declaring that genocide was the direct will of Odin, when he wrote *Mein Kampf,* but his emotive rhetoric served his hateful personal version of Divine Law: "Nations that make mongrels of their people, or allow their people to be turned into mongrels, sin against the Will of Eternal Providence." Hitler's Social-Darwinist apocalypticism, borrowing from the scientific racism of Herbert Spencer (*Social Statics,* 1850; Spencer himself being influenced by the Deism, Positivism, and Synthetic Philosophy of George Combe, who wrote the wildly popular *The Constitution of Man,* 1828), could be summed up thus: "And

Article I. Governing Principles and Essential Declarations of This TACA Diocese

thus their overthrow at the hands of a stronger opponent cannot be looked upon as a wrong but, on the contrary, as a restoration of justice." Armageddon, says Hitler, dispatches cowards to earthly damnation: "If a people refuses to guard and uphold the qualities with which it has been endowed by Nature and which have their roots in the racial blood, then such a people has no right to complain over the loss of its earthly existence" (*Mein Kampf*; Adolph Hitler; Chapter V, IX (l); 1924).

3) TED Talks host and author, Lesley Hazelton, self-professed agnostic, who authored a book extolling a great hater of Christians, the "prophet" Muhammad, arguing that he was good because he was Gnostic: "This is the basic insight of the Gnostics, the one known to the great mystical thinkers of all traditions: the divine spark is within each human being" (*The First Muslim: The Story of Muhammad*; Leslie Hazleton; Chapter 8; 2013). The idea of the "divine spark" of causality is derived by modern Gnostics from the vitalist doctrine of Henri Bergson, which contends that the world was created by the perpetual expansion of physical matter, replacing Divine origin with base physics stemming from increased temperature and high density, much like a powder keg, or a "big bang" (*Creative Evolution*; Henry Bergson; Chapter 1-Orthogenesis; 1907).

Article I. Governing Principles and Essential Declarations of This TACA Diocese

4) Eugenics (masquerading as "Crispr Ethics") proponent Henry T. Greely, a Stanford professor of Law and Genetics, who advocates "Easy PGD" as the alternative to controversial Crispr/Cas9 genetic editing,[1] thus creating "chosen babies" instead of "designer babies." Preimplantation Genetic Diagnosis (PGD) is how geneticists promulgate genetic testing within embryonic cells so that parents (or their handlers) can cherry-pick only certain embryos for implantation in terms of the quality of their genetic contents or, conversely, lack of anomalies. Greely falsely assures his audience that the Catholic Church does not itself consider the embryo to be "ensouled" until the third gestational month by refuting the logical disputation which Christians know to be in the Bible. He writes, "It is an additional blessing that those [Catholic] arguments do not rely on citations to scriptural passages, but to stress logical arguments," effectively attacking the truth of Psalm 139:13 that God "designs" the human contents of the womb. However, even the modernist Roman Catholic Catechism clearly *does* designate life as starting at conception (CCC, 2270-1). Additionally, Saint Jerome found source material written two centuries before his Vulgate, in Didache 2.2,

---

[1] Embryonic genes are edited, according to this method, by precisely cutting DNA and then allowing the gene to repair itself.

Article I. Governing Principles and Essential Declarations of This TACA Diocese

which orders, "Thou shalt not murder a child by abortion nor kill them when born." Greely wrongfully believes that this chromosomal intervention does not interfere with DNA's sole authorship by God, Who we know alone creates physical disabilities (Exodus 4:11) and blesses all "weaknesses" from which spiritual strength comes (2 Corinthians 12:9). Using specious argumentation to presume that religion should respect the anonymous author of what he refers to as the "book of nature", Greely concocts a persecution-delusion set against him, which he claims is depredated upon him coequally by Darwinist and Christian "heresiarchs"—enemies of Crispr science who somehow co-worship the Judeo-Christian "Deity," whose commands, or desires, are to be deduced from a source other than from the "Deity's" revelations, whether directly or through a prophet or holy book. The exasperated Greely unabashedly recommends government coercion: "If easy PGD really is easy, safe, and effective, why shouldn't a government require it or require that a prospective parent who uses it avoid intentionally choosing an embryo that is certain to have a very serious genetic disease?" To the extent that Greely wants to ensure that pure Gnosticism should dominate all the ethics of Crispr/Cas9 and easy-PGD Eugenics, Greely's personal prophet may as well be playwright George Bernard Shaw. Shaw's signature Gnostic theology famously concluded the outcome of

Article I. Governing Principles and Essential Declarations of This TACA Diocese

Genesis in the century-old play *Back to Methuselah*, in which Adam and Eve end up as evil spirits. Shaw resolved that the wicked Lilith should be paired with the Serpent as her eternal "Instructor," and that she should become Adam's second wife—the "mother of all mankind." Shaw boldly portends an end to life's enslavement to physical matter—voicing, through Lilith's soliloquy, the classic Gnostic eschatology of disentanglement from life's material "vortex" (*Back to Methuselah*; George Bernard Shaw; Part V; 1922). Also irresistible, when seeing Shaw's co-identification of Genesis with the imaginary mischief wrought by a demiurge snake (i.e., knowledge, understood alongside Greely's supplanting of God's hand with parental vanity), is our recognition of the influence of the satanic "Theosophy", which was well known to intrigue Shaw. Theosophy—a dark theme so boldly heralded by his contemporary Madame H. P. Blavatsky that it became the Luciferian precursor for Shaw's play's Gnostic denouement—was formed and developed by the infamous blaspheming by Madame Blavatsky, who put forth that "The Logos and Satan are One" (*The Secret Doctrine*; H. P. Blavatsky; Volume II; Section XIX; Page 515; 1888). Modern genetics thus employs strawman rhetoric, hoping to confuse Christians otherwise intending to avoid the idolatry of replacing God's creational intentions, by insinuating the proposition that parents are incapable of loving their impaired

Article I. Governing Principles and Essential Declarations of This TACA Diocese

or only slightly gifted children: "I am tempted to focus on the harms to be avoided by restricting parental choice." Sexual reproduction, proud Greely advises, will no longer occur at home, as the blessed nest where God should be worshiped, but in "safe, lawful, and free" laboratories (*The End of Sex and the Future of Human Reproduction*; Henry T Greely; Chapter 6, 7; Harvard, 2016).

5) Discreet survival or keeping a low profile: As the Oxford theologian Rev. William Sanday wrote in 1878 about protecting strong Faith among the "madness of the peoples" (Psalm 65:9), "reserve the exhibition of it to the privacy of your own direct communion with God, and do not display it ostentatiously in public where it may do harm." Survival and getting through the work day while discretely and shrewdly remaining orthodox is very important. Saint Paul, continued Rev. Sanday in discussing Romans 14:22, instructs us to exercise one's Faith boldly only when necessary. In present times, this could be the refusing an employer's demand to use "preferred-gender pronouns" at one's job, or refusing to acquire an industrially mandated harmful medical injection touted to be a "vaccine." "It is indeed, the Apostle continues, a happy thing to have no self-condemnatory scruples of conscience, but on the other hand, it is fatal to have scruples and to disregard them" (*Ellicott's Commentary on the Whole*

Article I. Governing Principles and Essential Declarations of This TACA Diocese

Bible; Vol. VII; Romans 14:22; Rev. William Sanday; Bp. Charles John Ellicott, Ed.; 1954).

6) The "Total View" of "Effect," or the "Culture of Death": The difficulty of arguing how it is a factual error to refer to Princeton University "Professor" Peter Singer as a "teacher of ethics" is not unlike the hardship of teaching a science-loving culture why it is morally and intellectually useful to know stories from the Bible (2 Timothy 3:16). For example, Beelzebub was known to the ancients as the "god of the flies" because anybody who sought his oracles (such as King Ahaziah of Israel), was considered by upright monotheistic men, such as the prophet Elijah, to be an enemy of eternal Truth (2 Kings 1:2-3,16). As the Gentiles learned, it was futile (and ultimately deadly, as the already mortally injured Ahaziah discovered) to replace God's Word with prophecies from a filthy, predatory entity such as this "Baal-berith"—aptly named because his insect likeness ate the sacrificed flesh at pagan temples (*Septuagint:* 4 Reigns 1:2-3;16; *Antiquities of the Jews*; Josephus; Book IX; Chapter 2, Section 1; A.D. 94; *Babylonian Talmud*; Tractate Shabbat; Chapter 9). For five decades since *Roe v. Wade*, misguided pregnant women have relied on smooth, specious reasoning to rationalize giving over their unborn and even newborn babies to death by dismemberment, neck-breaking, poisoning, or abandonment without medical care. Knowingly

Article I. Governing Principles and Essential Declarations of This TACA Diocese

or not, these women who have willingly slaughtered the fruit of their wombs have taken comfort in the teachings of Peter Singer, a prophet of hell, refusing to submit to God for strength during their perceived crisis. Singer, the "doctor" of the "science that is falsely so-called" (1 Timothy 6:20), who wrote the "groundbreaking" 1979 text titled *Applied Ethics,* employs an old-fashioned but infamous rhetorical device once described by Edgar Allen Poe as the "effect of the denouement being thus provided for." If, for example, a pregnant woman is dismayed by advice from her obstetrician that her amniocentesis results might predict a life of hardship caring for a person with Down's Syndrome, she can instead feel better that a famous contemporary "moral philosopher" has explained 44 years ago why killing her child could be her remedy, that she should feel secure in sacrificing innocent blood in order to solemnize a constitutional "right" that for 50 legislative years has simulated a rite of Moloch under the guise of serving the common good of citizens, whose imagined right it is to "pursue happiness" (1 Kings 11:7; *Roe v. Wade*, 410 U.S. 113). Denying the God-given dominion of humans over animals, Singer advances the anti-Christian concept of animal equality and is an activist for all that comes with that idea, including animal rights and animal liberation—and therein lies the important connection to abortion: Employing the term "Speciesism," or the assumption of

Article I. Governing Principles and Essential Declarations of This TACA Diocese

human superiority over animals, Singer builds his pernicious case that holds that protecting the life of developmentally impaired human infants reflects an "attitude of bias toward the interests of members of one's own species and against those of members of other species" (*Practical Ethics;* Peter Singer; p. 7; 1st Ed.; 1979). That is, after stoking an emotional reaction, a pseudo-scientist author like this one can present assurances using laboratory data and statistics as coaxing premises to substantiate his devious conclusion, or as Poe had put it (in explicating his poem about another scavenger of corpses, the Raven), "I immediately drop the fantastic for a tone of the most profound seriousness" ("The Philosophy of Composition"; Edgar Allen Poe; *Graham's Magazine;* Vol. 28; No. 4; pp. 163-167; April 1846). As mentioned earlier in the Constitution—a concept so ghastly that it deserves to be repeated—Singer assures the amoral mother of the rectitude of her decision: "Human babies are not born self-aware, or capable of grasping that they exist over time. They are not persons"; and therefore, "the life of a newborn is of less value than the life of a pig, a dog, or a chimpanzee" (*ibid.* pp. 122-123). Unmoored from the objective morality of an omnibenevolent Creator, Singer wrote, "The liberal search for a morally crucial dividing line between the newborn baby and the fetus has failed to yield any event or stage of development that can bear the weight of

Article I. Governing Principles and Essential Declarations of This TACA Diocese

separating those with a right to life from those who lack such a right" (*Practical Ethics*; Peter Singer; p. 142; 2nd Ed.; 1993). Seen as being incapable of awareness that they exist, newborn babies are downgraded by their intellectual murderers from their being actual persons to the status of non-persons, who are incapable "of seeing themselves as distinct entities, existing over time" (*ibid.* pp. 171, 188) Singer, the "bioethicist," then inserts a flaccid rejoinder calling for ethical oversight: "We should certainly put very strict conditions on permissible infanticide, but these conditions might owe more to the effects of infanticide on others than to the intrinsic wrongness of killing an infant" (*ibid.* p. 173). As a result of this type of Culture of Death rhetoric over these past five decades, whether the act of abortion is considered right or wrong boils down to the "wantedness" of the unborn child: If she wanted it and someone kills it, they have committed a crime of murder; if she didn't want it, and she decides to have it killed through abortion, then she has done the heroic thing and cannot be blamed because its worth was less than the worth of a pig or a chimp. This is the witchcraft of the modern pseudoscientific mind. Because killing an infant is eagerly comprehended by complicit humans to be less than the moral equivalent of killing an adult person or even an animal (*ibid.* p. 191), it follows that the majority of Americans, who have little to zero Faith in God, do not go to

Article I. Governing Principles and Essential Declarations of This TACA Diocese

Church, and cherish personal comfort and security over the lives (physical, moral, spiritual) of their offspring, are becoming increasingly tempted to adapt this murderous logic to a vision of all their dependents as potential scapegoats, assuring themselves that they are helping the cause of "population control" ("Innovating to Zero"; Bill Gates; TED-Talks; Transcript: TED2010). Being culturally nudged by soulless doctrine (1 Corinthians 5:6), the Godless might soon cheerfully widen the kill yard to include, for example, relatives with Alzheimer's Disease, autistic family members, poor relations, the psychologically-afflicted, or anyone whose lives they could arbitrarily accuse of being too costly and hence expendable, and assisted suicides of these vulnerable populations are already happening in certain hotbeds around the world, especially in European countries like the Netherlands ("Eligibility for medical assistance in dying for persons suffering solely from mental illness extended to March 17, 2024"; News Release, Department of Justice of Canada: March 9, 2023; "How Dutch Law Got a Little Too Comfortable With Euthanasia," Scott Kim, *The Atlantic*, June 8, 2019). Singer's chilling and gruesome brand of Utilitarianism is nothing more than cunningly packaged but garden-variety eugenics, which has been around for an awfully long time: "When the death of a disabled infant will lead to the birth of another infant with better prospects of a happy life, the

Article I. Governing Principles and Essential Declarations of This TACA Diocese

total amount of happiness will be greater if the disabled infant is killed" (*Practical Ethics*, Singer; 1993; p. 186). This winner of the 2021 Berggruen Prize computes, as though this were but a simple math problem: "The loss of the happy life for the first infant is outweighed by the gain of a happier life for the second" (*ibid.* p. 186). It is not interesting that even he can concede that the sick or disabled infant victim would have had a happy life, had he been allowed to live? Singer's heartless arithmetic concludes: "Therefore, if killing the hemophiliac infant has no adverse effect on others, it would, according to the total view, be right to kill him" (*ibid.* p. 186). The "total view" approach is therefore open to participants in the Culture of Death, but we orthodox Christians, who revile it as anathema, find ourselves crying, *maranatha*—O Lord, come! Regarding when Christ will indeed return, we must remember that "the Lord is not slack concerning His promise...but is longsuffering to us-ward, not willing that any should perish, but that all should come to repentance" (2 Peter 3:9), and so we "groaneth and travaileth in pain together" (Roman 8:22), waiting for the brightness of His glory in this present dark age. The best opposing philosophy against the philosophies that advance the Culture of Death—Hamartiology (i.e., the theological study of sin)—must be internalized to prepare one to oppose such "intellectuals." Herds of cattle may naturally neglect runts until they die, but

Article I. Governing Principles and Essential Declarations of This TACA Diocese

> we are not cattle; we were made in the image and likeness of God (Genesis 1:26). Knowing the difference between good and evil, and called "gods" and "children of God," we know the difference between, and are given the choice between good, and evil, life and death: "I call heaven and earth to record this day against you, that I have set before you life and death, blessing and cursing: therefore choose life, that both thou and they seed may live" (Deuteronomy 30:19). The saintly protection of human life calls for the biblical scrutinizing of any social principle to see whether it rightly places God above Nature; the saints must emulate the Father's goodness and firmness, separating from the godly all the disobedient worshipers of the Tree of Knowledge, tossing them out of Eden, so to speak, and thus removing their despicable ideas from all places of Innocence, just as surely as was done due to the immorality of Sodom and Gomorrah: "the cities about them in like manner" should be remembered only as ashes (Genesis 3; Jude 1:7; Revelation 18:4).

g) *Technological Singularity:* Ever since Simon the Sorcerer tried to "buy" the miraculous power of the Apostles (Acts 8:9-25), Gnosticism has tempted Christians. Attainment of the "gnosis" or "supreme knowledge" disqualifies any need for God's Grace in attaining Salvation, because, as the Gnostics Cerinthus and Carpocrates preached, "the Law and prophets have been given by the angels, and the law-giver [Jesus] is

Article I. Governing Principles and Essential Declarations of This TACA Diocese

one of the angels who have made the world" (*The Panarion;* Saint Epiphanius of Salamis; Section 28: Against Cerinthians or Merinthians; Parts 1,1-1,3). Christians must worship and serve the Creator and not the creature—unless God gives them up "to dishonor their bodies between themselves" (Romans 1:24-25), in which case they are given over to a reprobate mind and *cannot* worship Him while in that unrepentant state. It is horribly wrongful Christology to denigrate the Trinity by reducing Christ—or any of the Persons of the Trinity, for that matter—to the status of being a mere mortal or even a demigod—presumed as such by today's science-lusting Gnostics and/or Agnostics, who more readily abide the "Technological Singularity" of the Internet and Artificial Intelligence as being "part of a superior cosmic process" ("Gaia, God, and the Internet—revisited. The History of Evolution and the Utopia of Community in Media Society"; Oliver Krüger; *Heidelberg Journal for Religions on the Internet;* Vol. 8; pp. 56-87; 2015). Dr. Oliver Krüger, professor for the Study of Religions at Fribourg University (Switzerland), has detected a religious aim of Transhuman Science— to render biological life obsolete, and to create a "general intelligence," a new "God." Contemplating the 2015 *Time-Magazine* "Top-Ten" non-fiction book by Israeli homosexual atheist historian, Juval Noah Harari calling for "hackable humans" (*Homo Deus: A Brief History of Tomorrow*; Yuval Noah Harari; pp. 372-402; 2016), Dr. Krüger writes: "[Harari] envisions the development of an all-powerful, immortal human being and adapts this for his philosophical speculations on the future of humankind" *(Virtual Immortality—God, Evolution, and the Singularity in Post- and*

Article I. Governing Principles and Essential Declarations of This TACA Diocese

Transhumanism; Oliver Krüger; p. 23; 2021). This brazen Israeli heralds the present era as the dawning of "the age of the Anthropocene, an age in which hunger and diseases have been eliminated, and human beings are taking creation into their own hands" (*ibid. Virtual*, p. 23). But the "peace and safety" truly set the stage for the Tribulation (1 Thessalonians 5:3). "As a result," Krüger adds, "immortality and divinity will develop. The world will be conquered not by Islamic fundamentalism but by techno religions, because they promise salvation through algorithms and genes" (*ibid. Virtual*, p. 23). Harari sees two possible variants: One is data religion, which propagates the replacement of human beings by artificial intelligence (*ibid. Homo Deus*; pp. 372-402). "The other is techno-humanism, which seeks to transform homo sapiens into homo deus [thanks to technical upgrades of the brain and of consciousness]" (*ibid. Virtual*; Krüger; p. 23). Christ, to the "Homo Deus," is a different entity than our true God, who created the suddenly obsolete man, and simultaneously is, at best, a merely blessed man, albeit a flawed man, who is actually capable of sinning, or is even a creation of the Internet. Such Gnostic demotion of the Person of Christ in the Godhead of the Trinity is not unlike the modern employment of technology to replace the immortal and God-given soul, which has thereby reduced the definition of man, and hence of Christ, to mere computer terms, with computers now laying claim to objective morality. "Some religious people may argue that AIs lack souls and therefore can't count as descendants, or that we shouldn't build conscious machines because it's like playing God and tampering with life itself—similar sentiments have

Article I. Governing Principles and Essential Declarations of This TACA Diocese

already been expressed toward human cloning" (*Life 3.0: Being Human in the Age of Artificial Intelligence;* Max Tegmark; pp. 189-190; 2017). A "god as protector" could regulate such matters as "climate change" and population control (*ibid.* p. 48, 172). The desire to surrender Free Will to a false god is latent, desiring the "Protector god: [The] Essentially omniscient and omnipotent AI [who] maximizes human happiness by intervening only in ways that preserve our feeling of control of our own destiny and hides well enough that many humans even doubt the AI's existence" (*ibid.* pp. 163-164). Thus:

> 1) Destroying comprehension of the divine nature of Christ allows nonbelievers to enjoy a morality gap, alleging that if Christ thus sins, then humans should be expected to as well, and thus Free Will should not be expected to strive for God's perfection (Matthew 5:48). But because Christ is the Son of the perfect God (Matthew 3:17), what need do humans have for a "demiurge"—unless they are malevolently taught that the material world is cut off permanently from God the Father? How did people wrongfully come to believe that the false deity of the Internet or Artificial Intelligence "thinks" instead of rightfully knowing that it merely computes? An ancient idea, the "demiurge" was ignorantly explained by Plato to be "the Lord and Father of the Ruler [i.e., king] and Cause" (*Letter 6*; Plato; B.C. ~365). Plato mistakenly thought that this being is not God Himself, but nevertheless is the

Article I. Governing Principles and Essential Declarations of This TACA Diocese

causer of the τἀγαθόν, or the "good" (*ibid.*). By the demiurge's work of building the world, the demiurge thereby is alleged to be the founder of εὐδαίμων, the "nobility of spirit" (*Letter 8*; Plato; 354-c; B.C. ~365). His building blocks of the Universe and its corporeal inhabitants are the five ideals known as the "Platonic solids," or "polyhedra" (Timaeus; 53-c). These ideals are the so-called perfect Forms, which Euclid had earlier said were first taught to the Greeks by Theaetetus (*Elements;* Euclid; Book XIII; Props 13-17; B.C. 300). This "craftsman of the universe" (Timaeus 28a), the helpful demiurge, was thought to have benevolently breathed into each human a mind, the ψῡχή (i.e., the psyche), which Pythagoras of Samos, according to Plato, had taught was formed by the interplay between those elemental Forms, the polyhedra, and all its *a priori* truths (such as the Pythagorean Theorem and Geometry). Earlier than Pythagoras, and according to Aristotle, the world's very first secular philosopher, Thales of Meletus, had guided his brilliant student, Anaximenes, to contemplate certain more-concrete building blocks of nature, the totally-viewable στοιχεῖον, or the "stoicheîon," that is, the four basic "Elements" of existence—earth, fire, air, and water—from which a thinker could deduce that the actual source of Creation (the perfect being) and the Creator are one (with no demiurge being necessary). In electing which of these Elements would be the first principle of all existence—that is the all-mysterious *arkhé*,

Article I. Governing Principles and Essential Declarations of This TACA Diocese

from which we derive the word "archetype"— Anaximenes took a leap of Faith: he considered that his teacher Thales had taught him that it was water, but Anaximenes decided that it had to be the air, ἀήρ, the breathable life-sustaining gas portraying its role in Anaximenes's Cosmos model as actualizing the Infinite, the ἄπειρον, or the "apeiron" (*On the Heavens;* Aristotle; Section 294:b; B.C. 350). The flexing of the Infinite, according to the ardent monist Anaximenes, produces the soul, the Inborn Spirit, the πνεῦμα, the "pneuma symphuton," whereby babies are born and life is lived through the breathing of the celestial arche of air into the corporeal recipients (*Movement of Animals;* Aristotle; Section 703:a; B.C. ~350). A point of departure between Plato and Aristotle, with Aristotle's conception being closer to Christian thought (perhaps explaining, in part, the appeal of Aristotle among so many formative Christian theologians), became evident by Aristotle's idea of the "unmoved mover": the idea that God, not the demiurge, has created both the perfection conceived in the Platonic ideal of having the polyhedra Forms and the soul-bearing gewöhnlicher-Mensch, the baby-birthing, hard-working people who are manufactured by God out of those perfect Forms, but incorporated into a metaphysical architecture (*Metaphysics;* Aristotle; Chapter 11; Part 9; A.D. 350). That is, in associating the soul, rather than the mere psyche, as being an element actively shared by

Article I. Governing Principles and Essential Declarations of This TACA Diocese

humans with the Divine, all sentient beings were now said by these monists (Anaximenes and Aristotle) to "possess an inborn spirit (*pneuma symphuton*) and to exercise their strength in virtue of it" (*ibid. Movement of Animals*; Section 703:a-10). This Inborn Spirit, they said, produces desire (*orexis*) to perpetuate life, the ardent will to survive, which is portrayed in the Cosmos according to Aristotle as being the "middle cause" (*meson*) operating underneath the primary cause, the infinite (*apeiron*), which he stated is of "central origin to meson, which moves by being itself moved" (*ibid. Movement of Animals;* Section 703-a:5-6). Besides Plato's metaphysics being prosaic, his failure to associate human Form with God's purpose relegated the soul to being merely the intellectual psyche, a detached mind, a human thought chasm outputted by the demiurge from the well-drawn angles and lines of arbitrary interplay of the coldly perfect Forms of the polyhedra. But Plato's eschatology is even bleaker. Without creational connection with the Creator, his metaphysics consigns existence to the banal condition of perpetuating a ceaseless transmigration of the psyche, a recycling of unsaved souls—originally described for Plato by the writings of Pythagoras—as the "metempsychosis," also known as reincarnation perpetuated between human and animal life, forever. Or, if a good life is lived, the obedient mind can live within the upright realm of the *Hyperuranion* (pure

Article I. Governing Principles and Essential Declarations of This TACA Diocese

Forms). But in either case, Plato promulgates the idea that a person can never know or belong to God Himself (*The Republic;* Plato; Book X; Section 620:a-e; 621 B.C. 380; *Phaedrus;* Plato; Section 246:b, 247:c; B.C. 370). Still, Plato pondered that knowing God the Father is possible, but only by looking at causality— whatever has been caused to exist by that detached Father, a concept known as Teleology, which denotes the hope of believing in God not according to Faith, but by looking at the Father's "intelligent design" (*ibid. Timaeus;* Plato; Section 28:c). Resultantly, Plato also said that the disciplines of science and math are the purest forms of religious expression (*Epinomis;* Plato; Page 978; B.C. ~347). To the resolute Plato, God, who is not the Architect, but is the actual embodiment of the invisible realm of perfect math and principles, represents the ideals that are epitomized not merely by the abstract polyhedra, but by the goodness by which the Architect deigns to create people and the Universe, whereof the Father can only be knowable to the human psyche by contemplating how God's perfection is actualized by sharing good ideas and good things as they relate to one another, but not by Faith or even hopeful guesswork (*The Republic*; Plato; Book VI; Section 508:e-509:a; B.C. 380). It was against this bleak philosophical backdrop that Saint Paul of Tarsus preached regarding the futility of worshipping the "Unknown God": Paul declared the proof of God's omnipotent

Article I. Governing Principles and Essential Declarations of This TACA Diocese

Love, standing atop the Mars escarpment at the prestigious Council of Areopagus at Athens, and proclaiming: "Ye men of Athens, I perceive that in all things ye are too superstitious. For as I passed by, and beheld your devotions, I found an altar with this inscription, 'To the Unknown God'. Whom therefore ye ignorantly worship, Him declare I unto you" (Acts 17:22-23). Thus, the musings of Plato and Aristotle were not in vain. Nor should the respective "arches" of Thales and his pupil Anaximenes, of water and God's breath, be overlooked as signifiers of the Baptismal elements of John and later his cousin Jesus, the Christ (Matthew 3:11). Therefore, acknowledging the Prevenient Grace by which the ancient monists were intellectually endowed to foreshadow, through pagan metaphysics, belief in the perfect God of Israel, Who created humanity, our spirits through Christ—not our psyches—attest that life perpetuates not through reincarnation or high knowledge (γνῶσις or gnosis), but through the free gift of Salvation (σωτηρία, "sótéria," or deliverance). The elevation of the reborn in Christ (John 3:3) completes man's sublimation into the human "polyhedron," the ideal form of humanity, attained by witnessing the Revelation of Christ, who makes everything—bodies, souls, and minds—new (Revelation 21:5). Christ, the Son of Man, the seed of Abraham (Galatians 3:16), promises eternal life to His perpetual Tribe of Judah, to His catholic Church: for "He spake to our fathers, to

Article I. Governing Principles and Essential Declarations of This TACA Diocese

Abraham, and to His seed forever" (Luke 1:55). Salvation therefore actualizes the ultimate ideal state of man living in divine Fellowship, the *theosis* (θέωσις) with Christ, Who is the perfect, the root cause, the holy pneuma, Who redeems humans by His perfect sacrifice, Resurrection, and Ascension, saving the human for God, intending that reborn people shall one day be like gods with God, seeing Him as He is (Psalm 82:6; John 10:34; 1 John 3:2). This "science" is a more complete school of thought than all other science (1 Timothy 6:20). "Beware lest any man spoil you through philosophy and vain deceit, after the tradition of men, after the rudiments of the world, and not after Christ" (Colossians 2:8).

2) Heresy is the "ring" through which a science-lover can knot his followers. "But there were false prophets among the people, even as there shall be false teachers among you, who privily shall bring in damnable heresies, even denying the Lord that bought them, and bring upon themselves swift destruction" (2 Peter 2:1-3). An abortionist will subvert a parent's moral sensibilities through a fake dispensation from their fear of God. After all, overpopulation is *sinful*, he says. I mean, we don't want to breed like *rabbits*, do we? ("Pope Francis: No Catholic need to breed like 'rabbits'," *BBC News*, January 19, 2015).

Article I. Governing Principles and Essential Declarations of This TACA Diocese

> 3) Imitate Jesus, but be a sleuth, like Saint Irenaeus, who exposed heresies. Behind artful causes, those early Gnostics such as Cerinthus, Simon Magus, Carpocrates, Mani, Valentinus, Cainius, Ebionites, and Philo, along with other heretics such as Arius and Sabellius, each wrote wrongful doctrines, and even forged "epistles" and "gospels", but always to twist the intellects of their followers into following beliefs that differed from the true Word (*Adversus Haereses*; Saint Irenaeus; Book 1; Chapter 26; Part 1; 3.2.1, 2; 3.3.4; 3.11; 3.11.1; A.D. 180). Because the Word is God, in whom consists Life, any deviation from the Word positions itself in conflict against Life (John 1:1-4; 2 Timothy 2:16).
>
> 4) "Error, indeed is never set forth in its naked deformity, lest, being thus exposed, it should at once be detected. But it is craftily decked out in an attractive dress, so as, by its outward form, to make it appear to the inexperienced more true than truth itself" (*Adversus Haereses*; Saint Irenaeus; Book 1; Preface; Part 2; A.D. 100).
>
> 5) According to Saint Polycarp, Saint John's Gospel was written as a refutation of Cerinthus's Gnosticism (*Adversus Haereses*; *ibid.*; 3.11.1). TACA's mission today is to ensure that the Bible is revered as the unparalleled literary Deposit of Faith that lays the

Article I. Governing Principles and Essential Declarations of This TACA Diocese

foundation for the utter necessity to protect innocent life inside and outside of the womb.

6) New Age and Gnostic spiritualities are heresies. Each thrives and grows not only among modern non-Christians, but also wherever wayward Christians can be found, who tend to claim that Jesus has already atoned for any possible sin that they ever committed or ever will commit, and so they delight to commit sins now with "no regrets".

7) Advancing a perversely updated Antinomianism, New Age/Thought "Christians" intend that their interpretation of "blessed assurance" should excuse any sin (e.g., murder, adultery, pedophilia, sodomy)—as if their misguided understanding of Christ's offer of Redemption and Salvation through the Crucifixion and Resurrection should excuse any guilt for their filthy works. Instead, they take it to be "sin" that people even exist as mouth-breathers who have overpopulated "Mother Earth". Drawing moral scrutiny away from Mortal Sin, the focus is switched to how modern science can merge with religion to offset the "dominant technological paradigm" by which "fossil fuels" restrain betterment of "biodiversity," with the minister warning against "unprecedented destruction of ecosystems, with serious consequence for all of us if prompt climate-change mitigation efforts are not undertaken" ("Encyclical Letter: Laudato

Article I. Governing Principles and Essential Declarations of This TACA Diocese

Si—On Care For Our Common Home"; Abp. Jorge Bergoglio/Pope Francis; pp. 1-184; Vatican, Rome, June 2015).

8) Yoga, Veda, Reiki, Astrology, Scientology, Pantheism, Monism, Yoruba, Voodoo, Islam, Hinduism, Bahaism, Buddhism, and all other un-Christian religious practices, beliefs, and cults that are not in unity with Anglican Christianity do not belong on TACA church grounds. Each stem in various degrees from the worship of Hindu deities, demons, and other entities, and neither membership in them nor affiliation with them is permitted, whether publicly or privately, while being parishioners or members of the Episcopate or Clergy of this TACA Diocese, "for what fellowship hath righteousness with unrighteousness? and what communion hath light with darkness? And what concord hath Christ with Belial? or what part hath he that believeth with an infidel? And what agreement hath the temple of God with idols?" (2 Corinthians 6:14-16).

h) Membership in Satanic "churches" or organizations, Order of Nine Angels, Covens, Wiccan groups, Gnostic groups, and other secret or esoteric cults or orders is strictly forbidden while being parishioners or members of the Episcopate or Clergy of this TACA Diocese (2 Corinthians 6:14-16).

i) The New Thought Movement: This heresy extrapolates from the *Three Laws of Motion* by Sir

Article I. Governing Principles and Essential Declarations of This TACA Diocese

Isaac Newton that a person may gain inner peace, mastery over others, and a peculiar Apotheosis of the Self by engaging the "momentum" that he allegedly can draw from his terrestrial energy, to become the "Übermensch"—the "beyond-man" or superman. The goal of this spirituality is for Free Will to *think* the agent into that self-actualization of deification, the so-called ultimate realizing of his universalist potential. Dependent on the so-called "Law of Attraction," the "momentum" produced by intellectual vitality draws together for the superman all agreeable people and helpful things that are similar and complementary to himself, all participants thinking together in tandem with one another's life force, to overcome any unavailing obstacles of "inertia" (i.e., to eschew any adversity or doubt, in metaphorical accordance with Newton's First Law of Momentum, concerning *Inertia* versus the oncoming *Momentum* of Force). The impetus to draw *like* existents together in harmony was long ago voiced by the Stoic Roman Emperor Marcus Aurelius: "Such as thy thoughts and ordinary cogitations are, such will thy mind be in time. For the soul doth as it were receive its tincture from the fancies, and imaginations. Dye it therefore and thoroughly soak it with the assiduity of these cogitations" (*Meditations*; Marcus Aurelius; Book V; Section XV; A.D. 170). Proponents of the New Thought Movement believe that the "Law of Attraction" paves the way for the "Law of Resonance," whereby the synchronous joining of Free Wills affords a momentous resultant

Article I. Governing Principles and Essential Declarations of This TACA Diocese

harmony, like the balancing of a radio signal's amplitude with frequency. With Newton's Second Law of Motion in mind, an ambitious person, emotionally moved like a physical object to apply Force or Will, should expect the output of his resultingly satisfying Work to equal the input of the Force that he was willing to apply. Promising personal success, gurus steeped in this psychological drink are paid by eager masses to teach them all the hot rubrics: "In moving beyond Stage Two, it is vital to understand the necessity of surrender. Not to an external, dominating, punitive, anthropomorphic deity, for of what use is free will if that were the case?" (*Life Visioning: A Transformative Process for Activating Your Unique Gifts and Highest Potential*; Michael Bernard Beckwith; Chapter 10, 2012). To press one's will ahead of others, forgoing inhibition or fear of remorse about resultantly becoming cretinous, is key: "To surrender is to yield to the next stage of your evolution. It is saying, 'I'm available to what wants to evolve and emerge through me and I'm willing to practice and embody what that takes for it to do so'" (*ibid.*). So that positive thinking dominates the psyche and attracts other cheerful but pushy collaborators, the goal of the New Thought Movement reveals itself by touting the "Law of Assumption," to be the creating of the self as God, who overcomes each "equal and opposite reaction" of Newton's Third Law and strives forward with contrived radiance: "You are consciousness. You are the creator. This is the mystery, this is the great secret known by the

Article I. Governing Principles and Essential Declarations of This TACA Diocese

seers, prophets, and mystics throughout the ages. This is the truth that you can never know intellectually" (*The Power of Awareness*; Neville Lancelot Goddard; Chapter 27; 1952). At moments of doubt, whereof "opposite reactions" are the annoying kickbacks that bother the mind, the guru assures that God encourages the remedy of self-deification: "The image God has of me is a perfect image, and my subconscious mind recreates my body in perfect accordance with the perfect image held in the mind of God" (*The Power of Your Subconscious Mind*; Joseph Murphy; Chapter 3; p. 35; 1963; Reprinted 2018). Known as the "Law of Correspondence," cool self-worship intends that obedience by God toward a powerful human mind should help the eager Zarathustra/narcissist to adapt the Momentum of His Omnipotent Free Will, by His coercing all of Heaven into complicity with the agent's plight to upgrade his psyche comfortably beyond the possible pangs of an overwrought conscience, into the sharing of equal status with the Godhead—thus harnessing God's will into lockstep with man's own will: "Your guilt complex is a false concept of God and Life. God, or Life, does not punish or judge you" (*ibid.* Chapter 17; p. 173). The sinner is transcended from shame into the limitless zone of cheerful sociopathy, lest he suffer a single regret: "You do this to yourself by your false beliefs, negative thinking, and self-condemnation" (*ibid.* p. 173). All religion is relative, after all, to the Law of Attraction, says this spiritual movement—one that has elevated human will to become Law: "The

Article I. Governing Principles and Essential Declarations of This TACA Diocese

secret was *as within,* so without; as above, so below... This same truth was proclaimed by Moses, Isaiah; Jesus; Buddha; Zoroaster; Laotze, and all the illumined seers of the ages. Whatever you feel as true subjectively is expressed as conditions, experiences, and events" (*ibid.* Chapter 3; p. 30) Salvation is merely contentedness on Earth, making sure not to annoy the teacher, who reminds the student: "Motion and emotion must balance. As in heaven [your own mind], so on earth [in your body and environment]. This is the great law of life" (*ibid.* p. 30). Inspired by the metastasizing of this bold blasphemy, millions of people patronize New Thought courses and contribute to robust book sales annually (*American Veda: From Emerson and the Beatles to Yoga and Meditation—How Indian Spirituality Changed the West*; Phillip Goldberg; p. 62; 2010). It is perhaps scary to presume to criticize humanity, lest God's image in man be reproached, but "If we do not redefine manhood, war is inevitable" ("Public & Private: Life After Death"; Anna Quindlen; Quot.: Paul Fussell; *New York Times*; February 7, 1991; p. A25). Self-deification is of course madness. Mandating their Apotheosis, the worst of the Roman emperors expressed that they were gods during their lifetime. For example, Commodus, self-deified as Hercules, would wear a lion skin and hunt the wild prey his guards had had let loose in the streets (*History*; Cassius Dio; Book 73; Section 17-18; A.D. 225). Celebrated for his "Pragmatism," the American psychologist William James developed the humanist Ethics that

Article I. Governing Principles and Essential Declarations of This TACA Diocese

would later be used by the New Thought movement. He insisted that critical emotional analysis safeguard the psyche from thinking itself into such bestial psychopathy by assigning *practicality* as the goal whenever physiological stimuli occur, thereby declaring that the difference between humanity and animals is not that people were made in God's image, but that humans can employ rational thought to cause themselves to act "as if" a moral principle is being served until the principle is fully identified by a person's overall comportment: "In all our discussions about the intelligence of lower animals, the only test we use is that of their acting *as if* for a purpose. Cognition, in short, is incomplete until discharged in act; and although it is true that the later mental development, which attains its maximum through the hypertrophied cerebrum of man, gives birth to a vast amount of theoretic activity over and above that which is immediately ministerial to practice, yet the earlier claim is only postponed, not effaced, and the active nature asserts its rights to the end" (*The Will to Believe and Other Essays in Psychology;* William James; "The Sentiment of Rationality"; p. 85; 1896) Another famous quote, one stolen from the Bible, founded the title of the seminal New-Thought book, *As a Man Thinketh*, a prosaic tome written in 1903 by James Allen. Its heralding of the *Law of Attraction* has led to the conflation of man with God, the wrongful presumption that because a man has something in common with God, in that he thinks and has Free Will, and was

Article I. Governing Principles and Essential Declarations of This TACA Diocese

made in God's image, he is thus entirely God himself, an errant proposition presuming cohesion by examining one part of a whole, one that Aristotle would have cooly called the "Fallacy of Combination" (*Organon; On Sophistical Refutations;* Aristotle; Chapter 4; A.D. 350). However, even when proper rhetoric is allowed to trump Faith, heresy results when the "as-if" idea and Aristotelian rhetoric are used as the apologetics of Atheism. So, for example, because Grace comes from God, and because man was made in God's image, it is seen by atheists as being nothing more than the Fallacy of the Undistributed Middle to declare that man is God. Accordingly, if the Bible were mere linguistics, then there would be no heresy in promulgating *Metaphysical Naturalism,* the Atheism which, while warning rhetoricians about "Modo-Hoc" Fallacy (i.e., the informal error of assessing significance to an existent based on the constituent properties of its material makeup while omitting the matter's arrangement—in that a chopped-up cow is not the same thing as an intact cow despite having the same substance), what elevates thinking above rhetorical error could conveniently become the heresy of reasoning against the faithful Discernment of one's heart that God exists. Claiming that it is a merely crazy Combination Fallacy to dare to believe that Faith purports the existence of God disposes the Metaphysical Naturalist to accuse Christians of seeing themselves as merely "us hacked up into a stew" or a "bundle of rods," maybe not pretending

Article I. Governing Principles and Essential Declarations of This TACA Diocese

to be gods, but being still unable rationally to disassociate the causality of human existence from the causality of a deity's being (*Sense and Goodness Without God: A Defense of Metaphysical Naturalism*; Richard Carrier; p. 130; 2005). Having Faith that one cannot prove God's existence merely through the study of any kind of rhetoric, it should be noted that Carrier, who clumsily declared that "all belief in gods is caused by cognitive illusions with cultural and behavioral explanations" (*ibid.* p. 272) is himself engaging in Modo-Hoc fallacy, because he extracts one participle of Faith—that one's Christian Faith shares belief in the supernatural with, say, psychosis, polytheism, or UFOism—to promulgate an all-encompassing global always-true conclusion that "all" belief in God (or gods) implies overall societal failure. It is a wrongful presumption of such a discipline—of Cognitive Anthropology as such—to relegate all religions as collectively being a societal "spandrel" (i.e., a cognitive offshoot, or a Jungian type of collective social "parasite") by positing: "There cannot be a magic bullet to explain the existence and common features of religion, as the phenomenon is the result of aggregate relevance—that is, of successful activation of a whole variety of mental systems" (*Religion Explained: The Evolutionary Origins of Religious Thought*; Blaise Boyer; pp. 298, 311; 2001). In the face of sheer rhetoric, a hearty "no thank you" is therefore deserved. To Saint Paul the Apostle, the "bundle of rods" would correspond to the body parts miraculously comprising the

Article I. Governing Principles and Essential Declarations of This TACA Diocese

Church without the schism of rhetoric, while rebuking the argumentative, lawsuit-loving Athenians (1 Corinthians 12:21-28). "As a man thinketh" thus returns to its rightful position as a merely beautiful set of words in the King James Bible. The first usage came from King Solomon, witnessing insincere guests in his palace: "For as he thinketh in his heart, so is he: Eat and drink, saith he to thee; but his heart is not with thee" (Proverbs 23:7). The verse merely concerns a person who is always thinking about the cost of hospitality and is not sincere in obliging his host's offer to eat and drink, allowing his falseness to convey his duplicitous mindset. As such, one mere part of the Law sustains the entirety of the Law (James 2:10), whereof this is not the Fallacy of Combination, but rather Truth. Mere ordinances or disputation thereof cannot make man perfect or prove God's Love, which only the Blood of the Lamb can do (Hebrews 10:1-4). Christ, hurling the "second cup" of eschatology at the Pharisees, who were trolling Him because He did not wash His hands before supper, superbly addressed their wicked hearts, "Now do ye Pharisees make clean the outside of the cup and the platter; but your inward part is full of ravening and wickedness" (Luke 11:39)—thus, as a man thinketh, is demonstrated correctly by Our Lord. Christ reminds the lesser of Who created them: "Ye fools, did not He that made that which is without make that which is within also?" (*ibid.*). Sinners and dirty hands—to the faithless—are too unlike the purity of Heaven to be able to be redeemed by the

Article I. Governing Principles and Essential Declarations of This TACA Diocese

Blood of the Lamb. Moreover, Plato had espoused the Law of Attraction three centuries earlier, saying, "It would seem, Adeimantus, that the direction in which education starts a man, will determine his future life. Does not like always attract like? To be sure" (*The Republic*; Plato; Book IV; B.C. 375). Would Christ thus reject a dinner invitation from the sinful merely because He is sinless? Certainly not! Later, Plato gave a gloomy thumbnail of Cosmology in his dialogue *Parmenides*, purporting that being and unbeing, or life and death, or good and evil, are really two parts of the same thing, namely life, further jading receptiveness to Christ entering the heart through the indwelling of the Holy Spirit: to the Manichean, goodness and evil are merely part of the same God (Ephesians 3:14-21; *Confessions*; Saint Augustine of Hippo; Book V; Section 10; A.D. 397). "And therefore whether we take being and the other, or being and the one, or the one and the other, in every such case we take two things, which may be rightly called both" (*Parmenides*; Plato; Transl. Benjamin Jowett; Sec. 143:b-d; B.C. 370). The formative relativism of Plato may explain why "Good Works" is wrongly believed by Christians as a necessary additive to sustaining Faith in Christ's perfect Sacrifice, as if God's impossible coequality with Lucifer would necessitate that extra salvific work should be done by humans because Christ did not finish the job (John 19:30). Given such morally relativistic bleakness, should Faith merely reflect the alleged "Momentum" cited by the New Thinkers, who hold

Article I. Governing Principles and Essential Declarations of This TACA Diocese

that the Creator created Faith for people to enjoy, but that Faith is not potentially powerful enough to enable the Faithful to throw mountains into the sea (Matthew 21:21)? Is human Free Will, vulnerable as it is to sinfulness, merely the same momentous force as Faith? Is Faith therefore (erroneously) a mere mental energy, which, if relegated to such a trifling status, would make followers believe that New Thought gurus are correct whenever they mislead followers into believing that by merely cultivating intellectual similitude with God they are sufficiently equaling how God the Father made the Universe and saves souls? Of course not, on both accounts. Christians do not need New Thought to help themselves, because God does not tempt Christians beyond our capacity to cope. True, God can give people over to their sinful ways (Romans 1:24). And God did indeed put an evil spirit into King Saul (1 Samuel 18:10). Moreover, He surely hardened Pharoah's heart (Exodus 9:12). However, neither evil, nor meaninglessness, nor unbeing define Who God is, because God is Love (1 John 4:8, 16). Perhaps the foundational text that forms the basis of New Thought's cherished Law-of-Attraction theories should now be used to make their Intellection/Momentum tenets fall apart. Consider that the true inventor of the Law of Attraction was himself a less insane (albeit a self-professed demigod) ancient sorcerer named Hermes Trismegistus. He chiseled into his *Emerald Tablet,* "That which is below is like that which is above, and that which is above is like it which is below, to do ye miracles of one only thing" (*The Emerald Tablet;* Hermes Trismegistus; No. 2 of 14; Transl. Isaac Newton; B.C. 200). This satanic verse may be more familiar through its popular catch phrase: "As Above, So Below." Several syncretic-Christian terms by which adherents toy with this concept consist in: "Will or Chant Your Desire Into Existence"; "Live Your Best Life Now"; "Ask the Universe for What You Want"; "Name it and Claim It," and other derivations of the "Word of Faith" and "Prosperity Gospel" movements. But Hermes, who was an astrologer who worshipped the "Divine Pymander" (a.k.a. "the great dragon in the sky"), had very different thoughts about the tendencies of that coveted momentous brain force that would long to help common folk deify themselves by attracting ethereal likenesses of their corporeal wants. His actual words make the modern heresy of New Thought stagger and then drop on its face. Firstly, his Eighth Book of *The Divine Pymander* was titled, "The Greatest Evil is the Not Knowing God": right away the title signals the Gnostic principle of supreme knowledge, but Hermes's actual obvious disdain for his being surrounded by wealthy pupils defines him as being more indifferent to fame and money than the modern Amazon-selling book writers would want him to appear. That is, the First verse upbraids the vain: "Whither are you carried, O Men, drunken with drinking strong Wine of Ignorance? which seeing you cannot bear, why do you vomit it up again?" (*The Divine Pymander;* Hermes Trismegistus; Book VIII; B.C. 200). Hermes,

Article I. Governing Principles and Essential Declarations of This TACA Diocese

whose astringent pontifications were borrowed for the 12 "principles" for the foundational 1908 hermetic New Thought guidebook by William Walker Atkinson, *The Kybalion*, is not the author of those haughty esoteric ideas about "momentum"; in fact, he actually praised a singular deity whose greatness he insisted cannot be simulated and whose likeness cannot be found. Hermes attested: "But he that is One, that is not made nor generated, is also unapparent and unmanifest" (*ibid. Pymander*; Book V; Verse 7). In fact, the Free Will of "God," implied Hermes, posits an unmatched omniscience by which one cannot think himself into being God: "pray first to the Lord and Father, and to the Alone, and to the One, from whom is one to be merciful to thee, that thou mayest know and understand so great a God; and that he would shine one of his beams upon thee in thy understanding" (*ibid. Pymander*; Book V; Verse 2). In reality, Christians, although resembling God, are unlike God because they simulate an image of the "Form" God made for them, when He conceived them prior to life in the womb (Jeremiah 1:5). Thus, the "prime matter" (not the formless "ether" from which alchemists pretend they can create gold via the Philosopher's Stone) is the Form of human perfection that the Creator intends for Christians to attain by Faith (2 Corinthians 5:1-8). It is the actual Love of God—Who is Love itself—that created humans out of that Love (John 1, 1 John 4:16), to which the Faithful may attribute their "being," or *ousia*. In Aristotelian terms, Love is the cause for the

Article I. Governing Principles and Essential Declarations of This TACA Diocese

creation by God of human beings, made in His image and likeness. Love is the unique "[mould] ... out of which a thing comes to be and which persists, and may be called 'cause', e.g. the bronze of the statue, the silver of the bowl, and the genera of which the bronze and the silver are species" (*Physics*; Aristotle; Book II; Part 3; B.C. 338). Saint Thomas Aquinas applied these physics in designating that the human soul and thinking are not momentum, but rather are simultaneously incorporeal and substantial (*Summa Theologiae*; Question 75. Man who is composed of a spiritual and a corporeal substance: and in the first place, concerning what belongs to the essence of the soul; 1274). Therefore, there is no zeitgeist or revolution or "Law of Assumption" in which New Thinkers, New Agers, or Marxists ought to presume that they are sharing in a mystical "momentum," but it should be known that each true Christian is not merely God's workmanship (Ephesians 2:10), "wonderfully and fearfully made" (Psalm 139:14), but is reborn (John 3:3) from the "prime matter" of God's Love (1 John 4:8), conformed to the image of Jesus (Romans 8:29) and yet is each uniquely faceted (Ephesians 4:11-12), or as Aristotle wrote, "As regards material substance, we must not fail to realize that even if all things are derived from the same primary cause, or from the same things as primary causes; i.e. even if all things that are generated have the same matter for their first principle, nevertheless each thing has some matter peculiar to it" (*Metaphysics*; Aristotle; Book 8; 1044a; B.C.

Article I. Governing Principles and Essential Declarations of This TACA Diocese

350). As the "mover," God, applies Salvation, by which the Prime Matter of the Elect owes its redemptive image to the perfect Form of the loving God (1 John 4:7-12). Also, presuming that he was himself moved by Common Grace, Hermes implied a raw precursor of his possessing a homoousian ("one in being with the Father") consubstantiality (the Real Presence), by which Christians know that all humans are made by the real God. He was accidentally launching a concept that destroys the New Thought idea that people, using the Laws of Attraction and Momentum can magically use positive thinking, instead of having Faith, to become a momentous juggernaut whose quantum "vibration" or "particulate" is mystically like in substance with that of the Creator. He declared: "So, if thou forcest me somewhat too bold, to speak, His being is conceiving of all things and making [them]. And as without its maker it is impossible that anything should be, so ever is He not unless He ever makes all things, in heaven, in air, in earth, in deep, in all of cosmos, in every part that is and that is not of everything. For there is naught in all the world that is not He. He is Himself, both things that are and things that are not. The things that are He hath made manifest, He keepeth things that are not in Himself" (*ibid. Pymander*; Book V; Verse 9). As an embarrassment to the so-called "Attraction Lawyer" (if you will), New Thinkers forgot that Hermes engaged the consubstantiality idea to state unequivocally that non-similar things, such as God and sinners, do indeed attract each other.

Article I. Governing Principles and Essential Declarations of This TACA Diocese

This is epitomized by the Father's existence being conceivable to Hermes via coherent states of His conscious being—in contrast with the blind state of unbeing or non-existence—the darkness from which God separated the light (Genesis 1:4). "God," to these demonic persons, is not leading a likes-attracting-likes Universe, but according to Hermes himself, the Divine is instead composed of both being and unbeing stuck upon one another, along with all things that are not like itself. The proof of the damnable belief that confuses people is therefore in his own writing. This intellectual failure today defines the New-Thought movement, whose philosophers do not comprehend Christ's effulgence of the creational Logos that pierces all darkness (John 1:5), giving meaning to all things, knowable by this holy epistemology of His glory and virtue (2 Peter 1:3), because they mistakenly believe that they can deify themselves out of mere meaninglessness, so long as that meaninglessness is thought about fervently and long enough. In other words, only Christ, with His Reciprocal Indwelling, is truly God, intending to indwell in us (i.e., "At that day ye shall know that I am in My Father, and ye in Me, and I in you"; John 14:20). By contrast, lovers of the black semantically nihilistic void should step into the light to enjoy the Consubstantiation of God's Real Presence in the Eucharist during the Last Supper (Luke 22:19-20). As a "control set," it should be noted that a man, devoid of Scriptural exegesis, could begin to grasp the indwelling of God in the soul by utilizing the same Aristotelian metaphysics that was diligently

Article I. Governing Principles and Essential Declarations of This TACA Diocese

employed by an obscure Roman grammarian, a recently converted Christian, a former pagan finding himself to dispute Homoousianism with the heretic Arius, in praise of the ethereal handiwork of the "Unmoved Mover" (*Metaphysics*; Aristotle; Chapter 11; Part 9; A.D. 350). Beholding the Matter that came from the Form and was not the creature but God: "If this is so, then Jesus, who was from what He is, did not appear as an action out of nothing; when the action itself, and this was what it is to be: nor is it because of these two τὸ ὁμοούσιον [homoousion]·because it is the same as the substance of one is the same. Indeed, there is one action, since it is to act and to be. This is the Son, this is from the Father, this is about God, this is in the bosom of the father, this is within, this is without. For by work without, in that which is being within: and in the Father God Himself in God, who is entirely the same with Him: but by action who is the Son. And wherever He is, there is both being and action: and in this way, both the Father is and God is, and the Son is and the Word. ("On the Generation of the Divine Word, to Candidus Arianus"; Gaius Marinus Victorinus; Part 23; A.D. 357). It is otherwise a pathological heresy to elect oneself to be God, noting the "as above, so below," quote of Murphy, above. The offer of employing such willful thinking to make oneself equal to God was indeed the incentive given by the serpent to Eve to become a god (Genesis 3). As the malevolent Madame Blavatsky described, the "wicked" array of God is always "feeding" on the "necessary" ego

Article I. Governing Principles and Essential Declarations of This TACA Diocese

of men—a higher "astral plane" invested insatiably in man's inescapable lower "body of light" (*Collected Writings*; H. P. Blavatsky; Volume XII; p. 711; 2019). The Satanic plan for people to replace God with the self was evident to Saint Paul, who was the first to warn Corinth, "And no marvel; for Satan himself is transformed into an angel of light" (2 Corinthians 11:14). Familiar with demoniacs as Saint Paul was (Acts 16:18), it was contemporary with New Thought movement, that the Abbey of Thelema indoctrinated for its Satanists the false promise that "Every man and every woman is a star" (*The Book of the Law*; Aleister Crowley; Chapter 1; Verse 3; Samuel Weiser, Newburyport, MA:, 1976), a vain hope for darkness recognizable by the fruits of deceit, filth, and violence of Satanic accomplishments (Matthew 7:16). "Therefore it is no great thing if His ministers also be transformed as the ministers of righteousness; whose end shall be according to their works" (2 Corinthians 11:15). Governed by the willful "momentum" of heartlessness, "Love is the law, [but] love under will" (*ibid.* Crowley; Chapter 1; Verse 57). Christ had thus appropriately sent forth his exorcists, "And he said unto them, I beheld Satan as lightning fall from Heaven" (Luke 10:18). Knowing that man's time is short (Revelation 12:12), the devil has cunningly inverted the source of the Law, just as Murphy above wrote that God does not judge people, but man judges God. By its customized immoral theology, the alleged Momentum of Free Will allowed the Ethics of Modernism to be

Article I. Governing Principles and Essential Declarations of This TACA Diocese

conditionally contingent upon whether pleasure and convenience are comfortably served, disregarding as being merely arbitrary Christian discernment over whatever is good or foul, against which the Book of Romans cries out, "And thinkest thou this, O man, that judgest them which do such things, and doest the same, that thou shalt escape the judgment of God?" (Romans 2:3). The erroneous Law of Attraction was therefore the objectification of God's image in modern man, a faithless rascal who enslaves Truth to the depravity of the heart, to actualize whatever hell on Earth as it liked: "Do as thou wilt shall be the whole of the law" (*ibid.* Crowley; Chapter 1; Verse 40). Finally, as the merely sensible ideas of the pagan monist Aristotle, as well as the peculiar words of Hermes Trismegistus, can themselves refute the so-called Law of Attraction, it shall be maintained that Newton's Laws of Motion do indeed factor in here, because they ironically collapse the Modernist heresy upon itself. That is, because the words of ancient pagan thinkers can be impelled against pathetically faulty doctrine, they can also be enjoyed in a Newtonian vein, in that the "force of equal magnitude and opposite direction" of God's Word is always available to uproot epistemological error: All secret or hidden things will be disclosed, out in the open, in God's light (Deuteronomy 29:29; Luke 8:17). To be sure, "The thought of foolishness is sin" (Proverbs 24:9), while the obedient Christian wisely prays, "I hate vain thoughts: but thy law do I love" (Psalm 119:113).

Article I. Governing Principles and Essential Declarations of This TACA Diocese

"For it is written, I will destroy the wisdom of the wise, and I will bring to nothing the understanding of the prudent" (1 Corinthians 1:19).

j) Transgenderism, a heinous defiance of God's creation of the sexes (Genesis 5:2) must be prohibited along with special mention of the founder of its fake science. Dr. John William Money was a psychologist who in the early 1970s coerced twin male children to engage in sexual activity so that one of the boys could submit to a violently enforced version of the "female" role, and called his methods "therapy." He had overseen the surgical removal of the boy's penis and the boring into the pelvic cavity to create a simulated vagina, as the solution to the parents' disappointment about the failure of the routine circumcision that took place during the child's infancy. That mutilation had left the child unable to procreate and gave Money an opportunity to demonstrate that "gender reassignment" proves that gender roles are learned, not natural and innate. Not reporting that the "female" in the study would grow up with a male sexual identity— in fact as a husband and stepfather—Money also did not retract his theory after one of the brothers, who was long clinically depressed, overdosed on drugs, and the "female," who was suddenly separated from his wife, committed suicide by shooting himself in the face with a shotgun just two years later. Money substantiated his claim that naturally occurring, albeit rare, "hermaphroditism" refutes the viability of

Article I. Governing Principles and Essential Declarations of This TACA Diocese

society's cultivation of traditional gender roles—a paradigm he claimed was to blame for the "bipolarity of mind and body" (to Money, a determinant of "gender dysphoria") that should be corrected via applied "Sexosophy," or the "unipolarizing" of the creational identity of human beings entirely in terms of sexuality ("An Examination of Some Basic Sexual Concepts: The Evidence of Human Hermaphroditism"; John Money, Joan G. Hampson, John Hampson; *Bulletin of the Johns Hopkins University Hospital;* Vol. 97; No. 4: pp. 301-319; Oct., 1955). Concealing the truth that the two brothers by their fifteenth year had already quit his therapy and pursued masculinity through hunting, sports, and heterosexual courtships, he heartlessly penned his vile emotionally void version of Epicureanism, writing, "TELEOLOGY AND PRIMARY DATA. There is an emphasis throughout this book on behavior rather than on thoughts and feelings. The reason is pragmatic: if you can't see, hear, touch, smell or taste it, then there is nothing about another human being that you can know, the claims of the occult [i.e., Christianity and Judaism] notwithstanding" (*Love and Love Sickness: The Science of Sex, Gender Difference, and Pair-Bonding;* John Money; Chapter 2, "Teleology and Primary Data"; p. 13; 1980). He insisted that the "doctrine" of Teleology is older than the Bible (*ibid.* Chapter 2, "Mind/Body"; p. 8) and falsely claimed that the Bible nowhere refers to "genuine homosexuals" (Genesis 19:5; Romans 1:26-27), proposing that what used to be "sin and sickness"

Article I. Governing Principles and Essential Declarations of This TACA Diocese

is now a "sanctioned social alternative" (*ibid.* Chapter 5 "Gender Transpositions"; p. 87). Money's so-called "feelings" about people were not for the weak of heart: "If I were to see the case of a boy aged ten or eleven who's intensely erotically attracted toward a man in his twenties or thirties, if the relationship is totally mutual, and the bonding is genuinely totally mutual, then I would not call it pathological in any way" (*Paidika: The Journal of Paedophilia—interview*, Vol. II; No. 3; p. 5; 1991). Money never acknowledged the suicide and death of the men whose youth was the basis of his abusive seminal case study; instead he is celebrated today by the children of disobedience as the official scientific founder of Transgenderism. The monstrous affront to Truth that he caused has led to a huge recent spike in attempted suicides among LGBTQ+ high-school students—26.3% versus 5.2% for heterosexual high-schoolers ("Mental Health, Suicidality, and Connectedness Among High School Students During the COVID-19 Pandemic — Adolescent Behaviors and Experiences Survey, United States, January-June 2021"; Sherry Everett Jones, et al.; *Morbidity and Mortality Weekly Report;* Vol. 71; Suppl. 3; pp. 16-21. Centers for Disease Control, Washington, DC: 2022). The fatuous grooming of youth, so academically malignant, is today considered "play as praxis" and offers "embodied kinship" for children, innocents encouraged to become a different gender at "Drag Queen Story Hour" paraded in the libraries of elementary schools ("Drag pedagogy: The playful practice of

Article I. Governing Principles and Essential Declarations of This TACA Diocese

queer imagination in early childhood"; Harper Keenan, Li'l Miss Hot Mess; *Curriculum Inquiry;* Vol. 50; No. 1; pp. 1-21; Jan. 2021). The hatred for God, who created the mind, is propagated disgustingly throughout all of academia in these last days, as the souls of such "doctors" are perchance now discovering as they stare into the abyss of their own damnation. To the purveyors of all of these wicked fruits (Luke 6:43), "It were better for him that a millstone were hanged about his neck, and he cast into the sea, than that he should offend one of these little ones" (Luke 17:2).

k) Life is protected by a lifelong Reconciliation with God (James 5:15-16). The call to Repentance must be tirelessly repeated. Wherever Life becomes assailed by the secular enemies of God, the manic hordes or lone wolves who advance against our divided houses with Godless ideas or actions, TACA shall be emboldened to denounce the aims of their Culture of Death, everywhere, in every possible workplace, church, and school (Acts 2:38).

l) Saint Clement of Rome thusly cared to repeat St. Paul's own such exhortation to the wild Church of Corinth, 20 years after the Apostle's martyrdom. "Say to the children of my people, though your sins reach from earth to heaven, and though they be redder [Isaiah 1:18] than scarlet, and blacker than sack-cloth, yet if you turn to me with your whole heart, and say, Father! I will listen to you,

Article I. Governing Principles and Essential Declarations of This TACA Diocese

as to a holy people" (Epistle to the Corinthians; Saint Clement of Rome; Chapter 8; A.D. 96).

iv) Regarding Murder, such as Elective Abortion, and the Sinful "Prevention" known as Contraception and the Sinful "Alternative" Known as Masturbation:

a) As regards the Biblical definition of the creation of Life, there must be constantly vocally considered, with preaching and exemplary praxis, a careful definition not only of Life but also of Life's moral obverse, the willful destruction of Life—that is, murder and non-Life—of a refusal to be fruitful, for all Sacramental purposes of this TACA Diocese.

b) "Elective Abortion" or "Procured Abortion," executed for a reason other than to save the life of the mother, is hence murder. It is in fact infanticide, and shall be known here as Abortion Murder, a criminal act. More explicitly, the inexcusable decision of deliberately ending the life of a human being—a baby, a person made in God's image, who lives inside the womb, or later outside of the womb of his or her mother—when committed with the rationally-determined intention solely to kill the baby when the birth or gestation is of no threat to the life of the mother, is therefore a premeditated murder, performed to accommodate convenience, social or political beliefs, fashion, or any other Godless whim. Such abortion shall be considered Anathema by TACA. All murder is forbidden by the Fifth Commandment of our Lord. Although no Federal

Article I. Governing Principles and Essential Declarations of This TACA Diocese

or Statutory or Case law considers Elective/Procured Abortion to be a criminal act, no Sacraments of any kind or membership of any kind shall be given to an unrepentant Mortal Sinner who has committed such a crime. The homicidal mother and her accomplices shall be encouraged to attend Mass and Prayer Services, to seek Christian or Bible counseling, to accept evangelizing, and eventually hopefully to be admitted by a discerning Priest or Bishop along the path of Confession, Penance, Reconciliation, and Catechesis.

c) Death, the cessation of Life on Earth, shall not determine the separation of the sinner from God (Romans 8:35). Innocent Life must be allowed at all turns to cease itself, unto death, naturally (1 Samuel 26:10; Deuteronomy 34:7). To this end, "mercy killing" and assisted suicide are themselves acts of murder. As such, people must not avail themselves of modern medicine or other sciences, or use Godless discernment, to decide either on their own, or through their next of kin, to make themselves out to be authorities over the degree to which medical interventions should be employed as end-of-life care, as if they were deciding whether or not to have a terminally ill or suffering animal put to sleep: "A righteous man regardeth the life of his beast: but the tender mercies of the wicked are cruel" (Proverbs 12:10). The Sacrament of Last Rites, or the Anointing of the Sick, of any sinner—including an unrepentant Mortal Sinner—shall be provided by a Priest or

Article I. Governing Principles and Essential Declarations of This TACA Diocese

Bishop at their discretion, as an act of charitable mercy, to mediate the afflicted person's Reconciliation with God (1 Thessalonians 4:14-17; Romans 5:12; Colossians 3:3).

d) Sexual coitus outside of the marital bond is fornication. The use of an anti-pregnancy method or drug (i.e., contraceptive) that prevents gamete fertilization is to be avoided. The intentional destruction of the fertilized zygote or embryo is itself abortion and hence is considered murder. All non-marital sex is to be avoided, and the unmarried should remain celibate. It is better to marry than to burn (1 Corinthians 7:8-9).

e) Masturbation, which is sexual gratification through the stimulation of the genitals, is also always to be avoided, especially where it concerns refusal to sublimate one's passion for vitality into the fruitful procreation of human life by "seeding" life within Holy Matrimony (1 Corinthians 7:8-9).

f) Masturbation and Contraception destroy orthodoxy (see Article XIX. ADDENDUM C of this Constitution).

v) TACA Refusal to Serve Sacraments to Unrepentant Mortal Sinners

a) No adult unrepentant practitioner, supporter, promoter, executor, or recipient of, or participant in, Elective Infant Abortion, or of any other murder, or of any other Mortal Sin as described in this Constitution shall receive a Gospel

Article I. Governing Principles and Essential Declarations of This TACA Diocese

Sacrament, a Domenical (Sunday-given) Sacrament, or a Religious Sacrament within this TACA Diocese. "For he that eateth and drinketh unworthily, eateth and drinketh damnation to himself, not discerning the Lord's body" (1 Corinthians 11:29).

b) Confession to a Priest or Bishop, or the Anointing of the Sick (or Last Rites for the dying), that is, Sacraments meant to attain Remission of Sins and Reconciliation with God, are available to a Mortal Sinner; they may not access the other Sacraments. First they shall have been counseled by a member of the Clergy or Episcopate, who will advise regarding his or her Penance and pious amending of ways, and only then shall they be able to approach to receive the other Sacraments within this TACA Diocese.

c) It is left to the discretion of the counseling Priest or Bishop to determine the level of severity of the crime, apostasy, or offense, in order to best judge the appropriate remedy of the spiritual condition of the penitent in relation to whether the penitent may be considered fit to be a TACA member or a recipient of Sacraments in these TACA Diocese. "If we confess our sins, He is faithful and just, to forgive us our sins, and to cleanse us from all unrighteousness" (1 John 1:9).

Article I. Governing Principles and Essential Declarations of This TACA Diocese

vi) Denial of Membership in TACA for Unrepentant Mortal Sinners

a) Moreover, no unrepentant supporter, promoter, or executor of, or collaborator in, Mortal Sin, may become or remain a member of any religious Body within this TACA Diocese. "For without are dogs, and sorcerers, and whoremongers, and murderers, and idolaters, and whosoever loveth and maketh a lie" (Revelation 22:15).

vii) Regarding Mortal Sins and Venial Sins: Both Types Defined

a) Mortal Sins are the kinds of wrongdoings that darkly transcend the category of lesser sinfulness, into a far graver spiritual and cognitive circumstance. In that there is no question in such cases as to whether the sinful act(s) are even partially a mistake, or the result of a flaccid failure of the will, or of a small impairment of reason, a Mortal Sin is one in which the sinner knows that a grave sin that he or she is doing is wrong but commits it anyway. The lesser, Venial Sins constitute any of the myriad more minor offenses against God or man that stem from our fallen condition, but that do not rise to the level of a voluntarily entering into, or at least edging toward, a state of damnation for the souls perpetrating them.

b) A Mortal Sin is what the Bible calls a "sin unto death" (1 John 5:16), that is, is a sin so serious that it separates us from our Creator. Its severity

Article I. Governing Principles and Essential Declarations of This TACA Diocese

is tantamount to denying God to his face. Such sins are abominations, idolatries, and the like. A Mortal Sin is a deliberate act of rebellion against God in which the person fully understands the implications of the offense or crime and yet chooses willingly to engage in the sin and to persist in it without repentance.

c) Venial Sins are offenses committed from time to time against God or man that, unlike Mortal Sins, do not reflect a sinner who is adamantly determined to persist in a moral state that is incompatible with Redemption through God's Grace, but one who is pained by such sins and intends to correct them. They can be characterized as errors of morality or ethics, and even of fatuous ignorance, various disappointing mistakes of the will that are not held by the sinner to be irresistibly committed or necessary means or ends in themselves, or unavoidable actions. They may fall under the category of unfortunate personal dispositions of temperament or character, or sundry types of foibles that are common to fallen mankind. They may include unfriendliness, laziness, being given to luxury or gourmet food and delicacies, failure to fast or to engage in religious ritual or discipline, hurtful or disruptive boisterousness, or the engaging of fear, material desire, profanity, sordidity, vainglory, or other sensual or emotional aims, in refusing to tell the truth or to do what is right and to avoid doing what is wrong, cowardice, filthy speech, gossip, sloth, pettiness, and the like. Any Venial Sin, if committed constantly, pervasively, and deliberately and without Remission, and devolving into the refusal to cease engaging in it, or enjoying the hurt caused by it, may worsen itself, now being accompanied by a multitude of accompanying other sins, thus downgrading the Venial Sin into the realm of Mortal Sin, with Pride being the catalyst of that alchemy. In that regard:

d) The Near Occasions of Sin are circumstances making exposure to sinfulness by others to be certain and probable. Peer pressure and bullying, suffered at any age, seduction by others, or the wearying of the fatigued Christian at "well-doing" (Galatians 6:9) may convert the desire for safety, security, and comfort into the committing of sin. As if influenced by the ritualistic idolators of Egypt and Canaan, ancient Hebrews enforced the Laws of Exodus, Numbers, and Deuteronomy (the latter with its Code in Chapters 12 through 26) for all the Israelites, and those of Leviticus for the priesthood, just as Christians would later receive Christ's Great Commandment (Matthew 22:36-46) for everyone. It had been hoped that living one's life in a state of constant contrition ought to replace temptation with thanksgiving. However, belief in rules alone, rather than in God above all things, smothers Faith, the only means by which the Fruits of the Spirit (love, joy, peace, patience, kindness, goodness, faithfulness, gentleness, self-control) may grow, independent of Law (Galatians 5:22-23). Thus, above Sacred Scripture's juridical

Article I. Governing Principles and Essential Declarations of This TACA Diocese

Word against evil, undefiled Love must ensure that evil itself may not fester and grow into the base litigiousness of modern clericalism and phariseeism, or into any hypocrisy by which misguided religiosity would function to lord over the Beloved without genuine piety (Matthew 5:20; 23:1-39). Despite his righteousness, the Pharisee was not held by Christ to be more blessed than the sorrowfully guilty tax collector in the Temple (Luke 18:10-14). Still, the book of Romans asks sinners to use the Law to hold a mirror up to themselves: "But sin, taking occasion by the commandment, wrought in me all manner of concupiscence. For without the Law, sin was dead" (Romans 7:8). Put plainly, the societal strengths of health and vigor, together with the natural graces of beauty and might, may serve communities that thrive in a state of law and order, in order to foster fruitfulness and creativity, but sadly they also allow acts of rude competitiveness, spite, vanity, and for that matter, lust, greed, gluttony, sloth, intemperance, envy, bigotry, wrongful ideologies, and boisterous wrath to metastasize a "culture" very fatuously, as though these firstly timid outpourings from the cup of concupiscence could be passed off as trifling byproducts of productivity, of glowing youth, success, and of hard work. No—rules are not enough. Jesus must be known in Fellowship with the sinner and/or with the Beloved, gathered in His name, together (Matthew 18:20). The governor of Persian Judea, Nehemiah, joined with the brethren and nobles to oppose the temptation

Article I. Governing Principles and Essential Declarations of This TACA Diocese

by their families to stray outside of the Law, formally affixing a permanent curse to it (Nehemiah 10:29). Its ancient twofold paradox of being both a "blessing" and a "curse," just as it had been written by Moses (Deuteronomy 11:26; 30:1), requires the Messiah to rescue the sinner from his falling more deeply toward the deadliness of sin (Romans 6:23), the meaningless and darkness from which he cannot be delivered without Faith in Jesus (Galatians 3:10-13). He already knows what the Law commands, but he sins anyway because of his Total Depravity, the proclivity toward enslavement to sin against which he can only deliberate with hopes that he will choose good over evil by his mortal Gnomic Free Will (*City of God;* Saint Augustine of Hippo; Book 13; Chapter 14; A.D. 426; Ezekiel 18:20; Romans 6:12-16; 2 Peter 2:19; Romans 5:12; Romans 10:20; Isaiah 65:1; Second Council of Orange; Session 6; Canons 1-3; A.D. 529; Third Council; of Constantinople Session 13; A.D. 681). Matthew Henry, the British "non-conformist" minister, wrote, "The corrupt nature [of man] would not have swelled and raged so much if it had not been for the restraints of the law; as the peccant humours in the body are raised, and more inflamed, by a purge that is not strong enough to carry them off. It is incident to corrupt nature, in vetitum niti—to lean towards what is forbidden" (*Commentary on the Bible;* Matthew Henry; Vol. VI; Romans 7:8; 1706). Therefore, great industry and civic construction brought along with them the seducers of misguided minds by way of such

Article I. Governing Principles and Essential Declarations of This TACA Diocese

blind alleys as Marxism, against which the Christian must "shun profane and vain babblings: for they will increase unto more ungodliness" (2 Timothy 2:16). In 1 Corinthians 15:33 ("Do not be deceived: evil communications corrupt good manners"), Saint Paul appears to be borrowing from the alleged verse from the lost drama *Thais*, by Menander: "Do not be deceived: Evil company destroys good habits." Avoiding the children of disobedience and the scandal and wrath coming to them (Colossians 3:6) by and large causes increasing numbers of weary but hardy Christians to identify themselves as if they are the:

e) "Hero of Haarlem": As a consequence of present sociopolitical strife and the slow burn of global economic collapse, the bi-vocational Priest and Bishop and the Christian worker or homesteader now works ever harder to keep the Church buttressed and the finger held in the proverbial broken dike of Holland. One cannot hold down a job and raise a family while shunning all proximate but necessary occasions in the marketplace, school, and government. Given to the skullduggery of doctors, banking mountebanks, rioters, and thieves, today's societal collapse inflicts the Near Occasion of Sin so insidiously against the Christian, that orthodoxy would seem impossible if one, who wishes to keep the dam of industriousness and moral probity from bursting, did not have the Bible and the Communion of Saints from which to draw inspiration. Otherwise, at a time of mental

Article I. Governing Principles and Essential Declarations of This TACA Diocese

breakdown, in the absence of a Bible passage or remembered hagiography, consider that one's own basic Prevenient Grace may summon forth the basic Faith epitomized by the child in the old American tale, the lad who stayed awake, freezing all night holding his finger in the dike: "Then he called on God for help; and the answer came through a holy resolution—I will stay here till morning," whereupon at daylight the villagers repaired the dam and tenderly relieved him (*Hans Brinker or the Silver Skates*; Chapter 18: "Friends in Need"; Mary Mapes Dodge; 1865). It is not practical for a working Christian to think that he or she can make a living without God's help. Included as one of the so-called "conflicts of the law," as codified by the Byzantines, was a psychological approach to rolling with the punches, perchance that one should be forced to accept that he or she must do business with the wicked, just as Saint Paul, Aquila, and Priscilla had to sell tents to the wayward people of Corinth (Acts 18:2-3); that is, "*Nemo tenetur ad impossibile*," translates as, "no one is bound to do what is impossible" (*Digesto*; Emperor Justinian I; Book 50; Chapter 17; Part 185; A.D. 531). If one's soul were an aircraft, it would be possible to perform a "root-cause analysis" to research how the Near Occasion of Sin could be attributable to what Sociologists call "set-up factors" that led to a plane crash, but God asks sinners to hold themselves, not others, accountable for personal wrongdoing (Romans 2:1). The tentmaker had to make money just as American parents must today

Article I. Governing Principles and Essential Declarations of This TACA Diocese

earn wages to feed their children (2 Thessalonians 3:10), or send them to awful public schools so that they can work; he could not always preach to the polytheists while simultaneously laboring to earn staters (i.e., the silver coins of ancient Athens), but he often strived to keep his personal convictions about disputable matters within the Roman world between himself and God—while never condemning himself for serenely doing the things that he knew were blessed. "Hast thou Faith? have it to thyself before God. Happy is he that condemneth not himself in that thing which he alloweth" (Romans 14:22). In avoiding scandal, peacefully eschewing the company of the deliberately unrepentant, and staying Biblically minded and praying "without ceasing" (1 Thessalonians 5:17), it is possible to work peacefully for a living during the "Great Reset," just as Saint Paul survived Hellenistic upheavals during the *Pax Romana*, always trying to become perfect like the Father (2 Timothy 3:16-17).

f) Silent Strength: As the Oxford theologian wrote in 1878 regarding Romans 14:22, about calmly staying in the Faith while living among the "madness of the peoples" (Psalm 65:9), "reserve the exhibition of it to the privacy of your own direct communion with God, and do not display it ostentatiously in public where it may do harm." Saint Paul advises abiding one one's Faith courageously when necessary. In present times, this could amount to one's refusal to use "preferred gender pronouns" at one's job, or

Article I. Governing Principles and Essential Declarations of This TACA Diocese

>refusing to acquire an industrially mandated, harmful, purely experimental medical injection. "It is indeed—the Apostle continues—a happy thing to have no self-condemnatory scruples of conscience, but, on the other hand, it is fatal to have scruples and to disregard them" (*Ellicott's Commentary on the Whole Bible*; Vol. VII; Romans 14:22; Rev. William Sanday; Bp. Charles John Ellicott, Ed.; 1954). Nevertheless, be "ready always to give an answer to every man that asketh you for a reason of the hope that is in you with meekness and fear" (1 Peter 3:15).

viii) Regarding Penance

>a) Penance is the state of voluntary acceptance by the sinner of the spiritual and temporal punishments that are typically associated with profound moral guilt. It otherwise is hard "to kick against the pricks" (Acts 9:5). As shall be advised by a TACA minister, the psychological, social, familial, and/or professional types of downfalls are merely the redemptive journeying toward Reconciliation with Christ, who promises that self-imposed graceful willingness to suffer comeuppance helps bring about the happiest possible reward. "For godly sorrow worketh repentance to salvation not to be repented of: but the sorrow of the world worketh death" (2 Corinthians 7:10).

>b) The penitential disposition of this TACA Church is thus Mercy, applied with an unwavering fatherly strength upon the spiritually sick sufferer

Article I. Governing Principles and Essential Declarations of This TACA Diocese

of any and all wicked madness, "for indeed the school of the Church is an admirable surgery—a surgery, not for bodies, but for souls" ("Homily Against Publishing the Errors of the Brethren"; Saint John Chrysostom; Section 1; A.D. 407).

c) Priests and Bishops of this TACA Diocese shall open their doors carefully only to repentant Christians seeking God, freed from the spiritually contagious despair of Mortal Sin, by which, "I account you happy for the zeal, beloved, with which you flock into the Father's house" (*ibid.*), for "sacrifices of God are a broken spirit: a broken and a contrite heart, O God, thou wilt not despise" (Psalm 51:17).

ix) Regarding Safe Fellowship

a) A safe Congregation or Mission is then a religious Body of TACA whose members' graceful Christian service actualizes the redemptive aspect of "having something in common" (in Greek, *Koinonos*) with other Christians—sinners, enjoying Church life, who are assembled in a TACA religious Body in joyful fellowship (Philippians 2:1-2, Acts 2:42, 1 John 1:6-7). But because we are—and are among—sinners in this fellowship, it can happen that some, "having swerved aside unto vain jangling" (1 Timothy 1:6), fall into heterodoxy or heresy, profanity or sordidness, thus running the risk of leavening the "whole lump" (Galatians 5:9). Therefore it must be constantly preached to every religious Body that Christian Faith must never slacken into a denying

Article I. Governing Principles and Essential Declarations of This TACA Diocese

of the truth that the devil is like a lion, seeking to devour sinners (1 Peter 5:8). Because sickening evil may leave the state of that "empty" house in a such a state that it is worse than it was ever before (Matthew 12:44-45), the constant calling of a good minister of Christ is to "be sober and be vigilant" as an ardent Christian commander of sound biblical teaching, so as to protect the spiritual life of the congregation to which he is entrusted.

x) Leadership Restraining Christians from Sin, as the Restraining of Dogs From Returning to Their Vomit (2 Peter 2:22)

a) Christian leadership within every religious Body of this TACA Diocese shall thus imitate Christ, our perfect Redeemer, who triumphed over sin, and in that capacity must exercise the grave responsibility of deciding upon the type and means of penance: "Whence we learn that we must determine the Penance not only by the nature of the sins, but by the disposition and habit of them that sin" ("Homily 4 on 2 Corinthians 2:7"; Saint John Chrysostom; A.D. 407) An able Priest or Bishop must know how, through prayerful discernment, to keep a penitent's spiritual rehabilitation from sliding backwards.

b) Saint Augustine of Hippo's rehabilitation of Leporius, the wandering monastic heretic who had been kicked out of the Church of Marseilles, reinforces the position that Mortal Sin must be rebuked by an impregnable Bishop or Priest,

Article I. Governing Principles and Essential Declarations of This TACA Diocese

whose example of Mercy, for the Church, stems from his powerful disdain for heresy and filth. Any such willing penitent is able to receive the consolation—one that ought to be safely enjoyed within any Christian fellowship—if they firstly feel safe to be in its presence (Letter 219; Augustine; 436 A.D.), for "They that are whole have no need of the physician, but they that are sick" (Mark 2:17).

c) It is then the lifelong spiritual warfare and disposition of the Church Militant of this TACA Diocese to "be not conformed to this world: but be ye transformed by the renewing of your mind, that ye may prove what is that good, and acceptable, and perfect, will of God" (Romans 12:2).

xi) Regarding Sexual Morality and Marriage

a) Our TACA Diocese considers that the employing of a fidelitous, thoughtful, careful, respectful, and healthy approach to the usage of one's body to demonstrate affection is the wisest and safest means by which a person may physically interact with the world while remaining supernaturally connected with the heavens. Because the forbidden indulgence of lust may directly injure happiness and trust in both the desired human object and the betrayed spouse, or the disappointed parents or guardians, it serves the highest moral utility that sex never occur outside the bond of Holy Matrimony.

b) Moreover, sex between married partners solely must occur between a married man and a woman, instead of between members of the same gender, for it is impossible for such to be married except in their own imaginations. A clean mind that is free of the shackling to prurient intention is able to know the consolation of serving angelic aims. However, the mind of such a Christian should remain both humble and sober: When the 70 disciples, having returned from their commission, boasted about their new ability to rid their subjects of demonic possession, Jesus advised them not to commend themselves for their powers of exorcism, but rather to celebrate the truth that their "names are written in the heavens" (Luke 10:17-20). The same must also be like the Apostle Paul, who wrote even of himself: "But I keep under my body, and bring it into subjection: lest that by any means, when I have preached to others, I myself should be a castaway" (1 Corinthians 9:27).

c) While the calling to spiritual fidelity that is associated with Matthew 5:27-28 (that a lustful man effectively commits adultery against his wife in his own heart whenever he covets another woman) underscores the intrinsic importance of covenantal purity in marriage, salacious desire within all people—whether married or unmarried—also augments the severity of the sin with the physical self-destruction of that concupiscent agent, who by committing such acts is depriving himself of the fruits of the spirit that

Article I. Governing Principles and Essential Declarations of This TACA Diocese

are mentioned in Galatians 5:22-23: "love, joy, peace, longsuffering, gentleness, goodness, faith, meekness, temperance," setting apart these good spiritual gifts as having no causal dependence on the existence of Moral Law. Such may falsely conclude that they are "not under the law" despite not having, or living in, or committing to a spirit of obedience to the Holy Spirit, but they are self-deluded.

d) In that sexual immorality is also the author of such heinous acts as murder, rape, incest, and the like, against which Leviticus 20 lists sundry harsh punishments, we hold that 1 Timothy 1:9 rightly posits that the Law exists only for sinners rather than it is to be seen as being capable of creating wholesome sources of happiness—those fruits that instead can only be created by the Holy Spirit (Galatians 5:22-23).

e) A sexually moral Christian can more abundantly foster spiritual rewards for himself and others than one who is guiltily obsessed with thoughts concerning the loved one(s) whose trust he or she is infidelitously betraying—more than one who realizes that that he or she has violated the Moral Law that Christ promised in Matthew 5:18 that He has not changed.

f) Reconciliation is better than divorce. A man seeking divorce from his wife because of her adultery may assuage his guilt by contemplating Matthew 19:9, but his bitterness over the situation will surely outlive any artificial sweetness he may

Article I. Governing Principles and Essential Declarations of This TACA Diocese

concoct for himself, as if Christ's justice cited herein could somehow justify his immoral appetite for vengeance.

> 1) While always remembering that 1 Corinthians 7:12-16 urges reconciliation, the faithful spouse must strive to help God to purify all the hearts of the home. A man must forgive countless times (Matthew 18:22), and must recall that the Lord hates the treachery of divorce: "For the LORD, the God of Israel, saith that he hateth putting away: for one covereth violence with his garment, saith the LORD of hosts: therefore take heed to your spirit, that ye deal not treacherously" (Malachi 2:16).

g) It should also be emphasized that wrongful sexual behavior destroys the lives of the betrayed because the body is meant for God (1 Corinthians 6:13).

> 1) Sexual abomination is depicted in the destruction of Sodom and Gomorrah because of the sin of homosexuality (Genesis 19; Romans 1).

> 2) Sexual desolation is shown in Judges 19 through 20, in which the Levite priest's concubine is raped by Benjaminite tribesmen until she later dies. David's adulterous conspiracy (2 Samuel 11) against his loyal warrior Uriah should be noted also, whom David murdered by proxy in battle so that he could marry this innocent Hittite's wife,

Article I. Governing Principles and Essential Declarations of This TACA Diocese

Bathsheba, setting forth a blood curse upon his family, leading to the death of her unnamed son by this seducer king, and later the raping by Amnon by Tamar and Absalom's twofold sin of vengeance in murdering Amnon and leading a national rebellion against his father that ended in his own death during battle. For "the wages of sin is death" (Romans 6:23).

3) Illicit sex indeed destroys families (Proverbs 6:32). Contraception is to be avoided, and the unmarried should remain celibate. It is better to marry than to burn (1 Corinthians 7:8-9).

4) In the case of the Benjaminites, the genocide beset against them by the other 11 tribes razed their number nearly to zero. Solomon, the offspring of King David and Bathsheba, though full of wisdom at first, eventually descended into hyper-polygamy, which in turn created the ripe condition for pagan universalism-syncretism in Israel. The end result was that the abominable, cursed state of Moloch worship, which required infanticide and other demonic practices, caused the dissolution of his household and the spiritual corruption of his people, all due to unstemmed lust and desire for forbidden unions. The birth of his successor Rehoboam ultimately led to the disunification of the Twelve Tribes of Israel (1 Kings; 2 Chronicles).

h) God sees all our sinful behavior and permits the temporal punishments of the world to be our

Article I. Governing Principles and Essential Declarations of This TACA Diocese

comeuppance. As Christ revealed His Messianic omniscience to the Samaritan woman at the well in John 4, He reserves for each of us the twofold choice to repent of our immorality and to amend the damage to others caused by it.

i) Mend the marriage. God embarks our personal calling toward marital Reconciliation with Christ as it is rolled out by the Apostle Saint Paul in 2 Corinthians 5:18, asking us to help God rebuild the ethics of others, "not imputing their trespasses unto them." In a spirit of forgiveness while calling forward their accountability in an action of real Penance, one spouse should be urged by the other to return to meekness (Galatians 6:1-2), under the guidance of the TACA Priest or Bishop. The erring spouse should be admonished to recognize that the result of destroying a family, a church, and society at large would be but a cynical burnt offering to Satan. Let the filthy, whose ways God hates, be filthy still (Revelation 2:6; 21:11), but let the one who would be made clean repent, for "joy shall be in heaven over one sinner that repenteth, more than over ninety and nine just persons, which need no repentance" (Luke 15:7).

j) During both good times and bad, let marriage survive. Recall that the adulterous Gomer abandoned her three children, whereof her husband, the prophet Hosea, took it gravely to heart. So too, like Hosea, regard personal injury in marriage, borne patiently, to be as storing up

Article I. Governing Principles and Essential Declarations of This TACA Diocese

treasures in Heaven through such a positive, voluntary, long-suffering witness on account of our Faith. God does not despise us in our pain (Hosea 1:2; Psalm 51:17) but rather lifts us up. "Wherefore lift up the hands which hang down, and the feeble knees; And make straight paths for your feet, lest that which is lame be turned out of the way; but let it rather be healed" (Hebrews 12:12). Society, after all, does not reward fidelity toward an undeserving spouse. Nobly, Hosea embroidered his example of constant forgiveness into a sober warning to an unruly, licentious, depraved Israel with respect to her relationship with God, warning Israel to abandon its whoremongering and deceitfulness, lest she face the ultimate ruin and entropy that awaits the cheater (Hosea 4:9).

k) Comfort the spouses. Rewarding our Faith as Priests, Bishops, Deacons, and Laity, Christ bequeaths to us the Absolution and Remission of Sins in our 1928 Prayer Book, echoing the poignant openness of 1 John 1:9—interpersonal confession shared with one another about our multifarious peccadillos (James 5:16); patience and forgiveness despite the luxuriously frigid emotional indifference of Moral Relativism, whose disembodied spirituality emblazons a fatuous gnosis (Colossians 3:12-13); the peaceful settling of accounts before approaching the altar (Matthew 5:23-24; 18:15-20); and at times the rebuke of one another, at times encouragingly and at other times in hard Love (Proverbs 9:8; Titus 1:3, 2:15; 2

Article I. Governing Principles and Essential Declarations of This TACA Diocese

Thessalonians 3:15; Matthew 18:17; 1 Timothy 5:20).

xii) Regarding Gender Expectation and Morality for Office Holders and the Laity

a) All ordained religious offices of TACA, as within the provisional Communion it may share in future offices with other dioceses, and with all true Christian Congregations and Missions (i.e., Bishops, Priest, Deacons) may be held by male adults only. Women shall not be ordained in any capacity in any TACA religious office.

b) No religious office, whether appointed or ordained, may be held by any person whose sexuality is illicitly professed by him or her as being homosexual, bisexual, pansexual, and the like, and/or who is identified through his or her actions, choices, or self-professions to be of such identity, and/or who identifies himself or herself as possessing any one of the other nearly countless and ever-changing socio-politico-sexual orientations and "genders" or "orientations" that may be popularly named as "real" by persons of secular importance, or by holders of secular office, or by members of failed houses of lapsed Christian Faith. For that matter:

c) Any unrepented, perpetually committed, publicly paraded or privately cultivated Mortal Sin—these being the offenses known in the Bible as being Abominable Mortal Sins (1 John 5:6; Luke 12:10; Matthew 18:6)—shall disqualify any agent

Article I. Governing Principles and Essential Declarations of This TACA Diocese

from becoming a postulant or member of a religious office or a member of TACA.

1) Unrepentant and/or fatuous perpetual Mortal Sinners shall not be welcomed anywhere in TACA: They shall be immediately expelled unless they can be discerned as having renounced their possession by these sexual perversions of human nature—perversions not created and blessed by God (a blasphemous proposition), but rather ones that God did not intend for humans to have whatsoever. From this world we are called to "Come out of her, my people, that ye be not partakers of her sins, and that ye receive not of her plagues (Revelation 18:4).

d) The Bible alone interprets the concept of sexuality. It is only through an ironclad union with Scripture and Tradition that a compassionate fellowship with one another may endure the sinful destructiveness of a community at the hands of the dutiful practitioners of any sort of immorality, sexual or otherwise. Through the strength of Scripture and Tradition, TACA members may put on the "whole armor of God" (Ephesians 6:11) and may maintain a solidly modest heterosexual peace; this is why Traditional Anglicans cherish the vital, unparalleled importance of an active and hardy church life and Christian fellowship (Romans 1; 2 Timothy 4:2; 1 Peter 3:3-4).

Article I. Governing Principles and Essential Declarations of This TACA Diocese

e) All language used anywhere in TACA referring to any person, in writing or in live/recorded spoken word, in reference, or in direct address, and via the use of pronouns or honorifics, must solely concern the use of "him" or "her"—that is, as being "him" solely with reference to those born male or "her" solely with reference to those born female. Stated another way, pronouns shall only be used in TACA according to the gender in which a person was actually and biologically born, made in the image of the God who created them. In short, traditionally understood, conventional pronouns shall be solely and exclusively used in TACA. Moreover:

f) No ecclesiastical union or covenantal joining together of same-gender members may be permitted for any purpose, whether for carnal cohabitational purposes that are sexual, or whether for merely emotional, civic, social, or professional purposes. Such proposed unions may not be called "marriage" or "matrimony" in God's sight, because they represent an unholy bond that is an abomination in the eyes of our Lord (Romans 1:23-27; Leviticus 18:22-28, 20:13; Genesis 19; 1 Timothy 1:10; Jude 1:7; Deuteronomy 23:17-18; 1 Corinthians 6:9). Likewise, two same-gender people who have been declared by a State entity or by some other religious Jurisdiction to be "married" cannot have such a union blessed or convalidated by any TACA Body.

Article I. Governing Principles and Essential Declarations of This TACA Diocese

g) Marriage is then a holy Sacrament that can occur solely within a consecrated location known as a Church or Mission, and can happen only between a biological man and a biological woman. The would-be husband and wife are neither to be co-members of a nuclear family nor currently married to anyone else.

h) A minister who attempts to marry two people who are of the same gender and/or persons who are offspring of the same parents, or are half-siblings, or are adoptive siblings, or are first cousins, or closely related in any way to a family member by traditional standards will be expelled permanently and immediately, along with the intended candidates and supporters desiring an unholy and impossible union, from TACA.

i) The religious office of Deaconess or Lay Minister is an appointed, non-ordained office. A Pastor or Rector may appoint a Deaconess (i.e., a female adult member of the Diaconate) within a Parish only if he attains the mandatory approval to do so by his local Bishop or by the Archbishop.

j) A Deacon is a man, whether he is appointed or ordained.

k) Marriage is a Holy Sacrament that can only be transacted between a man and a woman identifying themselves as the genders God has made them to be, and who are not siblings or first cousins, or related in some other way that signifies abominable consanguinity, or currently

Article I. Governing Principles and Essential Declarations of This TACA Diocese

married to anyone else. No accidental or misunderstanding or purposeful neglect of this rule by TACA priests or bishops, or said misguided persons who are intending to be wrongfully and impossibly married in this disordered state, may result in a Holy Matrimony within TACA that would be intended to be forced by Statutory or Federal authority or participated in by TACA Religious or Lay members. A minister who attempts to marry anyone in blatant disregard of this rule, or who actually marries anyone in blatant disregard of this rule—whether intentionally or accidentally, not having done his due diligence—will be expelled permanently and immediately from TACA, along with all the intended candidates and supporters desiring one or other such impossible and unholy unions.

l) Gender rightly concerns the creation of a human being by God as either a male or female only. Any person who seeks new or retained membership or fellowship in TACA will be immediately expelled if he or she strives to commit or has committed, without sincere repentance and penance, the following Abominable Mortal Sins (or who gives support to or promotes these sins): incest, rape, or molestation; changing his or her gender through hormone replacement and/or surgery; engaging in transvestitism to reflect a real intended gender change; calling oneself and/or attempting to force others to call oneself a gender other than the gender God has created for him or her, or declaring oneself "nonbinary" and the like;

Article I. Governing Principles and Essential Declarations of This TACA Diocese

>practicing homosexual acts or living a homosexual lifestyle; engaging in transvestitism as a homosexual fetish or otherwise; engaging in the consumption and/or production of pornography of any kind (adult, child, animal, violent); and practicing any other acts of sexual perversion, false gender ideology, or so-called sexual orientation. Anyone who teaches children or instructs anyone that these abominable sexual sins are acceptable and worthy to be practiced and/or supported as an "alternate lifestyle" shall be expelled immediately from TACA.

xiii) Regarding Disqualification from Receipt of Sacraments by Unrepentant Sinners

>a) Although all Trinitarian Christians are allowed to receive a Holy Sacrament and participate in its Ordinal, a Priest or Bishop may refuse to give the consecrated Wafer and Wine, or Order of Matrimony, or provide any Sacrament to any adult person whom he deems to be deliberately possessed of a sinful nature, fatuously or consciously submitted to the desolate callings of a wrongful, immoral disposition and of Godless choices, and partaking consciously and actively in a culture or community that affirms or encourages his or her immorality (see Title III, Canon 4, Section C).
>
>>1) Confronted by such a petitioner, the presider may faithfully include an Exhortation in that person's regard, or may outright withhold the Sacrament; additionally:

Article I. Governing Principles and Essential Declarations of This TACA Diocese

2) Encouraging the petitioner toward Penance but only if his or her intention to confess with Faith shall be deemed by the Priest or Bishop to be commensurate with our church's expectations that they be satisfied, per Canon 4 of Title III, Section 3. Note:

3) "Wherefore whosoever shall eat this bread, and drink this cup of the Lord, unworthily, shall be guilty of the body and blood of the Lord. But let a man examine himself, and so let him eat of that bread, and drink of that cup" (1 Corinthians 11:17-34; Amos 5:22).

xiv) Divorce

a) Divorce is considered profane by this TACA Diocese unless for reason of infidelity. That is:

1) "And unto the married I command, yet not I, but the Lord, Let not the wife depart from her husband: But and if she depart, let her remain unmarried or be reconciled to her husband: and let not the husband put away his wife" (1 Corinthians 7:10-11).

b) To illustrate the preciousness of Holy Matrimony, it is useful to consider here what trials of sinful error may negate, impede, or destroy that priceless bond.

1) Because God has deposited His spirit into the marital bond between spouses, we hold adultery, divorce, and remarriage to sit at severe variance with our Father's expectation

Article I. Governing Principles and Essential Declarations of This TACA Diocese

for permanence and holiness to characterize the nuptial union (Malachi 2:14-16; Mark 10:9; Hebrews 13:4).

2) Moreover, because the eagerness for divorce followed by remarriage would tempt an irresolute spouse to lessen his or her devotion to God by hastening an unnatural exigency, we shall take the grave urging against divorce by Christ to be a momentous warning against the same demand by Moses's followers, that God did indeed oblige the hardened hearts of spouses who wish to sever the marital bond, but to their own spiritual detriment (Matthew 5:32; 19:10-11).

3) To tempt God, who was the witness and affirmer of one's original marriage, into sympathizing with the renunciation of the marital vow that He exhorted in 1 Corinthian 7:10 is also to presume that Divorce could ever be the advice of this TACA Diocese. Nay, TACA ministers instead urge Reconciliation between spouses as counseled by a Priest or Bishop to mitigate all disappointments associated with marital disagreement or strife (1 Corinthians 7:11; Ephesians 4:32). Thus:

4) TACA holds that the severing of the permanent covenant of matrimony would be indeed the breaking of the sacramental vow that is affixed in our 1928 Prayer Book and shall always be discouraged by the Clergy and Episcopate.

Article I. Governing Principles and Essential Declarations of This TACA Diocese

> c) Insofar as the Annulment of a marriage via writ or a blessing upon a separation would be concerned, such written dispensation from that vow of marriage shall be granted in this TACA Diocese only by the Archbishop, discretely considering extreme cases of abuse, neglect, or adultery.
>
> d) Thus, it must be the pastoral aim of the Clergy and Episcopate to employ Christian or biblical counseling whenever possible to reach both of the estranged spouses with the twofold condition of repentance and renewed faithfulness as the means of renewing their vow of Matrimony (Matthew 19:26; Genesis 2:24; 1 Corinthians 7:11). Also:
>
> e) In confronting a contention by a spouse that the avowal to honor the nuptial covenant was never fulfilled or "consummated," perchance owing to a spouse's lack of support and/or of intimacy, or some other irreconcilable condition, this TACA Diocese respects the oration by Saint John Chrysostom, in "Homily 19—On Marriage," in which marital consummation is being bemoaned as never having been dutifully served. Chrysostom posits in his homily that marriage the marriage is still valid, in that it is nevertheless a spiritual intercession between the married couple and the lifelong chasteness associated with Christ's Resurrection:
>
>> 1) "There are two reasons why marriage was instituted: to make us chaste and to give us

Article I. Governing Principles and Essential Declarations of This TACA Diocese

> children. Of these two reasons, the first takes precedence ... especially now that the human race has filled the entire earth. ... But now that the resurrection is at hand, and we do not speak of death but rather advance toward another life better than the present one, the desire for posterity is superfluous" (Homily 19 – "On Marriage", Saint John Chrysostom). Thus:
>
> 2) To stay married, even if celibately, regarding any charge of non-consummation, dissatisfaction, or neglect, is Chrysostom's and TACA's exhortation.

f) However, as literally pledged in the Ordinal of the "Solemnization of Matrimony" in our 1928 Prayer Book (i.e., that the one spouse must permanently cherish the other), any truly profound dishonoring of this vow must be charitably recognized by the TACA minister as grounds for Christian or biblical counseling.

> 1) Because divorce or Annulment of marriage shall never stand as the benchmark of this church's substantiation of any claim that a matrimony has never been physically consummated and/or has been betrayed, this TACA Diocese will neither support nor bless divorce nor issue an Annulment of Holy Matrimony (unless the latter has been issued by the Office of the Archbishop himself). "What therefore God hath joined together, let no man put asunder" (Mark 10:9).

Article I. Governing Principles and Essential Declarations of This TACA Diocese

g) Reconciliation shall be encouraged; remarriages shall be discouraged (Matthew 5:32).

h) Church membership, nevertheless, shall not be refused to a person involved in a marital divorce.

i) Ordination or appointment to the priesthood or Permanent Diaconate may not occur, nor shall consecration to the Episcopate, during a marital divorce.

> 1) Except under the Archbishop's dispensation from this rule, in relation to the seeking of priestly or episcopal vows, a candidate who is pursuing divorce shall be refused Holy Office in TACA until all attempts at marital reconciliation may be exhausted, the divorce has been finalized, and at least one full year has gone by since the divorce.

j) If a Priest or Bishop intends to serve the Eucharist to a divorced parishioner (i.e., a church member, who is divorced but not for a justified reason, such as due to adultery or spousal abuse or neglect), the first or second Exhortation of the Ordinal of the Holy Communion service shall be read.

> 1) A Priest or Bishop must always exhort the divorced sinner wishing to regain Grace to amend his or her life and examine his or her conscience, lest the remaining earthly life following the sinner's disavowal of marriage linger in regretful guilt and/or sustain the unrepented adultery through remarriage

against which we are admonished by Holy Scripture (Luke 16:18; Matthew 19:9; and Mark 10:11-12).

k) If repentance and recovery of Grace following divorce can be adjudged by the Priest, Bishop, or Archbishop to have substantially taken place a full year after its finalization, and if pastoral authority can thereby recognize that penitent contemplation has cultivated a tender and real charity that has become restored in the heart of the candidate, remarriage may be permitted (John 4:1-25).

xv) Identification of Psychological Afflictions and Moral Pathologies

Preface: Moral Pathology is a Metaphysical Error that owes its evil to the fallacy of Nominalism. It is the institutionalized madness that results when individuals turn their backs on Christ's ability to save, and the launch the Will into despair, falsely distinguishing identifiers, such as "diagnoses," to be imprimatur, teaching resultantly that an afflicted person is capable of only serving evil, or if the person has a condition that renders them an innocent, of being incapable of knowing how to serve good, just because it is written in a secular source that he or she is nominally whatever the creature (the party doing the labeling) states he or she "is."

Epigraph: A pathological person invents or identifies himself according to such a disturbing definition of his life as being a new subclassification of human

Article I. Governing Principles and Essential Declarations of This TACA Diocese

being that does not come from Sacred Scripture, which says that man was made in God's image, and after His likeness (Genesis 1:27), but is knowable instead only according to that designation—for instance, by a diagnosis or by some legal jargon that they must force themselves to swallow or to coerce upon others also suffering horribly under it (e.g., when people believe that God will not permit "herd immunity" or allow life on Earth to be "sustainable," or that that humans can only spread disease and famine and must stop breeding).

Exordium: Sometimes the classification that is designated against the person is conveniently coopted and enjoyed by him or her, and is thus fatuously or cowardly confessed in order to avoid accountability; at other times, it is fought against by the thus-labeled victim, even though his life has already been by the purveyors of the label. To accept or promote a "diagnosis," or to personify a slur, an aspersion, or a fallacy by projecting and professing it as defining one's very identity, existence, soul, and will, is the satanic inversion of Logos: It insists that the Creature, not the Holy Trinity, is the Word. Unfortunately, people believe that there is no escape from their being "drunks" or "losers" or "schizophrenics" or "whores" or "pedophiles." Moreover, each innocent person falsely believes that his diagnosis or epithet designates a new species of human, or a gender, or a new class of being, such as "autistic" or "transgender" or a "demon" or a "superman" or a "furry." For some, initiation into this new club made for them, or of their own making, is so intoxicatingly comforting that it is very difficult to reach them

Article I. Governing Principles and Essential Declarations of This TACA Diocese

with the idea that what they *do* (or don't do, or believe or don't believe) is not who they *are* as a person created in the image of God in their original state and, as a created being, falling under the Natural Law and Moral Law of the Creator.

Exortatio: Sadly, any meticulously measured empirical data should nevertheless be taken seriously if it can be assessed by Ecclesiastical Authority as having been honestly recorded, which is why a Bishop cannot reasonably ignore any diagnosis and case histories of a "pedophile" any more than he can eschew being kind and understanding toward a diagnosed mentally retarded or autistic person, but always disavowing the idea that "as a man thinketh" (Proverbs 23:7) should determine the ontological classification of a person as being reprobate or irredeemable or fixed forever in a particular state of being. Secular definitions are only data, not definers, because an innocent person such as a profoundly autistic or intellectually disabled person, or a rape victim, or a person with a harmless mental illness, should not be caused to be put together with or menaced within the same pew by deliberately evil people. There is no possibility of putting all of these different kinds of people in one bucket as though to broad-brush anything that falls outside the norm as being on equal footing. The Church can never be persuaded that the creature is able to redefine the essence of man's Creation: The Church distinguishes between the holy and the unholy, between the pure and the impure, and the Church is a mother, protecting the flock through the spiritual leadership of the Archbishop and Clergy from the wolves. "Ye cannot

Article I. Governing Principles and Essential Declarations of This TACA Diocese

drink the cup of the Lord, and the cup of devils: ye cannot be partakers of the Lord's table, and of the table of devils" (1 Corinthians 10:21). Our TACA Diocese can never permit the Near Occasion of Sin among our ranks. Although the below Nominal Fallacy involved in the subject of Moral Pathology encompasses definitions of both the innocent and the guilty, it is the responsibility of the TACA Diocese to protect the innocent and guard against the guilty, who in their unrepentant state cannot seem to cease from trying to drag other souls into hell. Our just God is forever (Psalm 48:14). Jesus, who saves, is the same yesterday, and today, and forever (Hebrews 13:8). Each person seeking Salvation, be he or she a rocket scientist or a profoundly autistic person, is fearfully and wonderfully made (Psalm 139:14). Otherwise, discerning that non-biblical Moral Pathology may or may not restrict a person from being appropriate for membership or ministry within TACA, Ecclesiastical Authority may view great error and sinfulness in candidates to membership or ministry. Thus:

> a) A person who may be deemed by TACA as being unfit for ministry or membership within any TACA religious Body is a person who demonstrates prolonged, overwhelming distress beyond his or her capacity or willingness to cope or to be trusted by others in TACA.
>
> b) He or she displays such an impairment of personality function, accompanied by non-functional or lacking coping strategies, that it makes his or her inclusion within Ecclesiastical life difficult or impossible to sustain.

Article I. Governing Principles and Essential Declarations of This TACA Diocese

c) Because a person's mental and/or physical deterioration may be attributable to the twofold etiology of psychological and moral pathology, this TACA Diocese pledges a merciful and prayerful disposition of charity toward their mental and physical well-being and salvation. It should not be assumed that exclusion from Ecclesiastical life on these grounds necessarily entails exclusion from all church life. Such determinations are at the discretion of the Ecclesiastical Authority.

d) The following list of Afflictions and Moral Pathologies that characterize spiritual and mental sickness, or reflect popular scientific diagnoses, or are careful euphemisms, may reasonably help Ecclesiastical Authority decide whether the afflicted person's degree of inability or refusal to recognize, or to abide, significant aspects of reality sit at irreconcilable variance with retention of his or her ministry or membership anywhere in TACA. (Note that the below list, as has been explained, combines conditions or states of being among people who are thereby either innocent or guilty, depending on their condition, and among the innocent, conditions that may or may not impact their ability to participate in the life of the church within the TACA Diocese). That is:

e) His or her mental and spiritual anomaly(-ies) may thus be discerned by Ecclesiastical Authority to be grounds for immediate expulsion from this TACA Diocese, and/or to require immediate

Article I. Governing Principles and Essential Declarations of This TACA Diocese

involvement of police or legally hired security. Moreover:

f) The below list of Afflictions and Moral Pathologies consists of, but is not necessarily limited to, charitable discretional use of both formal and informal terms—as well as both professional and colloquial descriptors—the listing of which herein reflects agape love cherished toward the afflicted, by Christians in this TACA Diocese, and the sincere intention by good TACA Christians to pray for a cure or a treatment, along with proper healing, rehabilitation, excellent catechesis, and the like—but most importantly the reconciliation with our Lord that leads the soul of the mentally afflicted and ecclesiastically unfit to ultimate Redemption and Salvation. This being said:

g) The entries on this list of Afflictions and Moral Pathologies do not signify blame, causation, or etiology for creating or regarding negative events or conditions, or regarding particular incidents that would be caused by the sufferer as though this were an effort by TACA to blame, judge, excommunicate, condemn, anathematize, socially ostracize, stigmatize, renounce, censor, reprimand, damn, or excuse him or her from this calling to healing and/or rehabilitation.

h) Instead, as they are listed here as of September 2023, these Afflictions and Moral Pathologies are set forth with the hope of aiding the religious and laity of TACA in identifying the existence of their disorderly affliction in order to reduce Ecclesiastical fear about them, as:

1) The first approach toward pastorally handling these abnormalities as being factors in identifying bodily, mental, and spiritual illness shall be set forth. And:

2) The sourcing and finding of the origins of social degradation, of vocational decay, of spiritual destruction, and of religious dysfunction can be arranged. Therewith:

3) Prevention and/or deterrence of criminality can also be attained.

4) To demonstrate to all people that the wise Church considers deliberately wicked people, who are destroying society to be in a state of intellectual and cognitive ruin, dangerous individuals and groups need to be identified here by putting their various types of deranged minds on a public list of the psychologically ill, the criminally insane, the sexually disordered, the homicidal, the mentally/cognitively impaired, and the like, because they cause harm to themselves and to others. Being that they injure and kill, using depraved sociopolitical programming and/or interpersonal manipulation and unrelenting aggressiveness bent on ridding the image of God from the souls of all people, and injuring, mutilating (e.g., castrating), kidnapping, looting, economically ravaging, raping,

Article I. Governing Principles and Essential Declarations of This TACA Diocese

corrupting (e.g., polluting innocent minds in schools via the media), and seducing, they are depicted in this list as being predators. They are insane and immoral assailants of the hearts, souls, minds, intellect, spirits, wills, and bodies of individuals, families, children, homes, cities, nations, workplaces, churches, communities, and any other such institutions that are the targets of their evil will. They wreak havoc consequentially upon themselves but do not attempt to arrest themselves. Rich or poor, Capitalist or Marxist, their malevolent character types will be meticulously placed throughout the following list, filed alongside all other nameable forms of mental sickness, all thinkable personality disorders, and any impairment of the mind and cognition in terms of their disobedient, willful retention of deliberately unrepentant morally pathological madness (Luke 17:2; Romans 1; 1 Timothy 1:10; 2 Timothy 3:13; Revelation 22:11-17).

5) It is not unreasonable to presume that because a person commits a certain sin that related sins may be attached to it. For example, as regards the activism by pedophiles to become part of the LGBTQ+ demographic, the creation of the term "Minor Attracted Person" is not merely a euphemism for their lust for children, but also denotes a violent depredation that is protected within institutional psychiatry, in considering it to be a mostly harmless subclass of same-sex

orientation. The examples of such treachery are disgusting and infuriating. Therefore, it is wise to avoid persons who are LGBTQ+, because one unrepentant sin would tend to normalize others, as, for example, one would be hard pressed to find an LGBTQ+ advocate who did not give a full-throated endorsement of abortion: "For whosoever shall keep the whole law, and yet offend in one point, he is guilty of all" (James 2:10). Christians, by loving God, Life, and family, are committing no evil in resisting friendship or any connection with persons whom they suspect are so dangerous. ("Minor-Attracted Persons: A Neglected Population"; Renée Sorrentino MD, Janette Abramowitz MD; Current Psychiatry; Vol. 20; Issue 7; pp. 21-27; July, 2021; "Pedophiles Believe They Should be a Part of the LGBT Community"; Jessica Jenkins; July 7, 2018; https://dailycaller.com/2018/07/09/pedophiles-lgbt-community; Accessed, July 28, 2023).

6) Hamartiology must therefore constantly account for the "madness of the people" (Psalm 65:7) and the deliberate mental sickness that is the aim of malevolent programmers who exploit and propagate unrepentant sinfulness. "I applied mine heart to know, and to search, and to seek out wisdom, and the reason of things, and to know the wickedness of folly, even of foolishness and madness" (Ecclesiastes 7:25).

Article I. Governing Principles and Essential Declarations of This TACA Diocese

i) So that Ecclesiastical Authority may chiefly draw hope from spiritual discernment about human behavior from God, instead of relying on science, this list of Afflictions and Moral Pathologies has been published for this TACA Diocese. **An important point of clarification to avoid any possible misunderstanding:** The perception that someone may possess some of these pathologies is often not enough to disqualify inclusion in TACA (e.g., an autistic person may be a good Bishop; someone with mental retardation may make an excellent Acolyte, Sexton, or Warden). However, such perception may be kept in mind to help an assessor determine, without prejudice or bias, why, or how, a person may be unfit or unsafe to engage in ministry or membership, based on the existence of the disorder or the degree to which his or her affliction hampers his or her ability to participate within the church and in ministry. The use of the term "Moral Pathology" shall also be appropriately employed upon discerning that one or more officials or parties are insisting or mandating that retention of an afflicted person in the Diocese should be rewarded or sustained simply because said individual has one or more of the following disorders, thus falsely putting them in a "protected class" without regard for the general welfare of the Diocese. Thus:

1) The following List of Afflictions and Moral Pathologies shall include diagnoses and disorder nomenclature from the first five

Article I. Governing Principles and Essential Declarations of This TACA Diocese

versions of the Diagnostic and Statistical Manual and revision(s) thereof, and from the American Psychiatric Association, along with popular descriptions held in common colloquial usage:

—Psychoses Consisting of Hallucinations, Delusions, and/or Disorganized Thinking or Speech;

—Schizophrenia that is Paranoid, Hebephrenic, Catatonic, Undifferentiated, Residual, Simple, or Unspecified;

—Brain Damage, such as Broca's or Wernicke's Aphasia; Closed or Penetrating Traumatic Brain Injury; Brain Deterioration from Cardiac, Ischemic, or Hemorrhagic Stroke; Diffuse Axonic Brain Injuries and Contusions (Severe Traumatic, Penetrating);

—Sociopathic or Psychopathic Disorders (e.g., Narcissistic, Borderline, Sadistic, Antisocial, Diabolical, Antisocial; Hubris Syndrome; see Personality Disorders, below);

—Behaviors consisting of, or associated with, Trolling, Harassing, Stalking, Terroristic Threat-Making, or Intimidation, Physical Molestation or Battery;

—Persistent and recurrent problematic gambling.

—Pathological Mental Disorders Associated with: Extreme Irrational Hatred or Fear of

Article I. Governing Principles and Essential Declarations of This TACA Diocese

Persons of Different Religions, Level of Reprobation or of Grace, Race, Ethnicity, Social System, Nationality, Preferences, Beliefs, Sexual Orientation, Gender, Income Status, Vocation, Career, or Family Type or Size.

—Membership in or Sponsorship of Groups Identified by or in Support of Pathology (e.g., Membership in Black Lives Matter, Naziism, Southern Poverty Law Center, Antifa, the KKK).

—Sociopathic/Psychopathic Personality Disturbances Associated With Sexual and Gender Deviation/Aberrancy that is: Pedophilia, Pederasty, Homosexuality, Bisexuality, Queerdom, Lesbianism, LGBTQ (and related sexual-identity acronyms), Sexual Orientation That is not Heterosexual, Bestiality, Incest, Tranvestism, Exhibitionism, Transgenderism, Gender Reassignment or any associated Genital Mutilation Activation, Coprophilia, Delusional Gender Dysphoria, Delusional Sexual Dysphoria, Compulsive Sexual Behavior, Nymphomania, Promiscuity, Sadomasochism, Sodomy, Sexual Violence, Genital Abuse, Scatophilia, Rape, Pornography Use, Pornography Addiction, Fetishism, Excessive, Public, or Exhibitionistic Masturbation, Frotteurism, Autogynephilia/Autoandrophilia (biological males/females who experience sexual arousal in response to imagining themselves as the opposite gender), Autoanthropomorphozoophilia (sexual arousal

Article I. Governing Principles and Essential Declarations of This TACA Diocese

while imagining oneself to be an animal); Autonepiophilia (*ibid.*, child or infant); Transvestite Fetishism, Polyamory, Voyeurism, Mania of Extra Gender Nomenclature and Mania of Extra-Sexual Orientation Nomenclature (Numerous Different Fake Sexual and Gender Orientations), Mania of Pronoun-Assignment, Affiliation With Sexual-Based/Gender-Based Groups and Ideation-Ruled Ideologies such as Feminism, or National Association of Man-Boy Love of America (NAMBLA), or Femen, or LGBTQ Associations, and all Social or Political Groups Assembled to Advance Legislative and Social Agenda That Regards Perverted Sexual Intercourse and Gender Reassignment; Ego-Dystonic Sexual Abnormality; Erotic Target Identity Inversion (Furies, and other varieties of this Paraphilia);

—Mental Retardation;

—Delusional Body Dysmorphic Disorder;

—Mood Disorders, consisting of Major Depression, Dysthymia, Bipolar Disorder, Induced Mood Disorder;

—Social Communication Disorder;

—Central Auditory Processing Disorder;

—Depression and Related Disorders, such as: Major and Episodic, Persistent or Dysthymic, Manic and Bipolar-I, Agoraphobia, Separation Anxiety Disorder, Social Anxiety Disorder,

Article I. Governing Principles and Essential Declarations of This TACA Diocese

> Conduct Disorder (or, that is, Disruptive, Impulse-Control), Oppositional Defiant Disorder, Related Disorders;
>
> —Eating Disorders, such as Bulimia Nervosa, Anorexia Nervosa, Binge-Eating Disorder, Pathological Morbid Obesity;
>
> —Sexualization of Minors, Sexually Corruptively Influencing Minors, Exhibitionism or Transvestism Exposure to Minors that is programmed or deliberate;
>
> —*Innocent* Intellectual and Cognitive Disorders, including Autistic Spectrum Disorder and Mental Retardation; Learning Disability; Brain Damaged/Injured;
>
> —Persecutory Delusional Disorder associated with affiliation with aberrant and hateful ethno-racial and sexual groups and ideologies such as Black Lives Matter, Antifa, Femen, Incel, Woke, Critical Race Theory, Darwinism, Satanism;
>
> —Grandiose Delusional Disorder, associated with affiliation with aberrant and hateful sociopolitical groups and ideologies, such as Marxism, Naziism, Socialism, Communism, United Civil Liberties Union, Darwinism, Satanism;
>
> —Personality Disorders, such as Paranoid, Borderline, Schizoid, Schizotypal, Antisocial, Histrionic, Narcissistic, Avoidant, Narcissistic-Diabolical;

Article I. Governing Principles and Essential Declarations of This TACA Diocese

—Severe Anxiety or Panic-Level Anxiety;

—Dementia, such as Alzheimer's, Vascular Dementia, Lewy Body Dementia, Frontotemporal Dementia, Mixed Dementia;

—Alcoholism, Drug and Entheogen abuse, or other Substance Addiction, and proliferation of and corruptively influencing adults or minors by offering or coercing them to ingest or inject such illicit substances;

—Kleptomania (e.g., stealing from collection plates; all forms of unremitted thievery; financial scheming; demographic-market targeting; grifting; looting; robbing; shoplifting; hostile corporate overtaking; larceny; burglary; all forms of pilfering including both "white-collar" and "low-life" misappropriation of funds and wrongful taking of the property or funds of others).

xvi) Corporeal Identity, Race, Ethnicity, and Human Dominion

a) All people are created by God and were made in His image (Genesis 1:27).

b) The Bible's expressing of "Race" according to different phenotypes, and Nationality, in terms of ethnolinguistic cultural identities, has long been in common usage and colloquial speech by speakers of English.

Article I. Governing Principles and Essential Declarations of This TACA Diocese

1) The List of Nations discussed in Genesis 10 was analyzed by Josephus, Saint Hippolytus, and Saint Jerome. But:

2) A human "race" must always be distinguished from other sentient life (Genesis 1:26-28; Psalms 139:16; Jeremiah 1:5).

3) While beagles are a race of dog that cannot freely choose to restrain sexual urges, and while parakeets are a species of bird that cannot freely decide to mate with larger members of the bird race, such as eagles, it must be seen that human beings have been given Dominion over the Earth because of our Free Will to be fruitful and multiply and to choose to serve the Lord (Genesis 1:26-28; Joshua 24:15).

—From Josephus, we learn that after the Creation and the Flood, descendants of Ham populate Canaan; descendants of Japheth populate Europe; and descendants of Shem populate Asia (*Antiquities of the Jews*; Book 1; Chapter 6; Josephus; A.D. 94).

—From Saint Jerome's update of *Antiquities of the Jews* (A.D. 94) by Flavius Josephus, we learn that Japheth's son Tubal founds the Iberians and hence Spaniards and then the Celtiberians and Italians ("Hebrew Questions on Genesis"; Saint Jerome; A.D. 390).

—From Saint Hippolytus comes the title of his chapter, *Diamerismos* or διαμερισμός (Strong's

Article I. Governing Principles and Essential Declarations of This TACA Diocese

Greek: 1267, defined as "Divisions," pertaining to the political stratifications of the Earth, according to Genesis 10), located in his book, *Chronicon* (A.D. 235).

—From Isadore of Seville come refined distinctions among Saint Jerome's definitions that highlight the cause of divisions in ancient and contemporary society (*De Viris Illustribus*; Isadore of Seville; A.D. 618). Two histories from Isadore, the second one suffering two famous redactions, help the reader understand how the devil's interference with language has led to the discord and wars traced by the writer as having built late-antiquity societies since Christ (*Chronica Maiora*; Isadore of Seville; A.D. 625).

—In the Codex Gigas, the "Devil's Encyclopedia," Isadore designates, for example, Japheth's descendants as the Scythians and Goths who terrorize Europe in barbarous fashion. In tracing Isadore's sheer objectivity in building natural classifications, as influenced by Pliny the Elder, we see the Barbarians placed within a framework of a study on the origins, or etymologies, of the sundry human languages— all arising from one original language shattered by Nimrod's damnable sin of blasphemy against God. For this abomination, humanity could no longer thereafter communicate with one another without pain, and the devil was free to further amplify these linguistic divisions as the father of lies and author

Article I. Governing Principles and Essential Declarations of This TACA Diocese

of confusion (*Etymologiae*; Codex Gigas/Sangallensis, Books XI-XX; Isadore of Seville; A.D. 625: Codex S. 1395; Genesis 11:1-9).

4) However, men and women are not the snakes and plants mentioned by Pliny the Elder (*Naturalis Historia*; Vol. III-VII; Books 8-27; Gaius Plinius Secundus; A.D. 79)

5) It is therefore an act of Free Will to choose to deny oneself of sins of the tongue and take up one's Cross (Matthew 16:28; 10:38) rather than using words like a warring or sordid dog returning to its vomit (2 Peter:22). "Let no corrupt communication proceed out of your mouth" and let "all bitterness, and wrath, and anger, and clamor, and evil speaking be put away from you, with all malice" (Ephesians 4:29-31).

xvii) Decision to be Anglican

a) Anglicanism is Older than the Old English Language

1) The Magna Carta of 1215 coined the term "Ecclesia Anglicana" to commend the authority of the Church of England to bless the landowners of England, and to limit the power of the Crown to encroach upon the biblical dominion over the Earth that was permanently granted by God unto mankind, rather than unto a monarch who is not the Christ (Genesis 1:26).

Article I. Governing Principles and Essential Declarations of This TACA Diocese

2) The Christianity of the ancient Britons designates English to be a consecrated Liturgical language, and English has been such since the era when Bishop Aristobulus, named in Romans 16:10, was numbered by Saint Hippolytus to be the twenty-ninth Disciple, whose Mission as one of the "70 Disciples" commissioned by Jesus was to evangelize Britain, for Christ ordered his 70 Disciples to go into "every city and place" (*On the Apostles and Disciples*; Pseudo-Hippolytus; A.D. ~230; Luke 10:1).

3) The English language is of exceedingly ancient origin, and one spoken by very early saints:

—A runic technolect from A.D. 200, "bidawarijaz talgidai," is written on the war shield of an Anglo-Frisian Viking to identify its rightful engraver. Earlier, Transalpine Gaulish is written in Iberian on pottery fragments in France, dated to B.C. 600. It declares the name of the owner having dominion over his properties.

b) Transalpine Gaulish, an extinct language, is the precursor to the Celtic languages of France and Ireland, as its Gaelic offshoot was spoken at the Saint Victor Monastery of Marseilles, France, to its founder Saint John Cassian.

Article I. Governing Principles and Essential Declarations of This TACA Diocese

—The Gaulish tongue was uttered hence by Saint John Cassian to his pupil, Saint Patrick of Ireland, in A.D. 420.

—Later Anglo-Saxon musicians in 860 pored over the Liber Hymnorum to read the interpretation of the "spiritual armor" of Ephesians 6:14 in the Gaelic translation of the "Lorica" (i.e., breastplate) of Saint Patrick.

—Then, scouring through the Caledfwlch (Medieval Welsh) of Culhwch and Olwen in 1150, crusader King Henry II could read how Excalibur was supposedly wrought mightily in God's sight by King Arthur.

c) There are truly "two swords" in English.

1) In reviewing interpretations of virility in Old English, it becomes the duty of Christians to contemplate the tactical language chosen in Luke 22:36. Employing the image of the "two swords," Scottish theologian William Barclay said the Christian must choose "to fight for your very existence" (*The New Daily Study Bible—17 Volumes Covering the Entire New Testament: The Gospel of Luke*; William Barclay; 1975).

2) Knowing when and how to use American English language to defend the innocent, or to use an actual physical weapon to do the same, defines our life of unwavering spiritual discernment, affirmed in strong Church Militancy, as Traditional Anglicans, who,

Article I. Governing Principles and Essential Declarations of This TACA Diocese

suffering in the flesh, with charitable language and a Christian duty to be ambassadors of peace, show that they have ceased from sin (1 Peter 4:1). For we know that against the fruits of the Spirit "there is no law"; therefore, "If we live in the Spirit, let us also walk in the Spirit" (Galatians 5:23,25).

xviii) Conclusion on Language and Identity: Thus stated, Anglicans set themselves apart by the partnering of words and action, definable as Anglican Praxeology, by which Traditionalist Anglicans are aware that:

a) Unaccountable people fall short of Grace but portray wickedness as goodness and vice versa, but TACA will not justify the wicked while condemning the righteous (Proverbs 17:15).

b) TACA will have no part in institutional error. By refusing to resist evil actions, but instead inventing ideologies and nomenclature that excuse or lionize wickedness, disobedient agencies pass off the ethical deterioration of the human will as something sublime (Isaiah 5:20). For example:

1) As being either a morally irresistible pastime, such as Internet obsession, monetary profligacy, and pornography, wrongfully claiming such immorality to be a "right";

2) As being social afflictions of the body or conscience, predicated to be a "pandemic" or "climate negligence," by which corrupt leaders

Article I. Governing Principles and Essential Declarations of This TACA Diocese

persecute the meek under the guise of "social justice" or "climate activism";

3) As an evil predilection or political affiliation, such as "LGBTQ" or "Marxist," being of superior quality compared to traditional norms, the gaslighters and purveyors of such ideologies insisting that perversion and corruption ought to be blessed or encouraged.

c) No one shall be an officer or member of TACA if they are morally corrupt, especially in a public and unrepentant manner, holding themselves unaccountable for the example they set to the innocent of making the Mystery of Iniquity more mysterious by deluding themselves and others into believing that they are decent, or simply living an "alternative lifestyle" (2 Thessalonians 2:7).

d) TACA shall take no part in the falling away of Christians from the holy catholic Church (Matthew 24:12-15). When the restrainer of the devil's fury is "taken out of the way," the collective moral pathology of nations, which declines into a state of madness (Psalm 65:7), shall bring about the ceasing of the sun's rising while the actual gravity holding certain humanity on Earth shall give way (1 Thessalonians 4:17) Thus:

1) Human depravity en masse shall ignite the revoking of Natural Law—whose ordinances (e.g., night, day, gravity) become deactivated

Article I. Governing Principles and Essential Declarations of This TACA Diocese

(Jeremiah 31:35-40; Mark 13:24; Revelation 6:13).

e) Although we are reassured that the Elect shall no longer be on Earth during this Wrath, there must nevertheless never be a failure among Christians to define evil as evil and good as good (Job 17:12; Isaiah 5:20; 2 Thessalonians 2:3-8). For "Woe unto them that call evil good, and good evil; that put darkness for light, and light for darkness" (Isaiah 5:20). Thus, in a spirit of truth and charity, members of TACA are to follow this rule:

1) "Them that sin rebuke before all, that others may fear" (1 Timothy 5:20); for,

2) "Open rebuke is better than secret Love" (Proverbs 27:5).

L. American Orthodox Ecclesiastical Polity

i) The purpose for all forms of Law is this: "... And the government shall be upon His shoulder" (Isaiah 9:6), and the written Law is God's Word, Who is Christ (John 1:1-3).

ii) The Bible is the means by which the Church interprets God's will openly for the faithful, since "no prophecy of the scripture is of any private interpretation" (2 Peter 1:20).

iii) The set of written rules governing biblical interpretation, for all TACA members and clergy, shall be the Constitution and Canons, which thus:

Article I. Governing Principles and Essential Declarations of This TACA Diocese

    a) entails a huge responsibility: "Hold fast the form of sound words, which thou hast heard of me, in faith and love which is in Christ Jesus" (2 Timothy 1:13).

iv) The goal of this Constitution shall be to apply God's Word, the Bible, to Ecclesiastical Authority such that:

    a) The Constitution and Canons shall be known by this TACA Diocese headquartered in North America to be the literary "rook" by which the TACA Archbishop, his Episcopate, his Clergy, and the Laity of this TACA Diocese shall practice civility and ministry in this TACA Diocese.

    b) Traditional Anglicans may even delight to parallel such rules to the codification of ancient Christian Roman Law where it concerned, for example, bishoprics:

    c) "Let the profane ardor of avarice cease to threaten our altars, and let this disgraceful crime be banished from our holy sanctuaries. Therefore, in our times, chaste and humble bishops are selected, so that, wherever they may go, they will purify everything with the morality of their own lives" (*Codex*; Book 1, Title 3; parts 30-31; Emperor Justinian I; A.D. 469).

        1) While one's own *amor iuris* (love of law) may seek to accredit the above example of Justinian I's political power merely to an august Pax Romana, only a higher calling could have motivated that great Emperor to affirm the

Article I. Governing Principles and Essential Declarations of This TACA Diocese

Chalcedonian position by convening its famous Council in A.D. 450.

2) The orthodox apologists of the early Church, having endured cultural persecutions and martyrdoms (especially under Western Roman Emperor Diocletian), were eloquent not merely in subjugating both Natural and Human Law to Divine Law, but in sobering fellow Christians into not being taken with the *zeitgeist*, or "spirit of the age"—the mindset by which contemporary artists and intellectuals were content to envision themselves as being glorified by people as if they and their audiences were gods: "For we do not see what is so wonderful in these arts [of grammar, music, oratory, and geometry], that because of their discovery the soul should be believed to be above the sun as well as all the stars, to surpass both in grandeur and essence the whole universe, of which these are parts" (*Adversus Nationes*; Book II; Section 19; Arnobius of Sicca; A.D. 304).

d) While hoping to catechize new members into the Church, a litmus test by which a minister may determine whether a visitor is open to receiving the Word is to ask the newcomer whether he or she would want to know just how a complex idea such as Logos could possibly be fathomed by a catechumen who is clueless as to why Jesus Christ could be God and is the only Mediator between the Father and mankind. Of

Article I. Governing Principles and Essential Declarations of This TACA Diocese

course, the approach is always the choice of the Pastor. Yet only a visitor who has become disgusted at living the Godless life of the disobedient in this modern age would want to seek this knowledge. "And they shall teach my people the difference between the holy and profane, and cause them to discern between the unclean and the clean" (Ezekiel 44:23-24). This question welcomes him or her to admit freely whether he or she would wish to malinger in a state of willful ignorance, whereof it is herein known to the good Anglican that "Sin is voluntary, and its penalty, which includes moral inability, is just. But Salvation is possible" (*Of True Religion*; Saint Augustine; Analysis: Section 14; No. 27; A.D. 390). Sometimes the willfully ignorant convince themselves that they are stuck in their rueful unknowing, therefore making them agnostic about whether or not they are sinning, which would seem to be a loophole supported by Augustine: "Sin is so voluntary an evil that it is by no means sin if it is not voluntary" (*Retractions*; Saint Augustine; Chapter 12; Part 5; A.D. 427). However, sometimes it is impossible to welcome the unwilling toward a Discernment of real Faith: "and as such, even those sins which are not unjustly called involuntary, because they are committed by those who are ignorant or constrained, cannot be committed entirely without the will, since, in truth, he who sins through ignorance in any case sins voluntarily because he thinks he should do something that should not be done" (*ibid.*). To be

Article I. Governing Principles and Essential Declarations of This TACA Diocese

able to detect whether ignorant newcomers may be ready for inspiration, the minister may wish to ponder such feats of ignorance as were historically reviewed by the Apostles in the writings of Philo of Alexandria, which were excellently corrected by Saint John of Patmos (John 1). Philo, a Jewish former pagan, had enticed the Hellenistic world to believe that God indeed had an ambassador to the people, but one who is not the homoousion Christ, but the lesser, the creature, the Demiurge. Saint John, 50 years later, correctively taught that Jesus, Who is God Himself (John 10:30) rose from the dead to take on the "Mediator" role forever for the saved (Luke 24:3). Nevertheless, Philo's idea of the Mediator became the incentive for misguided Jews to believe that man could reasonably "strive to reach Heaven," but via attaining the so-called highest knowledge, the *gnosis*, awarded by a lesser being, that Demiurge, whom Philo called "Logos," as he framed the promise: "And even if there be not as yet anyone who is worthy to be called a son of God, nevertheless let him labour earnestly to be adorned according to his first-born word, the eldest of his angels, as the great archangel of many names; for he is called, the authority, and the name of God, and the Word, and man according to God's image, and he who sees Israel." ("On the Confusion of Tongues"; Philo of Athens; Part XXVIII; Section 146; A.D. 33) However, as the misbegotten ideas of Arius the Presbyter would later reverberate, this heresy that Christ was Himself a creature

Article I. Governing Principles and Essential Declarations of This TACA Diocese

created by God and was not God Himself was forever anathematized (Council of Constantinople; Canon 1; A.D. 381). Indeed, the correct homoousion Christology taught that the "Son of God [is] coeternal and consubstantial with the Father" (Council of Chalcedon; Session II; A.D. 451). Of course, both the ancient and the modern person confess that he or she, "desirest truth in the inward parts: and in the hidden part thou shalt make me to know wisdom" (Psalm 51:6). This makes for an interesting meditation to review the vain but hopeful attempts of the hungry mind, given to emulate thinking such as Philo's, to contemplate how a Mediator between God and man could possibly exist: "And this same Word is continually a suppliant to the immortal God on behalf of the mortal race, which is exposed to affliction and misery; and is also the ambassador, sent by the Ruler of all, to the subject race (206). And the Word rejoices in the gift, and, exulting in it, announces it and boasts of it, saying, 'And I stood in the midst, between the Lord and You'" ("Who is the Heir of Divine Things"; Philo of Athens; parts VII, XLII; Section 205-206, 35; A.D. 33). The now-contemplative future Lector is invited by the Continuing Anglican minister to arrive at the Bible, reading, "For there is one God, and one mediator between God and men, the man Christ Jesus" (1 Timothy 2:5).

e) Most people, who could otherwise become happily catechized parishioners, do not firstly

Article I. Governing Principles and Essential Declarations of This TACA Diocese

recognize that their being dead in their sinfulness signifies that their true identity will remain lost to them (Colossians 2:13). They must firstly be helped to realize that they have been made in the image of God (Genesis 1:27). They could therefore become future converts and reverts, who will have learned that they were not created by God to remain unrepentant sinners (Matthew 4:7), such as those self-professed "cretins" (Titus 1:12), the rascals whose darkness they finally learned to escape (2 John 1:10-11; 2 Thessalonians 3:6)—rascals and mountebanks, who mock the followers of God's expectation that everyone must not merely repent but must become reborn and "put on the new man" (Ephesians 4:24). The reality that God alone creates justice and inner righteousness was long ago written by Isaiah and King David (Isaiah 51:4; Psalm 33:5), centuries before Plato. Plato, that historic sage to the vast many of the godless, determined that the sole source of all goodness was the human psyche (*The Republic*; Book IV). Without belief in God, could a merely "psychological" person, during riotous times, ever advance Social Justice, the kind that is coincidently prayed for, on page 44 of the 1928 Book of Common Prayer—noting, for instance, the material expense alone to society of their remaining, even for a short time, mired in spiritual malfeasance? The cost of insurance claims, for example, exceeded $2 billion concerning the 2020 George-Floyd Riots, which destroyed huge parts of 140 U.S. cities ("How

Article I. Governing Principles and Essential Declarations of This TACA Diocese

2020 protests changed insurance forever"; Thomas Johansmeyer; Word Economic Forum; https://www.weforum.org/agenda/2021/02/2020-protests-changed-insurance-forever; Retrieved April 28, 2023). The goal of employing philosophically determined qualities to explain all worthwhile endeavors was famously said by Plato to be *Eudaimonia*, also known as Platonic "happiness" (*Apology*: 30:b; *Euthydemus*: 280:d-282:d; *Meno*; 87:d-89:a; *Republic*: d, B.C. 348). Different from mere sensual Epicurean pleasure, as Aristotle later clarified, *eudaimonia* can only reasonably arise entirely out of *aretē*, or human-conceived "virtue" (*Nicomachean Ethics*; Aristotle; Book 1; Chapter 7; Section 1-82; B.C. 350). To Plato, "perfection of the soul" (Apology; Plato; 29:e) and "care for virtue" (*ibid.* 31:a-b), should become the master work of what he called the *Logistikon* (the interior Logos of the Psyche), the will to reason the self toward the creating of goodness, the achievement of a mindset that is generated within a person after he has actualized the three Platonic Cardinal Virtues, of wisdom, courage, and temperance (*The Republic*; Plato; Book IV; Section 426-442)—and, added later by Plato, piety toward the gods ("Protagoras"; Plato; 330:b; B.C. 370). The soul—in fact, a "Tripartite Soul"—is an invisible element that is governed by the very highest of its three constituent parts: the aforementioned rational *Logistikon* (λογιστικόν; *ibid. Republic*; 435:e), which guides the other two invisible parts—the spirit or *Thymoeides* (θυμοειδές; *ibid.*

Article I. Governing Principles and Essential Declarations of This TACA Diocese

439:e) and the concupiscence or *Epithymetikon*, the latter being that carnal and sensual urge that endows all human appetites to satisfy the physical self, including the *Eros* (ἐπιθυμητικόν; *ibid.* 441:e-442:b). This "concupiscible part of the soul," though it is profane and sordid, was sadly not eschewed by ambitious English speakers but later ambitiously snatched up in the famous philosophical overreaching by Scottish economist, Adam Smith. Smith keenly drew from Aristotle and Plato in addressing the "different passions and appetites," which he argued ought never be deprived of inflicting the economic power that they could wield, writing: "Carelessness and want of œconomy are universally disapproved of, not, however, as proceeding from a want of benevolence, but from a want of the proper attention to the objects of self-interest" (*The Theory of Moral Sentiments*; Adam Smith; Part VII; Section II; Chapter 1; 1759). It is within this weirdly spiritualized context of exaggerated self-advancement that "the pursuit of happiness" would in 140 years excuse the craft of the arrogant past-is-dead Transcendentalists, who inspired the psychopathy of Industrialist moguls, not to mention the wicked "Ethical Egoism" of Ayn Rand and her charity-dooming *Fountainhead*. However, early American enterprise had firstly enjoyed a brief literary check against its power, one very important but all-but-forgotten delimitation notable for its much nobler expectations that Americans should

Article I. Governing Principles and Essential Declarations of This TACA Diocese

avoid idle speech (Ephesians 4:29) and guard against the unbridled ambition of kings (1 Samuel 8:10-18). By voicing the exigency to fulfill demand with supply while preserving the peace of God in the nascent United States, important warnings were spoken by Founding Father James Wilson, the Scottish-American jurist who in 1790 stood before President George Washington and both houses of Congress, lecturing them on the authority given to ancient and modern rulers via the "covenants and agreement" that can only be daily mandated by the American people when they are authorized by "the laws of nature and of nature's God"—his voicing the actual juridical theology that had been written 14 years earlier in the Declaration of Independence, which Wilson himself had signed (*The Works of the Honourable James Wilson, L.L.D., Late One of the Associate Judges of the Supreme Court of the United States, and Professor of Law in the College of Philadelphia*; Ed. Bird Wilson, Esq.; Vol. 1; Chapter 2; pp. 101-102; 357; Philadelphia: 1804). Wilson reminded the first President, his wife Martha, and all the legislators about the words of the English theologian Richard Hooker, who wrote: "The lawful power of making laws to command whole politick societies of men, belongeth so properly unto the same entire societies, that for any prince or potentate of what kind soever on earth to exercise the same of himself, and not either by express commission immediately and personally received from God, or else by

Article I. Governing Principles and Essential Declarations of This TACA Diocese

authority derived at the first from their consent, upon whose persons they impose laws, it is no better than mere tyranny. Laws they are not, therefore which publick approbation hath not made so" (*Of the Lawes of Ecclesiastical Politie*; Richard Hooker; Book I; Chapter 10; 1594; *ibid.* Wilson; p. 102). The errors/partial truths of Socrates and his friends therefore are, in this view of American Liberty, assuredly worth listing here, only in determining by contrast that Jesus Christ is the truest source of *Dikaiosyne* (i.e., justice)—His real Logos disqualifying the mistakes of misbegotten ideologies that always end up leading desperate people toward sociopolitical rebelliousness and collateral loss. Consider, for one, how *The Republic* had correctly attributed *Adikia* (i.e., injustice) to the immorality of every such wayward person as his selfishness is reflected by the whole state (*The Republic*; Plato; Book IV; Section 443:a) but do remember to acknowledge the ultimate failure of all of these pre-Christian classical ideas: Thrasymachus wrongfully believed in an inversion of virtue, possible only through brutish Machiavellian might and cunning, like a modern murderous Washington insider; Glaucon and Adeimantus advocated for a social contract akin to modern Marxism could be said to be the forerunners of groups like Antifa; for Polemarchus, justice meant causing harm to his enemies but benevolence to his friends, like a misanthropic pharmaceutical mogul advancing "gain-of-function" laboratory tests to realize

Article I. Governing Principles and Essential Declarations of This TACA Diocese

profits for his family by secretly inflicting a pandemic (*ibid.* Books I-VI). Plato, writing the words spoken to him by his teacher, Socrates, had indeed designated justice to be derived from the *Logistikon*, but mistakenly venerated the Logos of the inner person as if the all-moral God was not needed to guide man's Cardinal Virtues of wisdom, courage, temperance, and piety, but instead adding that ordinary people and the mighty gods, are given—in an arbitrary manner—varying degrees of virtues and vices (*ibid.* Book IV; Section 426-335). Plato knitted this pagan predestination that he famously allegorized as "the Charioteers," with Zeus having the very best horses among all humans and all the other gods ("Phaedrus"; Section 246b; B.C. 370). However, as studious Christians now love to study the steps taken towards Truth by those mistaken but "Virtuous Pagans" (*The Inferno*; Dante Alighieri; Canto IV; 1320), the ancient fourfold reward of inner righteousness can be appropriately consecrated: the grasped Truth, partnered with that longed-for Happiness that stems from Agape Love, and enjoined by that hoped-for justice of Revelation. All these elements of virtue attested by Plato and Aristotle, became the gifts of the Spirit in a reborn Christian identity, hoped-for joys that are really only attainable through Faith in the Blood of the Lamb (Revelation 12:11). Jesus, as God, has elevated Love above Law, Mercy above Justice, and is the Holy Word, the Son of the Father, coequal with the Father, Who created

Article I. Governing Principles and Essential Declarations of This TACA Diocese

everything and everyone (Genesis 1-3; John 1). Christ, simultaneously being fully man and fully God, gave His people actual Fellowship with the Creator "by abolishing in His flesh the law of commandments and decrees" (Ephesians 2:15), and models human perfection by being *homoousion* with the Father and the Spirit (*On the Trinity*; Saint Augustine; Book V; Chapter 8; A.D. 416; John 10:30; Council of Chalcedon; Session II; A.D. 451). He did this to make in Himself of twain one new man, so making peace" (Ephesians 2:15). Jesus thereby delivers people from their riotous nature if they seek Him, "For Christ is the end of the law for righteousness to every one that believeth. For Moses describeth the righteousness which is of the law, That the man which doeth those things shall live by them" (Romans 10:4-5).

f) There are not enough pages available within a catechetical Christian book such as this to present the woefully unprovable case that Karl Marx and Frederick Engels were satanists, albeit a small sample of evidence will be provided here by means of support for this position. If a Christian were to test the spirits and sample the fruits of Communism's trajectory in history, he would make his decision based on the genocides of nearly 200 million people directly executed by its adherents; the Soviet Gulag and Pitesti Prison in Romania; paeans to Satan in Marx's poetry and plays; the suicide pacts of Marx's daughters and their spouses; the biographical arc of Marx's

Article I. Governing Principles and Essential Declarations of This TACA Diocese

conversion from Judaism, to Christianity, and then to atheism; the frequent use of words such as "nigger" and "Jew" written in the letters between both founders to integrate Social Darwinism and Eugenics into their socialist mindset; and the unholy dialectic by which they ensured that law and order and ownership of property would project the "inversion" principle of Satanism. A number of outstanding Christian and Messianic Jewish authors will be listed below, whose books are indispensable in compiling the evidence against these two. For the moment, it can be helpful to entertain, ironically, the systematic study of the revisionist-history tool of *Semiotics* to build that case—that same ubiquitous weaponized mode of scrutinizing, doxing, and canceling opponents of Marxism for decades, wielded by most modern academicians. Semiotics is merely the linguistic magic that makes a college professor sound intelligent when he insinuates, for example, that because he has overheard a florist using a certain "Signifier" of, perhaps, describing most cleverly a "fractal curve," she thus is probably not merely a florist but also a mathematician who liberally engages in usage of the "sign" of simultaneously specializing in both floral arrangements and teaching all the permutations of the Mandelbrot Set! Semiotics is thus a logical fallacy resounding in educational failure.

However, one does not need Semiotics to actualize what the Bible has, for millennia,

Article I. Governing Principles and Essential Declarations of This TACA Diocese

taught. As the philosophical means of showing how a merely spiteful personality influences social upheaval, one needs only to review the ancient quote: "And since men also cause revolutions through their private lives," Aristotle said, they are "unsuited to democracy in a democracy, to oligarchy in an oligarchy" (*Politics*; Aristotle; Book V; Section 1308:g-20; B.C. 330). Bitter and disenfranchised, they will cause revolution "even if they have not run through all their property," Aristotle continued, by "being allowed to do whatever they like; the cause of which [Plato] states to be excessive liberty" (*ibid.* 1316:b-3). Plato, having earlier presented a dialectic less suitable to the materialism loved by Marx than would Georg Wilhelm Friedrich Hegel with his antithesis model, forebodingly had postulated a sociopolitical descent away from Democracy, toward Oligarchy, into theft of personal property by the oligarchs, men exploiting the indolence and insolvency of the unruly, whose "excessive and unseasonable liberty has clothed itself in the garb of the most cruel and bitter servile servitude" (*The Republic*; Plato; Book VIII; Section 569:c; B.C. 380). Today, the Communist Signifier of The Great Reset has utilized the Sign of Marxism to begin to wage the wicked Dialectical Materialist Revolution through the creation of public riots, inflicted by bitter unemployed people unwittingly, as useful idiots, practicing Disaster Capitalism—a term used to describe the practice of destroying cities so that the elite can buy up all the razed property at low

Article I. Governing Principles and Essential Declarations of This TACA Diocese

prices, actualizing the dark ethos of, "Everyone who participates profits from it," a terrible trend reported by former House and Human Services Director Catherine Austin Fitts and her editors ("Corruption—A Pandemic Emergency of International Proportion"; Wolfgang Wodarg; *Solari Report,* March 19, 2023). The current Social Revolutions are thus a Marxist art shaping the *Great Reset*, in which "sustainable development" is make a priority against the backdrop of economies ravaged by the COVID-19 lockdowns ("Pandemic is chance to reset global economy, says Prince Charles"; Phillip Inman; *The Guardian,* June 3, 2020). The concept of "you will own nothing, and you will be happy" is intended to entitle modern Marxist oligarchs to possess your private property and to assume executive control over the desperate masses who are becoming increasingly dependent on them, in addition to their technocrat friends—an intention that is not being concealed but rather is now boastfully presented by its adherents represented by entities such as the World Economic Forum (Ida Auken, "Welcome to 2030. I own nothing, have no privacy, and life has never been better" *World Economic Forum.* Archived from the original on 2016-11-25; Retrieved 2021-09-20).

Books describing the Satanism of Marxism, Communism, and Socialism, written by Christian authors (which also mention infiltration of government, schools, and churches, and the coercive advancing of LGBTQ "rights") include:

—*The Devil and Karl Marx: Communism's Long March of Death, Deception, and Infiltration*; Paul Kengor: TAN Books, Gastonia, NC: 2021

—*Marx and Satan*; Rev. Richard Wurmbrand; Crossway Books, Wheaton, IL: 1986

—*Tortured for Christ*; Rev. Richard Wurmbrand; Living Sacrifice Book Co., Bartlesville, OK: 1998

—*The Meaning of Karl Marx*; Bruce Mazlish; Oxford Univ. Press: 1984.

v) Divine Law for Christian Americans supersedes all other forms of Human Law; evidence for this principle is manifest everywhere, as follows:

a) American Christians, seeing the modern holocausts of our arts and sciences, cannot argue against the Creator's moral expectation that we are to keep His statutes and testimonies, by whose creation are configured all the laws of Nature, and by Whom the Moral Law of the Bible must configure all the laws of government (Isaiah 28:29).

b) "Nature's God," and the "Lord" and "God" are respectively cited in:

1) The first paragraph of the American Declaration of Independence, and:

Article I. Governing Principles and Essential Declarations of This TACA Diocese

    2) In Article VII of the United States Constitution; and:

    3) On the face of the U.S. Dollar.

c) "God" and "Creator" to Americans must be known and interpreted solely as the Triune God as revealed by Divine Inspiration in the Holy Scriptures—God the Father, God the Son, and God the Holy Ghost, Three in One—who created and orders the "Laws of Nature" and gives Americans the "self-evident" truths of the Bible, by which the Declaration of Independence and all formative American documentation shall solely be spiritually discerned and properly understood—irrespective of any personal opinion or belief that may have been held, whether publicly or privately, on the part of any or all of our founding fathers.

d) Richard Hooker defines the moral context whereby nature among Anglicans is perfected by Grace: "When supernatural duties are necessarily exacted, natural are not rejected as needless" (*Of the Laws of Ecclesiastical Polity*; Book 1; Chapter 8; Richard Hooker; 1594) This means that:

    1) As Americans, Christian Americans are to daily forge lives through cities of asphalt and concrete that are not really that far removed from the wild forests, which themselves have long proved homesteaders' mettle, but always requiring God's moral laws to keep families safely working in good spiritual health no

Article I. Governing Principles and Essential Declarations of This TACA Diocese

matter where they are situated (2 Thessalonians 3:8).

e) Hooker continues, "The law of God therefore is, though principally delivered for instruction in the one, yet fraught with precepts of the other also." That is, living morally according to biblical conviction is necessary for surviving and sharing the abundance or tumults of nature, or as Hooker notes, "The Scripture is fraught even with laws of Nature" (Jeremiah 31:35-40; Isaiah 51:5; *ibid. Of the Laws,.*). It is by God's enduring eternal mercy that the sun, moon, and water operate for our benefit within nature (Psalm 136:6-7).

f) Hooker further posits that God endowed humans with reason so that goodness may prevail over evil, whereof Romans 13 promotes our moral indebtedness to the blood atonement, which frees our will from the mercilessness or exploitation of others: "Owe no man any thing, but to love one another: for he that loveth another hath fulfilled the law" (Romans 13:8). Hooker concurs, "But the nature of Goodness being thus ample, a Law is properly that which Reason in such sort defineth to be good that it must be done" (*ibid. Of the Laws*). Thus:

g) American Anglicans, knowing themselves to be Traditionalist or orthodox Christians, are thus morally expected by God to engender our civility and obedience to upright rules of the homes we occupy, rationally securing communities built from chaste agape love for our neighbors, to foster health and fruitfulness in society (Romans 13).

    1) Hooker commends the Anglican religion as instilling for our Free Will vigilant thoughtfulness, ethically achieved through the simultaneous rational obedience to the moral, legal, and supernatural supremacy of Divine Law, to be held above Natural and Human and Statutory/Case Law: "The rule of voluntary agents on Earth is the sentence that Reason giveth concerning the goodness of those things which they are to do" (*Of the Laws*, ibid.). As always:

    2) "All scripture is given by inspiration of God, and is profitable for doctrine, for reproof, for correction, for instruction in righteousness: That the man of God may be perfect, thoroughly furnished unto all good works" (2 Timothy 3:16).

h) Still, human depravity threatens to derange self-control toward bending Natural, Human, and Moral Law to the dictates of our depraved human will and the fulfillment of our concupiscence. The translator of the Bible into the English of King James—Launcelot Andrewes—preached, "We see it is a Thing very agreeable to our Nature, to have what We shall have by Justice (to choose): and that way do even the mightiest first seek it; and when that way it will not come, they overbear it with Power." People, hinged only to Natural and Human Law, sadly become tyrants inside and

Article I. Governing Principles and Essential Declarations of This TACA Diocese

outside of their homes (Sermon, Whitehall; III. Jehovah Righteousness; Launcelot Andrewes; 1600, Nov. 23).

1) Traditionalist Anglicanism embraces the Bible as humanity's prophylaxis against evil so that Natural, Moral, and Human Law may be subjected at all times to the Will of God, for "the government shall be upon His shoulder (Isaiah 9:6), and yet we are to "Fear God. Honour the king" (1 Peter 2:17). This is the *via media* of Traditional Anglicanism, and to be followed and held by all members and clergy of TACA, with respect to interpretation of the relationship between Natural Law, Human or Statutory/Case Law, and Divine Law.

2) Regarding how orthodoxy was epitomized by the daily praxis of Andrewes, the Russian Orthodox scholar Nikolay Lossky wrote, "An authentic witness ... is someone for whom theology is not a system of thought or intellectual construction, but a progression in the experience of the mystery, the union with God, in the communion of the church" (*Launcelot Andrewes, the Preacher: The Origins of the Mystical Theology of the Church*; Chapter 3: "Christmas"; p. 78; Nikolay Lossky; A. Louth, transl.; Oxford Press, 1991)

3) King David, that sacerdotal monarch, sang to this end, "Blessed are the undefiled in the way, who walk in the law of the Lord" (Psalm 119:1). "Theology is for the understanding an ascetic

Article I. Governing Principles and Essential Declarations of This TACA Diocese

way, a way of the Cross," Lossky adds (*ibid., Launcelot*).

4) The King James Bible, representing the apex of the English language, exemplifies the orthodoxy of its interpreter—the American orthodox Christian. Mindful of the English-speaking Andrewes, Lossky wrote, "Theology and life are inseparable; there is no orthodoxy without orthopraxy. Christianity demands the four virtues [mercy, truth, righteousness, and peace]" (*ibid. Launcelot*).

ARTICLE II. Our Evangelistic and Spiritual Heraldry Brought Forth for all Potential and Ongoing Worshippers

A. Staying Humble, Lowly Teachers

i) Ministers shall instruct sinners not to confuse goodness with evil (1 Corinthians 1:27-31; Isaiah 5:20; Romans 1:18-32).

a) Teach from a low estate (Romans 12:3; Ephesians 4:2); God chose the poor and lowly to teach about the kingdom (James 2:5). Saint Philip the Apostle, who, along with the apostles Peter and Andrew, hailed from the poor northern shore of Bethsaida, Galilee, received God's order from an angel to approach a certain spiritually ignorant but very powerful eunuch of Ethiopia, a man "of great authority" (Acts 8:26-39). He preached to the eunuch about the prophecy of the profoundly redemptive humbleness of the Messiah, reading from the scroll the Book of Isaiah: "He is brought as a lamb to the slaughter, and as a sheep before her shearers is dumb, so he opened not His mouth. He was taken from prison and from judgment: and who shall declare His generation? For He was cut off out of the land of the living" (Isaiah 53:7-8).

b) Credit inspiration to God, not to oneself (Ephesians 2:9). Learned in Scripture, and not moved by vanity to appear learned, Saint Philip stayed with the eunuch, who began to grasp the reason for the peculiar meekness of the long-

Article II. Our Evangelistic and Spiritual Heraldry Brought Forth for all Potential and Ongoing Worshippers

suffering servant-Messiah (Isaiah 53:7-8). Through Philip's serviceable pedagogy, God received the rich Eunuch of the Queen of Ethiopia into the Faith; now gladly humbled by the Word, the eunuch persuaded Philip to baptize him in a waterway nearby (Acts 8:36-40). Although wisdom is better than weapons of war (Ecclesiastes 9:18), "the Word of God is quick, and powerful, and sharper than any twoedged sword, piercing even to the dividing asunder of soul and spirit, and of the joints and marrow, and is a discerner of the thoughts and intents of the heart" (Hebrews 4:12).

c) Plumb ignorance immediately in search of Faith. Without Saint Philip acting quickly upon the Spirit's order, how could the eunuch have been gifted with the understanding of why his Savior, the all-powerful Christ, should have bothered to suffer peacefully along with all hagridden sheep—enduring all the abuses normally meant to crush the meek? (Acts 8:31-33). Abused by modern Herods and Pilates, we are nonetheless called to teach God's word peacefully and boldly (Acts 4:29). There is very little time because our "night"—our biological death—is coming (John 9:4). Because the devil himself has limited time to send or reveal the beast, we must accelerate our humble willingness to teach (Revelation 12:12).

d) We the clergy must help our parishioners find the confidence to live faithfully in an unfair, corrupt world in which the wicked prosper but the righteous suffer and God seems inactive or aloof.

Article II. Our Evangelistic and Spiritual Heraldry Brought Forth for all Potential and Ongoing Worshippers

Christians may happily refer to this concept as theodicy, defined in the Merriam-Webster dictionary as "defense of God's goodness and omnipotence in view of the existence of evil," as Joseph said: "But as for you, ye thought evil against me; but God meant it unto good, to bring to pass, as it is this day, to save much people alive" (Genesis 50:20).

e) Neither Sacred Scripture nor Sacred Tradition can be taught or understood in a vacuum. It was the Holy Ghost, not humans, Who inspired the writings of Sacred Scripture, and all Sacred Tradition depends on Sacred Scripture. "Therefore, brethren, stand fast, and hold the traditions which ye have been taught, whether by word, or by our epistle" (2 Thessalonians 2:15).

f) Sympathy shall be accorded to Faithful witness. If a Christian suffers for good and endures it, this is commendable by God (1 Peter 2:20).

g) All are welcome who come and go in Christ's peace (Judges 18:6; 1 Thessalonians 3:11). The merciful Father, Who will not tempt Christians beyond their capacity to cope (1 Corinthians 10:13), grieves the horrors that men cause (Psalm 78:40). Just as King David bewailed his own series of exiles (which his mentor Saul and son Absolom respectively impelled), it should be recognized by all Christians that prophecy or God-inspired warning, such as the Baptizer's exhortation to "Repent," is never a private matter because God intends to save us (Matthew 3:2; 2 Peter 1:20; 1

Article II. Our Evangelistic and Spiritual Heraldry Brought Forth for all Potential and Ongoing Worshippers

Timothy 2:4). Thus, let us feel bold in our witnessing, to give lessons from our own learning of humility, knowing that our "old man" has been crucified with Jesus, and so that by our words we can draw others away from serving sin (Romans 6:6).

h) Take your "lumps" in this life charitably and with patience. God cannot be fooled by attempts to eschew correction and downfalls, nor can He be mocked or deceived (Galatians 6:7; Hebrews 12:6-7).

i) Renounce hatred and bitterness (1 John 4:20-21; Ephesians 4) and draw strength from infirmities (2 Corinthians 12:9). The Book of Kings presents a penitent, merciful, powerful father in King David (2 Samuel 12:13-15; 19:1). He lamented the "curse of Eli" as it would pertain to his dead sons in his great prayerful sorrow. By contrast, the High Priest Eli, the ineffectual father of two foul and adulterous sons, the idolator priests Hophni and Phinehas, exhibited no penance but only flaccid fatherly regrets (1 Samuel 2:27-36). Morbidly obese, but not glorifying God in his weakness, he fell aghast off his stool to his death upon his being told that the Ark of the Covenant had been stolen by the Philistines (1 Samuel 2:27-36; 4:18). Moreover, a father must not become so cynical, paranoid, and horrible that God would give him over to his sins or sends a demon to go into him (1 Samuel 18:10; Romans 1:24); instead he should accept temporal and spiritual hardship peacefully,

Article II. Our Evangelistic and Spiritual Heraldry Brought Forth for all Potential and Ongoing Worshippers

for "it is hard for thee to kick against the pricks" (Acts 9:5) when there is the great duty to be simultaneously strong but kind and patient (1 Corinthians 13; Galatians 5:22-23). If hatred and bitterness are directed toward you, do not render "evil for evil, or railing for railing: but contrariwise blessing" (1 Peter 3:9). For these hated Christ before they hated you (John 15:18). A church without the Love of God, Who is Love itself (1 John 4:8), is like a body without a head, "For the husband is the head of the wife, even as Christ is the head of the church: and He is the savior of the body" (Ephesians 5:23). "So we, being many, are one body in Christ, and everyone members one of another" (Roman 12:5).

j) Do not take refuge in illicit unions, communions, consultations, and the like. One example of such illicit union is Saul's seeking communion with the Necromancer of Endor (1 Samuel 28:5-25). Instead, we are to seek refuge in traditional orthodox churches, and so it shall be taught. Any admixture of good with evil by the solicitation of evil influences or forces on the part of members of this TACA Diocese is strictly forbidden. First, it makes a person's situation worse than it was in the beginning (1 Samuel 31:3-6). Second, it makes a mockery of God, and God shall not be mocked (Galatians 6:7). Third, it scandalizes the faithful, Christ's "little ones": "Whoever therefore shall humble himself as this little child, the same is greatest in the kingdom of heaven ... but whoso shall offend [i.e., scandalize] one of these little ones which believe in me, it would be better for him that a millstone were hanged about his neck, and that he were drowned in the depth of the sea" (Matthew 18:4-6).

ii) Heeding Scriptural Warnings to Accept Eternal or Temporal Consequences

a) Not long after his victory over the Ammonites, the temporal repercussions of King David's depraved concupiscence resounded when the unnamed infant son he sired with Bathsheba was taken by God as punishment for his adulterous proxy homicide of her husband Uriah (2 Samuel 2:11). Not even his lifelong Penance could prevent the temporal punishments documented in 2 Samuel. Even after Absolom committed the revenge-killing of his half-brother Amnon, and after Adonijah tried to supplant David's heir apparent Solomon, David remained repentant and hopeful. After Adonijah was himself summarily executed, the Davidian family and kingdom of Israel continued to fall to its own idolatry and dissolution until the time of Josephus, when Judah was finally a puppet of Rome, which in turn destroyed her in A.D. 70. Nevertheless, vengeance belongs to the Lord, and it is He who will repay (Romans 12:19; Isaiah 59:18).

b) Even after David's greatest general and nephew Joab betrayed him with libel and sedition, the sorrowful David respected God's throne and took his lumps, all throughout his dotage, all because God is no respecter of persons (2 Samuel 7:16;

Article II. Our Evangelistic and Spiritual Heraldry Brought Forth for all Potential and Ongoing Worshippers

    Acts 10:34). Humility shall thus define penitent Anglicans.

    c) There are no "plenary indulgences" in Anglicanism. Purgatory is doctrinally revoked in Article XXII of the Thirty-Nine Articles. If one sins, but confesses, performs Penance, and strives fervently to make amends, one still must penitently accept the consequences that the world and possibly also the government may deign fitting toward oneself and family—irrespective of the remission of sins granted by God. Contrariwise, unrepented sins put one in danger of hell fire (Matthew 5:22), or of being cast away from God (Matthew 7:23), or of being thrown into outer darkness (Matthew 8:12, 22:13, and 25:30). Although God desires not the death of a sinner but would that he would repent and live (Ezekiel 18:23), the world does not forgive even pious acts, such as those of Saint Stephen (Daniel 3:20; Daniel 6:16; Acts 7:57-60).

iii) Curbing Ambition and Envy

    a) Thus, take heart, Christian shepherds of souls: it is Christ who is seated at the right hand of the Power, and not we ourselves. Who can doubt that our treacherous hearts need Him to lead us through the narrow gate (Matthew 7:13-14), lest we find ourselves being judged by Him more harshly as teachers of Scripture than He would our most petty parishioners? For you must "give an account" (Hebrews 13:17) and it is you who (shall receive the "greater condemnation" (James

Article II. Our Evangelistic and Spiritual Heraldry Brought Forth for all Potential and Ongoing Worshippers

3:1). Stay low in estate, as the Theotokos is herself thus graceful, in the hope that you will find God's favor (Luke 1:48), for God reduces princes to nothing (Isaiah 40:23).

iv) A Broken Spirit and Contrite Heart Shall Rule

a) God calls all sinners home, just as King David, longing for Absalom to come back home, displayed that he was indeed a man after God's own heart (1 Samuel 13:14). To whatever degree King David was myopic about the prophet Samuel's warning that David's family would fall apart because of his adulterous killing of Uriah (2 Samuel 12:11), David's sense of guilt may have left the heartsick monarch appearing weak to his own son, and it was in this state that he welcomed Absalom home.

1) The father, the compassionate patriarch, was recognizing the gravity of his own mortality, not wishing to allow his time on Earth to pass before reconciling with his boy, wanting his family to become lovingly united once more, just as God wants us to live together in fellowship: "For we must needs die, and are as water spilt on the ground, which cannot be gathered up again; neither doth God respect any person: yet doth he devise means, that his banished be not expelled from him" (2 Samuel 14:14). This ideal is perfected in the parable of the Prodigal Son (Luke 15:11-32).

Article II. Our Evangelistic and Spiritual Heraldry Brought Forth for all Potential and Ongoing Worshippers

v) Commitment to Moral Strength

a) This TACA Diocese recognizes that the true Universal Church worships Jesus Christ fervently during these very confusing times, a truly morally terrible era, which, if visualized as a timeline hosting our journey through a riotous, poisoned wilderness since the time of the Cross, convinces us that Christians are navigating through the very foothills of the Apocalypse (Matthew 24:7; Matthew 25:7; 2 Thessalonians 2:3). We must endure hostility and abound in the work of the Lord (1 Corinthians 15:58).

b) Being that violence, perversity, and deceit throughout society are truly the handiwork of the "powers and principalities," and that these are thus now fatuously programmed institutionally by governments and corporate officers serving Luciferian political aims, Christians shall labor with one hand to fit spiritual stones into the wall around the Church Militant, while with the other hand holding a weapon of Christian duty, never fatiguing to keep the agents of Satan ably resisted (James 4:7; Nehemiah 4:7; Galatians 6:9).

1) Mistrust and spite are rationally witnessed by Christians to rule and pollute the sidewalks, workplace, and classrooms of our children: "And because iniquity shall abound, the love of many shall wax cold" (Matthew 24:12).

vi) Charity through helping the poor, the needy, the broken-hearted, or the downcast on Ember Days,

Article II. Our Evangelistic and Spiritual Heraldry Brought Forth for all Potential and Ongoing Worshippers

Rogation Days, or on any days of the year is a worthy expression of Christian Faith.

> a) Programming for Charitable Good Works shall be part of the written Customary in every TACA Congregation or Mission.
>
> b) Deacons and Deaconesses, Priests, and Secretaries are appropriate senior ministers of charitable works (Acts 6:1-4).

vii) Grace Shall Protect the Church's Faith and Characterize Its Harmless Pews and Wise Doorways (Ephesians 2:8-9; Matthew 10:16; Luke 13:24-25)

> a) This TACA Diocese now publishes its Constitution, Canons, and 50-year History in order to posit that loving-but-authoritative theology that ought to be modeled for the polity of the Christian world to view by permission, not by commandment (1 Corinthians 7:6). Logos, exemplified for the Laity, shall be practiced by the Episcopate without arrogance or caprice, and shall be followed by the Clergy and Laity alike, so that heartlessness and wicked ploys shall be restrained by humble Christian men and women from disordering the pews and doorways of churches and homes (John 17:12; 1 Thessalonians 5:14; 2 Thessalonians 3:6-11).
>
> b) There shall be no favoritism among Christians, because actions and rank do not bring the Faith that is required for Salvation. "For there is no respect of person with God" (Romans 2:11; Ephesians 2:8-9). Sanctuaries planted by mere

people should not be considered to be owned nor rented outright by a small few: we should instead consider that we are able to avail ourselves of our beautiful structures only because God has supplied them to us. "There is a way that seemeth right unto a man, but the end thereof are the ways of death" (Proverbs 16:25).

c) A Christian cannot redeem or save another Christian through the Roman Catholic concept of "redemptive suffering," which comes from Colossians 1:24, wherein Paul describes himself thus: "Who now rejoice in my sufferings for you, and fill up that which is behind of the afflictions of Christ in my flesh for his body's sake, which is the church." On the subject, Thomas Aquinas wrote: "Contrition is ordained against the guilt which affects a man's disposition to goodness or malice, so that one man is not freed from guilt by another's contrition." One cannot employ "redemptive suffering" as an Act of Contrition to help the salvational state of another, as Aquinas further adds: "In like manner, by confession a man submits to the sacraments of the Church: nor can one man receive a Sacrament instead of another, since in a sacrament grace is given to the recipient, not to another." A Christian act is satisfiable solely in accordance with God's good pleasure in relation to the one engaging in such act. "Consequently, there is no comparison between satisfaction, contrition, and confession" (*Summa Theologica;* Supplementum; Question 13; Answer to Objection 2; Aquinas, Saint Thomas;

1274). One should consider that each is responsible for his own sin (Ezekiel 18) and, contrariwise, for his own "calling and election" (2 Peter 1:10), though we must certainly and always pray for one another: "Confess your faults one to another, and pray one for another, that ye may be healed. The effectual fervent prayer of a righteous man availeth much" (James 5:16). There is also no sin in asking of God that deceased persons be forgiven, as in the case of the brethren who persuaded Judas Maccabeus to send their donation of twelve-thousand drachmas to the Temple, begging God to forgive the idolatry of their fallen comrades, "to offer a sin offering, doing therein very well and honestly, in that he was mindful of the resurrection: For if he had not hoped that they that were slain should have risen again, it had been superfluous and vain to pray for the dead. And also in that he perceived that there was great favour laid up for those that died Godly, it was an holy and good thought" (2 Maccabees 12:43-46). Therefore, praying for the beloved dead while tithing in the spirit of one's Love for the faithful departed is an act of piety without material indulgence, to which God is not indifferent.

d) Anglican Elders must help other Christians achieve Salvation "not by constraint, but willingly; not for filthy lucre" (1 Peter 5:2). In doing so we will we lay up for ourselves treasures in Heaven (Matthew 6:20). Bearing one another's burdens tirelessly fulfills the Law of Christ (Galatians

Article II. Our Evangelistic and Spiritual Heraldry Brought Forth for all Potential and Ongoing Worshippers

6:2,9). The Bible restrains "lording over" religious followers (1 Peter 5:3). Despite the Papal Letter of 1984 by Pope John Paul II, "*Salvifici Doloris*," designating God's Grace as the redemptive agent, the codification has, since the Council of Trent remained in the Catechism of Rome, "*Qui divina gratia præditi sunt alterius nomine possunt, quod Deo debetur, persolvere*" (CCC; Part 2; Section 2; Chapter 2; Article 5; Pars. 1501-1505). The Roman doctrine translates as, "Those endowed with divine Grace can pay in the name of another what is owed to God." However, although we love our neighbors as we love ourselves (Galatians 5:14; Matthew 22:39-40), our own personal Prevenient Grace is not a determinant of, nor should it be held responsible for, the redemption of another; such teaching is not biblical. Christians, lest they should expect to suffer profane or sordid exploitation by clericalists laboring under such a misapprehension of Fellowship, shall instead know kindly biblical counseling, caritas, and agape love from the Traditionalist Anglicans of our TACA Diocese.

e) If a Christian lacks a Bible, let Grace inspire Faith in others in response to our Good Works. "But my God shall supply all your need according to his riches in glory by Christ Jesus" (Philippians 4:19). The Saints who preceded Christ (e.g., Isaiah [Isaiah 53], Job [Job 19:25]) did not have a New Testament until the testator died (Hebrews 9:16), but they all had faith in the Living Christ. Likewise, John the Baptist even from the womb of

Article II. Our Evangelistic and Spiritual Heraldry Brought Forth for all Potential and Ongoing Worshippers

his mother Elisabeth, or Mary Theotokos, as made clear in her Canticle (Luke 1), had no written Word setting forth the teachings of the Gospel, and yet she and all the saints had a Living Faith through Grace. Likewise shall it be for any Christian who has no access to the Holy Bible. Saint John Chrysostom, in his homily on the Gospel of Saint Matthew, reassures: "οἱ πνευματικοὶ πάντα πράττουσιν ἐπιθυμίᾳ καὶ πόθῳ, καὶ τοῦτο δηλοῦσι τῷ καὶ ὑπερβαίνειν τὰ ὑποτάγματα," or, "For neither to the apostles did God give anything in writing, but instead of written words He promised that He would give them the grace of the Spirit: for He, says our Lord, shall bring all things to your remembrance. [John 14:26] And that you may learn that this was far better, hear what He says by the Prophet: 'I will make a new covenant with you, putting my laws into their mind, and in their heart I will write them,' and, 'they shall be all taught of God.' And Paul too, pointing out the same superiority, said, that they had received a law not in tables of stone, but in fleshy tables of the heart" ("Homilies on Saint Matthew's Gospel"; Saint John Chrysostom; Homily 1; Part 1; A.D. 407).

f) No Laity shall have rank one over another. No amount of money—by tithing, or in-kind gift, or monetary favor—will earn nobility or status in a Congregation or Mission. No pew will be reserved for purposes beyond charity or as accords participation in a ceremony (e.g., Confirmation, Baptism). This distinction between "precept and council" differentiates between the obligatory expectations in our Decalogue and our non-obligatory recommendation by God to be helpful or edifying. Even the anti-Reformer, Robert Bellarmine made this distinction, writing, "*nee praecepta nee indifferentia, sed Deo grata et ab illo commendata*," which is translated as, "neither precepts nor indifference, but pleasing to God and recommended by him" (*De Monachis*, Chapter 8; Robert Bellarmine; 1593). God does not show favoritism or partiality to anyone (Romans 2:11). Just as King Amaziah of Judah annoyed King Joash of Samaria by boasting that he had conquered the Edomites and was himself idolatrous (2 Chronicles 25:19), a proud churchgoer who is arrogantly puffed up will only stir up contention within the pews (Proverbs 28:25). Amaziah was slain in a conspiracy following his crushing defeat by the Samaritans (2 Chronicles 25:27), demonstrating the truth that neither money, nor status, nor muscle power can change the fact that we are debtors to the Spirit, not the flesh (Romans 8:12).

g) Loving acts shall be meritorious and favored by God. "For God is not unrighteous to forget your work and labour of love, which ye have shewed toward His name, in that ye have ministered to the saints, and do minister" (Hebrews 6:10). When Christians do good works, it is God using our "fingers," as Saint Ambrose explains, "So, then, the works of the hands are the same as the works of God. There is not therefore any distinction of

Article II. Our Evangelistic and Spiritual Heraldry Brought Forth for all Potential and Ongoing Worshippers

the work according to the kind of bodily members, but a oneness of power" (*On the Holy Spirit*; Book III; Saint Ambrose; Chapter 5; Section 32; A.D.). It was famously argued against Bellarmine that Saint Ambrose had been wrongfully employed by the Jesuits to promote Supererogation (i.e., doing more than God expects, without merit, for vainglory or "virtue-signaling") to increase coffer cash via plenary indulgences (*A Challenge Concerning the Malignant Church of Antichrist, and False Doctrine, and Lewd Practises of Papists*, Directed to Robert Parsons, Frier Garnet, George Blackwell the Archpriest, and all Their Adhaerents; Matthew Sutcliffe; Chapter VII, p. 152). However, the guilty pleasure of polemics should be avoided by contemplating the Psalmist: "For thou, Lord, hast made me glad through thy work: I will triumph in the works of thy hands" (Psalm 92:4). Likewise, we know that the Lord strengthens our own hands (Psalm 144:1).

h) Christians shall courageously correct people who disavow or denounce the Bible, the Church, or the saints (Ephesians 5:11-13). "The elements are worshipped—the air by Diogenes, the water by Thales, the fire by Hippasus," Saint Clement of Alexandria writes, making the case for remaining unyoked with polytheists, who seek their dead ends, whereas Christians have the true Faith (2 Corinthians 6:14). Citing Saint Paul and Proverbs, Saint Clement implores Christians to test the spirits and know people by their works (1 John

Article II. Our Evangelistic and Spiritual Heraldry Brought Forth for all Potential and Ongoing Worshippers

4:1; Matthew 7:16-20). "'Prove all things,' "the apostle [Saint Paul] says, 'and hold fast that which is good,' speaking to spiritual men, who judge what is said according to truth, whether it seems or truly holds by the truth. 'He who is not corrected by discipline errs, and stripes and reproofs give the discipline of wisdom,' the reproofs manifestly that are with love. 'For the right heart seeketh knowledge ... For he that seeketh the Lord shall find knowledge with righteousness; and they who have sought it rightly have found peace'" (*The Stromata/Miscellanies*; Saint Clement of Alexandria; Book I; Chapter XI; Hebrews 5:13; 1 Thessalonians 5:21; Proverbs 2). It is better to suffer for doing God's will than to suffer for wrongdoing (1 Peter 3:17).

viii) Bonding Together in Orthodoxy

a) TACA shall inspire its parishioners to be a mutual witness standing in opposition to the iniquity of this era, encouraging one another to present ourselves as "a living sacrifice, holy, acceptable to God" (Romans 12:1; Psalm 139:23-24).

b) Every Ordinal's final benediction shall be sincere and heartfelt, and every "goodnight" bade to the beloved shall be uttered with untiring hope so that strength may grow for the morrow.

1) Resisting sin and folly, TACA Christians are ready to gather in one accord with a peaceful,

Article II. Our Evangelistic and Spiritual Heraldry Brought Forth for all Potential and Ongoing Worshippers

loving disposition one toward another, being of "one mind" (2 Corinthians 13:11).

2) TACA Christians shall hold that the time is now, not tomorrow, to fight off the devil using the "whole armor of God," knowing that we are engaging daily in Spiritual Warfare (Ephesians 6:11-24).

c) TACA Priests are to exemplify to their flocks a bold renewal of true discipleship, making this long-neglected form a priority and a prominent expression of *caritas* in this calling, for the devil is working with a "great wrath" now, "because he knoweth that he hath but a short time" (Revelation 12:12).

ix) Logos Taught by Priests and Officers

a) The typical Christian today needs Truth to be explained: that Logos in all its mystery is also in essence a simplicity. Its "simple math" distils into one small, perfect equation: Everything good and perfect stems from the Word of God—from He who was with God and is God, Who spoke the world into existence (John 1).

b) Christian Bible education and Anglican formularies shall be taught by TACA officers or formal teachers in classrooms of all sorts—from pulpits or ambos, to church vestries or private homes—at all age levels and appropriate to each age level.

Article II. Our Evangelistic and Spiritual Heraldry Brought Forth for all Potential and Ongoing Worshippers

1) TACA ministers must teach both the educated and the simple, the greatest and the least (Matthew 5:19).

2) TACA ministers must teach by taking note of their proper role, guided by their bishops, as pedagogy is no trifle but framed by ardent moral accountability (2 Timothy 2:24).

3) Women in TACA are not to have spiritual authority over men, not only with respect to ordination, but also with regard to the role of teaching, with the implied meaning that the subject at hand is teaching in a public and official capacity in the context of church life: "Let the woman learn in silence with all subjection. But I suffer not a woman to teach, nor to usurp authority over the man, but to be in silence" (1 Timothy 2:11-12). Therefore, women in TACA may teach other women in the church, or they may teach children.

c) God's promise of the joy of Revelation is the teaching that good things are promised to those who stay on the "narrow road" (Matthew 7:13-14)—if only each mother and father were taught exactly what and who God is and why God exists so that they may teach Logos to their children (John 1; Genesis 1; Revelation 1)! But "how shall they believe in Him of whom they have not heard? And how shall they hear without a preacher?" (Romans 10:14). Therefore, we are called to teach and to preach.

Article II. Our Evangelistic and Spiritual Heraldry Brought Forth for all Potential and Ongoing Worshippers

x) Slaking the Thirst for an "Equation"

a) The "holy math" that supplants all other science, therefore, would be thus: God equals His promise, equals Love, equals the Word or Bible, equals the promise, equals Jesus, equals the Holy Spirit, equals God, equals His promise, equals Love, equals the Word or Bible, equals the promise, equals Jesus, equals the Holy Spirit, equals God, equals His promise, equals Love, equals the Word or Bible, equals the promise, etc. (John 1:1; 1 John 4:16). Without this knowledge, our followers shall die of dehydrated epistemology (Hosea 6:4).

b) Without correct teaching, it is otherwise very hard for a modern person who is used to equating Truth with the temporary gratification of his five senses, the satisfaction of his sense of *a priori* or *a posteriori*, to believe that God created the world out of Love for people, especially when there are otherwise so many seductive sources of fake miracles—ones usually consisting of electronic, biological, and pop-cultural blind alleys—which he already venerates or worships, whether knowingly or unknowingly (Romans 8:12-13). What will devote their energies toward glorifying God (1 Corinthians 10:31)?

xi) Penetrating the Gnostic Lie of Today

a) Remove the spoiled leavening: Before wiping the sand off his feet, a TACA member may wish to inspire a doubtful worldling to question his

Article II. Our Evangelistic and Spiritual Heraldry Brought Forth for all Potential and Ongoing Worshippers

apathetic, agnostic, or atheistic stance toward God instead of welcoming predators seeking his own cultural and spiritual death, which are:

1) Media sources that tell untruth (Matthew 24:6-13).

2) Candidates or holders of public office that incite him to riot. "Why do the heathen rage, and the people imagine a vain thing? The kings of the earth set themselves, and the rulers take counsel together, against the Lord" (Psalm 2:2). The Byzantine Emperor Justinian thought it prudent to forbid any admixture of the Clergy in politics: "It pleases our Clemency that the Clergy shall have nothing to do with public matters or matters pertaining to the municipal senate to which they do not belong" (*Codex*; Book 1, Title 3; Part 17; Emperor Justinian; A.D. 469).

3) Entertainments that waste his mind (2 Timothy 2:22). "The young lions do lack, and suffer hunger: but they that seek the Lord shall not want any good thing" (Psalm 34:10). "For all that is in the world, the lust of the flesh, and the lust of the eyes, and the pride of life, is not of the Father, but is of the world" (1 John 2:16).

4) Lewd or violent practices and vile ideologies that falsely promise social relevance. "But foolish and unlearned questions avoid, knowing that they do gender strifes" (2 Timothy 2:23).

Article II. Our Evangelistic and Spiritual Heraldry Brought Forth for all Potential and Ongoing Worshippers

b) Sensually redundant science offers only, at best, the tasteless fruits of secular academic genius (Ecclesiastes 12:12; Matthew 11:25; 1 Timothy 6:20). TACA elders offer the Word—a fruit far longer lasting than the vacuous momentary rewards always relished by the dispassionate or the nihilist.

    1) "O taste and see that the Lord is good: blessed is the man that trusteth in him" (Psalm 34:8).

c) The Gnostic lie is age-old: the wrongful science and its embedded sociopolitical horrors are daisy-chained across past millennia to ancient teachers, such as Cerinthus or Philo of Alexandria, whose surviving works excuse and inspire moral relativism (Acts 4:9-24). The evil fruit of this lie is multifarious, cabbalistic, and ubiquitous.

    1) God's ordinance for a redeemed Creation is that sources of joy—not of worldly impermanence or connection with a lesser "creator" or demiurge—can instead be touched and felt (Colossians 20:20-22).

d) The refreshing simplicity by which the Bible conflates God with His own credibility is most salient in the book of Hebrews, which sets forth God's greatness and limitless Love. Therein we learn that God made himself as low as men, a little "lower than the angels," so that He could become the "Captain of their Salvation" (Hebrews 2:9-10).

Article II. Our Evangelistic and Spiritual Heraldry Brought Forth for all Potential and Ongoing Worshippers

> 1) "The Lord preserveth the simple: I was brought low, and He helped me" (Psalm 116:6).
>
> 2) "For the day of vengeance is in mine heart, and the year of my redeemed is come. And I looked, and there was none to help; and I wondered that there was none to uphold: therefore mine own arm brought salvation unto me; and my fury, it upheld me" (Isaiah 63:5).

e) "His burden is light" should be ground-level catechesis (Matthew 11:28-30). The road to endless happiness is achieved by the most basic lesson of metaphysics—that, all man's ponderings are answerable within the Fellowship of collaboratively yearning hearts that are hoping to be loved by the Father (John 15:9-12). As Saint Augustine put it so perfectly and so famously, writing, "Thou hast made us for thyself, O Lord, and our heart is restless until it finds its rest in thee" (*Confessions*, Saint Augustine). The perfect ontological state of God, who created humans in His image and is therefore also omnibenevolent, sets forth His moral expectation. Thus, says Immanuel Kant:

> 1) "Where do we get the concept of God as the highest good from? Solely from the idea of moral perfection that reason lays out for us a priori and which it ties, unbreakably, to the concept of a Free Will" (*Groundwork for the Metaphysic of Morals*; Immanuel Kant; Chapter 2.; 1785).

f) Fatherly Love shall impeach the laborious error of this era of so-called quantum nihilism, as Saint John Chrysostom says:

> 1) "[God] has done what is worthy of His love towards mankind, in showing His First-born to be more glorious than all, and in setting Him forth as an example to the others, like some noble wrestler that surpasses the rest" (Homily on Hebrews; Part 4; Hebrews 2:10; Saint John Chrysostom; A.D. 407).

> 2) Therefore, TACA members must lovingly exemplify and teach the Word, because God wants all of us to be Christlike. The very term "Christian" means "little Christs" (*christianos*, Gr.); let us live, therefore, according to our title, whether such title be an epithet to some or an honor to others.

g) Neither money nor its ideologies bring happiness in life or Salvation. "For the love of money is the root of all evil: which while some coveted after, they have erred from the faith, and pierced themselves through with many sorrows" (1 Timothy 6:10). Therefore, all prosperity preaching must be viewed as anathema.

xii) Creating Catechists

> a) So that potential or reverted Christians may exchange their cynicism and animosity for the sweetness of having new parents, brothers, and sisters in God's sight, TACA members should always be godly and approachable, "having the

same love, being in full accord and of one mind" (Philippians 2:1-5).

1) Kindly, sweet instruction is especially appealing both to lonely and failed people and to currently lapsed Christians who should wish to revive their Faith, all of them comforted by our empathy for a "broken spirit and contrite heart" (Psalm 51:17).

2) Grief shall be promoted to them as coming from our "godly sorrow" instead of arising from the useless "sorrow of the world that worketh death" (2 Corinthians 7:10).

3) By illustrating this inversion of emotional purpose, evangelism teaches that it is better to weep over good deeds than to weep over wrongdoing (1 Peter 3:17). The sorrow over not being clever, powerful, rich, or beautiful enough to avoid shame shall now be exchanged for the sorrow that "worketh repentance to salvation not to be repented of" (2 Corinthians 7:10).

b) So that the spiritual fruits of Galatians 5:22-23 may replace every spiritual speck of one bad leaven after the other, an "unleavened" person shall begin to resemble the image of God in which they were made (Genesis 1:27; 1 Corinthians 5:7-8). Over time they will be able to say along with Saint Patrick in his beautiful Lorica, "Christ in the heart of everyone who thinks of me, Christ in the mouth of everyone who speaks of me, Christ in every eye that sees me, Christ in every ear that hears me" (The Lorica of Saint Patrick).

xiii) The Happy State of Being Reborn in TACA

a) The reborn catechized person is a far happier man or woman; no amount of cleverness, power, wealth, or beauty, falsely promised by pop culture and all its empty "multiverses," could have otherwise overcome the evil from which Christ alone has saved all of us. The old pagan evils of bygone days—and yet new again in these end times—shall no longer have a stake in any of us (2 Corinthians 5:17).

b) TACA members shall together die to the uses of sin (Romans 6:11).

1) A person born again shall thus be loveable, forgiving, hardworking, and fearless (Luke 6:30-42).

2) The "Gospel of Nice" must be avoided, because it is deadly. On March 27, 2018, the Dean of the Cathedral Church of Saint James of Toronto, Canada, was present at the medically assisted dual suicide of George and Shirley Brickenden. The Rev. Canon Andrew Asbil, who, as of September 2023, became the Bishop of Toronto, also presided at the funeral for the couple, who died in front of Rev. Asbil in their beds, at home ("Medically Assisted Death Allows Couple Married Almost 73 Years to Die Together"; Kelly Grant; *Globe and Mail;* April 1, 2018;

https://www.theglobeandmail.com/canada/article-medically-assisted-death-allows-couple-married-almost-73-years-to-die; Accessed, April 29, 2003). One month prior to the double suicide, the Anglican Church of Canada published a pastoral manual, along with a companion study guide, providing religious advice concerning "termination of life support," "termination of treatment," and "euthanasia" (*In Sure and Certain Hope: Resources to Assist Pastoral and Theological Approaches to Physician Assisted Dying; Resource & Study Guide;* The General Synod of the Anglican Church of Canada: February 2018). Assigning scripture from the English Standard Version of the Bible to its homicidal vision of the *summum bonum,* the despicable enchiridion shamelessly isolated a verse from the Prophet Jeremiah as an italicized pull quote to support its aims: "But seek the welfare of the city where I have sent you into exile, and pray to the Lord on its behalf, for in its welfare you will find your welfare" (Jeremiah 29:7; *ibid. Resource*, p. 4). The 48-page *Resource* and its 36-page *Study Guide* technically do not advocate for assisted suicide, nor is the word "suicide" even used in the latter. Even worse, they restrict the minister from issuing the biblical prohibition against suicide, as the taking of one's life regards the destruction of Eternal Life of Christians, whom God intends shall never perish: "Say unto them, As I live, saith the Lord God, I have no pleasure in the death of the wicked; but that the wicked turn from his way and live" (Ezekiel 33:11). The *Study Guide* reads, "In the first place, it is important to note that *In Sure and Certain Hope* is not intended to provide moral arguments for or against a decision to resort to medically-assisted dying" (p. 7). "There may be reasons why, for example, it may not be the parish pastor, other clergy, or the best teacher in the parish who is best-suited to serve in this role" (p. 14). Both Old and New Testaments clearly hold us accountable as regards confronting the sins of an offender: "go and tell him his fault" (Matthew 18:15); and "if thou dost not speak to warn the wicked from his way, that wicked man shall die in his iniquity; but his blood will I require at thine hand" (Ezekiel 33:8). So, too, the Bible is the source for helping God make man perfect by issuing such instruction and reproof (2 Timothy 3:16). The *Resource* advises that the participant ask God to bless the suicide, praying, "Help me know that you will bless my choice to me" (p. 30). Note that this practice is not unlike the prayers that have been offered up to bless abortion and abortion clinics ("Clergy Bless Ohio Abortion Clinic in Show of Solidarity"; www.nonprofitquarterly.org; October 12, 2015; accessed May 30, 2023). Instead of accepting as "prophecy" that the State should have the authority to allow a person to kill himself, the TACA Diocese must instead decide that Sacred Scripture, not secular legislators,

Article II. Our Evangelistic and Spiritual Heraldry Brought Forth for all Potential and Ongoing Worshippers

proclaims God's authority: "For the prophecy came not in old time by the will of man: but holy men of God spake as they were moved by the Holy Ghost" (2 Peter 2:21). Fellowship with such churches as the Anglican Diocese of Toronto shall be entirely avoided, remembering the stern admonition: "Be ye not unequally yoked together with unbelievers: for what fellowship hath righteousness with unrighteousness? and what communion hath light with darkness? And what concord hath Christ with Belial?" (2 Corinthians 6:14-15)? Judged as harvesting wrongful fruit (Matthew 7:20), the Anglican Communion, which retains this Synod as a Province, should take note of the public, synodal mandating of assisted suicide as publicized by its Canadian Diocese. To traditionalist Anglicans, noting the misuse of Jeremiah 29:7 to justify religious approval of state-sanctioned suicide (*ibid. Resource*; Appendix I; Submission to the Special Joint Committee on Physician Assisted Dying; pp. 37-43; The Anglican Church of Canada: 3 Feb. 2016), any such "Communion" with the Anglican Church of Canada is forbidden, as it bears no resemblance to a traditional continuance of real Anglicanism. "Be not deceived; God is not mocked: for whatsoever a man soweth, that shall he also reap" (Galatians 6:7)—"Wherefore come out from among them, and be ye separate, saith the Lord, and touch not the unclean thing; and I will receive you" (2 Corinthians 6:17).

Article II. Our Evangelistic and Spiritual Heraldry Brought Forth for all Potential and Ongoing Worshippers

3) Our Triune God, who is One, is watching the Faithful (Psalm 37:23-25). "And Jesus answered him, The first of all the commandments is, Hear, O Israel; The Lord our God is one Lord: And thou shalt love the Lord thy God with all thy heart, and with all thy soul, and with all thy mind, and with all thy strength: this is the first commandment. And the second is like, namely this, Thou shalt love thy neighbour as thyself. There is none other commandment greater than these" (Mark 12:29-31).

c) The conclusion of all approaches is patience: Our TACA Diocese is like a boat in a sea of grievous storms, which welcomes and affirms the unconditional Faith of all seekers of Christ's hand (Matthew 14:28-31).

xiv) Richness of Anglicanism

a) Now, because the Bible is more enjoyable than any episode of the TV program "Game of Thrones" (we speak of the tales of Jehu, of Elisha, of Gideon, of King David, and of Moses, to name a few), through proper and thoughtful teaching we can enjoyably win over the attention of any lost lamb, who needs to grasp why the world was created and what purpose humans serve, and therefore what purpose he personally serves in the world.

b) The hymns contained within our 1940 U.S. Episcopal Hymn are of such sweetness that they could captivate even the most jaded and secular soul. The profundity of the Athanasius Creed,

Article II. Our Evangelistic and Spiritual Heraldry Brought Forth for all Potential and Ongoing Worshippers

which exposits the hypostatic union, is worthy of the contemplation of even the most intellectual and philosophical person of our present day.

c) Anglicanism's ancient history of the See of Glastonbury and the Archbishopric of Canterbury—storied churches of the Celtic and Anglo-Saxon languages—is framed by speculation that Joseph of Arimathea was not only one of the 70 disciples but also the one who founded the Apostolic See in Glastonbury.

> 1) Saint John of Chrysostom, in his Homily on John 19, wrote: "After this came Joseph of Arimathea, being a Disciple. Not one of the twelve, but perhaps one of the seventy."
>
> 2) Chrysostom's speculation may add gravity to the account given in 1125 by William of Malmesbury about the Bishop of Rome, Eleutherius, in A.D. 189, about whom Malmesbury claims that Joseph of Arimathea had been sent to England by Saint Philip the Apostle to found Saint Mary's Church at Glastonbury, "affirming that the church was built by no other hands than those of disciples of Christ; this is not unlikely, for if the Apostle Philip preached in Gaul, as Freculf avers [*Twelve Histories*; Freculphus Lexoviensis; Book II; A.D. 852], he would naturally have desired to sow the seeds of discourse also beyond the sea" (*Chronicle of the Kings of England. From the earliest period to the reign of King Stephen;*

Article II. Our Evangelistic and Spiritual Heraldry Brought Forth for all Potential and Ongoing Worshippers

William of Malmesbury; Book I; Chapter I; p. 21; 1847).

3) Antiquity's portrayals of British Christians should refute anyone who may wrongly associate Traditional Anglicanism with the infamy of King Henry VIII. There is no current spiritual or historical connection between the English Reformation and the Anglican Communion and Traditional Anglicanism other than a profound hope that the ancient foundational parishes of Canterbury and Glastonbury will once again adopt the orthodoxy with which Anglicanism was in ancient times founded, but which has been (except for about the last 50 years or so) all but totally abandoned (*The Affirmation of Saint Louis;* Article 1. "Principles of Doctrine"; Footnote-1: "1992"; Congress of Concerned Churchmen, St. Louis, MO: 1978). TACA derives its examples from antiquity and the rich spiritual Christian tradition of the Celts and the Britons that even predates the arrival of Rome, albeit its chancery is located in Newton, North Carolina, in the United States of America.

4) Although TACA and the English Reformation spring from different religious traditions, the stories and lessons of that English Reformation era ought not to be ignored, for all Anglicans should attempt to reach people's hearts by being "all things to all men, that I might by all means save some" (1 Corinthians 9:19-22).

Article II. Our Evangelistic and Spiritual Heraldry Brought Forth for all Potential and Ongoing Worshippers

>Christ's example is timeless, and we can draw from many lessons from the past in seeking and saving the lost. Thus TACA should not alienate those Christians who have come from the tradition of the English Reformation, should they desire to enter TACA, so as not to erect a stumbling block to them in their understanding of where TACA fits into the overall framework of Christian tradition as they understand it. The common English heritage and overall spiritual tradition should serve as a point of commonality.

d) Let it also be no small cause to overcome any source of superstition, pseudoscience, "fake news," paranoid hoaxes, "false flags," or paranormal fanfare, all of it framed by twists of hyperbole and fallacious rhetoric employing the English language (Matthew 12:36) bent on creating the fear of "wars and rumors of wars" (Matthew 24:6). Let Faith, Hope, and Love stabilize the soul (1 Corinthians 13:13), imbuing the heart with discernment, to avoid the "divers and strange doctrines" (Hebrews 13:9), all of it rooted in a dependence on ignorance and a lowered tolerance against crafty linguistics:

>1) Faith, more than the vacuous promises of revisionist text or media, assures the mind of the great promise given to those who call upon the name of Father: they "shall be saved" (Romans 10:13). Faith, "being the substance of things hoped for, the evidence of things not

seen" (Hebrews 11:1), consoles the heart (John 14:1). A comforted heart and mind can embrace a comparison of oneself to the woman at the well, she who shares our confession that Christ is God because He knew everything we ever did (John 4:29). There is nothing ever to fear while, with trust and joy, we "draw water out of the wells of salvation" (Isaiah 12:2-3).

e) A prospective politically conservative parishioner should feel enticed by the hard, unapologetic Love exhibited in our Commination exorcism—an intense Litany that has been available in our lexicon since 1549. TACA means tough Liturgical business! (*Book of Common Prayer*; Scotland; 1637).

xv) Leavening the Whole Lump for God

a) Traditional Anglicanism gives us all the tools we need as Christians to go anywhere we want and speak Truth to anybody, especially to persons whose Prevenient Grace has not been darkened, and thus a spiritual state that is still open to Salvation and yet precedes conversion. The inborn capacity in all humans to choose good over evil necessarily includes the Free Will to choose belief in Jesus, so that oneself and one's family may be saved (Acts 16:31). This Prevenient Grace allows us to freely choose the gift of God's own Grace, which is the only power to redeem us (Titus 2:11). "For by grace are ye saved through faith; and that not of yourselves: it is the gift of God" (Ephesians 2:8).

Article II. Our Evangelistic and Spiritual Heraldry Brought Forth for all Potential and Ongoing Worshippers

> b) Thus, anyone who seeks Salvation can be saved, and can be a member of TACA, only if he or she chooses unconditionally to believe wholeheartedly in Christ (John 3:16). The Great Commission has been handed down to TACA and to any other traditional orthodox Christian churches with whom TACA is united in fellowship:
>
>> 1) "Go ye therefore, and teach all nations, baptizing them in the name of the Father, and of the Son, and of the Holy Ghost: Teaching them to observe all things whatsoever I have commanded you: and, lo, I am with you always, even unto the end of the world" (Matthew 28:19-20).
>
> xvi) Prevenient Grace Trumps Idolatrous Cynicism
>
>> a) Good ministers shall know that each sincere person seeking Jesus enjoys the ability, on whatever individual level of his or her Grace, to join the evangelistic and charitable mission of the Church—or, just to be part of TACA in happy consolation. *Sola fide* existed long before there was a Vatican or a Reformation. One of the interesting characters of the so-called Pre-Reformation was the iconoclast Bp. Claudius of Turin, a most hardcore polemicist, who, upon his elevation to the Bishopric of Turin in A.D. 817, was known to match his enthusiasm over Penal Substitutional Atonement (the idea that Christ suffered bodily injury and death as punishment for human sin) with his penchant for smashing the "sluttish abominations" of sculptures within

Article II. Our Evangelistic and Spiritual Heraldry Brought Forth for all Potential and Ongoing Worshippers

the churches of Turin—that is, until the congregations cursed and "nearly swallowed me whole." He was also known for rigorously defending against Muslim invaders in armed combat along the shores of his native Spain (*Early Medieval Theology*; *Defense and Reply to Abbot Theodemir*; Claudius of Turin; Trans. Allen Cabaniss; Vol. IX; p. 242; Library of Christian Classics, 1958). His disdain for the expensive extravagance of the Holy Roman Empire and his love for the doctrine of *sola fide* were matched by the passionate freedom he felt while contemplating the exquisite perfection of the Atonement. His refusal to abide the "Declaration of Faith" allowing the use of religious iconography in churches during the Seventh Session of the Second Council of Nicaea kept alive the controversy of Iconoclasm that had been formally reviewed at the Second (A.D. 553) and Third (A.D. 681) Councils of Constantinople; the Quinisext Council (A.D. 692); the rejected "Emperor's" Council of Hieria (A.D. 754); and, of the Second Council of Nicaea (A.D. 787) which legislated finally in support of iconography. He thus made it his own cause to protect the Church against idolatry, albeit very loudly and with some real spillage. His passion cost him many friendships and hurt his reputation. In his Preface to the *Commentary to the Book of Kings,* he wrote that he was "living among scorpions" and always penned his other commentaries with like intense hyperbole: "[God's] anger did not blaze carnally for a carnal observance and sustain the penalty

Article II. Our Evangelistic and Spiritual Heraldry Brought Forth for all Potential and Ongoing Worshippers

set for those who did not keep it, but that believers might be in themselves entirely free from fear of such penalty..." (*ibid. Commentary on Galatians*; p. 229-230; Library of Christian Classics, 1958). The writings of Claudius of Turin influenced *Satisfaction Doctrine of Atonement* by Saint Anselm, who defined the substitution that was undertaken by Christ for sin—albeit the latter theologian engaged in semantic intensity in a more eloquent manner: "Therefore the honor taken away must be repaid, or punishment must follow; otherwise, either God will not be just to Himself, or He will be weak in respect to both parties; and this it is impious even to think of" (*Deus Homo*; Book 1; Chapter 13; Saint Anselm of Canterbury; 1094).

> 1) "So then because thou art lukewarm, and neither cold nor hot, I will spue thee out of my mouth" (Revelation 3:16).
>
> 2) It is less shameful to love the Gospel fervently than to stay glued to the void of the Internet or other media, or to be transfixed in horror at world events, or to sin boldly (1 Peter 3:14). The members of TACA shall boldly and shamelessly warn future Christians worldwide to renounce the apple-gazing that the devil always feverishly encourages (Genesis 3; 1 John 2:16; James 1:14-15).
>
> b) Saint Prosper of Aquitaine recognized that Prevenient Grace, rather than meritorious works (e.g., handing out free turkeys and coats), is the

Article II. Our Evangelistic and Spiritual Heraldry Brought Forth for all Potential and Ongoing Worshippers

> mark of each person's inborn calling to seek to belong to God. This Grace transcends all worldly and legalistic trappings, and if the agent is properly catechized, leads the soul toward that longed-for *theosis* and his hardy service for God that becomes a natural outgrowth of that Faith, resulting in a religion that is "pure and undefiled" (James 1:27). Saint Prosper remarks thus:

> c) "No wonder either, that pagan philosophy opposes the Gospel of the Cross of Christ, when Jewish learning also resists it. We conclude that neither the learned nor the illiterate of whatever race or rank come to God led by human reason; but every man who is converted to God is first stirred by God's Grace. For man is no light unto himself, nor can he inflame his own heart with a ray of his own light" (*The Call to All Nations*; Ch. 8; St. Prosper of Aquitaine; A.D. 529).

xvii) The Holy Ghost Conquers Artificial Intelligence

> a) There is true joy in the knowledge that the Holy Ghost cannot be defeated. The father of desert monasticism, Evagrius Ponticus, ably penetrated the doubts of his postulants by showing that one's soul can be indwelled with the Holy Ghost, as is assured in 1 Corinthians 3:16, wherein the Corinthians were admonished: "Know ye not that ye are the temple of God, and that the Spirit of God dwelleth in you?" God, thus enjoying Fellowship inside of us, cannot be conquered, because the Spirit is not a "creature" (whereas an AI hobgoblin is merely a monster).

Article II. *Our Evangelistic and Spiritual Heraldry Brought Forth for all Potential and Ongoing Worshippers*

So saith Ponticus of the Spirit: "He consists of essence and sanctification, and is therefore composite. But who is mad enough to describe the Holy Spirit as composite, and not simple, and consubstantial with the Father and the Son?" (*Epistula Fidei*; Section 32; Evagrius Ponticus; Rev. Blomfield Jackson, transl.; 1895).

b) Human attention must be rescued by the Gospel messages, delivered in every instance in which the mind has been taken captive by the demonic infestation (Matthew 12:44-45), the vain whisperings of "philosophy and empty deceit" (Colossians 2:8) into each brain that is hounded by "irreverent babble"(2 Timothy 2:16)—as if the person is a kind of "Schrödinger's Cat," her soul, sitting near a fragile vial of poison inside a dark box, not knowable to her own family as being alive or dead, but obliged by everybody as being both (*In Search of Schrödingers Cat*; John Gribbin; Part Two: "Quantum Mechanics"; Chapter 9; p. 203; 1984). Indeed, if a loved one is saved from the Culture of Death, after she is revived (like the cat being rescued from the box), the human bullies or mind pimps at the other side of the Internet will seek vengeance against the Christian discipleship by which their captive is rescued from them, just as the enslavers of the fortune teller were so angry that the Apostle exorcized their captive (Acts 16:16-18). Today's mind captors will try ever harder, with the sleeplessness of the ubiquitous Internet always calling out to her, to repossess its programmers' subject, as a demonic foray that demands constant sober and vigilant Christian advocacy over all the church and the home (1 Peter 5:8-9). Availing a delivered person, one who is seeking the contemplative life, Ponticus's ministry, as it is mentioned in his work *The Praktikos*, offers a sweet window into the rebirth of hope in a saved person. She is removed from seducers of the appetite, and has now willed herself to learn that it is true that God will not tempt her beyond her ability to resist sin, and that hope for happiness can indeed be restored with help against any demonic discouragement (1 Corinthians 10:13). "No other demon follows on immediately after this one but after its struggle the soul is taken over by a peaceful condition and by unspeakable joy" (*The Praktikos*; Part 12; Section 6; Evagrius Ponticus; Luke Dysinger, transl.; A.D. 399). Therefore, TACA encourages the contemplative life, whether in following the direct teachings or derivations from the saintly examples and writings of the Desert Fathers, such as Ponticus; of the Cappadocians such as Saint Gregory of Nyssa or his brother Basil the Great; the Conferences and Institutes of Saint John Cassian; the sermons of Saint John Chrysostom; or the Rules of Saint Benedict or Augustine, or in the honoring of traditions left for the Church, the Abbey, the Deanery, or the home, as given to us by such saints as Brigid, Francis, Patrick, and countless others in the Communion of Saints.

xviii) Conclusion of TACA Evangelism

    a) Our Traditional Anglican Church of America has long persisted with confidence, though seeking only modest mention in books or periodicals via the Internet, or over airwaves—for half a century, armed with the security, maturity, scholasticism, charitable works, and confidence of the fatherly men who are its ministers and founders—a spiritual heraldry proven out of these truths, that all people have the capacity to understand Sacred Scripture and Holy Tradition and ought to desire it for themselves.

B. Catholic Calling of All Christians

i) The word "catholic" comes from the Greek adjective καθολικός (*katholikos*). It translates as "general" or "universal". The Greek adverb καθόλου (*katholou*) comprises the preposition "κατά," translated as "according to," and the adjective "ὅλος," meaning the "whole." The word *katholou*, then, from which we derive the word "catholic" indicates each Christian's (or Christian Body's) ecclesiastical position "according to the whole"—enjoying commonality with all true believers in Christ, and standing in general collaboration with the many denominations of Trinitarian Christians.

ii) Therefore, the modifier "catholic" signifies that the totality of the Christian Faith within all of Christendom is perfectly complete, embraces the fullness of devotion to Jesus, and without shortages of or defects in that Faith in or knowledge of

Article II. Our Evangelistic and Spiritual Heraldry Brought Forth for all Potential and Ongoing Worshippers

Logos—in other words, without heresy. The word "catholic" has nothing whatsoever to do with the bishopric of Rome, Italy, by which "Catholic" has been coined and "trademarked," as though the Roman Catholic Church had the right to wrest this most wholesome term from the rest of Christendom and reserve it for themselves as a brand. Today, the word "catholic" is usually taken to mean "Catholic," and hence "Roman Catholic," and it is viewed unfairly by many Protestants to be equivalent to "popery." TACA Clergy should make the effort to contextualize the term as it was always meant, and should not feel any reservation about using it. We would do well to remember the words of St. Vincent Lorens, who wrote in his *Commonitorium* that a test of the truth of a matter within the Christian Faith was whether it has been believed "everywhere, always, and by all" (*Commonitorium*, St. Vincent of Lorens, Chapter 2). It simply isn't true that "catholic" has always been understood to mean "Roman Catholic." In fact, the English convention of capitalizing proper nouns and using lower case for general nouns did not yet exist in the language in which the first known instance of "catholic" in relation to "church" was ever found in Christianity: Greek. At the time that the Letter to the Smyrnaeans was written by Saint Ignatius of Antioch circa 110 A.D., the Greek text was written in all capital letters. The important excerpt on this subject is this: "wherever Jesus Christ is, there is the catholic church [καθολική εκκλησία]" (*ibid.* Chapter 8). If you reference this same sentence from any Roman Catholic source, it will read "... there is the Catholic

Article II. Our Evangelistic and Spiritual Heraldry Brought Forth for all Potential and Ongoing Worshippers

Church." A discerning mind will take note of his or her source material in drawing spiritual conclusions about any important Christian matter, this being just one of many such matters.

iii) The word "catholic" may refer to all the Church (*ecclesia*) as spread throughout the globe, with no essential lesson or participle of Logos missing from it. Thus, one's "catholicism" means that he or she is part of the genuine and universal Church of Jesus Christ. "Fulfil ye my joy, that ye be likeminded, having the same love, being of one accord, of one mind" (Philippians 2:2). St. Vincent elaborates thus: "[Catholic] comprehends all universally. This rule we shall observe if we follow universality, antiquity, consent" (*ibid. Commonitorium*). The Faithful must not allow themselves to be confused or brought to shame over dubious allegations by the Roman Catholic Church (or any other) of "heresy" if you aren't counted among their ranks. Using the principles established by Irenaeus in *Adversus Haereses,* the Christian must self-protect against having their "conscience seared" (1 Timothy 4:2) by those who desire to vaunt their "Church™" above all other churches. That which divides orthodoxy from heresy is not as long of a list as such denominations pretend to be the case.

B. Good Tidings of Great Joy (Luke 2:10)

i) Give thanks for the catholicism that has been hard won: Since A.D. 50, there have been 12 pre-Ecumenical Councils and 21 Ecumenical Councils, seven of the latter known as *canonical* by

Article II. Our Evangelistic and Spiritual Heraldry Brought Forth for all Potential and Ongoing Worshippers

Traditionalist Anglicans and both Western and Eastern Orthodox. Along with the nearly countless ancient regional councils (e.g., the Council of Arles, the Council of Orange) and Traditionalist Anglican and Episcopalian synods, these global assemblies were invoked to mediate, for the universal *ecclesia*, "an expression of the mind of the whole body of the Faithful both clerical and lay, the sensus communis of the Church" (*A Select Library of the Nicene and Post-Nicene Fathers of the Christian Church, Second Series*; Vol. 14: *The Seven Ecumenical Councils;* Henry R. Percival; Philip Schaff, Ed.; Part II; p. 4; 1886).

a) The good catholic news (i.e., the Gospel) is announced through the combined use of Sacred Scripture and Sacred Tradition, without excluding any class or kind of persons, each of whose members is made in the image of God, and thus has Prevenient Grace, given by God alone (John 3:16; Acts 4:12).

b) Chastening, levied through generations of Church fathers to create good children is at first unpleasant but "yieldeth the peaceable fruit of righteousness unto them which are exercised thereby" (Hebrews 12:9-11). As was Israel, the catholic Church is a "city of righteousness, the faithful city," the Bride of Christ, worthy to be protected and defended. And to that end, our Church fathers and our TACA Clergy today have asked, and do ask, Almighty God to "purely purge away thy dross and take away all thy tin" (Isaiah 1:24-25). Let this embolden Faith (1 John 5:14).

Article II. Our Evangelistic and Spiritual Heraldry Brought Forth for all Potential and Ongoing Worshippers

1) The Nicene Creed, one of the ancient professions of our Christian ecclesiastical Faith, commits Christians to holding a belief in the Four Marks of the Church—that it is "One, Holy, Catholic and Apostolic." This denotation was added after the Creed was first promulgated at the Council of Nicaea in 325 A.D., and it is one of the tenets of our catholic Faith.

2) The Four Marks of the Church were also inserted at the Council of Constantinople in 381 A.D.

3) Catholicism was thereby defended from such heresies as Pelagius's idea that one's Salvation has no need of God's redemptive Grace. Moreover:

4) Keeping a conciliatory but steadfast attitude toward Truth in ministry is epitomized by ancient catholic assemblies, such as the councils of Ephesus and then Chalcedon. When a Diocese or Synod of today seeks inspiration to preserve precious interior uniformity, it should consider the past sacrifices that affirm our permanent precious understanding of Christ's nature: After traveling to Ecumenical Councils from numerous points within the Roman world, "many of the bishops and clerics were overtaken with illness, and much burdened by the expense, and some even died," handling heat, cold, and squalid accommodations, striving to heal divisions in

Article II. Our Evangelistic and Spiritual Heraldry Brought Forth for all Potential and Ongoing Worshippers

the catholic Church (Letter of the [Ephesus] Synod to Pope Celestine; A.D. 431). Our sources concern conciliation between the Five Ancient Patriarchates, or Apostolic Sees, of that more unified catholic Church, whose constituents longed to standardize a rational definition of the Godhead that could be readily understood by the human mind (*A History of the Councils of the Church: From the Original Documents, to the Close of the Second Council of Nicaea A.D. 787*; Karl Josef von Hefele; Vol. 1-7; 1855-1874; *Sacrorum Conciliorum Nova et Amplissima Collectio*; Giovanni Domenico Mansi; 1758-1798). As such, Chalcedon strove to sustain Catholic cohesion by affirming that man will "profit unto salvation," by abiding the reality of the hypostatic union (ὑπόστασις, *hypóstasis*)—that there are two natures in Christ united unchangeably, inseparably, unconfusedly" (Council of Chalcedon; Session II; A.D. 450; John 14:20). Yet there is much utility in reviewing just how the affirmation of the hypostatic union was promoted through patriarchates with differing views about Christ's nature. Firstly, refuting the Monophysitism of the heretic Eutyches (that God portrayed Himself as a human, but is not human, His humanity having been absorbed by His divine nature, that of being God Himself) and the flawed "Dyophysitism" of Nestorius (that Christ is simultaneously truly God and truly human, but is a new kind of God-person, known as the "Prosopon"—which is why

Article II. Our Evangelistic and Spiritual Heraldry Brought Forth for all Potential and Ongoing Worshippers

Nestorius considered Mary the Christ-bearer and not the *Theotokos*), this Council promulgated the Christology of Christ's holding the two natures—fully divine and fully human—simultaneously and in complete unity (*ibid.* Chalcedon, Sessions I, II). Joined together as God and man, simultaneously, in hypostatic union, Christ's two natures came to be understood as follows: "each nature being preserved and being united in one Person and subsistence, not separated or divided into two persons, but one and the same Son and only-begotten, God the Word, our Lord Jesus Christ, as the Prophets of old time have spoken concerning Him, and as the Lord Jesus Christ has taught us, and as the Creed of the Fathers has delivered to us" (*ibid.* Chalcedon, Session III). Proceeding not from the Father alone—"but the Spirit Himself of God and the Father, who proceeds also from him, and is not alien from the Son, according to his essence"—the concept of the *filioque* (Latin: "and from the Son") was also thereby acknowledged at Chalcedon (*ibid.* Chalcedon, Session II). Twenty-nine of the original thirty Canons were ratified by Abp. Leo I of Rome, the twenty-eighth, which had given the Patriarchate of Constantinople equal temporal status with Rome, being nullified by Leo. Although Canon 28 was issued during the day of his absence, Leo protested against 28, arguing that it violated Canon 6 of the Nicene Council, which placed Rome first, Alexandria second, and Antioch third, and established that

Apostolic Sees had to have been founded for Christendom by an actual Apostle (Constantinople did not meet this condition). This canon was denounced by the papal legates, who themselves had not been present during its passing by the other bishops, but although 28 was never ratified by Leo, it was also never nullified beyond its receiving Leo's mere line-item veto. Leo himself acknowledged, in a letter written to his ally, the Eastern Roman Empress Aelia Pulcheria, Letter 116, about a year after the Council, that his hopeful nullification was being ignored by the Illyrian bishops, who had already subscribed to Canon 28, awarding their obedient sole subsidiarity to Patriarch Anatolius of Constantinople. Although the text of this letter appears to have been suppressed (it does not appear in publicly available collections beyond a brief recently written summary under its nominal listing), it is clear that Leo's vetoing of Canon 28 was never obeyed en masse throughout the Pentarchy. Letter 106 displayed Leo's reproaching of Anatolius in regards to the Patriarch's leadership in the violation of Canon 6 of Nicaea I, but Anatolius would never add his own nullification of Canon 28. The daughter of Roman Emperor Theodosius I, Galla Placidia, in accordance with her late father's splitting of the Empire into West and East, had already bequeathed the Pannonian Diocese of Illyricum to Pulcheria's brother, Eastern Emperor Theodosius II in A.D. 425. This gift temporally

Article II. Our Evangelistic and Spiritual Heraldry Brought Forth for all Potential and Ongoing Worshippers

placed the Illyricum Episcopate under the Patriarchate of Constantinople. The records of this Balkan Diocese were lost when, starting in A.D. 454, the Huns, and then the Ostrogoths, conquered Pannonia (*ibid.* Chalcedon, Session XVI). As a side note, it is worth remembering that the much rockier earlier Council of Ephesus, which had convened 20 years earlier, had used the term "catholic" definitively twice—firstly, with tactical wisdom, to signal affection for the disgruntled Bp. John of Antioch, famous despite his sudden hostility toward the Synod. John retaining stalwart loyalty to a heretic named Nestorius, even to the point of his creating the schismatic "The Holy Synod," advertised boldly on a placard in Ephesus—not to defend Nestorius against that Council's charges of heresy, but to satiate John's own bitterness at the presiders over his having been excluded from the Council for his late arrival (Council of Ephesus; Session IV; July 16, A.D. 431). Matters could have stayed bitter, but the Ephesus bishops politely countered that their president, Patriarch Cyril of Alexandria, and the bishops at Ephesus "could not be understood in anything but a catholic sense" (*ibid.*). As days progressed, they began to coax John away from Nestorianism toward Cyril's Miaphysitism (the Alexandrian view of Christology that is very similar to Chalcedonian Dyophysitism, but which depicts Jesus as having one solid nature)—the idea that the Lord is composed of His being fully God plus being

Article II. Our Evangelistic and Spiritual Heraldry Brought Forth for all Potential and Ongoing Worshippers

fully man, instead of separately having two constituent natures that are unified in a single hypostasis; (to the Miaphysites, these natures are dually compounded as a single element—the "physeis" version of Christ's nature). The bone of contention really was not due to John's fervent loyalty toward Nestorius, but was rather borne of the vagueness of the Nestorian version of Christology and its harsh demotion of Mary, as mentioned earlier, from Theotokos to her being a mere ordinary sinner who happened to be the Christ-bearer (*The XII. Anathematisms of St. Cyril, and Nestorius's Counter-anathematisms*; Excursus to Anath. I., On the word Qeotovko; A.D. 431). John became reconciled with Cyril two years after the Council of Ephesus, via the "Formula of Reunion," by which the spirit of catholic confraternal reconciliation may for history's eyes be said to have been exemplified, but which also may be interpreted as diplomatic pretext to convey some of the affectionate finesse that was ably demonstrated at the Council of Ephesus concerning the relationship between the Apostolic See of Rome and John's own Antiochian Patriarchate, its leader, John, now being anxious to renounce the heretical Nestorianism in keeping his patriarchate buoyant. In commending the Apostle Saint Peter (the actual founder of Antioch) as the key-holder, the Council's three legates, who were acting as judges in Ephesus under the Council president, Patriarch Cyril of Alexandria, wrote

Article II. Our Evangelistic and Spiritual Heraldry Brought Forth for all Potential and Ongoing Worshippers

the non-biblical exegesis of Matthew 16:19 that speciously elevated Rome above its long-held role of patriarchal moderator upwards into the temporal role of portraying a rhetorically "consecrated" supreme pontificate: "It is doubtful to none, nay it has been known to all ages, that holy and blessed Peter, the prince and head of the Apostles, the column of the Faith, the foundation of the Catholic Church, received from our Lord Jesus Christ, the Saviour and Redeemer of the human race, the keys of the Kingdom, and that to him was given the power of binding and loosing sins, who until this day and for ever lives and judges in his successors. His successor in order and his representative, our holy and most blessed Pope Celestine" (Council of Ephesus; Session III; July 11, A.D. 431). Finally, the Nicene Creed was prominently declared at Ephesus to be the sole profession of ecclesiastical belief shared throughout the catholic Church, and the presbyter, Abp. Nestorius of Constantinople, was promptly laicized—his doctrine formally condemned as a heresy at Chalcedon in A.D. 451 (*ibid.* Session VI, VII; July 31, A.D. 431). Also, because Nestorius's treatment of the Theotokos had finally repulsed John, the Miaphysite Cyril now welcomed John and his bishops of Antioch—those who were still loyal to John—back into catholic fellowship with the rest of the Pentarchy (i.e., altogether, Constantinople, Alexandria, Jerusalem, Rome, and Antioch). This confraternity, aiming its

Article II. Our Evangelistic and Spiritual Heraldry Brought Forth for all Potential and Ongoing Worshippers

subsequent decretals toward Chalcedon eighteen years anon, was by then, because of the Council of Ephesus, shared ever more strongly between the Miaphysite Patriarchy of Alexandria and the Dyophysite Bishopric of Rome. Where Jesus is concerned, the catholic Church is excellently defined as the brotherly coexistence of all Trinitarian churches, because "My Father's house has many mansions" (John 14:2). *The Formula of Reunion,* penned on the heels of Ephesus, is printed here, because its Christology ought to suggest the conciliatory aim of Theology, whenever the threat of schism or dissolution is foreshadowed within Christendom:

— "We confess, our lord Jesus Christ, the only begotten Son of God perfect God and perfect man of a rational soul and a body, begotten before all ages from the Father in his godhead, the same in the last days, for us and for our salvation, born of Mary the virgin, according to his humanity, one and the same consubstantial with the Father in godhead and consubstantial with us in humanity, for a union of two natures took place. Therefore we confess one Christ, one Son, one Lord. According to this understanding of the unconfused union, we confess the holy virgin to be Theotokos, the mother of God, because God the Word (Logos) took flesh and became man and from his very conception united to himself the temple he took from her. As to the evangelical and apostolic expressions about the Lord, we know that theologians treat some in common as of one person and distinguish others as of two natures, and interpret the god-befitting ones in connection with the godhead of Christ and the lowly ones with his humanity" (*The Formula of Reunion;* A.D. 433).

5) Mention of these Councils meanwhile serves to underscore the irreplaceable necessity of resisting every heresy with every possible rigor. As Saint Paul the Apostle wrote, "Watch ye, stand fast in the faith, quit you like men, be strong" (1 Corinthians 16:13).

6) Dying to the self (Romans 6:11): Before he demanded that the "bloodthirsty beasts" devour him in front of Emperor Trajan in the arena, Saint Ignatius of Antioch armed the Church with an exegesis of Isaiah's verses of comfort for Israel (*Codex Colbertinus: The Martyrdom of Saint Ignatius;* Philo of Cilicia; Chapter 3; A.D. 108; Johannes Engebretsen Belsheim, Ed.; 1888). He proclaimed the Visible Catholic Church to be the seat of Christ as the "ensign to nations" (Isaiah 5:26), under which the "sons" and "daughters" will be embraced in the arms of Christ under the "standard" (a military flag as is an ensign) of the Cross (Isaiah 5:26, 49:22; *Epistle to the Smyrnaeans;* Saint Ignatius of Antioch; Intro.; A.D. 108). Ignatius beheld the authority of the Bishop in all ecclesiastical matters (Baptism, Eucharist,

meetings, "love feasts," etc.), without whom the Church can do nothing. "Wherever the Bishop shall appear, there let the multitude [of the people] also be; even as, wherever Jesus Christ is, there is the catholic Church" (*ibid.* Chapter 8). Despite God's enemies, the role of the Bishop is to ensure that the Church Militant shall "stand aloof from such heretics" (*ibid.* Chapter 7) and that the flock shall "exercise repentance towards God" (*ibid.* Chapter 9).

c) TACA members shall also benefit from the teachings of John the Apostle, Polycarp, Irenaeus, and John Chrysostom. Each of these saints protected Christianity from the worst enemy of Catholic unity—Gnosticism—and the moral indecency permitted by its many unholy tenets, all of which form the basis of what we see today in their modern and "New Age" manifestations, described throughout this Praxeologion.

Article II. Our Evangelistic and Spiritual Heraldry Brought Forth for all Potential and Ongoing Worshippers

C. A Katholikos That is a Low, Medium, or High Church

i) That "Niceno-Constantinopolitan Catholic Creed" was meticulously given the ageless stewardship of such saintly exemplars as St. Athanasius, who, alongside so very few kindred spirits (St. Nicholas of Turkey, Saint Hilary of Poitiers, and Abp. Liberius being three of the very few) defended our catholic Faith against teachings by the heretic Arius—that wayward Bishop who, complicating the plain message of Christ's salvation, falsely confirmed the Gnostic ideology of a non-saving Christ.

a) But since God is not the author of confusion (1 Corinthians 14:33) we can rest in the knowledge that "the Lord preserves the simple" (Psalm 116:6) and believe the simple message of the Gospel as "little children" (Matthew 18:3).

b) When it comes to matters of theology, let Christians encourage one another to appreciate godly simplicity and peace, and let this mindset be modeled by the TACA Clergy: "As I besought thee to abide still at Ephesus, when I went into Macedonia, that thou mightest charge some that they teach no other doctrine, Neither give heed to fables and endless genealogies, which minister questions, rather than godly edifying which is in faith" (1 Timothy 1:3-4).

ii) Heresies die hard. Consider, for example, the "Oneness" heresy, taught by the priest Sabellius, that the Godhead is not a Trinity but is merely one

Article II. Our Evangelistic and Spiritual Heraldry Brought Forth for all Potential and Ongoing Worshippers

God. Relegating the ontological status of Jesus to anything that is less than God threatens to call Christians away from the morality of the true Faith, withdrawing Christology away from the perfectness of Jesus, and thus misleading Christian minds toward the immorality and arrogance sired by the confusing false glow of human knowledge (Proverbs 3:5-6).

> a) "But there were false prophets also among the people, even as there shall be false teachers among you, who privily shall bring in damnable heresies, even denying the Lord that bought them, and bring upon themselves swift destruction. And many shall follow their pernicious ways; by reason of whom the way of truth shall be evil spoken of. And through covetousness shall they with feigned words make merchandise of you: whose judgment now of a long time lingereth not, and their damnation slumbereth not" (2 Peter 2:1-3).

iii) Saint Athanasius, himself being orthodox, was exiled six times by a lapsed theocracy, whose adherents gave no quarter to the merciful Truth of God's Word.

> a) Athanasius and other saints, martyrs, and heroes, such as true Christian veterans of American wars, and our own long-suffering Parish elders, shall be acknowledged, emulated, and thanked for their unwavering fidelity to the living promise of Salvation that is best comprised in a

Article II. Our Evangelistic and Spiritual Heraldry Brought Forth for all Potential and Ongoing Worshippers

single person, Jesus (Revelation 6:9-11). "Greater love hath no man than this, that a man lay down his life for his friends" (John 15:13).

b) The Church Militant is indeed grounded in the blood of martyrs, which is the seed of the Church (*Apologeticus*; Tertullian; Part L; Section 13).

iv) Conclusion about High vs. Low Church: Whether a High Church—known for the unfeigned sweetness of *Te Deum Laudamus* at morning, or the solemn vigil of *Nunc Dimittis* at night—or a Low Church, whose usage of the 1940 Hymnal still allows the most Tridentine-sounding organ—the whole Church must seek joy in Fellowship (*koinonia*) but guard against spiritual pride. To relax the "scrupulosity and spiritual gluttony" of legalism of the Law is to give way to the Fruits of the Spirit (Galatians 5:22-23, Ephesians 5:9). "But He giveth more grace. Wherefore he saith, God resisteth the proud, but giveth grace unto the humble" (James 4:6).

D. Contra Mundum

i) Our saints and martyrs endured harsh persecutions and slaughter. The unwavering St. Athanasius inspired the Council of Chalcedon 74 years after his five exiles and death, as he affirmed boldly the permanent conclusion of Atonement reached at Nicaea. Any error staged later at Chalcedon would be tinged in part by Eutyches's tricky Monophysitism: foolishly believing in one *physeis* of Christ's being divine, vaguely affirming that the human being is totally subsumed by the divine, thus emitting a false Christology that negates Christ's humanity and cheapens His sacrifice and death. In truth—to utter the official Chalcedonian/Nicene Christology in one swallow for all reference purposes—let it forever be known: The consubstantial homoousion God-man Jesus, that Jesus the Christ whose Dyophysite human and Godly nature are united in *hypostasis,* is seated at the right hand of the God the Father in glory, and together with God the Holy Spirit is God—blessed Trinity— and it is the Holy Spirit Who, proceeding from the Father and the Son, indwells all who have been born again, as he is our promised Comforter (John 10:38; John 14:11-18; Council of Chalcedon, Sessions I-III, XVI; Canon XXVIII; A.D. 451). Just imagine if the First Seven Ecumenical Councils had not done away with all of these alternative, misleading, evil teachings that wrongfully define Jesus, thus darkening and eroding our faith—imagine if St. Irenaeus had never written *Adversus Haereses*! But "the Lord hath done great things for us; whereof we are glad" (Psalm 126:3).

ii) Much has been done by the Ecumenical Councils to help Christians understand the person and nature of Christ. Because of our religious forebears, Christians throughout the ages are able to stand more firmly opposed to the unbeing of the lukewarm, the despair of the nihilist, and the evil of worldliness. The major principles of the first four Ecumenical Councils are summarized as follows:

Article II. Our Evangelistic and Spiritual Heraldry Brought Forth for all Potential and Ongoing Worshippers

- Nicaea I (A.D. 325) affirmed the deity of Christ, who is not a creation but is God;
- Constantinople I (A.D. 381) clarified the nature of the Holy Spirit as being coequal with God/Jesus;
- Ephesus (A.D. 431) clarified the personhood of Christ as having two natures (i.e., *diaphysis*);
- Chalcedon (A.D. 451) clarified that Christ is consubstantial with (i.e., *homoousion*) the Father and defined the hypostatic union to explain the Dyophysite nature of Christ.

   a) Therefore, because, Christ is simultaneously fully man and fully God, gladdened Christians may enjoy sufficient hope that they too can become perfect, because Christ has a unique personality, just as each person does, despite His being God, and despite His being consubstantial with God the Father and God the Holy Spirit (2 Timothy 3:16-17; John 10:34; Matthew 5:48).

   b) The Church Triumphant will be built by a kingdom of priests. We, the reborn, will be ordained at the moment when we will have found ourselves reconciled, in *theosis*, in the ultimate fellowship of oneness with Him (Revelation 1:6; Exodus 19:6; Psalm 82:6). This Good News gives us joy and unity, standing along with Saint Athanasias against the world (*contra mundum*)—a world that thirsts for the devil's "fake news" (the old man's lies, deception, manipulation, propaganda), which can bring nothing but wrath and dissolution.

Article II. Our Evangelistic and Spiritual Heraldry Brought Forth for all Potential and Ongoing Worshippers

> "Love not the word, neither the things that are in the world. If any man love the world, they love of the Father is not in him" (1 John 2:15).

iii) Much shall be expected: Let us defy the tellers of lies by professing brave belief in Jesus, never being yoked to untruth. "Be not unequally yoked with unbelievers: for what fellowship hath righteousness with unrighteousness? and what communion hath light with darkness?" (2 Corinthians 6:14).

iv) A Clean, Godly House: We shall sanctify our adulthood with loving brethren, cauterizing lesser Christology (Colossians 2:8), eschewing lukewarm theology (Matthew 7:21; Revelation 3:15), avoiding prosperity preaching (Matthew 6:19-24) and licentiousness (Jude 1) in all the churches, evading sorcerers and diviners (Acts 8:18), deposing ministerial whoremongers (Revelation 2:6), rebuking false teachers (2 Peter 2), toppling collared and mitered pedophiles (Mark 9:42), giving our cleanest imitation of Christ's perfection (Revelation 21:8):

> a) Ours is a beautiful aim that owes its ready availability to the honesty of John 4:24: "God is a Spirit: and they that worship Him must worship Him in spirit and in Truth."

v) Simple Truth: This simplicity, whether given in High or Low Church worship may best be mentored by our Bishops and Priests, who are sincerely strong in their mighty respect for the greatness of things that are invisible (Hebrews 11:3). Why spend money on bread that is not bread? (Psalm 55:2).

Article II. Our Evangelistic and Spiritual Heraldry Brought Forth for all Potential and Ongoing Worshippers

a) As anonymously expressed in *The Cloud of Unknowing*, neither science nor metaphysics can fulfill the heart: "For of all other creatures and their works, yea, and of the works of God's self, may a man through grace have fullhead of knowing, and well he can think of them: but of God Himself can no man think. Therefore I would leave all that thing that I can think, and choose to my love that thing that I cannot think" (*The Cloud of Unknowing*; E. Underhill, transl.; Chapter 6; c. 1390).

E. Showing Christians That All Goodness Comes God's Grace

i) The Salvational Map of Holy Communion: So that a Christian may recognize the theology of Soteriology, or the "doctrine of Salvation," the technical terms describing the steps taken toward reaching Salvation are said to be *kenosis, epiclesis,* and ultimately *theosis. Kenosis* is the "emptying-out" process (i.e., κενόω) by which one's human nature is moved aside by the Christian who asks God to replace his nature with the Father's perfect Will (Matthew 26:39; Luke 22:43). To deny the self of one's choices and wants perfectly is known as *epiklesis* (i.e., "Invocation" or ἐπίκλησις), emulating the self-sacrifice of Christ known to Anglicans hearing or speaking the Words of Institution, that come after the Propitiation (the appeasing of God) through the Comfortable Words, the thanking of the Father for the perfect sacrifice of His Son and then invoking the Holy Spirit during the Consecration of the Bread and Wine, on pages 76

Article II. Our Evangelistic and Spiritual Heraldry Brought Forth for all Potential and Ongoing Worshippers

and 80 of the 1928 Book of Common Prayer. Saint Basil elaborated on the *kenosis* and *epiklesis* in his Divine Liturgy, "not because of our righteousness, for we have not done that which is good on the Earth but because of Thy mercies and Thy compassions" (A.D. 378). Suffering as a man, Christ "made himself of no reputation, and took upon him the form of a servant, and was made in the likeness of men," sacrificing His life, "Wherefore God also hath highly exalted him, and given him a name which is above every name" (Philippians 2:7,9). In Pneumatology, the system of theology concerning the Holy Spirit, the Holy Ghost moves Christians to allow God's redemptive work to commence, which Saint John Chrysostom commemorated in his Divine Liturgy, at the very moment of Anaphora—the giving thanks for the Consecration of the Gifts: "Send down Thy Holy Spirit upon us and upon these Gifts set forth" (A.D. 407), an imploration of God's work, which has its parallel in the Sursum Corda dialogue in the 1928 Prayer Book, on page 76, reading the heart for the Holy Spirit's Institution at the altar, whereby "we lift up [our hearts] to the Lord" asking for this unparalleled Grace. It is after this dialogue with the Faithful that we celebrate the Mass, to anticipate the hoped-for Salvation and the reaching of that *theosis*, the "divine state" (i.e., θέωσις), the transformative process of one day becoming holy and fully restored to God, who has known us since before our conception in the womb (Galatians 1:15-16). "Beloved, now are we the sons of God, and it doth not yet appear what we shall be: but we know that, when He shall appear, we shall be like Him; for we shall see Him as He is" (1 John 3:2). Our emptying of our worldly desires and self-sacrifice was therefore perfectly modeled by Christ after His perfect *kenosis* in the Garden of Gethsemane (Luke 22:39-46), leading to His perfect *epiklesis* of the Crucifixion, exemplified by His announcement to God that "It is finished," and thus of His death—and finally by his Resurrection and Ascension into Heaven, having ultimate restoration with the Father, sitting at His right hand—all of this transacted for Christians as if it were a salvational "map" directing our "narrow path" (Matthew 7:13)—the route of Holy Communion with God, as plotted by Jesus Christ. Hence, the avenue of the Eucharist leads us to the Father, so that Christians may share one day in His perfection, by Whose Grace a Christian may become holy while navigating the narrow path *contra mundum*— shunning all that is impure: "According as He hath chosen us in Him before the foundation of the world, that we should be holy and without blame before Him in love" (Ephesians 1:4).

ii) Jesus, the "Last Adam," is the beginning and end of man (1 Corinthians 15:45; Revelation 1:8).

> a) Indeed, Church history and theology are aids, but only the Bible contains the simplest, most irresistible statements. Whether in the collar or the miter, we are to offer those who seek it the choice to believe in the Father's perfect sacrifice of His Son, which sacrifice alone saves us, and which no law, history, theology, or doctrine can

teach independent of Sacred Scripture (Romans 8:3).

iii) Let the intellectual "uncles" test the lock. St. John Cassian subdued the fatalism by which many Christians have long explained the Total Depravity of Augustinian theology. God, in Cassian's *Conferences* (13.9), "all day long outstretches His hands" so that man's "Free Will" may answer Christ's "knock" on man's "door": "Whence human reason cannot easily decide how the Lord gives to those that ask," and "is found by those that seek." Such knowledge should encourage the men and women of TACA to explain to eager Parishioners how God wills to redeem his or her voluntarily opened heart.

iv) Conclusion: Because Simplicity, Sincerity, and straightforward Integrity are best helped by human speech's basic "figs" and "grapes," as opposed to its "thorns" and "thistles" (Matthew 7:16), large ecclesiastical assemblies—especially the First Seven Ecumenical Councils—have always been remedial, but only whenever they are led by honest, modest, and dignified ministers of great Apostolic integrity (Acts 15; 1 Peter 2:5), and only with respect to the fundamental tenets of the Faith that distinguish orthodoxy from heresy. As to the rest, it is merely *adiaphora* (i.e., a matter not central to Christian belief) as to whether Martha would have kept a fancily decorated Upper Room or if Mary would have instead chosen a modest tablecloth, or none at all.

Article III. Patriarchal Governance, Formal Meetings, and Elections of this TACA Synod

ARTICLE III. Patriarchal Governance, Formal Meetings, and Elections of this TACA Synod

A. Custom and Subsidiarity

i) Throughout the Diocesan Year (see Article V, Part B, Section viii), sundry decisions with respect to Christian praxis and quotidian church life are made on the Parish level: Each Parish decides over its own basic matters. At the highest level, the Archbishop will be the supreme executor and public voice over the major workings of the Diocese of TACA and will manifest his rule with charitable fatherly service toward each legislative or delegative assembly.

ii) It is part of his evangelistic mission as Archbishop to call forth a Yearly Synod or other Formal Meeting(s).

    a) He may either affirm the status quo or decide over a diocesan matter in a group or by himself, *ex officio* and unilaterally.

B. Formal Meetings

Preface: A "Formal Meeting" is defined hereof as any important grouping of Parish members within this TACA Synod. It may contain members of more than one Parish or religious Body of TACA (e.g., a Congregation or Mission), and it speaks or votes on behalf of his or her respective TACA religious Body.

    i) A Council Meeting is a type of Formal Meeting that is held by bishops only. A TACA Synod Meeting, which is usually held at the start of September,

Article III. Patriarchal Governance, Formal Meetings, and Elections of this TACA Synod

includes members of the Clergy, Episcopate, and Lay delegates from various TACA religious Bodies discussing or voting on topics or elections that affect the entire TACA Diocese. A Regional Synod contains TACA members representing a limited number, or cross-section, of the TACA Diocese. "Synod" has technically the same meaning as "Diocese," but Synod is predicated in sentences that convey the Diocese acting as a legislative religious Body.

ii) A Synod is thus henceforward expressed as the legislative religious Body of all delegates—Lay, Episcopal, and Clerical—who are known to meet formally for important purposes, such as to vote, or to engage in an Ecclesiastical Court.

iii) The TACA Synod: Sometimes, a given Jurisdiction within a greater church or church movement, or Diet, or Confession, such as perhaps within the Lutheran Church, is referred to by the degree of orthodoxy of its governing body—hence, the "Missouri Synod of the Lutheran Church," or the "Independent Anglican Church of Canada Synod of 1934," the latter of which was a representative Body of Continuing Anglicanism. Now, because a formal all-unifying Synod has never been created (although it was initially proposed) for our *Continuing* most upright version of Anglicanism 45 years ago (*The Affirmation of Saint Louis;* Article 1. "Principles of Doctrine"; Footnote-1: "1992"; Congress of Concerned Churchmen, St. Louis, MO: 1978), the Synod that TACA shall be said to occupy is

Article III. Patriarchal Governance, Formal Meetings, and Elections of this TACA Synod

eponymously named provisionally herein as "the TACA Synod."

iv) Greater Synods: In the future, it is also possible that TACA's provisional Communion with another Jurisdiction(s) would permit provision for a combined "Synod". Thus, Traditionalist Anglican prelates rule themselves patiently, today, in theological lockstep with such an envisioned united Body.

a) It is an aim in the Bible that "rooms" within the mansion of the Church (John 14:2) thusly can become collaborative within a "pure religion and undefiled before God the Father" (James 1:27).

C. Relevance of Meetings

i) The House of Bishops will meanwhile decide over its interior doings as are accorded to their respective Jurisdictions. All in all, for each part or delegative Body mentioned below, the Constitution and Canons will be abided meritoriously, according to Subsidiarity, as follows:

a) Yearly Synods: As regards items affecting the entirety of this TACA Diocese or Synod, a Formal Meeting—yearly, seasonal, provisional, or extemporaneous—may be held. Such meetings may be held in person or by live Internet conference, but the proceedings must be recorded electronically and/or written (e.g., as minutes) by any member, logging it and/or transcribing it as it happens.

Article III. Patriarchal Governance, Formal Meetings, and Elections of this TACA Synod

>b) A smaller partial Body meeting sometimes is convened, such as when the Western Diocese meets on its own, although all discussions and decisions must be summarized for the Archbishop so he can ratify them.

ii) A wise, godly decision solely made by the Archbishop may be reached regarding any matter within this TACA Diocese, independent of any Formal Meeting, and always being made mindfully with the principle of Custom and Subsidiarity in mind (see Article VI; Part C; Section i).

D. TACA Religious Bodies

i) A TACA "religious Body" is defined as a religious entity within this TACA Diocese whose delegates attend such Formal Meetings, within entities known to be Congregations, Ministries, Churches, Church Plants, Missions, Parishes, Deaneries, or Schools, or any religious entity formally officiating within a Yearly Synod, Regional Synod, Bishops' Council, or other kind of Formal Meeting of TACA.

E. Formal Communication Within This TACA Synod

Exordium: Because we are expected at Judgement Day to give an account to Christ for how our sinful nature has compelled us to speak idly (Matthew 12:36), we must be exceedingly careful to guide our verbal dispatches according to Sacred Scripture and Tradition. Saint Paul exhorts all Clergy, Episcopate, and Laity to "keep that which is committed to thy trust, avoiding profane and vain babblings, and oppositions of science

Article III. Patriarchal Governance, Formal Meetings, and Elections of this TACA Synod

falsely so called" (1 Timothy 6:20) and to let "all things be done unto edifying" (1 Corinthians 14:26).

i) All important communication must be recorded/logged that there is an incontrovertible record. From the human voice to the technological devices that are used to broadband our language, it is the physical world that becomes weaponized by false science to supplant the "true science" of Truth. "Beware lest anyone cheat you through philosophy and empty deceit, according to the tradition of men, according to the basic principles of the world, and not according to Christ" (Colossians 2:8).

ii) Confident, sober, vigilant mindfulness is key. Though we daily strive to shunt our minds away from God's enemies—those rascals who unite to seduce our households and church families—let us also take comfort in knowing that our adversary is a coward whose scoffing minions disband and flee in the face of our godly strength through faith (Deuteronomy 28:7). "Resist the devil, and he will flee from you" (James 4:7). Thus, the Archbishop presides over us, speaking from the narrow roadhouse of our TACA Diocese (Titus 1:5; See "Our Archbishop Unilateral Rule per Subsidiarity and Custom" in Preamble Parts I and II).

iii) Keep records of decisions: All Formal Communication of record (that which can be recorded and published and used for Formal Meetings or Voting) in this TACA Synod/Diocese may occur in person by in-person meetings; in a journal;

Article III. Patriarchal Governance, Formal Meetings, and Elections of this TACA Synod

by publishing; by handwritten or typed recording; by e-mail; by telephone; by text messaging; and by Internet-streamed conferencing. All recorded data can be useful only if it is recorded according to the mutual agreement and assent by participating communicators and by an understanding that the communications are being logged, transcribed, and/or published.

iv) Public speech is TACA's. If public communication shall represent, or relate to, this TACA Synod/Diocese in any way, the Archbishop shall retain the right of first refusal as regards its relevance and worthiness to be quoted, paraphrased, published, logged, retransmitted, (re-)published, or (re-)printed anywhere, and at any time. He alone may share this discretionary power with any TACA member whom he chooses. It is only by the light of Sacred Scripture that we should talk; we must not lean unto our own understanding, but "In all thy ways acknowledge Him, and He shall direct thy paths" (Proverbs 3:5-6).

v) Only humans shall talk. TACA may not at any time be represented by use of Artificial Intelligence or pre-recordings or computerized speech. Carefully speak only with human beings regarding matters of God.

    a) God and His saints hear the tumultuous noise of unhappiness inside the technological walls of modern "Jericho", but God speaks in whispers

Article III. Patriarchal Governance, Formal Meetings, and Elections of this TACA Synod

(Exodus 32:17; 1 Kings 19:12) and can be found outside the camp (Hebrews 13:13).

vi) God hears and reads everything. "Of these things put them in remembrance, charging them before the Lord that they strive not about words to no profit, but to the subverting of the hearers" (2 Timothy 2:14). Neither person nor Artificial Intelligence can equal the omniscience of God, whose understanding is unfathomable by all (Isaiah 48:28; Psalms 33:13-15). "For the eyes of the Lord run to and fro throughout the whole earth, to shew Himself strong in the behalf of them whose heart is perfect toward Him" (2 Chronicles 16:9).

vii) Faith determines Salvation, not fractional agendas. "Study to shew thyself approved unto God, a workman that needeth not to be ashamed, rightly dividing the word of truth" (2 Timothy 2:15). We are entrusted with the Gospel, not to please man in our communication, but to please God who alone tests our hearts (1 Thessalonians 2:4). "For do I now persuade men, or God? or do I seek to please men? for if I yet pleased men, I should not be the servant of Christ" (Galatians 1:10).

viii) Trust the one who has the fatherly rule over us. The Archbishop was commissioned by Christ at his Consecration to speak, just as Saint Paul consecrated Timothy to speak, in order to pass down the holy truths that have been entrusted to his House of Bishops. The Bishops, in turn, teach other Christians, who themselves will employ the message

Article III. Patriarchal Governance, Formal Meetings, and Elections of this TACA Synod

of the Gospel to contradict the teaching of the devil as they go out into the world.

a) Bishops guard us from the devil's "oppositions of science falsely so called" and thus refute heterodoxy and heresy. "But shun profane and vain babblings: for they will increase unto more ungodliness" (2 Timothy 2:16).

b) "Obey them that have the rule over you, and submit yourselves: for they watch for your souls, as they that must give account, that they may do it with joy, and not with grief: for that is unprofitable for you" (Hebrews 13:17).

F. Archbishop Allows All Meetings and Elections, and Manner Thereof

i) The wise patriarchal Archbishop is therefore he who guides and represents all his Bishops, who are persons who fully identify and speak as moral orthodox conservative Christians. Thus:

ii) All ministers must take ownership of their every thought, word, and deed, and always be sober, sincere, and vigilant in all communication and action (1 Peter 5:8-9; 1 John 3:18); otherwise, the devil will make the minister's confusing language into the beast's dominion, with listeners becoming increasingly confused. "And what concord hath Christ with Belial? or what part hath he that believeth with an infidel" (2 Corinthians 6:15). The "Patient" in *The Screwtape Letters* is tempted into donning unbecoming pettiness at the hands of the

Article III. Patriarchal Governance, Formal Meetings, and Elections of this TACA Synod

demon Wormwood, the journeyman ghoul who seizes upon the pert boisterousness that is momentarily employed by the "Patient" during a party (akin to a Church Council). Wormwood's objective was to substitute the young man's foolishness in place of the clement ownership over reality that the sinner's otherwise sober executive function ought never leave vacant. "Cowardice is acceptable so long as one brags about it in a comical manner," wrote he, thus reminding the reader to avoid vainglorious revelry. Wormwood designated "Flippancy, however, [to be] the best of all," calling to mind the ruthless verbal ironies diverting attention away from godly things toward buffoonery packaged in both printed and electronic media, recognizing that "Flippant people don't actually laugh, they just assume everything is laughable. They take nothing seriously, not even virtue. This isolates them from the Enemy [God], and, contrary to what they believe, it does not make them more intelligent (*The Screwtape Letters*; C.S. Lewis; Letter 11; 1942). A serious Customary must be published by each Congregation and Mission, whereby proper administrative praxis will deter the ministers and laity from having corrupt and foolish ways and secret lives. Emotional insecurity and immorality form the vapor of formless vanity (Ecclesiastes 1:2) but "He that handleth a matter wisely shall find good: and whoso trusteth in the Lord, happy is he" (Proverbs 16:20). Delegates at a Diocesan Council must project the same utter seriousness, gentility, and courage that they are known to display within

Article III. Patriarchal Governance, Formal Meetings, and Elections of this TACA Synod

their own wisely run Parishes, to the end that "all the members of that one body, being many, are one body: so also is Christ" (1 Corinthians 12:12).

iii) Our TACA Diocese thus has various delegated parts, each with a unique function, in that "all these worketh that one and the selfsame Spirit, dividing to every man severally as he will" (1 Corinthians 12:11).

iv) Although the TACA House of Bishops acts as the heads of this religious Body, they fulfill a vocation that only a few men could ever merit. While they are consecrated to serve Jesus, they must "be *not* many masters, knowing that we shall receive the greater condemnation" (James 3:1). Eagerness to serve must never interfere with humility and vigilance to be orthodox, lest after death God will punish bishops more harshly than other men (James 3:4-6).

v) If the Priests and Bishops of TACA are deemed to be wise and good men, then the Archbishop, seeing his Diocese at peace, may deign to allow the various kinds of voting styles shown in Article V, and to take satisfaction in presiding over the kinds of Formal Meetings, Bodies, situations, and rubrics that are discussed in Articles IV and VI through VIII.

ARTICLE IV. Primus Rule, Literature, Discipline, Ecclesiastical Court, Primate Discretion, Modesty

A. Verbal and Written Moral Probity in Law

i) The Archbishop, who leads this TACA Diocese, shall always ensure that neither the lesser Bishops, nor any governing Body, nor any Minister, nor any member of this TACA Diocese shall make, enforce, or emulate any rule or take any action within TACA that is contrary to Sacred Scripture, as the Church has received it, and/or that is outside of the oversight or contrary to the approval of the Archbishop.

B. Primary Canon Library

i) The following literature constitutes the Sacred Tradition of TACA, by actualizing the perfection of the Bible; by providing a framework in which to preach the Gospel and administer the Religious sacraments; and by guiding the daily lives of all Christians within our *ecclesia*: The 1928 Book of Common Prayer; the 1940 United States Episcopal Hymnal; the Thirty-Nine Articles of Religion; the Apostle's Creed; the Nicene Creed; the Athanasian Creed; the St. Louis Affirmation of 1978; all revisions and translations of the Book of Common Prayer published in the United States of America and England, up until 1928, including the Book of Lesser Feasts and Fasts (until 1964), and the Book of Offices: Services for Certain Occasions (up to and including 1940). Together with these, our sources of

Article IV. Primus Rule, Literature, Discipline, Ecclesiastical Court, Primate Discretion, Modesty

Sacred Tradition, TACA holds that the King James Bible is our Sacred Scripture, without which the foregoing sources of Sacred Tradition cannot be interpreted or applied.

ii) No "Alternative Service Book" may be utilized for worship other than the official canonical revisions of the Prayer Book up to and including 1928.

iii) Adjunctive worship books such as the Book of Occasional Services (up to and including 1973) may be permitted only with Bishop approval, per use of each of its given liturgies or rites (e.g., Exorcism Rite).

C. Cardinal Canon Library:

i) By means of supplemental literature, its orthodoxy supported by its antiquity, TACA shall ensure that this Diocese employs the Bible's perfect aims and projects God's irresistible Grace to the outside world.

ii) Noble reading may include all acceptable histories, theological tomes, and essays or treatises in our greater canon, such as, but not limited to, The Saint James Apocrypha; St. Bede's *Historia ecclesiastica gentis Anglorum*; Gildas' *De Excidio et Conquestu Britanniae*; Richard Hooker's *On the Laws of Ecclesiastical Polity*; St. John Cassian's *Institutes* and his *Conferences*; St. Augustine of Hippo's *Confessions* and *City of God*; St. John Chrysostom's complete *Homiletics*; St. Albertus Magnus's *De Bono*; St. Patrick's *Confessio* and his *Epistola ad Coroticum*;

Article IV. Primus Rule, Literature, Discipline, Ecclesiastical Court, Primate Discretion, Modesty

Evagrius Ponticus's *The Praktikos* and *The Making of a Gnostic*; Irenaeus's *Adversus Haereses*; Josephus's *History of the Jews*; the First and Second Epistles of St. Clement, Bishop of Rome, St. Thomas Aquinas's *Summa Theologica*; the Didache; the historical documents of the first Seven Ecumenical Councils; the writings (letters, homilies, treatises, etc.) of the Church Fathers; the various Liturgies and Rites of the East and West; and multifarious others.

D. Customaries

i) Each Congregation and Mission is expected to have its own written Customary, properly blessed by the Archbishop, to run itself.

ii) The fundamental agency of decision-making is the local Congregation, acting within and with the support of Ecclesiastical Authority, and of the Archbishop's benediction.

iii) The order protecting Church Custom shall be the governance and fine discipline of, and exemplified by, this TACA Diocese as a whole as it is vested by the men of the House of Bishops, whose rule defines Ecclesiastical Authority. Their power derives from the Archbishop, who protects Church Custom and the House of Bishops, thus completing the Subsidiarity.

> a) Ecclesiastical Authority exists in the Subsidiarity that the Archbishop deigns to extend to his House of Bishops so that each Congregation and Mission may govern itself via conformity with

Article IV. Primus Rule, Literature, Discipline, Ecclesiastical Court, Primate Discretion, Modesty

these Constitution and Canons and all the Anglican formularies listed here, operating according to its own Praxis, as defined in its Parish or Mission Customary.

E. Modest Rule as Witnessed in the Nativity

i) The model for Ecclesiastical Authority may be likened to the setting of Luke 2, consisting of the Holy Family (the Clergy and Episcopate); the shepherds and Wise Men (the Wardens and Ministers); the stable and manger (the churches and pews); the sheep and Border Collies learning the Bible to attain Salvation (parishioners, abiding Genesis 28:12 and Luke 2:13: "Glory to God in the highest"); the quiet awe and respectful veneration of all who adore Jesus (shepherds and Wise Kings); and love of Scripture and prophecy (Simeon, in Luke 2:25-26). Outside is the world (Herod's census and his killing of the innocents).

ii) Peaceful, self-controlled reverence must always order our calling to administer public adoration with our fellows, as if we are shepherding our own children, or the infant Jesus Himself (Matthew 2:1-6).

iii) One's attire, writings, and speech must be modest and tasteful, from opening to closing of the mouth, from head to toe. All uses of, and references to, information inside and outside of our Canon must be made without trace of profane or sordid utterance, display, or reference. There can be no doubt on the part of others that we are like the Wise Men on our way to see the infant Jesus, wearing our

Article IV. Primus Rule, Literature, Discipline, Ecclesiastical Court, Primate Discretion, Modesty

adoration in a dignified way, reserving even our most well-meaning passion for Truth until the meek and the innocent have their chance under our loving, watchful care to increase in Christlike expressiveness (1 Corinthians 3:2). Our addresses one to another, our gifts, our possessions, our brethren, and anyone representing us must be humble, reverent, and unpretentious, both inside and outside of the church and everywhere, always (1 Timothy 2: 9-10; 1 Corinthians 6:19-20; Matthew 15:11-18).

F. Primate Discretion or Rule of this Canon as Emulated En Masse

i) The tone, the idiom, the judiciousness, and the overall culture of our Jurisdiction are set forth, demonstrated, and warranted for daily adoption by the Archbishop, who is our diocesan Primate, and by his nobly influenced House of Bishops (Luke 17:7-10).

ii) What is a Primate? The use of the term "Primate" refers to the executorship played by the Archbishop heading a multilayered Diocese. It also refers to a theologically united Primature, perchance a joint Archbishopric, or to one presiding man (e.g., an Archprimate or Co-Archprimature of, say, a future provisional Communion Synod).

iii) Provision for Collaborative or Co-Archprimature in a Communion Synod: Joining fishing boats together implies that said Communion Synod would

Article IV. Primus Rule, Literature, Discipline, Ecclesiastical Court, Primate Discretion, Modesty

also enjoy Custom and Subsidiarity and display hearty theological collaboration by all members.

    a) Such shepherding by an honorable Primate would propagate a fine example of spiritual partnership in the greater Anglican Continuum and all of Christendom (Luke 5:4-7).

iv) Humility would characterize collaborative Primates of a future provisional Communion Synod. In that there is no respect of persons with God (Romans 2:11), the humility of all participants—including the Archbishops of a co-Archprimature—would manifest itself through pastoral charity, through administrative skill, and via each member's orthodox application of their charisms. According to St. Augustine (paraphrasing Plato), the Cardinal Virtues that the Archbishop projects are prudence, justice, fortitude, and temperance (Augustine of Hippo, *De Moribus Ecclesiae Catholicae* 1.25; *Letters* 155.12; 155.16; *De Libero Arbitrio* 1.27).

v) The charism of the Primates of a future provisional Communion Synod would be a gratuitous gift of God. It would stem from the Word itself, and its doings would be ably reflected by the first rule in the Rule of St. Augustine (i.e., "to live harmoniously in your house, intent upon God in oneness of mind and heart") and by Acts 4, to wit, that Traditionalist Anglicans, witnessing the miracles of Christ and of their own rebirths, shall loyally take direction from Ecclesiastical Authority

Article IV. Primus Rule, Literature, Discipline, Ecclesiastical Court, Primate Discretion, Modesty

in said Synod and within one's independent autonomous Diocese of TACA.

a) A provisional Communion Synod including this TACA Diocese shall strive to be of one mind and one heart on its members' way to meeting God as fellow travelers, sharing one pilgrimage together. On this sea, Christ is Anglicans' constant Companion, Navigator, and Admiral, whereby each Anglican has found his or her calling to ministry to be irresistible (Acts 4:32-35).

vi) Said Communion Primate shall be a kindly monarch. Therefore, the Discretion of our Archbishop or Primate in deciding all matters, or delegating any choices or power, will prove that his wisely conducted life and vigorous ministry shall keep the Diocese pursuing the same direction.

a) Christians within the *ecclesia* shall each advance more stably toward salvational *theosis*—the very oneness with Christ (see Article XVII, Anglican Primer).

vii) Said Communion Primate's rule shall ensure that his Clergy, Episcopate, all Ministers, and parishioners will persist most excellently in this very Anglican Traditionalist Faith, sharing the same rubrics and the identical Bible, Eucharist, Liturgy, Sacraments, Canon, Constitution, and Traditions.

viii) The Communion Primate shall emulate the long-suffering intention of Saint Athanasius. In his Easter Epistle, Athanasius teaches that such must rule

Article IV. Primus Rule, Literature, Discipline, Ecclesiastical Court, Primate Discretion, Modesty

biblically—to preserve the Old and New Testament as "fountains of salvation," defending for the "thirsty" the "living words they contain." An Athanasian Primate will "Let no man add to these, neither let him take ought from these" (Epistle Number 39: Festal Easter; Saint Athanasius; Part 6; A.D. 367). All godly ministers must accept suffering and abandonment, lockdowns, and agonies, as did the blessed Saint Athanasius, who endured five grueling exiles, safeguarding that Canon and confessing defiantly that the Bible itself is a perfect document for the ordering of humanity and cannot— shall not—be changed or neglected in making any choice on any matter concerning the Church (2 Timothy 4:16).

ix) The Clergy shall copy the Archbishop's imitation of Christ. Finally, the Primate is to be copied in his fortuitous Humility by all of his Bishops and Priests. To ensure this, he should employ the most winsome, discerning, and vigorous parts of his nature to enrich Church life, his choices for comportment always emulating his exemplary imitation of Christ. Thus:

x) "For a Bishop must be blameless, as the steward of God; not self-willed, not soon angry, not given to wine, no striker, not given to filthy lucre; But a lover of hospitality, a lover of good men, sober, just, holy, temperate; Holding fast the faithful word as he hath been taught, that he may be able by sound doctrine both to exhort and to convince the gainsayers" (Titus 1:7-14).

Article IV. Primus Rule, Literature, Discipline, Ecclesiastical Court, Primate Discretion, Modesty

xi) Pastoral Metaphysics Mediating Unrest

"Woe to the multitude of many people, which make a noise like the noise of the seas" (Isaiah 17:12). Sacred Scripture bemoans that our people's failure to obey God results in the "tumult of the people" (Psalm 65:7). Mediation using Scripture so that man may become perfect like God shall begin by blessing our peaceful incapacity to understand the fullness of the Godhead and affirming our place in the creational order that is so huge that we can only begin to grasp it. For the "secret things belong unto the Lord our God: but those things which are revealed belong unto us and to our children forever" (Deuteronomy 29:29). The Father's thoughts and ways are not our ways, but are higher (Isaiah 55:8-9). This Ontological Order, which positions Heaven above Earth and God above Heaven, is aptly taught in Medieval discourse to admonish disruptive souls peddling contagious darkness and to comfort the ignorant. Truly, no one could reasonably hope to substitute a better idea about the Father for a discerning Church. "Therefore, Lord, not only are You that than which a greater cannot be thought, but You are also something greater than can be thought" (*Proslogion*; Chapter 15; Saint Anselm of Canterbury; 1078). And yet, though it is most wise to embrace one's proper ontological estate in relation to God, recognizing a sense of "unknowingness" in contemplating the fullness of God in a spirit of humility, Christians are promised that, in Christ, certain hidden mysteries are revealed unto us and

Article IV. *Primus* Rule, Literature, Discipline, Ecclesiastical Court, Primate Discretion, Modesty

not to the unfaithful and ungodly (1 Corinthians 2:7-14). We rejoice together with our Savior in saying, "I thank thee, O Father, Lord of heaven and earth, because thou hast hid these things from the wise and prudent, and hast revealed them unto babes" (Matthew 11:25).

xii) Logos Triumphs Over the "Multiverse"

a) Because it is possible that today's rascaldom is less disorderly than Medieval skullduggery, a good Priest may easily discern which supernatural species (devil or God) is doing the "ghostly work" in his parishioners' spirits as they contemplate naively their interior purpose versus that of the Cosmos, noting the inability of arrogant churchgoers to test the spirits (1 John 4:1) and find the Holy Spirit (John 14:17); or discern whether a sullying influence comes from within (Mark 7:23); or if Lucifer himself is corrupting the mind (2 Corinthians 11:3-4). "How these young presumptuous disciples misunderstand this word 'in', and of the deceits that follow thereon ... [and] 'up' ... Some of these men the devil will deceive full wonderfully" (*The Cloud of Unknowing*; E. Underhill, transl.; Chapter 52, 57; c. 1390). The Metaphysics of this anonymous theologian are often consumed together with Saint [or "Pseudo"] Dionysius the Areopagite, who besides publishing his *Ecclesiastical Hierarchy* had attributed to the cosmic order the necessity of Salvation, placing the roles of the Episcopate and Clergy just below the "angelology" of the celestial order, because

Article IV. Primus Rule, Literature, Discipline, Ecclesiastical Court, Primate Discretion, Modesty

"ours is a Hierarchy of the inspired and Divine and Deifying science, and of operation, and of consecration, for those who have been initiated with the initiation of the sacred Revelation derived from the hierarchical mysteries" (*Ecclesiastical Hierarchy*; Areopagite, Pseudo-Dionysius; Caput I; Section 1; A.D. 450). *The Cloud* meanwhile warns about malcontents infesting various corners of ministry: "They read and hear well said that they should leave outward working with their wits, and work inwards: and because they that know not which is inward working, therefore they work wrong" (*ibid. The Cloud*, Chapter 52).

b) In the very last paragraph of *Celestial Hierarchy*, Dionysius enlists pastoral guidance as the salve for a loosely catechized man's myopic refusal to accept their incapacity to comprehend God's omniscience: "If you should point out that we have not mentioned in order all the Angelic powers, activities and images described in the scriptures, we should answer truly that we do not possess the supermundane knowledge of some, or rather that we have need of another to guide us to the light and instruct us." It shall hold, then, that the patient TACA Patriarch, thus seeing pretext for his role as Pastor by Dionysius, shall disabuse a troublemaker of his or her self-mind-worship. Hubris is merely that person's errant part played out somewhere within that cosmic hierarchy: "the hidden Mysteries which lie beyond our view we

Article IV. Primus Rule, Literature, Discipline, Ecclesiastical Court, Primate Discretion, Modesty

have honored by silence" (*De Coelesti Hierarchia*; Pseudo-Dionysius the Areopagite; Chapter 15; A.D. 450). Indeed, God is likely indifferent even to our very best opinions about religious reality, which are better left unformulated. "Him that is weak in the faith receive ye, but not to doubtful disputations" (Romans 14:1). A TACA shepherd must compassionately advise impregnable ignorance whenever appropriate (Hebrews 5:2) and when necessary must admonish the unruly, while always upholding the core tenets of the Faith without wavering. "Now we exhort you, brethren, warn them that are unruly, comfort the feebleminded, support the weak, be patient toward all men" (1 Thessalonians 5:14).

c) Ordination of priests and deacons finds a beautiful parallel in the Areopagite's poetic treatment of the Salvational process as man's sponsorship by the Son completes the celestial order:

—"But he, though religiously longing for his Salvation, when he measures human infirmity against the loftiness of the undertaking [of Reconciliation with the Hierarch of Heaven], is seized with a shivering and sense of incapacity. Nevertheless, at last, [Christ] promises with a good Grace to do what is requested, and takes and leads him to the chief Hierarch. He then benevolently receives the man, as a sheep upon His shoulders, and admits the two men [such as a sponsor leading his Deacon friend toward their

Article IV. Primus Rule, Literature, Discipline, Ecclesiastical Court, Primate Discretion, Modesty

Bishop for ordination] and worships, and glorifies, with a mental thanksgiving and bodily prostration [as in the Ordination Rite], the One Author and Finisher of Good; from Whom those who are being called, and those who are being saved, are saved. He then collects the whole religious Order into the holy Choir for co-operation and common rejoicing over the man's Salvation, but also for thanksgiving to the Divine Goodness (*Ecclesiastical Hierarchy*; Areopagite, Pseudo-Dionysius; Caput II: "Concerning Those Who are Being Initiated in Illumination"; Section 2; A.D. 450).

—The "marriage of the Lamb is come, and His wife hath made herself ready," and He "omnipotent reigneth" (Revelation 19:6-7).

G. Definition of Ecclesiastical Authority

i) Ecclesiastical Authority (meaning the supremacy of the Archbishop delegating powers to the Episcopate and Clergy) is a reflection of the Dominion given to the Church by Jesus Christ (Matthew 18:17-18; Matthew 28:18-20). As His voice, Sacred Scripture and Sacred Tradition are the Rule enjoyed by Jesus over any Primate and all constituent religious officers.

ii) Because the power and authority of our TACA Diocese are vested ultimately with the Archbishop/Primate, then, as per his sole discretion to share them, it holds that all church power and authority may manifest from him to his Bishops and

Clergy with excellent Subsidiarity (see Preamble Part II). Thus, as per the conjuncture of his sharing his supremacy with his House of Bishops and/or Clergy, and/or by means of the Formal Meetings he allows, he will always, and without any intentional variance, operate in excellent accordance with Sacred Scripture and Sacred Tradition. Topical or disputational discourse hence shall be always in conformity with the Constitution and Canons, just as they, too, are authorized and ratified by the Archbishop/Primate as being biblically sound, always according to his authority.

iii) Rule-oriented Patriarchs may lead. Just as a shepherd competently navigates the countryside, so too shall the Primate rule over a Diocese(s); a Bishop over a Bishopric(s); and a Pastor over his Vestry and Congregation or Mission. Likewise, the Permanent Diaconate shall help the Parish, the father shall rule his home, and a manager shall run his department or store. By this Dominion set forth by the Holy Trinity, activated by Church, and helped by the angels, may the Word expect to hold sway over the hearts, souls, minds, wills, intellects, and bodies of the Laity and all Ministers thereof.

H. Teaching of Anglican Theology

i) Theology on any level must be taught patiently so that Christians may understand God through Scripture. The latest "Systematic" schools—by no means exhaustive—advancing Anglican Theology, as listed below, can be expressed to children or adults,

Article IV. Primus Rule, Literature, Discipline, Ecclesiastical Court, Primate Discretion, Modesty

in methods suited to each, by means of nothing more complicated than the Bible:

a) Christology, Soteriology, Trinitarian Theology, Pneumatology, Mariology, Ecclesiology, Sacramental Theology, Ecumenism, Interreligious Dialogue, Theological Anthropology, Protology, Grace, Redemption, Atonement, Predestination, Theological Virtues, and Eschatology.

b) Wherever determined needful, Ecclesiastical Authority shall teach church history, including the Reformation, and shall include Anglican formularies and higher rubrics from our 1928 Prayer Book in teaching postulants and students.

c) At the time of this writing (September 2023), the educational office of Training Director for TACA is chartered via the Archbishop to Father Michael DellaVecchia.

I. Ecclesiastical Court

i) A Body formed for the purpose of deciding an emergent church matter is defined as a "Court" (see Meetings and Voting, Article V, Part A, B; Article VI, Parts A-F).

ii) Neither the Bishops nor any governing Body of this TACA Diocese shall make any edict or take any action that is contrary to the Scriptures. As with any Synod or Assembly that elects a Bishop or votes on alterations to the Constitution and/or Canons or on any other matters, all Ecclesiastical discussions are

Article IV. Primus Rule, Literature, Discipline, Ecclesiastical Court, Primate Discretion, Modesty

always a biblical endeavor. The same Authority that writes rules also defends them.

iii) Any modification or changes to this Constitution and/or these Canons; any adoption of doctrine; any proposed diocesan partnership; or any suggestion to mutate the sacramental, cultural, or foundational conventions and traditions of this TACA Diocese must be proposed according to Scriptural bases and be in compliance with Traditional Anglican formularies.

iv) Disciplinary Action against violations of ministerial duty and the proper following of the Rule of the Constitution and Canons is a biblical endeavor.

v) Joint Hearing or Review: By a Joint Hearing or Review by Ecclesiastical Authority and all concerned parties and offices, all pertinent accounts and testimony may be reviewed according to any given proposed change or violation, at the pleasure of the Archbishop.

vi) Ruling: All Court Decisions will be handled by a vote in a Formal Meeting, such as a Yearly or Regional Synod or Bishops' Council and ratified by the Archbishop.

vii) Discipline: As the Rule, the Archbishop of TACA herein recommends a four-fold way of Juridical Review for Discipline:

> a) First, to review a violation in terms of whether to examine a minister in terms of suspending or

expelling him from various services, from overall duty, from title, or from incardination.

b) Second, to review a violation in terms of whether rehabilitation would be useful or appropriate—through the requiring of education or counseling (afforded at zero expense to the Church, and fully paid for by the disciplined party).

c) Third, to review a violation in terms of whether the minister must be expelled, i.e., excardinated unconditionally and permanently from our TACA Diocese.

d) Fourth, to review a violation in terms of whether to commit the minister to the enforcing power of civil authorities because of a presumably criminal component to the case.

viii) There shall be a Juridical Review by the Court regarding any disciplinary, expulsive, or corrective action, as determined and/or warranted by the Archbishop.

ix) Vote of Loss of Clerical State Against the Archbishop: If there is a situation of mass discontentment within the House of Bishops over the suitability of the Archbishop for his office, and if circumstances are peaceful enough, then the Archbishop may meet with the House of Bishops to reconcile as brothers, and thus his office may resume as before. However, if a Ballot of No-Confidence may be called forth and presided over by

Article IV. Primus Rule, Literature, Discipline, Ecclesiastical Court, Primate Discretion, Modesty

the Coadjutor (by his sole right to do so), the vote would choose whether the Archbishop ought to resign immediately on the grounds of Loss of Clerical State. If the vote is that he should thus vacate office, the result can nevertheless be vetoed by the Archbishop, and in his doing so, the Bishops must hence forbear the matter and not contest it again. There is no override allowed that would nullify the Archbishop's veto of the No-Confidence vote. As an alternative, and as a last resort, each discontented bishop may opt to resign and forfeit his incardination. However, they may not defect and regroup or call themselves "Traditional Anglican Church of America" or "TACA" or use a previous appellation of our TACA Diocese for the rump party (e.g., "Anglican Diocese of the Good Shepherd," etc.) or thereafter assume authority of any kind whatsoever over any of the Congregations, Missions, or other religious Bodies of this TACA Diocese. It holds, that:

— The Archbishop, like any man, does not have the Impeccable Will of Jesus, but instead the Gnomic human Will. The Infallibility doctrine concerns the Church and the Apostolic Sees of the Church, not the fallible men who occupy positions within the Body. Although the Church had anathematized Archbishop Honorius I at the Third Council of Constantinople (Session 13; A.D. 681), alternately known as the Sixth Ecumenical Council, his expulsion came after his death—an action that certainly did not represent the

Article IV. Primus Rule, Literature, Discipline, Ecclesiastical Court, Primate Discretion, Modesty

expulsion of the *Seat* of the Archbishop of Rome itself (Matthew 16:18), the office to which "Pope" Honorius had been elected and anointed. In that Christ has the Hypostatic Union of his two natures of fully man and fully God, a Bishop thus does not reflect the false idea of the singular Will of Christ, that of the so-called Monothelite Will, which was declared heretical at this Council (Rome was the first to disavow it). He alone deliberates on behalf of his Chair, or Seat, in terms of what the perfect Dyophysite Will of the Savior expects during his tenure. Saint Maximus the Confessor had ardently fought against the false doctrine of the singular Will of Christ; an even more ancient example of orthodoxy associated with the Infallibility of the Archbishopric can be found in the book of Acts, Chapter 15, when the Apostle James gave a final sentence that put to rest the first significant religious controversy to plague the fledgling Church: how to handle the objections of the Judaizers against the Gentile converts. Interestingly it was not Peter who declared the definitive position and gave the final sentence; it was James. If anyone was "pope" in the Church of Jerusalem, it was actually James—a not inconsequential detail, particularly in light of the papacy and how the Church of Rome went off course, as discussed in this Constitution. "And after they had held their peace, James answered, saying, Men and brethren, harken unto me: ... Wherefore my sentence is that we trouble not

Article IV. Primus Rule, Literature, Discipline, Ecclesiastical Court, Primate Discretion, Modesty

them, которые from among the Gentiles are turned to God" (Acts 15:13-19). Only very few men could ever hope to fulfill the inviolability of the Seat of Archbishop Therefore, while the House of Bishops, the Clergy, and all of TACA honor the sincere humility and orthodoxy with which the Archbishop of TACA officiates, vacating the Seat of said living Archbishop should only occur by the voluntary resignation by that minister, or the continuation of his ministry until his death—feats deliberated by the shepherd's Gnomic human will. He hopes he is making the right choice at every move, but his choices are his alone: to abdicate or to die while occupying the Chair. Thus:

"Since, then, I have in the persons of those above mentioned beheld as it were your whole multitude in faith and have loved you, I exhort you to be careful to do all things in the unity of God, since the bishop sits in the place of God, and the presbyters in the place of the synod of the Apostles, and the deacons, who are most dear to me, have been entrusted with the ministry of Jesus Christ, who was with the Father before the world began, and was manifested in the end" *(Epistle to the Magnesians;* Saint Ignatius of Antioch; Chapter 6:1; A.D. 108).

The example of the voluntary lapsing, and later repentance, of Rome's Archbishop ("Pope") Liberius should stand with authority. A defender

Article IV. Primus Rule, Literature, Discipline, Ecclesiastical Court, Primate Discretion, Modesty

of the great Saint Athanasius of Alexandria in his opposition against the heresies of Arius the Presbyter, Liberius was coerced by Emperor Constantius II to sign the terrible Second Creed of Sirmium to support the heresy of Arianism lest he else face removal by Constantius. Liberius was wise enough to know that being removed would have automatically initiated an antipope crisis to weaken the Church. Later, however, upon the death of Constantius II, Liberius annulled the Second Creed of Sirmium and restored Athanasius and the other homoousian bishops, now engaging in a tireless episcopate of orthodoxy against Arianism until his death. We see in these examples, therefore, that the concept of "Bishop" as it is found in the epistle of Saint Ignatius of Antioch holds securely: "Wherever the Bishop appears, there let the people be; as wherever Jesus Christ is, there is the Catholic Church" (Letter to the Smyrnaeans, Saint Ignatius of Antioch, Chapter 8, J.R. Willis transl.). It is only through this blessed Office of Bishop, executed solely via the Bishop himself, that error in the Office's occupant can be rightly corrected. Any such correction must reflect the infallibility of the Invisible Church so that the Visible Church can continue without schism (*Contra Constantium Augustum liber;* Saint Hilary of Poitiers; Part X; Section 577-587; A.D. 355). Therefore, Truth cannot possibly stem from the false doctrine—one that would have no biblical precedent—that a vote was ever held among the

Article IV. Primus Rule, Literature, Discipline, Ecclesiastical Court, Primate Discretion, Modesty

Apostles to declare that one of their fellow Apostles was incapable of healing a situation within his jurisdiction or of correcting himself; a Jurisdiction is the Bishop's to lead and his alone. As explicated just above, the Apostle James in the Council of Jerusalem—the first Council of the Church—had declared the unsettling position of its most unpopular Apostle, Saint Paul, to be the winning decretal (Acts 15). As an extreme and merely speculative example, it could be argued that Judas Iscariot, as one of the Apostles originally, had the choice either to repent and continue as an Apostle or to refuse to repent and thus abdicate, but his suicide negated all of his episcopal authority *ex post facto* (Matthew 27:3-8; Acts 1:18-19).

ARTICLE V. Archbishop Primacy Over Voting, Synods, and Meetings

A. The Archbishop Shall Permit Voting and all Procedure Styles and Delegation of Powers Thereof

i) As concerns voting and assembling, and all matters, the Archbishop may abolish, change, overrule, nullify, or approve, at any time and at his pleasure, any part of, or all of, the Constitution and Canons of our TACA Diocese, with or without consultation of any person.

ii) Typically, a balloting event occurs for the election of a Bishop or Archbishop. If the incumbent Archbishop should generously allow a given matter to be decided or voted upon by delegates of the constituent members of this TACA Synod, we are given to explain how such voting could occur. Such a vote could include the election of a new Bishop if he so desires not merely to appoint a Bishop. Alternatively, the creation of a new office or administrative species, such as a general fund or a Constitutional Amendment may be decided by a vote or a focus-group called forth by the Archbishop, only if he does not wish to decide the matter by himself.

iii) The Archbishop permits voting by majority (or he may choose according to his pleasure any different method, such as the option shown in Article VI, Section iii, presenting limitations on the number of voters). Because typical Anglican-Continuum Jurisdictions are almost always small, it is sagacious

Article V. Archbishop Primacy Over Voting, Synod, and Meetings

to guard against the possibility that one Parish that may be larger than all the others may be tempted to think only for its own needs, and due to its size may have sufficient votes to unfairly "win the day" at TACA. Can every section, then, despite its size, have equal say? Thus:

iv) The Archbishop permits the type of voting Body: Because a certain part or cross-section of members in the Diocese, small or large, may seek a decision and may act as the legislative Body on a given issue (e.g., regarding whether to create a new Deanery that would develop TACA acolytes and altar boys into theology students), an enhanced voting method could be optioned. (An alternative style known as "manor voting" is suggested as an option for the Archbishop to choose for his Diocese; see below in Article XVIII. Addendum B). However, the conventional voting system (Article V, Part B) is the following basic standard:

B) The Archbishop's Traditional Voting and Assembly Standard:

i) As is his privilege, the Archbishop shall at any time request the standard voting by majority. He may want to host a formal discussion or focus group to influence balloting, and may ask for think-tanking, immediately to precede an election. Thus, he will issue a "Calling Forth" (defined below in Article VI, Part A, Section iv). Delegates may be drawn from all the parishes, congregations, and missions of this TACA Synod. The voters may be allowed by the Archbishop to be smaller in number

Article V. Archbishop Primacy Over Voting, Synod, and Meetings

than the number of persons invited to discuss such matters.

ii) Each Congregation or Mission shall be allotted up to eight delegates per Parish, consisting of Clergy and Laity.

iii) Of that eight, if a Congregation or Mission has fewer than ten Lay members, it may allow one Lay delegate at a Synod or Formal Meeting to vote; the limit of Lay delegates shall equal two delegates if the Laity numbers ten or more members (see Title I, Canon 2). Each Lay delegate must be a member of a TACA Congregation or Mission if he or she wishes to vote and/or participate in discourse.

iv) To replace an absent Archbishop, the House of Bishops shall call forth the entire Synod (all of TACA's religious and Lay members) into an assembled session, known as an Assembly or a Synod Meeting. They vote on who the new Archbishop will be, with up to eight delegates voting per Parish as set forth above.

v) At times it is only the Bishops who vote. That is, at such times, regarding any balloting purpose, the Archbishop and the House of Bishops decide to restrict the decision-making process to the convening of a Council. That is, the House of Bishops, including the Archbishop, shall thus meet to make a final decision on a matter.

> a) The Yearly Synod may thus be convened only as a Council convocation, a provisional, ad hoc, or rump Body, and so could such a Council thus be

Article V. Archbishop Primacy Over Voting, Synod, and Meetings

invoked regarding a partnership with a new ministerial entity or for any decision whatsoever. It is up to the Archbishop, as with all matters—unless he must be replaced, in which case the decision rests within the downward change of command, the Coadjutor, or in the latter's absence, the Suffragan.

vi) At times only the Archbishop decides (see Article VI; Part C; Section i: "*Archiepiscopi Unilateralis*"). No voting, meetings, or assemblies would happen in such a case. Any decision with respect to the elevation of a new Archbishop, the current Archbishop's decision on his own successor, may be made entirely and unilaterally by the current Archbishop alone. His appointment of the imminent Archbishop would typically be his Coadjutor Bishop, whom he would have either already appointed to that assumed pre-slotting or allowed to be voted into office. Alternatively, the Archbishop may decide to choose the Suffragan Bishop, whom he would have appointed in the event of the Coadjutor's vacancy. By the Archbishop's blessing—or in his absence or death—the House of Bishops would traditionally formally elect the Coadjutor/Suffragan. But if it must convene a Council or vote by itself, after the departure or death of the preceding Archbishop, then it will temporarily possess the unilateral authority that would then be passed to the new Archbishop, or to the Coadjutor, or the Suffragan, as outlined above. In any case, he must be formally elected at the Yearly Synod or Formal Meeting (see Article VIII; Part C; Section i).

vii) If the Archbishop's seat is vacant, then typically after the Coadjutor or Suffragan Bishop completes his interim term as Acting or Interim Archbishop by the end of the Diocesan Year (see Article V, Part B, Section viii immediately below), the Acting Archbishop incumbent is then permitted to be elevated to Archbishop by the House of Bishops.

    a) If, under a state of *epikeia* (see Article XVII, Addendum A), the House of Bishops may convene as a Conclave, rather than waiting until September 1, to select the next Archbishop.

viii) The Archbishop's Diocesan Year begins formally on September 1 at midnight, but it may change provisionally according to diocesan need. It ends every August 31, one second before midnight.

ix) Let it also be known that an appointed Deaconess, although she is not ordained, is, for Meetings and Voting purposes, considered by this TACA Diocese to be a member of the Clergy.

ARTICLE VI. Ecclesiastical Authority in Action

A. Meetings and Votes

i) Quorum: The minimum number of members by which a ballot or vote can happen with soundness and validity is 50 percent of all who have been called forth to vote and expected to assemble to so decide.

ii) Synod or Yearly Synodal or Council or Formal Meeting: It shall be held on September 1 of any given year, or the date may be changed by the Archbishop or Interim Archbishop. It may be known as the Yearly Synod. Or if it is a lesser assembly, it can be known as a Regional Synod, Synodal Council, Bishops Council, or other, and still retain the rules of this Article VI and may be called a Formal Meeting.

> a) The Formal Meeting, permitted by the Archbishop, shall operate as the governing Body. It can be co-named "Yearly Synod" if it selects Bishops or votes on this Constitution and/or these Canons or intends a Jurisdictional change for this Jurisdiction. Each religious Body in TACA shall be represented in said Formal Meeting, according to the Canon.

> b) The Synod is a Unicameral Legislature, which means that it is a single legislative chamber. In simpler language, it has no equal chamber to check or to challenge its final vote other than the Archbishop's ratification or veto. Its Diocesan

Article VI. Ecclesiastical Authority in Action

Year technically begins on September 1, which can be changed at the discretion of the Archbishop.

iii) The limit of ordained and consecrated delegates, per Congregation or Mission, who may vote in the Synod, Yearly Synod, or Formal Meeting shall number no more than eight ordained and consecrated delegates, and of that number one Lay delegate if that Body numbers less than ten members, and two Lay delegates if that Body comprises ten or more members. (Or the Archbishop may otherwise choose the number of authorized voters, such as using the basic majority-vote option; see Article V; Part A; Section iii.)

iv) Calling Forth: The Archbishop announces the Yearly or Formal Meeting. Or, for smaller bodies:

a) Formal Meeting within a Regional Diocese or Parish: The Regional Bishop or the Archbishop, Coadjutor, or Suffragan may call forth a meeting to be held within the Regional Diocese or the Church Vestry, under approval of the Archbishop.

b) Lay Representation: A Bishop shall utilize the Laity in a spirit of consultation; or they may be heard and/or vote. Given:

v) Lay Delegation in Formal Meeting or Yearly Synod: Each Congregation, Parish, and Mission, numbering fewer than ten Lay members, may be entitled to the limit of one Lay adult delegate for any Formal Meeting, for voting, or for any discursive purpose. If the number of Lay members in a represented body is ten or more, this limit may be increased to two.

However, each delegate who wishes to vote must be a member of a TACA Parish. His or her inclusion in or exclusion from discussions is at the discretion of pastoral leadership. The Archbishop may increase or decrease the number of Lay participants as he deems necessary, and he may choose to lend his authority to the presider over any group to oblige the same option.

vi) Journal: Sometimes called a Legislative Journal or *imerológio* (ημερολόγιο), a Journal is to be used to date and log all matters and minutes of any such Meetings or Votes.

a) Meetings, Votes, or Elections of any type shall be recorded in said Journal. Such recording concerns the discussion and resultant outcome or decision, and it is to be signed, dated, and thus ratified by the Archbishop or presider given the Archbishop's authority.

vii) Full Body Vote: This constitutes a vote in which all members of each Body within every Parish, within each regional Diocese, and within the entire Archdiocese participate in the vote, so long as every voter is a TACA parishioner. It is convened only by the Archbishop or Interim Bishop, may regard any matter, and may be convened at any time of the Diocesan Year (see Article V, Part B, Section viii). Such Vote reflects a suspension of the delegate process at the discretion of the Archbishop or Interim Archbishop.

Article VI. Ecclesiastical Authority in Action

B: Ratification of a Vote

Preface: All elections of a candidate or decisions on any possible topic, anywhere in this TACA Diocese, shall be ratified by the Archbishop or Interim Archbishop, or delegated by him at his discretion or at any time to the House of Bishops or to any other religious Body of his choice.

> i) Ratification by the Archbishop or Interim Archbishop, or that of any other party of Ecclesiastical Authority, constitutes his Final Approval and qualifies that a given election has occurred with proper adherence to the Constitution and Canons, and was discussed and decided according to the majority of called-forth voters, voting in a 50-percent quorum. All decisions must be ratified by the Archbishop or Interim Archbishop.
>
> ii) Ratification shall happen only with unanimous decision by the majority of the quorum of 50 percent of called-forth voters. A ratification must be recorded in the Journal or *imerológio*, and subsequently signed, dated, and attested to by the Archbishop or Interim Archbishop (or if the Archbishop or Interim is absent, then by the Coadjutor, or in the absence of all higher authority as such, the Suffragan).
>
> iii) Only the House of Bishops may appeal to overturn a vote or decision.
>
> iv) If the House of Bishops shall motion to deem an election flawed or shall argue that some immorality or impracticality has disqualified ratification by the

Archbishop, said Episcopal party may appeal the decision. In such a case:

  a) A House of Bishops' Council shall be called forth to review the appeal, if the Archbishop or Interim Archbishop shall deem such a meeting to be a proper means of settling an appeal against a vote or decision.

  b) The Archbishop or Interim Archbishop shall ratify or veto a vote, or he shall ratify or veto the vote on the appeal.

v) The Archbishop or Interim Archbishop shall ratify or veto, thereby approving or nullifying, respectively, any vote or appeal of a vote made within any part of this TACA Diocese.

C. Archbishop Discretionary Non-Voting Decisions

i) *Archiepiscopi Unilateralis*: A non-voting decision shall be made for the benefit of any part or whole of the Jurisdiction of this TACA Diocese, executed by the Archbishop himself, and made at any time. Said motion is conventionally made by his consulting with the Coadjutor, Suffragan, or anyone he may choose, and is self-ratified via the help of a Journal or *imerológio*.

ii) *Episcopi Unilateralis*: A non-voting decision shall be made for the benefit of a Parish(-es) or Regional Diocese by its head Bishop, in accordance with his best ministers, keeping all pertinent information within a Journal or *imerológio* that can be viewed at any time by the Archbishop.

Article VI. Ecclesiastical Authority in Action

D. Vetoes and Overrides

i) Archbishop Veto: The exercise of such is a highly unusual exception taken by the highest authority of the Church, who normally votes without protest and in respectful regard to the majority of a given decision. His voiding of any vote thereof would be enacted only in matters that could be as grave as with St. Athanasius opposing all of the ancient Bishops' supporting of the wicked presbyter Arius. He is presumed to vote and veto only with the harmonious assent of his brethren in the Episcopate, Clergy, and Laity.

ii) Override of Archbishop Veto: Following the Archbishop's veto, should it be exercised, a Referendum Memo must be written, dated, and signed by a two-thirds majority of the House of Bishops to calendar an override vote.

    a) Only ordained Clergy and Bishops may vote to override by two thirds majority the Archbishop's veto of a vote. The vote must occur no less than 24 hours after the veto has occurred.

iii) The Archbishop may, at his sole discretion, ratify or nullify the override conclusion for any reason or purpose.

E. Episcopal Discretionary Decisions:

i) All decisions or votes that do not occur in the form of a Synod or Yearly Meeting—such as are made within a Bishops' Council, Regional Synod, or

Article VI. Ecclesiastical Authority in Action

other Formal Meeting—are given authority by the Archbishop or Interim Archbishop as reflecting:

a) A choice to be made between the Archbishop and an individual Bishop; and/or:

b) A choice decided for a Jurisdiction, Region, Parish, or other religious Body of TACA, made between its Bishop, Archbishop, and/or consulting an Administrator(s) of appertaining Clergy (e.g., Pastor, Registrar, and/or Vestry); and/or:

c) Any choice affirmed in accordance with the Customary of that religious Body; and/or:

d) Any choice needing Patriarchal guidance or discretion, whatsoever. Ecclesiastical Authority and subordinates must always be mutually approachable, attentive, fair, well-informed, and involved.

F. Episcopal Deference to Customaries

i) Humble respect shall accord each written Customary of every religious Body of this TACA Diocese, given for:

a) All votes and decisions;

b) All Formal Meetings, meetings, conferences, and assemblies;

c) All religious Bodies that are Traditionalist Anglican, in conformity with this Constitution and these Canons.

Article VI. Ecclesiastical Authority in Action

ii) Ecclesiastical Authority holds that each written Customary reflect the established spiritual and practical activities that occur every day within an upstanding traditionalist Anglican Parish. A written Customary helps a Congregation or Mission be objectively understood according to its own ministerial and administrative paradigm. By this noble Subsidiarity, the most charitable consultations may be given by Ecclesiastical Authority to each Parish and Congregation.

> a) The Archbishop may deign to change how a ratified vote is levied, or alter a decision, as regards preserving the healthy independence of a Congregation or Mission as reflected by its Customary and particular need(s). That is, if the Congregation or Mission could be made exempt from a change that affects the rest of Diocese so that its healthy independence may be better preserved, it is only by the sole authority of the Archbishop that such an exemption may occur. Such Congregation or Mission must nevertheless protect orthodoxy and all the proper Anglican formularies, including abidance with these Constitution and Canons.
>
> b) It is thus healthy self-governance, according to the principle of Subsidiarity, that determines the Custom by which an orthodox traditionalist conservative Continuing-Anglican religious Body keeps itself worthy of autonomy and makes itself eligible for official elevation or promotion.

ARTICLE VII. Offices of the Episcopate and Clergy

A. The Archbishop's Vocation

i) An Archbishop is called by the Holy Spirit to head his Diocese, acting through his Jurisdiction as the shepherd, and to nourish the flock entrusted to his care with advocacy and guidance. He is the overseer of the entire Diocese and all its houses, subsidiaries, being given by God the authority and power teach, propagate, buttress, and defend the Faith and the Order of the Diocese under his care.

> a) The Archbishop shall be motivated not merely according to his Free Will but also by his calling to serve God without lording over the people entrusted to his care or expecting to be rewarded with money.
>
> b) A wholesome model of excellence to the whole flock of Christ, the Archbishop is authorized to expand the material presence of the Jurisdiction, its properties, its number of houses, the size of the Clergy, and the like, and to model the Daily Offices and Sacraments of the Diocese.
>
> c) The Archbishop's legacy will be to have advanced the Four Marks of the Church—One, Holy, Catholic, and Apostolic—so that TACA will continue to thrive.
>
> d) The Archbishop is the senior Missionary, head Pastor, guardian and teacher of doctrine, and the

Article VII. Offices of the Episcopate and Clergy

administrator of godly governance and discipline in TACA.

e) The Archbishop consecrates other Bishops, ordains Priests and Deacons, and appoints Deaconesses.

ii) Qualification for the Episcopate

a) To be an acceptable candidate for the Episcopate, a future Bishop must:

1) Be a Priest who is at least 35 years old;

2) Have good morals, be pious, and display godly character;

3) Be prayerful and have great Faith;

4) Zealously care for souls;

5) Exhibit undeniable proof of possessing the Fruits of the Spirit;

6) Have the knowledge, skills, and personal gifts allowing him to fulfill the duties of the office;

7) Be known as an upstanding person by the Faithful;

8) Prove to have administrative experience in leading and growing a Church or Parish.

B. The Priest's Vocation

i) A Priest, well versed in the Liturgy and all of the Bible, must administer the two Gospel Sacraments of

Article VII. Offices of the Episcopate and Clergy

Holy Baptism and Holy Communion, and the Religious Sacraments of Confirmation, Confession, Matrimony, and the Anointing of the Sick/Dying. Priests also must visit the sick, oversee religious education, and give pastoral care to their parishioners.

ii) To be an acceptable candidate for the Priesthood or Deaconate, respectively, a future Priest or Permanent Deacon must:

a) Prove to have strong, unwavering Faith in Christ and impregnable moral integrity;

b) Be a Traditional Anglican (abiding the Thirty-Nine Articles of Religion; the St. Louis Affirmation, and the complete TACA Primary Canon (see Article IV; Section B);

c) Have completed bachelor's degree (only for a prospective Priest);

d) Be able to demonstrate an appreciable degree of education in Theology, Philosophy, the Bible, and Religion;

e) Possess a minimum of one year of experience as an ordained Deacon (or the equivalent);

f) Exemplify leadership, public speaking, compassion, and charity;

g) Have no arrest record;

h) Possess no moral perversion;

i) Be of sane mind;

Article VII. Offices of the Episcopate and Clergy

j) Have a stable work history;

k) Be in good physical health;

l) Not be in the process of a Divorce or Annulment;

m) Be a man who is at least 25 years of age (only for a prospective Priest); a man who is at least 24 (for a prospective Ordained Deacon); or a man or woman who is at least 21 (for a prospective Appointed Deacon or Deaconess).

C. Selection of a Bishop for the TACA House of Bishops

i) Bishops must either be elected in compliance with the Constitution and Canons or unilaterally appointed by the Archbishop. The nominating by any members of the House of Bishops of one to three nominees for the following episcopal offices may be conducted during a Yearly Meeting or a Formal Meeting called forth for that purpose: Archbishop/Primate, Bishop, Diocesan Bishop, Ordinal Bishop, Suffragan Bishop, Coadjutor Bishop, or Metropolitan.

ii) The Archbishop, who may appoint a Bishop on his own, without the need for an Election, will thus elevate an upstanding man, who besides fulfilling the requirements of age, education, formularies, and so forth, projects a character that should inspire unity, hope, and growth within his jurisdiction.

iii) The nomination of potential bishops, and the voting upon of those nominees, must be approved

Article VII. Offices of the Episcopate and Clergy

by the Archbishop (or, if he is being replaced, then by the Coadjutor), and such approval must be written, signed, dated, and added to the Meeting Journal.

iv) Upon the tally and receipt of the vote at a Formal Meeting, the election is automatically ratified by the dating, attestation, and signage in the Journal by the Archbishop and the quorum of the House of Bishops. (If the Archbishop is being replaced, the senior signee is then the Coadjutor.)

v) If only one suitable candidate arrives for the Office of Bishop, his elevation to incumbency may occur only after a discretional consultation has been conducted between the House of Bishops and the Archbishop, and only upon the written, signed, and dated approval in the Meeting Journal by the Archbishop (or, if he is being replaced, by the Coadjutor) that this consultation may take place.

vi) In the event that all the nominees are rejected by the House of Bishops, another Meeting shall be called forth, convened, and concluded, and its results enacted and formally logged.

vii) Upon the selection of a Bishop-Elect to the House of Bishops, the Archbishop shall ratify or veto the choice, with his decision formally logged in the Meeting Journal.

Article VII. Offices of the Episcopate and Clergy

D. The House of Bishops

i) The Bishops together with the Archbishop are known to constitute the House of Bishops of this TACA Diocese.

ii) The House of Bishops is created by gift of prophecy and the laying-on of hands. The gift is the prophetic understanding exemplified and taught to encourage and comfort ministers and all the flocks that the Deposit of Faith, Hope, and Love shall bring forth Revelation and Salvation (1 Timothy 4:14-16; Jeremiah 3:15).

  a) Bishops are expected to consult with the Archbishop upon his request.

  b) As a group, the House of Bishops are godly men whose great integrity and confident leadership characterize them as strong, fit, friendly, and helpful with one another and the Clergy, never interfering with one another's Jurisdiction or lives. Their roles and Jurisdiction are decided by the Archbishop.

  c) Bishops exemplify the stature of the senior shepherd for the priesthood. "And I will give you pastors according to mine heart, which shall feed you with knowledge and understanding" (Jeremiah 3:15).

E. Consecration of a Bishop

i) It is traditional that at least three Traditionalist Anglican/Episcopalian Bishops may consecrate a Traditionalist Anglican/Episcopalian Priest into the

Article VII. Offices of the Episcopate and Clergy

TACA bishopric, if permitted by the Archbishop of TACA.

ii) It is hereby acceptable as Custom that the Archbishop of TACA may be the sole consecrator of a Traditional Anglican Priest into the TACA Bishopric.

F. Election of an Archbishop

i) To be elected Archbishop, a Bishop should have been a member of the House of Bishops of TACA, or a member of a Jurisdiction in Communion with TACA, for at least one year.

ARTICLE VIII. Sede Vacante

A. On the Vacancy of the Seat of the Archbishop

i) If the Archbishop dies, retires, or is expelled—i.e., if his seat is vacant—it is the responsibility of the Coadjutor to take his place as Interim Bishop until a Yearly Synod or Formal Meeting is held to officially elect the new Archbishop or elevate the Coadjutor, by ballot. He votes for himself.

ii) If the Coadjutor is unavailable, the most senior or most capable Suffragan Bishop becomes the Interim Bishop after the other bishops nominate him by mutual agreement or ad-hoc vote to fulfill the office until a formal election can be held. He then becomes formally affirmed by the House of Bishops at the Yearly Synod or Formal Meeting that will officially elevate this Suffragan by regular ballot, and votes for himself, or said Body will at that time nominate and elect a rival Episcopal candidate to be the Archbishop by ballot.

iii) Although there is a formal nomination to populate the ballot with Bishops or Priests eligible to be consecrated, with no minimum mandated as to the number of candidates who can be nominated, it is presumed that the Coadjutor (or, as needed, the most senior Suffragan) will be nominated and imminently elected. But the matter always is formally put out to said vote.

iv) If a lesser Bishop dies, he can be immediately replaced by his nearest or most available and relevant Suffragan permanently or until a

Article VIII. Sede Vacante

replacement is elevated, elected, or appointed by the Archbishop or Interim Archbishop.

v) If there is no replacement available for a vacant Bishop, the Jurisdiction administered by the late Bishop will be handled by the Archbishop and Coadjutor until a Formal Meeting can be convened to nominate a new Bishop to be elected, elevated, and consecrated.

vi) The office of a vacant Bishop may, by the *Archiepiscopi Unilateralis* principle, be appointed by the Archbishop or Interim Archbishop. However, the vacant seat of the Archbishop can only be filled by the aforementioned vote by the House of Bishops traditionally voting imminently on the Coadjutor or otherwise.

vii) The Interim Archbishop shall not engage the *Archiepiscopi Unilateralis* principle or employ any other motive to abolish the requirement that he must be formally elected at the next available Yearly Synod or Formal Meeting. He must be formally elected by said vote (see Article VIII; Part C; Section i).

B. On the Absence or Disability of the Archbishop

i) If the House of Bishops concurs that the Archbishop is fraught with some disability, has been absent from his office, or has failed, neglected, or refused to execute his duties for more than 30 days without providing arrangements with the House of Bishops for coverage during such temporary interregnum, the House of Bishops may declare a

Article VIII. Sede Vacante

state of *sede vacante*. This may be resolved by the return of the Archbishop, and if circumstances are peaceful, then his office resumes as before. If there is an irreconcilable matter associated with the return of the Archbishop, and an Ecclesiastical Court that is summoned forth by the Coadjutor causes a Loss of Clerical State vote that is annulled by a veto by the Archbishop, the Bishops may forbear the matter and not contest it again, or may opt to resign their incardination, but they may not defect, regroup, or call their rump party "Traditional Anglican Church of America" or "TACA" or thereafter assume authority over any of the Congregations, Missions, or other religious Bodies of this TACA Diocese.

ii) In so being determined by a vote of the House of Bishops, the Coadjutor Bishop becomes the de facto Interim Archbishop.

iii) Or, if he is unavailable, the nearest/most relevant Suffragan Bishop thus takes the office.

iv) In the absence of both a Coadjutor and Suffragan, the seat of Interim Archbishop becomes empowered to the House of Bishops corporately until a new Archbishop can be nominated, elected and consecrated).

Article VIII. Sede Vacante

C. The Interim Archbishop Must be Formally Elected

i) The Interim Archbishop shall not be permitted to engage the *Archiepiscopi Unilateralis* principle or employ any other motive to abolish the requirement that he must be formally elected at the next available Yearly Synod or Formal Meeting. He must be formally elected by said vote.

ARTICLE IX. Diocesan Identity, Archbishop's Purse, and Nominal Exclusivity

A. Traditional Anglican Church of America, or TACA, is Solely Religious and is not Financially or Legally Incorporated

i) This TACA Diocese is not a secularly legal or financial corporation of any kind.

ii) A common-law or grassroots "chartering" defines all designations of parishes and other religious Bodies.

iii) The Archbishop affirms that he administers this TACA Diocese according to a broad-based Customary that is published in the office of the home residence or church that he designates as his base of operations, and one that is in compliance with the Constitution and Canons.

iv) No financial or legal responsibility over subsidiaries, agents, agencies, or parties now exists, as they would be subordinate to an otherwise federally- or state-chartered legal entity known as Traditional Anglican Church of America, or TACA.

v) Neither the Archbishop of this TACA Diocese nor any commonly named party operating as Traditional Anglican Church of America, or TACA, of or by itself, or as a religious subsidiary of itself, shall be expected to pay or compensate any financial expectation or debt in full or part, as a party being so named, or to engage in fiscal or formal legal business or activities while being so named.

ARTICLE IX. Diocese Identity, Archbishop's Purse, and Nominal Exclusivity

B. Provision for Fiscal and Legal Incorporation and Federal Codification Under the TACA Diocese Name

i) The Archbishop may provisionally deign to create or to inherit the ruling chair of a corporate entity that encompasses all of TACA, typically a nonprofit structure, over which he himself would be the senior officer, with a secretary, treasurer, and so forth, as is ordinarily done in a nonprofit setting.

ii) The corporation would have the same name as our TACA Diocese, "Traditional Anglican Church of America."

iii) A provisional allowance is made for said TACA corporate entity, but this entity has never existed in TACA prior to and including September 2023, nor shall it exist without a proper legal filing of the appropriate statutory documentation by the Archbishop, using his own church as its operational center or his personal home address.

iv) Said provisional future central entity would be a body incorporated within his local State Department, and, for banking and tax-filing purposes, simultaneously registered as a 501(c)3 corporation through the U.S. Internal Revenue Service.

v) At the Archbishop's discretion, as he consults his trusted associates, he may in time decide on how funds, tithes, collections, financial gifts, or other revenue may be disbursed within the greater Jurisdiction of TACA, and/or disbursed within any particular Body, Parish, or Regional Diocese over which he supremely presides.

ARTICLE IX. *Diocese Identity, Archbishop's Purse, and Nominal Exclusivity*

C. Incorporation of TACA belongs to the Office of the Archbishop

i) No other Body or person within TACA—neither a Parish, a Regional Diocese, a Ministry, nor any other member or constituent of TACA except for the Archbishop—shall publicly file or publish for itself a publicly incorporated leadership role as a 501(c)3 organization or other, or use the name "Traditional Anglican Church of America," or "TACA," to name itself in any way, whether in whole or in part.

ii) No Parish or any other ecclesiastical Body may publicly file any name besides its own distinct individual name, as that individual ecclesiastical name should exist in writing within TACA's religious chartering of it as recorded within the Archbishop's Chancery. If chartered religiously as, for example, "St. John's Church," then so may a nonprofit corporation be named as such, albeit without the use of the name "Traditional Anglican Church of America" or "TACA" within or beside the name, whether in whole or in part.

iii) No religious subsidiary Body shall ever file the name of our whole TACA Diocese for any legal, financial, or publishing purpose or for any membership causes.

iv) The name "Traditional Anglican Church of America" (herein "the TACA name") may only be publicly registered or published, verbally promoted, printed, or electronically reproduced solely for the issuance of material that is authored or directly controlled by the Archbishop.

v) As usage of the TACA name in connection with some other venture would regard the referential naming of our TACA Diocese or imply the representation of our TACA Diocese, the TACA name may only be used to refer to our TACA Diocese within the flow of regular speech or expository, religious/spiritual, and theological writing.

vi) The TACA name shall not be used to endorse or promote any idea or entity other than this TACA Diocese.

vii) Only the Office of the Archbishop, when identifying the whole of this TACA Diocese, shall use the name, "Traditional Anglican Church of America," or "TACA," in a way that denotes the nominal identity of our TACA Diocese for any legal, journalistic, promotional, or transactional purpose.

viii) Otherwise, all uses of the TACA name as such can only be made available for use solely according to the expressed written permission of the Archbishop of TACA.

D. Financial Responsibility Belongs to Each Religious Body

i) This TACA Diocese, the Chancery of TACA, the Archbishop or Archdiocese of TACA, or any party or agent bearing the TACA name shall not give, apportion, or transfer any salary, or payment of fees, or debt that is whole or in part, or any other

ARTICLE IX. Diocese Identity, Archbishop's Purse, and Nominal Exclusivity

money or stipend, proffered in-kind or monetarily, to any individual, or party, or agency—whether religiously or non-religiously chartered, consecrated, ordained, or sanctified, or whether operating, serving, or helping anywhere within this TACA Diocese.

ii) Each religious Body is related to TACA solely theologically as accords the spiritual dominion possessed by the TACA Archbishop to invisibly incardinate and sanctify its Clergy, Ministers, and religious Bodies.

iii) A voluntary or free-will monthly gift is given outright to the Archbishop of TACA for his own personal funds in order to offset the costs of his provision of broad-based volunteer administration of this TACA Diocese. As of September 2023, this gift is set at $25 for its incardinated TACA Priests and $50 per month for its consecrated TACA Bishops.

ARTICLE X. Regional Dioceses of TACA, and Its Subsidiaries, During the Pre-Apocalyptic Era

A. Impetus for Geographical Relocation of TACA Bodies Determined by the Practical Demands of Bi-Vocational Life

i) A religious Body of TACA shall change location as befits its Pastor's habitational and/or geographical needs; such flexibility epitomizes a flexible Church that is simultaneously of a Confessional and Tabernacle-like nature. The TACA Jurisdictions as of September 2023 are listed below (see Article X; Part A; Section vi; Item d).

ii) That is, because the bi-vocational Bishops and Priests of TACA are Pauline men, they perform the Liturgy and homiletics wherever life dictates that they must plant, and sometimes move, their ministry.

iii) At such times of relocation, the Diocese of TACA and/or any of its Subsidiaries may thus change its physical boundaries. Saint Paul of Tarsus, himself a tentmaker, funded his ministry chiefly in Corinth (Acts 18:1-4) but became increasingly dependent on fiscal and in-kind help from wealthier Christians, who were thereby sanctifying their social praxis (Philippians 4:17).

iv) Inching along via the dirty fingernails of work life toward the white gowns of Paradise, we TACA ministers shall work in order to eat (2 Thessalonians 3:10-12) as we fulfil our salvific work as Ministers of God and. There may be times when tithes and

Article X. Regional Dioceses of TACA, and Its Subsidiaries During the Pre-Apocalyptic Era

donations shall need to be sought from faithful nearby Christian parishioners and supporters, wherever they may be, regarding whom TACA ministers have never had to wipe the dust off of their priestly feet.

v) However, such loving parishioners and TACA supporters, who have been nobly catechized not to be avaricious lovers of the Mammon of Caesar and his image, are sadly becoming increasingly impecunious: many are struggling financially and otherwise right alongside their Priests, trying to survive in today's socio-politically hyperpolarized, globalized world.

a) A bi-vocational Priesthood sets stakes deeply, knowing such polarity descends toward the Apocalypse: The more that survival increasingly coerces confused persons to behave bestially towards the meek (Proverbs 22:22-23), the more sympathetic hearts must thus be angled for by Anglicans. There is a remnant in every Age: "Even so then at this present time also there is a remnant according to the election of grace" (Romans 11:5).

b) At the evaded evil pole, the institutional churches are thus the more financially richer, as they continue confessing a homosexual, transgender, pedophilic, and bucolic worship— hence, a religious ethos that comforts and enables the spiritual sickness of the wealthier reprobate, as if God cannot see this (Psalms 10:2-18; Psalm

94:7). Their heartless pleasure, proffering false mercy to those headed for damnation, will thus be short-lived (Psalms 37:12-15).

c) God also made His hard-working Elect to feel abundantly satisfied, resting in his goodness: "How excellent *is* thy lovingkindness, O God! therefore the children of men put their trust under the shadow of thy wings. They shall be abundantly satisfied with the fatness of thy house; and thou shalt make them drink of the river of thy pleasures" (Psalm 36:7-8).

vi) All of these stated truths help explain why TACA is not a wealthy enough Diocese to have permanently stationed geographical locations. However:

a) Times being what they are, many rich "institutional" cathedrals are themselves going under the wrecking ball.

b) Only the churches of Smyrna and Philadelphia stand the test of God's time (Revelation 2:8-11; 3:7-13), and not for reasons of wealth. Thusly:

c) A few examples below shall illustrate how a TACA Bishop or Rector has thus sometimes needed to move his religious office wherever he had to go to find paying work in this world. (They show how each minister has moved his ministry as if he were a version of Moses moving from one town to another the Tabernacle containing the Ark, rather than compromising his confessional

Article X. Regional Dioceses of TACA, and Its Subsidiaries During the Pre-Apocalyptic Era

devotion to Bible Truth, on which all solid Traditional Anglican principles are based):

1) In 2010, Bishop Paul Leeman moved his heavy-equipment operator business from Montague, California, to Klamath Falls, Oregon, where he soon became the leader of the Western Diocese of TACA at Saint Mark's.

2) In 1992, Bishop Robert Baker, who had assisted TACA co-founder Bishop Melvin Pickering in running Saint Chad's Church and its adjunct seminary, Saint George's, in San Antonio, Texas, returned to Saint Mark's as TACA's Archbishop, chaired there in his hometown.

3) Bishop Howard Edwin Caudill, the earliest co-founder of TACA, was born in West Virginia, began his operations in 1967 within the American Episcopal Church in San Antonio, supported himself as an author, and eventually became the Archbishop of the Central and Western Provinces (an early formative version of TACA), finally locating himself in the Ohio Valley.

4) The impetus for all of these early or current manifestations of TACA has been the bi-vocational nature of the TACA Priesthood and Episcopate.

Article X. Regional Dioceses of TACA, and Its Subsidiaries During the Pre-Apocalyptic Era

d) Bi-vocational and Tabernacle-like in its operations, TACA is divided into the following regions, as of September 2023:

1) The Eastern Diocese, where the Chancery and Archbishop Rick Aaron Reid sit, at Saint Andrew's, in Newton, North Carolina.

2) The Western Diocese, where Bishop Paul Leeman sits, at St. Mark's, in Klamath Falls, Oregon.

3) The Southwestern Regional Diocese, occupied by the Bishop Francis Fontenot in St. Martinsville, Louisiana; Right Reverend Ashley Edward, of McKinney, Texas; Right Reverend Donald Nozawa of Bridgeton, Missouri.

4) The Northeastern Diocese, maintained by Father Michael DellaVecchia, of Perkasie, Pennsylvania, a Jurisdiction whose bishopric is currently *sede vacante.*

5) The Canon Prelature, helmed by Right Reverend, Kenneth Walsh, in White Stone, Virginia.

6) The Coadjutor/Suffragan Prelature (non-geographic), occupied by Coadjutor Bishop Fontenot and Suffragan Bishop Fleming.

B. Availability for Convocations, Ministries, Orders, Working Groups, and Deaneries

i) Parishes are encouraged to produce internal associations and ministries that participate in, or

Article X. Regional Dioceses of TACA, and Its Subsidiaries During the Pre-Apocalyptic Era

lead, a local cause, such as would concern a charitable goal or a virtuous social interest. Fund raising and recruitment as well as hiring of volunteers and workers must not interfere or conflict with, or lessen the influence of, regular Church drives and goals, or be utilized to diminish the worship life and holdings of the Parish(-es) in any way.

ii) A Working Group (e.g., volunteers running a coat drive, a club that routinely goes on leisurely outings) may also be encouraged to continue as per, or even grow into, an active ministry. A Dean of such potentially budding ministry may thereby be appointed—perhaps the Pastor himself, or a Deacon or Priest—to oversee and foster the development and continuing function of such ministry.

iii) While a club or ministry may be created at such grassroots level, and sometimes may comprise a society or cause that involves collaboration between two or more parishes or dioceses (e.g., such as Anglican Association of Biblical Scholars, or Guild of All Souls), it is also foreseeable that the prayerful life and good works of such a Body may beg the question of how best to abide the growth of such a fruit on the vine.

iv) Upon the Pastor's request, a Bishop, such as a Suffragan, may review the blessed *cultus* of such growing entity and create a Deanery for it, envisioning it as a potential mission or Church.

Article X. Regional Dioceses of TACA, and Its Subsidiaries During the Pre-Apocalyptic Era

v) No legal, statutory, financial, or federal registration may be filed, registered, or published on behalf of any religious Body, or, for any interest, within TACA, other than a Parish that is filing solely in its own name and accepting all financial and legal responsibility for itself.

ARTICLE XI. Holy Ordination, Consecration, and Appointment

A. Chaste, Conservative Male Ordinations

i) Affirming the ministry of men in the offices of the Church, TACA will ordain and consecrate only heterosexual men and no women, as regards the Transitional and Permanent Diaconate, the Priesthood, and the Episcopate (Exodus 28:1; Hebrews 5:1; 1 Timothy 2:12). Regarding Bishops specifically, "a bishop must be blameless, as the steward of God; not self-willed, not soon angry, not given to wine, no striker, not given to filthy lucre; But a lover of hospitality, a lover of good men, sober, just, holy, temperate; Holding fast the faithful word as he hath been taught, that he may be able by sound doctrine both to exhort and to convince the gainsayers" (Titus 1:6-9).

ii) Women may be appointed, although not ordained, as Deaconesses, whose "permanence" is relevant in insofar as their Grace is sufficient to retain their incumbency as Deaconesses (Romans 16:1-15; 1 Peter 3:5).

iii) Religious offices abide the Scriptural warrant and fulfill the mission of the Church and its Four Marks: One, Holy, Catholic, and Apostolic Church, as exemplified by this TACA Jurisdiction.

iv) The roles of Priest, Bishop, and Deacon are formally defined above in Article VII, along with various forms and uses.

ARTICLE XII. Reserved Rights of all Independent Constituent Congregations and all Bodies

A. All property—real, personal, tangible, and intangible—owned or held by, or on behalf of, an Officer, Parishioner, Parish, Regional Diocese, or this entire TACA Jurisdiction, now and in the future, is and shall be solely and exclusively owned by the holder of the deed, the title, or the receipt of the property, who has or shall have acquired it for himself or herself independently, or shall have been acquired by the recipient(s) to whom it has been publicly or personally recorded as having been bequeathed or given, or by the agency which has acquired it for itself, or for the recipient(s) to whom it has been recorded as having been bequeathed or given. All such owned property is hereby free of any trust, right of assessment, or other claim in favor of any Church, the Diocese, the Archdiocese, an Archprimature, or any other Congregation or religious Body of TACA.

B. Each constituent Congregation, religious Body, and person reserves the right to withdraw from TACA at any time.

C. A withdrawing Congregation or religious Body should give notice of its withdrawal simultaneously to the House of Bishops and Archbishop, including the effective date, and shall retain all its own property—real, personal, tangible, and intangible—owned, rented, leased, or held by or on behalf of that departing Congregation or Body, and which is not owned, leased, held, or rented by TACA or an agent of TACA.

ARTICLE XIII. Reserved Rights of the Archdiocese of TACA

A. All property of the Archdiocese of TACA shall not be subject to any trust, right of assessment, or other claim by any member of, or constituent body or entity within or outside of the Jurisdiction of TACA, or within or outside of any future provisional Communion Synod as an independent Jurisdiction thereof. The Jurisdiction of TACA reserves the right to withdraw from any church partnership or Communion at any time with the consent of at least a 51-percent majority vote of the voters or delegates convened at a meeting of the Synod that is called for that purpose, or by unilateral decision of the Archbishop of TACA. In the advent of a withdrawal, the Archdiocese shall give notice to the partner, including the effective date of withdrawal, and shall retain all property—real, personal, tangible, and intangible—owned or held by or on behalf of this TACA Archdiocese.

ARTICLE XIV. Incorporation; Operation; Guarantees; Derivatives

A. The Archdiocese shall firstly incorporate in accordance with the laws of the State (e.g., Department of State) where a predominant number of its churches and ministries are located and file its public legal identity with the U.S. Internal Revenue Service (typically as a nonprofit charitable institution or church). The Archbishop conventionally shall be the President of the corporation, while the House of Bishops would populate the chairs of its Board of Directors.

B. Alternately, the Archbishop may incorporate his Cathedral as a singular Parish within the Jurisdiction and deign to share regularly his house's endowment and abundant tithes meritoriously with the other parishes of TACA.

C. As a religious Subsidiary of the Archbishop's very Archbishopric, the Chancery/Cathedral is itself a freestanding Parish simultaneously, which therefore may accord itself the same perfunctory workings as are enjoyed by any other individual TACA parish. Meanwhile, it can oversee the sustained magisterial framework of a theological and divinity-based polity. By and large, the U.S. government may view all the churches of TACA as independent nonprofit corporations, while it is our hope that God sees the Cathedral and all its parishes, being shepherded by a Presiding Episcopal Overseer, as faithful, vigorous, thriving campuses shepherded, in turn, by other faithful and stalwart shepherds.

Article XIV. Incorporation; Operation; Guarantees; Derivatives

D. Unless firstly approved by a Synod vote, the Archdiocese shall not act corporately "as TACA" to guarantee, whether directly or indirectly, any loan or other commitment for the benefit of any Parish, Congregation, or any other religious Body or person. Likewise, the Archdiocese or any religious Body or agent, presuming to act "as TACA," may not enter into any investment or contract commonly referred to as a "derivative," or any type of financial contract whose value is dependent on an underlying asset, group of assets, or performance benchmark, unless consent is firstly given by a Synod vote.

E. Any Parish known to this TACA Diocese as one of its Congregations is responsible for all of its own business and legal endeavors, including seeking incorporation, proprietorship, partnership, certification or licensure of any kind, or any other business legal status and may not legal and publicly file its name, whether whole or in part, as "Traditional Anglican Church of America" or as "TACA." Its collaboration with this TACA Diocese is within the broad-based fellowship of a theological union that recognizes the Archbishop and House of Bishops as its Ecclesiastical Authority, a union that is wholly spiritual in nature.

ARTICLE XV. Parishes, Congregations, and Dioceses of TACA, or in Communion with TACA, as of September 2023 *(except where noted)*

A. Saint Andrew's Anglican Church and Cathedral of TACA, Newton, North Carolina

B. Saint Mark's Anglican Church of TACA, Klamath Falls, Oregon

C. Saint Patrick's Anglican Church of TACA, Perkasie, Pennsylvania

D. The Reformed Anglican Church, Saint Augustine, Florida *(Communion annulled, July 2023)*

E. Cathedral of the Province of Santa Maria Virgen, Santo Domingo, Ecuador

F. Cathedral of the Independent Mexican Episcopal Church, Tlalpan, Mexico

G. The Emmanuel Communion, Diocese of Indiantown, Florida

H. Additional parishes and congregations to be added as provided by Canon. Subject to their prior right of withdrawal, a Parish or Congregation may be removed from membership as provided by Canon.

ARTICLE XVI. Adoption and Amendment

A) The Constitution and Canons will be adopted by this TACA Synod by the consent of a majority vote of all eligible delegates and/or voters present at the Yearly Synod Meeting or other Formal Meeting convened for its purpose or by the Archbishop's approval by his exercise of *Archiepiscopi Unilateralis*. The Archbishop's final signed approval shall constitute Ratification of the Adoption of the Constitution and Canons of TACA.

B) The Constitution and Canons may be amended provisionally by this TACA Synod by the consent of a majority vote of all eligible delegates and/or voters present at the Yearly Synod or other Formal Meeting convened for its purpose.

C) The Constitution and Canons may otherwise be adopted or vetoed *Archiepiscopi Unilateralis* by the Archbishop.

D) The Archbishop's signed approval shall be located at the bottom of the Constitution and Canons of TACA and thereby shall count as the Ratification of this Constitution and these Canons and of any provisional or conclusive Amendment. The Archbishop's signed approval shall be the Final Ratification of any Draft of the whole, or of any revision within, of this Constitution and these Canons of TACA, or any Amendment thereof.

E) The Final Draft of this Constitution and these Canons of TACA shall be submitted prior to the next Yearly Synod Meeting or prior to a Formal Meeting convened for the purpose of voting to adopt, nullify, or amend it. Any decision on whether to adopt, nullify, or amend the Constitution and Canons, if not made *Archiepiscopi Unilateralis,* shall be voted on in a Formal Meeting inclusive of the appropriate consultants (e.g., the Canon), who will be chosen by the Archbishop to convene together with the Archbishop to discuss their contents.

F) If ratified, or if there is a need for amendment, the Constitution and Canons may be discussed during an in-person Formal Meeting or remotely held through interactive video conferencing (e.g., Zoom), convened for the purpose of consultation with the Archbishop and solely by his permission.

ARTICLE XVII. Addendum A—Anglican Primer: Organization, Hierarchy, Christian Terms, and Administration

A. Definitions not in alphabetical order, but in order of relevance to the subjects in the Constitution and Canons.

Customary: A written set of rules published by a Parish or religious Body, by which a pattern of spiritual and practical activities that can be objectively verified within the particular setting can be established. It is the written set of each Custom of that religious Body.

Subsidiarity: The principle of allowing the religious Bodies of a Traditional Anglican Diocese to make decisions on issues that affect themselves, so long as the decisions are in conformity with the Constitution and Canons under which their Jurisdictions are governed. Hence, TACA is a Diocese of both Custom and Subsidiarity.

Traditionalist Anglican/Episcopalian: A Reformist Christian who not only fully accepts no later version of an American or British Book of Common Prayer than 1928, but also holds as being extraordinary the Thirty-Nine Articles of Religion and the St. Louis Affirmation of 1978. He or she lives an orthodox life in solemn witness of the Bible as being the primary sufficient means of Salvation, and considers no historical Ecumenical Council to be canonical that is later than first seven Councils, while raising or being a part of a family, whether married or unmarried, and living chastely—i.e., keeping "unspotted from the world" (James 1:27).

Synod or Assembly: The entire legislative body of this Jurisdiction. TACA, as a whole, is the Synod or Assembly (sometimes referred to as the "Synod Assembly"), whereas the term "Council" only refers to all the Bishops and Archbishop as a group.

House of Bishops: The Archbishop or Primate and all the other Bishops of this TACA Synod. Whenever they meet together by themselves for a Bishops' vote or meeting, or when referred to as a group, they are referred to as the House of Bishops, or the Council, or the Archbishop's Council, etc. The House of Bishops may also be called, any of the other following appellations: Council, Tribunal, Ecclesiastical Authority, Trial Court, dependent on the context.

Arch-Synod: The entire legislative body of a provisional future Communion with all of its constituent Jurisdictions, including TACA and all others. It more often defines an Eastern Orthodox larger jurisdiction but is pertinent for use when there are two Primates jointly holding a jurisdiction.

Parishioner or Traditionalist Anglican Parishioner: A Christian member of a TACA parish, or other Anglican house known for its orthodoxy, who adopts our Canon and participates in the Daily Office, Holy Communion, and Sacramental life, with happy Fellowship.

Bishop: The senior adult male shepherd serving all the parishes, Priests, and members of a region appointed

Article XVII. Addendum A—Anglican Primer: Organization, Hierarchy, Christian Terms, and Administration

to him by an Archbishop or Primate. The Bishop is the inheritor of the Apostolic Succession of such elders who have each been committed to his respective divine purpose by a Consecrator, who himself has been consecrated via a continuous, unbroken chain of Bishops, through the holy *cheirotonia*, or the "laying on of hands," upon each Bishop's person, ever since the brotherly bonding of the Twelve Apostles, whose unity framed the Church Universal. Each had been physically and spiritually touched by Jesus, and were empowered by the Holy Spirit at Pentecost, to pursue and to build their ministries, and thereafter to ordain Priests and consecrate new Bishops.

Archbishop or Primate: The head of Traditional Anglican Church of America (TACA) in a given country. In terms of his theological synodal partnership within a Communion with other churches, the Primate rules as our own Archbishop of TACA, for all of our interior purposes. His incumbency is elected at any Yearly Synod Meeting or a Formal Meeting that would be called for that purpose. As of July 2023, the head of TACA for the nation of Mexico is Archbishop/Primate Jorge Martinez. The head of TACA for the United States of America is Archbishop/Primate Rick Aaron Reid, who, from the Archdiocese or Chancery of TACA in Newton, North Carolina, presides over the entire Jurisdiction of TACA. The Archbishop/Primate of the Reformed Anglican Church is the Right Reverend Robert Bierman, whose chancery is in Saint Augustine, Florida. (Although no longer in communion with TACA,

Article XVII. Addendum A—Anglican Primer: Organization, Hierarchy, Christian Terms, and Administration

his former collaborative theological primacy with TACA is mentioned herein for illustrative purposes.)

Regional Bishop: The Metropolitan head of a regional Diocese within TACA. This office pertains to two offices for TACA as of September 2023: namely, the Eastern Diocese, which is helmed by Archbishop Rick Aaron Reid; and the Metropolitan of the Western Diocese, led by Bishop Paul Leeman.

Coadjutor Bishop: A Diocesan, typically Regional, Bishop who collaborates with the Archbishop in the administration and religious leadership of the Archdiocese. While in other Anglican Jurisdictions, he may be considered a "Vicar General," his significance in terms of experience and tenure instills in his office a second-in-command connotation. Thus, the Coadjutor at TACA conventionally influences voters at the Annual Meeting or Special Meeting to nominate and then elect a minister unanimously to become the Archbishop after the latter's retirement, removal, or death. Although there is a necessary formal nomination to populate the ballot, with no minimum number of men mandated as regards the number of candidates who can be nominated, the general understanding is that the Coadjutor has long been the most trusted and experienced prelate outside of the preceding Archbishop. That is, it is presumed that the Coadjutor would be nominated and unanimously elected. However, if there is no Coadjutor, the most senior or most equipped Suffragan Bishop will instead tend to be nominated to the candidacy of this imminent seat. The Coadjutor Bishop is often simultaneously a

Article XVII. Addendum A—Anglican Primer: Organization, Hierarchy, Christian Terms, and Administration

Metropolitan at TACA while being the Coadjutor, presiding over a whole region within the Jurisdiction, as is Bishop Paul Leeman, who is the Metropolitan of the Western Diocese, just as Archbishop Rick Aaron Reid, who had been the Coadjutor Bishop and Metropolitan Bishop of the Eastern Diocese, was but is now the Archbishop of TACA. The current Coadjutor Bishop of TACA is Bishop Francis Fontenot.

Secretary of Chancery, Diocese, or Parish: Appointed by a Bishop or Pastor, a Secretary is the assistant and/or Registrar in all administrative matters. A Secretary of a Parish is a staff member of an individual Parish. At the time of this writing, the Secretary for the Archdiocese is Deaconess Virginia Reid, who thus works in the Chancery. The Secretary of the Western Diocese is Deaconess Grace Leeman.

Treasurer: Bookkeeper and senior depositor of all money coming and going out of a religious Body.

Cathedral: The main church, or Chancery, where the Archbishop presides, and which is the administrative center of a Jurisdiction. In TACA, the Cathedral is St. Andrew's Anglican Church, in Newton, North Carolina. For the Reformed Anglican Church (RAC, which was in provisional Communion with TACA until July 2023), the Cathedral/Chancery is in Saint Augustine, Florida. The concept of a Cathedral/Chancery of such an Communion, as of July 2023, exists in this Constitution, and may be substantiated as a future matter at the discretion of the Archbishop.

Article XVII. Addendum A—Anglican Primer: Organization, Hierarchy, Christian Terms, and Administration

Provisional Future Communion and Synod: A theological confraternity and fellowship within which two or more mutually exclusive independent and autonomous Traditionalist Anglican dioceses and all its members may share the same Eucharistic and Liturgical prayers, the 1928 BCP, ordinals, hosts, and meetings. It is a theological union without a shared physical property and without shared fiscal or administrative responsibilities. Each member of such fellowship would govern his own Diocese by its own Custom.

Archprimature: The Archbishopric of a provisional future Communion of Traditional Anglican dioceses, held either by one Archbishop, or jointly by two. Traditional Anglican Church of America would therefore theologically be a constituent synodal partner of this Communion. The Archprimature thus describes a theological co-leadership without shared physical property and without shared fiscal or administrative responsibilities. Each partner would govern his own Diocese by its own Custom.

Church: Where priests and/or Bishops preside. It may be the presiding church of a Regional Diocese, or it may merely house a Parish. Depending on context, it may also refer to the entirety of all Trinitarian Christians worldwide, otherwise known as the Universal Church.

Jurisdiction: The geographical region served by the Diocese. The United States and Mexico each fall within the Jurisdiction of TACA.

Article XVII. Addendum A—Anglican Primer: Organization, Hierarchy, Christian Terms, and Administration

Diocese: The administrative center of a Jurisdiction. These terms go back to ancient Rome. By 305 A.D., the "Praeotorian Prefecture" ruled over a precinct, or an area known as a "diocese," that was governed by a "Vicarius," from which derive the word "Vicar." Today, a Diocese is the territory from which a Bishop administrates all the local and regional parishes that fall under him.

Regional Diocese of the East: St. Andrew's Anglican Church of Newton, North Carolina is the headquarters of the Eastern half of TACA; it is thus the Eastern Metropolitan hemisphere, and the place where the Metropolitan Bishop for this eastern hemisphere is stationed, namely Rick Aaron Reid, who also happens to be the Archbishop/Primate of all of TACA.

Regional Diocese of the West: St. Mark's Anglican Church of Klamath Falls, Oregon, is the headquarters of the Western half of TACA. It is the western Metropolitan hemisphere. It is thus where the Metropolitan of this Western Hemisphere is stationed, namely Bishop Paul K. Leeman, who also happens to be the Coadjutor Bishop of all of TACA.

Regional Diocese of the Midwest: As of September 2023, TACA is has its eye on an emergent Traditional Anglican witness in the midwestern United States and is open to receiving a qualified Bishop, who conventionally would be a Suffragan, to preside over an active nearby ecclesial post in this region prior to naming him as a Metropolitan. This office, therefore, is open.

Article XVII. Addendum A—Anglican Primer: Organization, Hierarchy, Christian Terms, and Administration

Regional Diocese of the Southwest: This Diocese is nearest to one of TACA's founding locations of San Antonio (i.e., St. Chad's Anglican Church). With respect to this Diocese, TACA focuses on continuing Traditional Anglican witness to unite with emerging forms. Any future local Bishop, conventionally a Suffragan, would reside in active nearby *ecclesia* prior to being named as a Metropolitan. As of September 2022, Bishop Francis Fontenot, founder of Portiuncula Franciscan Hermitage and Retreat Center, residing in St. Martinsville, Louisiana, is the Coadjutor of this Diocese and is available to all TACA Dioceses.

Anglican Church Suzerainty: A Parish or Regional Diocese that is in equal status with other such Bodies within a Jurisdiction and is equally affected theologically by all decisions across that body, but is also simultaneously the ruling Metropolitan body or the Cathedral for its own original diocese. For example, the Reformed Anglican Church, which had been in provisional Communion with TACA until July 2023, was not merely a Parish in Saint Augustine, Florida, but during said Communion was also the seat of the suzerain ruling house as a Parish/Diocese within TACA (as TACA was a suzerain Diocese within RAC), as all mutual bodies are able to collaborate within a Communion. Accordingly, St. Andrew's Anglican Church is not merely a Parish in Newton, North Carolina, but was also the suzerain ruling house in Primacy over the Archdiocese within said Communion.

House of Bishops: All the bishops within a Jurisdiction or Diocese, also known as the Episcopate, which

Article XVII. Addendum A—Anglican Primer: Organization, Hierarchy, Christian Terms, and Administration

includes the Archbishop. As of September 2023, this TACA Episcopate consists of Archbishop/Primate Rick Aaron Reid; Bishop Paul Leeman; Right Rev. Kenneth Walsh; Bishop Francis Fontenot; Right Rev. Ashley Beckham; Bishop David Fleming; Right Rev. Don Nozawa; and Archbishop/Primate Jorge Martinez. (Note: In Anglicanism, there is no office of "Presbyter" or a "Presbytery," although "Elder" is a term that is informally bandied about as an affectionate reference to a beloved senior, consultant, or founder of a church or religious Body).

Chancery: The executive center of a Church or Cathedral, where the Office of the Archbishop is located. It is the senior administrative religious office of our Diocese and is also referred to as the Archdiocese, located in the state in which this TACA Diocese is incorporated. The Chancery of TACA is St. Andrew's Anglican Church, in Newton, North Carolina, as of September 2023.

Archdiocese: The same as Diocese (see above definition), except that it is helmed at the TACA Cathedral by the Archbishop, who administers all parishes and regional dioceses under him. TACA is then our Archdiocese, where presides (as of September 2023) Archbishop Rick Aaron Reid. He is also known as Primate when referred to in the context of a Provisional Future Communion or Arch-Synod). Archbishop Reid presides over TACA from his Chancery (see above definition) at Saint Andrew's. It is often a matter of convenience to refer to his office as the Archdiocese of TACA.

Article XVII. Addendum A—Anglican Primer: Organization, Hierarchy, Christian Terms, and Administration

Ecclesiastical Authority: The Chancery or Office of the Archbishop acting alone or in consultation with his House of Bishops.

Canon, Chancellor, or Prebendary: The Bishop or Priest who specializes in Canon Law, who advises the Archbishop and sits in physical and/or administrative residence at the Cathedral. If he were paid a stipend or salary from the coffers of the Chancery or Cathedral, he would also be referred to as the Prebendary. The Canon of TACA as of September 2023 is the Right Reverend Kenneth Walsh. The appointment of a Canon may be ratified via the Ratification for Imminent Vote (see next entry, below).

Ratification for Imminent Vote: For all appointments or inherited offices to which the Archbishop does want to appoint his own shepherd, a formal ballot may be conducted. The office may contain the presumed incumbent immediately, but his official appointment must be finalized by a Council Meeting of the House of Bishops to nominate him and/or anyone else desired for the seat, and then by putting the matter out to vote. The Archbishop retains the authority to veto the outcome. The Ratification vote by the House of Bishops will be presumedly unanimous in favor of the inheritor or the appointee, conventionally speaking. If there is a desired override, however, the Ordained Clergy may participate in the voting, and the rules for Vetoes and Overrides must be followed (see Article V, Parts A, B; Article VI, Parts A-F, but particularly Part D).

Article XVII. Addendum A—Anglican Primer: Organization, Hierarchy, Christian Terms, and Administration

Suffragan Bishop: A Bishop elected to be an interior consultant for the Archbishop, especially one to assist a Regional Bishop/Metropolitan in administering a given Diocese or the Archdiocese as a whole. (In the latter case, a Chancery Suffragan would be an already-consecrated Bishop who is appointed by the Archbishop to help administer the entire Jurisdiction.) A Diocesan Suffragan also may help the Coadjutor act as the de facto Interim Archbishop until an election can occur, formally nominating him and confirming his imminent assumption by ballot. Bishop David C. Fleming is jointly a Suffragan of TACA and of St. Mark's Church of Klamath Falls, Oregon. Bishop Charles Klughart, who resides in Springfield, Illinois, is also a Suffragan of TACA.

Interim Archbishop: A Bishop who is usually imminently the Coadjutor or nominated by the House of Bishops to replace the Archbishop, or who is named as successor of the Archbishop.

Interim Bishop or Archbishop: A Bishop who replaces a member of the Episcopate, while another Bishop is being sought. If the Archbishop is being replaced, it is presumed that the Coadjutor will take over the role and imminently become the new Archbishop.

Ordinal Bishop: A Bishop who is a member of a Religious Order such as an Abbey, Seminary, or Academy within a Jurisdiction. This office is being developed as of September 2023, but its incumbency is contingent on the development of a Religious Order. An Ordinal Bishop can also be called a Right Reverend.

Article XVII. Addendum A—Anglican Primer: Organization, Hierarchy, Christian Terms, and Administration

As with any religious Body other than a School, Congregation, or Mission, which are begun by the Diocese, an Order, as well as many Abbeys, Monasteries, Deaneries, and Seminaries, begins with an independent ministry inside the Diocese that becomes a recognized *cultus*, gains helpers and adherents, has its own Bishop, and then becomes a larger entity.

Diocesan Bishop: A Bishop in charge of a region within a Diocese. For example, Suffragan Bishop Charles Klughart is the Diocesan Bishop of TACA in the provisional Midwest Diocese. Coadjutor Bishop Francis Fontenot presides over the Southwest. A Diocesan Bishop can also be called a Right Reverend.

Diocesan Canon Bishop: a Bishop or Priest who is a specialist in Canon Law, who advises the Bishop of a Diocese.

Diocesan Priest: A Priest, ordained by a Bishop, whose ministry presides from within a Parish. Also referred to as Secular Priest.

Priest and Priesthood: The parish or ordinal office of a male adult heterosexual Deacon, who has been ordained by a Bishop as a Priest and is thus a member of the Priesthood. The Bishop confers upon the Priest this office if he can be assured that he is sane, moral, and so well educated in the Bible, in Traditionalist Anglicanism, in Theology, in Divinity, in the Liberal Arts and Sciences (including Philosophy), and in Ministry that his daily priestly office should irresistibly lead followers toward Salvation. A Priest is a Priest for life; his Incardination by a Bishop allows him to engage

Article XVII. Addendum A—Anglican Primer: Organization, Hierarchy, Christian Terms, and Administration

in public ministry within a Jurisdiction. The order for priestly ordination is in the 1928 U.S. Book of Common Prayer.

Priestly Titles: Father, Reverend, Pastor/Rector (head of a Parish), Vicar, Chaplain, Prior. Father Gary Mullica is a Priest at St. Mark's Church in Klamath Falls, Oregon. Father Mike DellaVecchia is the Rector of St. Patrick's Church in Perkasie, Pennsylvania. Bishop David C. Fleming is the Rector of St. Mark's.

Pastor/Rector: While a Pastor may be elected by a Parish Council, he may also be appointed by the Ecclesiastical Authority. While a Parish Priest/Reverend is incardinated by the Archbishop and/or House of Bishops to serve in a given Parish, a Rector is the title that is typically used to identify a Priest who has been appointed or approved to be the head of a Parish by the Ecclesiastical Authority. In short, one who is ordained a Priest may be both a Parish Priest/Reverend and a Pastor/Rector.

Junior Priest: Just after his ordination, the Junior Priest practices the Liturgy and writes sermons, assisting on the altar as a second Father to the presider, while developing the focus of his lifelong service, be it in charity, education, counseling, etc. After one year of good priestly service within TACA, the Father receives Incardination within the Parish where he serves. It is presumed that he will thereafter remain at said Parish, or the Archbishop or House of Bishops may suggest to him (if he is free to relocate or

Article XVII. Addendum A—Anglican Primer: Organization, Hierarchy, Christian Terms, and Administration

can change his type of ministry), that he serve TACA in another Congregation or Mission, or in another way).

Episcopate: The Episcopate is another word for the House of Bishops, namely all of the bishops of this TACA Diocese.

Episcopal Office/Bishopric: The office of an adult male, who having served as a Priest may be deemed by the House of Bishops to merit consecration to the Episcopate. A Bishop is, as explained above, consecrated by the laying-on of hands by other Bishops, who are themselves inheritors of the Apostolic Order. The order for the consecration of a Bishop is in the 1928 U.S. Book of Common Prayer. "This is a true saying, If a man desire the office of a Bishop, he desireth a good work. A Bishop then must be blameless, the husband of one wife, vigilant, sober, of good behaviour, given to hospitality, apt to teach" (1 Timothy 3:1-2).

Convalidation of Sacrament: The conferring of Anglican validity to a union or office that was previously validated by an outside Christian Jurisdiction. A Priest may use his discretion to decide whether the conditions were canonically sound and licit as regards the antecedent validity of a given Sacrament that was officiated outside of our Jurisdiction, as that Sacrament might pertain, for example, to a Baptism or a Matrimonial Covenant, and thus whether it could be Convalidated in the eyes of TACA.

Article XVII. Addendum A—Anglican Primer: Organization, Hierarchy, Christian Terms, and Administration

Convalidation of Office: The conferring of Anglican validity to a Priest who has been excardinated from an outside Jurisdiction and who intends to become incardinated by TACA. He may be convalidated using an office in our 1928 Book of Common Prayer. A Priest, if he is deemed to be in need of additional instruction in order to graduate into a new office, may afterward be ordained first into the TACA Diaconate and then into the Priesthood, using the offices contained within the 1928 Book of Common Prayer. Likewise, an applicant Bishop, needful of more instruction, may also follow steps leading him toward the Episcopate, following a full review of his credentials, resume, curriculum vitae, and oral interviews with TACA Ecclesiastical Authority.

Permanent Diaconate: The body of appointed and ordained Deacons and Deaconesses. As Christians of unwavering orthodox mindset, who are upstanding established members of society, they advocate, initiate, and exemplify outstanding active Christian life within their community. An Ordained Deacon is a Christian man who is ordained by a Bishop. A Priest first must become an ordained Deacon before he may become a Priest, and he is expected to pursue at least one year of service in the Diaconate before his priestly ordination may occur; however, he remains a Deacon even after subsequently holding any higher office. An Appointed Deacon or Deaconess is a Christian whose appointment to a Parish by its Pastor or Rector is approved by a Bishop or Archbishop.

Article XVII. Addendum A—Anglican Primer: Organization, Hierarchy, Christian Terms, and Administration

Ordained Deacon: A male adult minister, aged at least 24 years, upon whom holy orders have been conferred, for active membership in the Diaconate. His ordination is conducted according to the 1928 ritual, and his diaconal incardination is given by a Bishop. His role is to be a role model and leader for all parishioners as an accomplished dignified man. He sets up the Hosts and Wine for Communion and may preside over any part of the Mass or Daily Office (especially reading the Gospel and giving the Sermon), except for the Liturgy of the Eucharist and the serving of Communion. After one year of serviceable membership in the Diaconate, the Deacon may apply to the House of Bishops to become a Priest. To enter the Diaconate, he must be interviewed and/or tested for his knowledge of Bible truths, his understanding of theology, and screened according to his employment and vocational background. If a shortage of available priests and deacons within the Jurisdiction causes a condition of serious liturgical and sacramental exigency or a Diocese-wide *epikeia*, the Episcopate need not wait as long as a year to elevate a Deacon to the Priesthood.

***Epikeia*:** A state of emergency within TACA or within the Church at large requiring that certain rubrics be broken or made less rigorous.

Appointed Deacon/Deaconess: A Minister, aged at least 21 years, who is appointed to the Diaconate by a Priest or Bishop, instead of being ordained. His or her appointment must be approved by a Bishop. He or she will have received the Office of General Instruction and, ideally, is a member of the Parish, is of

Article XVII. Addendum A—Anglican Primer: Organization, Hierarchy, Christian Terms, and Administration

respectable familiarity to its Clergy and Laity, and is seen as a Christian community leader with much integrity. He or she may serve on the altar exactly as an ordained Deacon does. The method of selection of the applicant may reside at the Parish level and may, therefore, be a matter of assessing his or her written and oral aptitude, background in Lay ministry, and/or overall employment and vocational history.

Bi-vocational Priests and Deacons: Priests and Deacons who have an income-earning, secular job outside of their Ecclesiastical duty. No salary or stipends are allotted to the Clergy, Episcopate, or any Minister of TACA. Although Bishops may request small free-will monthly dues to offset the cost of managing the Diocese as a whole, all offices are to be led by those who identify with everyday working Christians, whose purse need not be continually opened to support someone else's life so that they may pursue a religious vocation. TACA Clergy exemplify the diligent integrity that has helped qualify them to be religious leaders. Saint Paul the Apostle, who built tents in Corinth alongside his friends Aquila and Priscilla (Acts 18:1-3), wrote: "Neither did we eat any man's bread for nought; but wrought with labour and travail night and day, that we might not be chargeable to any of you: Not because we have not power, but to make ourselves an ensample unto you to follow us. For even when we were with you, this we commanded you, that if any would not work, neither should he eat" (1 Thessalonians 3:10).

Article XVII. Addendum A—Anglican Primer: Organization, Hierarchy, Christian Terms, and Administration

Warden: A man or woman, holding the highest Lay office in the Church. A Warden is the senior-ranking member of the Vestry. He leads, *ex officio*, the Church Vestry (i.e., Lay Council) and initiates calls for all votes and meetings. He is in charge of the entire buildings and grounds of the Parish, ensuring that financial stability and physical integrity of all edifices and rooms are optimal. The Warden is responsible for all governmental filings with the Department of State and the Internal Revenue Service, for maintaining the nonprofit 501(c)3 status of the Parish and annually disclosing all revenue data, and for filing all nominal and status changes. In the appointment or replacement of a Pastor, the Warden is responsible for creating a memorandum that advises the House of Bishops on the best choice or needs of the Parish. If the Warden, acting as a Sequestrator, desires to nominate the next Pastor (after of course consulting with, and possibly even via tallying the votes of, his Vestry), that nomination as well as the appropriate associated information will be included in the memorandum.

Church Vestry: The body of Lay officers and staff members of the Parish. Because TACA parishes tend to be small and familial, the Vestry also contains the operations staff. It consists of the following offices (not all of which may always be filled at any given time): Warden, Chapter Warden (i.e., Warden of a Cathedral Vestry), Junior Warden, Secretary, Treasurer, Registrar, Sexton (i.e., officer of church and altar material, following established rubrics), Sidesman (i.e., usher, etc.), Virger (i.e., event planner), Lector,

Article XVII. Addendum A—Anglican Primer: Organization, Hierarchy, Christian Terms, and Administration

Deaconess, Minister (charitable and other), Musician (Music Director, Choir Director, Cantor, Organist, etc.), Catechist, Youth Minister, and Beadle (ancillary service helper/officer). The Vestry is also the official "office of the Parish, where administrative and financial decisions are made. The Warden may delegate his or other duties among any other competent members of the church.

Charter: The issuance in writing by the Archbishop to a religious Body that it may become a formally recognized group within TACA.

Nonprofit Corporation: The United States allows a Parish to define itself in secular terms as a legal entity organized and operated for a collective, public, or social benefit, by filing as a Nonprofit Organization (NPO) that functions as a charitable organization. For our TACA Diocese, any individual TACA Parish, TACA Diocese, or the TACA Archdiocese itself may be given Ecclesiastical Authority to identify itself as an independent autonomous NPO. It may do so by filing special applications with the United States Treasury and with the state in which the new NPO shall operate. Such a legal entity is contrasted with a business aiming to generate a profit for its owners. A nonprofit is therefore exempt from taxation but is subject to the following non-distribution constraint: any revenues that exceed expenses must be committed to the organization's purpose, not taken by private parties. A tax-exempt church entity is legally filed under Section 501(c)(3) of Title 26 of the United States Code. Use of the name "Traditional Anglican Church of America," or

Article XVII. Addendum A—Anglican Primer: Organization, Hierarchy, Christian Terms, and Administration

"TACA," to identify the incorporating Body in any Federal, State, or other public documentation is not permitted except by the expressed written permission granted by the Archbishop's Office (see Article IX, especially with respect to Nominal Exclusivity).

Nonprofit Master Entity for TACA: As of September 2023, the Office of the Archbishop has never sought to file a nonprofit status, or to create a corporate type of fund for our TACA Diocese, in order to help preside over our TACA Diocese as a collective association or convention that would encompass all its TACA churches and all other TACA bodies. As it daily secures the very Subsidiarity that preserves autonomy for each of its individual congregations and missions, the Ecclesiastical Authority of TACA has also never created a nonprofit fund, a foundation, or a distinct 501(c)3 entity that would cover the entire TACA Diocese or any partition or region within it. However, Canon 12 does make the provision for such an entity to exist.

Nonprofit Officer Titles: 501(c)3 paperwork, such as Form 1023-EZ or a 990-N tax-exemption document, have fields that may be filled in with the names of the President, Senior Director, Treasurer, Secretary, and/or any number of other titles. If an NPO were started at the Parish level or at the greater Ecclesiastical-Authority level, then the Nonprofit Officers would be whomever the Archbishop chooses or he can entrust delegating of titles to a competent Chancery or Vestry member or minister; he may also opt to make himself President or take a different title. (Note: Nonprofit Officer titles are not necessarily going to be the same

Article XVII. Addendum A—Anglican Primer: Organization, Hierarchy, Christian Terms, and Administration

titles that are used at a more basic proprietary Parish or Diocesan level, and a person with one title at the Parish or Diocesan level, such as "Secretary" or "Treasurer," may be given a different Nonprofit Officer title, as appropriate or as needed).

Laity: the entire body of Christian Parishioners (see definition below) within the TACA churches, including its regional dioceses, prelatures, and other religious Bodies. They can have up to two votes per Body in Formal Meetings, and they may be consulted via assemblies, suggestion boxes, or individual meetings.

Parish-Level Council or Parish Council: The group of all ordained and appointed religious ministers plus all the Lay Church Vestry members, whom the Pastor or Rector allows to have a say in important Parish matters and who can thus vote on issues such as the election of a new Pastor.

Consiliarius: A Medieval title, lately meaning "advisor," used only for transitional periods or as regards a project or temporary situation, made nearly obsolete by the greater availability and permanent willingness of Coadjutors, Canons, and Suffragans to advise on important matters. The Consiliarius's role in the Old Sarum Cathedral was to be a chief advisor of the Archdiocese. A Consiliarius of a modern Archdiocese could be an usher or an elder who operates as a kind of religious ombudsman who checks against government overreach affecting the average churchgoer, or perhaps a wise churchman or activist who advocates, for example, against the futility of

Article XVII. Addendum A—Anglican Primer: Organization, Hierarchy, Christian Terms, and Administration

shutting down a Parish during civil overreaction to a public crisis, or when the government censors First-Amendment-endued religious speech.

Catechists and Religious Educators: Qualified and appropriately vetted Ministers who teach lessons from the Bible to adults and youth.

Youth Ministers: Appointed or ordained religious men or women who host children at a given church, guiding their attentions toward Christian play and teamwork, so that they may be receptive to Gospel lessons meant for their salvation, and so that they may be inspired to go forth as a light in this present darkness.

Sexton: The Minister keeper of the Sacristy, Altar, graveyard, vestments, icons, relics, candles, bells, incense, censer, fabrics, thurible, books, holders, water, wine, unconsecrated wafers, and all material items that have a sacred relevance to the Parish, according to all established rubrics.

Charitable Ministers: Lay, appointed, or ordained officers in the Parish, or as part of an inter-Parish/Diocesan group or religious/secular order, who are appointed to work with the poor, needy, and stricken. Although such ministries may be ecumenical and openly volunteer-based, appointment of Charitable Ministers is contingent on such officers being Traditionalist Anglicans.

Christian Parishioners: All Christian Parishioners may attend services and take an active role in the life of a Parish. The consecrated Eucharist and Wine are served

Article XVII. Addendum A—Anglican Primer: Organization, Hierarchy, Christian Terms, and Administration

from the Open Table and are welcomed to all Christian Parishioners unless they are known to be in a state of unrepentant Mortal Sin (see Venial and Mortal Sin below).

Congregation, Parish, Individual Church: These titles are almost always used interchangeably, except that "Congregation" sometimes refers to the grouping of the faithful in a Mission or a Church Plant, a physical location that is intending to become a Church. "Parish" is sometimes meant to refer to a church and its campus, along with the geographical area and that area's people, whom it serves.

Religious Bodies of TACA: Known to be Congregations, Ministries, Churches, Church Plants, Missions, Parishes, Deaneries, or Schools, a TACA Body is a religious entity within this TACA Diocese that has received expressed written permission from the Archbishop to operate as a constituent part of this TACA Diocese. A TACA religious Body has also agreed in writing to be subject to the Constitution and Canons of this Diocese. Delegates from a TACA religious Body may attend a Formal Meeting and are thus allowed to participate within a Yearly Synod, a Regional Synod, a Bishops' Council, or other kind of Formal Meeting of TACA.

Church Militant: The idea of Christians, in catholic fellowship, armed in spiritual warfare against Satan, prayerfully resisting the Luciferian seduction of the world (Ephesians 6:12). The concept has long been said to stem from ancient Latin society since the Roman

Article XVII. Addendum A—Anglican Primer: Organization, Hierarchy, Christian Terms, and Administration

decadence, where those subject to moral degradation sought deliverance, as epitomized by the comedy *Persa*, written by Plautus. The characters were seeking a way to sidestep enslavement by a creditor, a pimp, using coy trickery. During the drama, an artful slave boy, defending the appearance of his emaciated body, sardonically quips, "*At confidentia militia illa militatur multo magis quam pondere*," which translates as, "Still, that warfare is waged much more successfully by spirit than by weight." Thus, two hundred years before Christ's ministry, the Gentile soul sought a spiritual rescue from immorality, ripe for Saint Paul's eventual visit (*Persa*; Act 2; Scene 2, Ver. 50; Titus Maccius Plautus; 184 B.C.). Tertullian later asks Latins to trade their togas for the Greek priestly Pallium worn by Christians, its central-torso knot signifying the contemplative zeal of the philosopher, likened to armed might, "*et aries iam Romanus in muros quondam suos audet, stupuere illico Carthaginienses*," or "a beam-like engine is a ram, which does military service in battering Carthage's walls" (*On the Pallium*; Part 1; Tertullian; A.D. 200). The other two classifications of Christian soldiery are the Church Triumphant that has reached Heaven (1 Corinthians 13; Revelation 22) and the Church Penitent, the number of those Christians who are in state of perpetual repentance (Matthew 12:32).

Fellowship: To be close with God and to share God's agape (parental or charitable, unconditional) love with one another. Although the outcome of our fallen nature is to die one day, all Christians share in common that

Article XVII. Addendum A—Anglican Primer: Organization, Hierarchy, Christian Terms, and Administration

we intend to end up in Heaven with one another by following Christ (Romans 6:23). In terms of Fellowship with God, any theological vagary improperly perceived in Psalm 82, i.e., that God wants us to "become Gods" is clarified by Saint John the Apostle, who explains that God has given Christians the "power to become the sons of God" (John 1:11-13), and He has done so out of his agape love for us: "Behold, what manner of love the Father hath bestowed upon us, that we should be called the sons of God" (1 John 3:1). It is very important to preserve Fellowship during this lawless era, when agape love otherwise so quickly waxes cold (Matthew 24:12). Fellowship is then a usage of this free gift of *gratia praeveniens,* which is the human but God-instilled free gift of Grace that is actualized for our life through our Baptism into the Church, where our Fellowship with God and Trinitarian Christians may be enjoyed. "But if we walk in the light, as he is in the light, we have fellowship one with another, and the blood of Jesus Christ his Son cleanseth us from all sin" (1 John 1:7).

Theosis: While the Greek term for θέωσις or *theosis*, also known as divinization, is not found in the Bible, the attainment of Fellowship with God after death, as his sons and daughters, is a goal toward which all Christians should strive. It is by the death of Jesus that God has upgraded Moses's Covenant with God into a new and better Testament (Hebrews 9:16). Therefore, Christian witness is not to be lived in a vacuum but rather shared with others (Matthew 5:16; 2 Timothy 4:2). We are baptized into Christ's death in order to,

Article XVII. Addendum A—Anglican Primer: Organization, Hierarchy, Christian Terms, and Administration

like Christ Himself, lighten one another's burdens and never to weary in doing good things (Galatians 6:2,9). Neither the Revelation of Christ's second coming (John 14:3) nor the Fruits of the Spirit (Galatians 5:22-23) are a private matter (2 Peter 1:20). We join together to help one another to avoid the "second death," that is the damnation of unrepentant sinners (Revelation 21:8). It is God's Grace, not ours, that redeems us, and thus saves us, from that fatality, and it is His Grace that impels us to seek and to save the lost (Luke 19:10; Romans 3:22-26; James 5:20).

Kenosis: Another Greek term, κένωσις or *kenosis* (defined as "emptying"), is a concept specifically mentioned in the Bible (Philippians 2:5-8). It describes how Christ emptied his soul of all traces of thought, and will, and even His own deposited Grace, so that His Father could will—and the Son could accomplish—the salvational work of the Crucifixion, the Son voluntarily suffering a "spiritual poverty" to show us how redemption is achieved for us (Philippians 2:7; Corinthians 2:8-9).

Grace, Discernment, and Free Will: So that our Free Will may choose to give sway to God's Grace, especially at difficult times, such as at our deaths, we can be glad that all humans are made in God's image, and are thus each supplied with Prevenient Grace. It is our Discernment, arrived at through Faith alone, to choose goodness over evil (Deuteronomy 30:19; Proverbs 3:5-6). This *gratia praeveniens* can help us abundantly if we discernibly choose to allow God's Grace, *gratia Dei*, to operate in us. Firstly, our initial justification to be

Article XVII. Addendum A—Anglican Primer: Organization, Hierarchy, Christian Terms, and Administration

called a "Christian" occurs at our Holy Baptism. Thereafter, God's Grace takes reign all throughout our sacramental life. Further, it is by His Grace that our sins are forgiven: Reconciliation with God is achieved through true repentance, taking heed to the call of St. John the Baptist, who admonished, "Repent ye, for the Kingdom of Heaven is at hand" (Matthew 3:2). Finally, through our exercise of Free Will we may show ourselves worthy of Salvation (Matthew 10:38; Luke 9:62), allowing God alone to confer the judgment of Christ at the Last Judgement in hopes that we may enter Heaven (2 Peter 3:9; Council of Orange; Chaps. xiii-xv, xxviii; A.D. 529; *The Call of All Nations*, St. Prosper of Aquitaine; Bk. 1: Ch. 25.; A.D. 450).

Property Ownership and Sanctification: Unless reflecting a written change in convention that would be reflected in a future version of the Constitution and Canons, this TACA Diocese, which identifies at divers times as a Jurisdiction, or an Archdiocese, or a Chancery, or a House of Bishops, or a Synod, or a Council, or a Diocese, or an Office of Archbishop, or any other Ecclesiastical Authority, shall not own physical property of any kind other than its own religious documents that name it as a Church. Other said property would be formal occupiable structures, buildings, houses, vehicles, or hard assets such as equipment, or land). However, each of the aforementioned property types, whose occupants and/or users call themselves members of TACA, shall be owned only by its individual owner(s), such as by an actual person(s), or by an individual Parish or Church

Article XVII. Addendum A—Anglican Primer: Organization, Hierarchy, Christian Terms, and Administration

under said Parish's or Church's name only, or by any other agency owning it, or shall be rented for occupation and/or usage by TACA from an outside party. No lease, deed, mortgage, rental agreement, or contract of any kind involving material possessions may be put in the name of "Traditional Anglican Church of America," or of "TACA," or of any version of the TACA name. Any property's existence, creation, identity, function, physical modifications, and appearance shall not be considered in any way or time to be the responsibility of this TACA Diocese. All notes of debts, mortgages, rent, upkeep, alterations, cleaning, maintenance, insurance, and liability that pertain to all property in which TACA members may at any time or duration of time occupy or use is wholly the responsibility of the independent owner(s) of that property and is none of TACA's. As of September 2023, TACA shall remain solely a constituent member of the universal Church Militant, an invisible "bride of Christ" that concerns itself only with the salvation of souls, rather than with any ecclesiastical dominion that could otherwise be held over material property within this world of any kind. Only under the authority of the Archbishop shall this condition or provision ever change. That being said, the religious Sanctification of any property occupied and/or used by TACA shall be conducted according the rule of the 1928 Book of Common Prayer, whereof Sanctification stands to be a consecrational religious sanctioning by our TACA Ecclesiastical Authority of that property to be used and/or occupied for our beautiful Traditional Anglican religious purposes that do not include TACA formal or

Article XVII. Addendum A—Anglican Primer: Organization, Hierarchy, Christian Terms, and Administration

legal secular ownership or proprietorship of it, of any kind or at any time.

Truth: Everything found in the Bible is Truth (2 Timothy 3:16). The Bible, in turn, is the Word, and the Word is Christ (John 1). Therefore, Christ is Truth, as He said: "I am the way, the truth, and the life" (John 16:6). Truth shall be exemplified in the saintly life of a person seeking Fellowship with God, for hell is reserved for those who "loveth and maketh a lie" (Revelation 22:15), following the devil, the father of lies (John 8:44).

Venial Sins and Mortal Sins: Mortal Sins are the kinds of wrongdoings that darkly transcend the category of lesser sinfulness, moving into a far graver spiritual and cognitive circumstance. In that there is no question of the act of the sinning being even partially a mistake, or a flaccid failure of the will, or a small impairment of reason, or some other consideration or mitigating circumstance, a Mortal Sin is one in which the sinner knows that what he or she is doing is gravely sinful but intends to commit the sin anyway. The lesser, the Venial Sin, is any offense against God that stems from our fallen condition but does not rise to the level of someone deliberately consigning the state of their eternal salvation to it, or stated another way, is not voluntarily entering into a state of damnation. A Mortal Sin is what the Bible calls a "sin unto death" (1 John 5:16)—that is, a sin that is so serious that it separates us from our Creator, its severity tantamount to denying God to His face. Such sins are abominations, idolatries, apostasies, and the like. A Mortal Sin is a deliberate act

Article XVII. Addendum A—Anglican Primer: Organization, Hierarchy, Christian Terms, and Administration

of rebellion against God in which the person fully understands the implications of the offense or crime and yet chooses willingly to engage in the sin and to persist in it without repentance. Such an act is a sign of hatred of Almighty God, which makes the judgment that much graver: "If I whet my glittering sword, and mine hand take hold on judgment; I will render vengeance to mine enemies, and will reward them that hate me" (Deuteronomy 32:41).

Contraception: Sexual coitus outside of the marital bond constitutes the sin of fornication (1 Thessalonians 4:1-6; 1 Corinthians 6:9-11). The use of anti-pregnancy aides (i.e., contraceptive agents) that prevent gamete fertilization, whether that use is inside or outside of marriage, is to be avoided. The deliberate destruction of the fertilized egg, or zygote, or embryo, or fetus constitutes abortion and hence infanticide—the murder of an innocent baby. Since all non-marital coitus is fornication, and since contraception is to be avoided, the unmarried should remain celibate or be married. It is better to marry than to burn (1 Corinthians 7:8-9). (See also Article XIX. Addendum C.)

Abominable Mortal Sins: Such sins are willfully committed, terrible Mortal Sins that are an affront to God in that their immorality and falsity is posed or blasphemously uttered directly against God, against Jesus, and against the Holy Spirit. As regards Nature, which is solely created by God, Abominable Mortal Sins are ones defined by a conscious, unrepentant, and hardened opposition to Truth, "because the Spirit is truth" (1 John 5:6), which often is manifested as a

Article XVII. Addendum A—Anglican Primer: Organization, Hierarchy, Christian Terms, and Administration

direct opposition to the Divine Laws and Creation. Any of these sins leads a person away from humility and repentance and hurling toward a state of unforgivable damnation or state of Reprobation (Romans 1; 1 John 5:6; Luke 12:10; Matthew 18:6). Such unrepented Abominable Mortal Sins would be Homosexuality; Gender Reassignment (i.e., mutilating the human body through hormones and/or surgery to create a fake alternate "gender"); Incest, Bestiality, and other grave sexual sins; Satanism; Atheism; teaching anyone that sexual perversion of all kinds is a good and a basic human right; teaching Darwinian Evolution as truth and a means of denying God and the Bible; Elective Abortion; Homicide; Pedophilia; Idolatry; Paganism; Witchcraft, Sorcery, Necromancy, and the like.

Unforgivable Sin: There is no definitive answer as to what this particular sin is, and what is implied by "unforgivable" (i.e., does this mean the person goes to hell, or does it mean they enter into a lesser level of Heaven?). Jesus said: "Wherefore I say unto you, All manner of sin and blasphemy shall be forgiven unto men: but the blasphemy against the Holy Ghost shall not be forgiven unto men" (Matthew 12:31). How does one sin against the Holy Spirit? Although the answer is unknown, it must be understood that the Unforgiveable Sin nevertheless does exist. We already work out our salvation with fear and trembling (Philippians 2:12). Is not fear of the Lord the beginning of knowledge and the start of ceasing to be a fool (Proverbs 1:7)? Thus how much more "dares" are we willing to take? Did God, because of our penchant to be foul, not reduce

Article XVII. Addendum A—Anglican Primer: Organization, Hierarchy, Christian Terms, and Administration

our lifespan, firstly to 120 years (Genesis 6:3) and now today to far fewer years? Did not God, because people disobeyed the Law, bring all the illness and madness to the world (Deuteronomy 28:28, 58-61)? From priests did God not remove the power to issue curses, such as the "tzaraath" (causing of leprosy; 2 Chronicles 26:18), and the vision of God's judgement over Israel through the Urim and Thummim of the Breastplate (Exodus 28:15-30), and the cursing of the Law (Nehemiah 10:29)? Was the Old Covenant with Moses not ended with God at the Crucifixion in His tearing of the Temple veil that had separated men from the Holy of Holies (Matthew 27:51; Mark 15:38; Hebrews 10:19-22)? Was not the Temple and Israel destroyed by Titus (*The Wars of the Jews*; Flavius Josephus; Book V; Section 9; A.D. 94)? Where are those great prophets of God, such as Elijah, who could perform great miracles now (1 Kings 18:16-46), except in Heaven awaiting us? Are not evil prophets of the beast meanwhile slated to do miracles of horror (Revelation 13:14)—after the Holy Spirit, or the cherubim with the flaming spears (Genesis 3:24), who have long been restraining the devil's wrath, while God remains merciful, is taken out of the way (2 Thessalonians 2:7)? Does humankind not tempt God to anger (Deuteronomy 6:16-18) by dishonoring His miracle of human conception (Psalm 139:13-18) via the allowing by modern "civilization" of millions of abortions since 1973? Will birth itself be one of the miracles permanently removed, after the final mothers nurse their infants during the Abomination of Desolation (Mark 13:14, 17)? Will God bother to restrain Himself from removing the Sun and Moon and all the "ordinances" of physical laws of Earth when the love of man turns cold enough (Jeremiah 31:35-36; Matthew 24:12)? Will the Apocalypse not initiate this End Time when the number of reborn souls (John 3:6-8) becomes enough in God's eyes to populate the Church Triumphant (2 Corinthians 2:14) while the cry for God's revenge, for the return Christ—"Maranatha!"—by the faithful is fulfilled (Psalm 143:12; Didache 10:14)? Therefore, exactly which Mortal Sin would be the Unforgiveable Sin? Is it not the blaspheming of the Holy Ghost? (Mark 3:28-30). How does one commit this, except that this sin is the "one" overall aggregate sin that the Lamb of God takes away (John 1:29)? Because any sin makes one guilty of all sins (James 2:10), it is better to avoid sinning entirely. When we are saved, finally cleansed of our sins, and are with God in Heaven, all our sins and every evil will be removed from Eternal Memory (1 John 1:9; Jeremiah 31:34). Thus, onward and upward (Philippians 3:14)!

Discernment: This is a spiritual gift from God to judge situations and intuit the intentions of people by Faith in God (1 Corinthians 12:10). The Apostle John advised us to "test the spirits" of people and of things involved in one's life (1 John 4:1). Christ told us that we can comprehend people's real motives and situations by assessing the virtues or ills associated with their deeds, a wisdom by which any "tree" can be known "by its fruit" (Matthew 12:33; Luke 6:43-45). Grace and peace will be multiplied unto us through the knowledge of God through His Son, Jesus Christ, as we avoid sin, and thus build our character: "And beside

Article XVII. Addendum A—Anglican Primer: Organization, Hierarchy, Christian Terms, and Administration

this, giving all diligence, add to your faith virtue; and to virtue knowledge; And to knowledge temperance; and to temperance patience; and to patience godliness; And to godliness brotherly kindness; and to brotherly kindness charity. For if these things be in you, and abound, they make you that ye shall neither be barren nor unfruitful in the knowledge of our Lord Jesus Christ" (2 Peter 1:2-6).

ARTICLE XVIII. Addendum B—Optional Provision for Voting by "Four Manors" of Legislature

At the discretion of the Archbishop (or the House of Bishops in case of his blessing, absence, or death), a certain Medieval option for voting may be used. It concerns the means of dividing the Synod into four sections. A sectioning by Office and Body can ensure that a fair percentage of votes gets reflected, rather than sheer number of church members. In other words, Bishops and Priests have a higher percentage of voting power than Lay members, but sheer number may rule the day. It is according to the discretion of the Archbishop (or, upon his vacancy, the Council's) as to whether it ought to be employed. First, let us name the parts or Manors that compose this TACA Synod.

i) The following parts compose the TACA Synod's Full Body—all the "manors," of TACA, for voting and transactional balloting purposes:

— The Archbishop;

— The House of Bishops;

— The Clergy of Ordained Priests and Deacons and Appointed Deacons; and

— The Vestry and Laity, of all secular and religious Officers and Ministers, and the Parishioners.

ii) Manor President: The person invoking an election, a meeting, or transaction. It is the senior member of the Manor or Legislature who calls it into session, such as the Archbishop, or a Bishop of a smaller region. For a Yearly Synod Assembly, for example, it would be the Archbishop. For a Diocese, it would be the Diocesan Bishop or Suffragan. Within a Parish, it could be the Pastor or the Warden.

iii) Calling Forth of a Meeting Body: A vote or transaction, or topical discussion, or decision-making body of any kind, must be invoked by a "Calling Forth," which is literally a message or memo that is written, dated, and signed (electronically or handwritten) with an RSVP by the Manor President, delivered to all Manors concerned in the topic of interest, for their participants to review. A more formal version of Calling Forth may occur in the form of a Hearing so that the presiding agent(s) may decide the kind of Council in which a decision should be disputed and balloted and who should attend it. Such a "Hearing" can occur in person or through interactive video conferencing (e.g., Zoom). The Calling Forth may be as simple as an e-mail message sent by the Archbishop to his ministers. It is simply a communication record of the conversations about the matter at hand so that a quorum can be arranged (see Article VI; Part A; Section iv).

iv) Yearly Meeting Voting: A meeting may therefore be called forth into commission by the Archbishop, whereof voting on a given subject shall allot a percentage value to each of the following branches of the Archdiocese, for balloting purposes.

Article XVII. Addendum A—Anglican Primer: Organization, Hierarchy, Christian Terms, and Administration

a) The Archbishop shall account for 30 percent of a Synod decision.

b) The House of Bishops, meaning all the Bishops voting within their house as a single Body, shall be accorded 30 percent.

c) The Clergy, which contains all Priests and ordained and appointed Deacons, if it numbers four or more members voting in an election, shall be given 25 percent representation of that vote (but 15 percent if fewer than four members vote, with the untaken 10 percent staying "unclaimed").

d) The Vestries and Laity (i.e., the Lay ministries: Wardens, Sextons, Lectors, Acolytes, Parishioners, etc.), and other appointed Lay Ministers, if they add up to four or more members, shall be given 15 percent of the vote (but 5 percent if fewer than four members vote, with the untaken 10 percent staying "unclaimed").

v) Discretionary Non-Voting Decisions: Other decisions or votes that do not occur in Yearly Synod form may be:

a) A choice to be made between the Archbishop and an individual Bishop, or within a Jurisdiction between its Bishop and a member(s) of its Clergy, or between a Priest and his Vestry and/or Lay officers. It shall occur with Patriarchal Discretion; the presiding administrator overseeing any given topic or decision shall be of higher episcopal or ecclesiastical title.

b) The Archbishop may talk concerning all matters, whereupon he may also, or instead, deign to concede or consult according to the good advisement of his minister(s)—persons, whose thoughts regarding any case he should fairly judge by virtue of his excellent leadership to be worthy, beneficial, and sound.

vi) Instead of using the Manor System, the Archbishop may elect to use the voting rules described in Article V of this Constitution. A wise leader may deign to announce that decision-making power can be given to his subordinates, under his assenting and watchful but caring authority and approval.

vii) Additional voting and meeting guidelines, such as relate to a Quorum and means of voting can be found in Article VI of this Constitution.

XIX. ADDENDUM C: Destruction of the Human Seed by Behaviors That Destroy Orthodoxy (Essay)

Genesis tells the story of Onan, who in refusing to procreate with his brother's widow as his new wife, deprived his father Judah of an heir and instead interrupted coitus by ejaculating his seed onto the floor (Genesis 38).

Such examples of willful disobedience, profanity, and sordidness have always epitomized the enmity between the seed of Eve and that of the devil (Genesis 3:15), inspiring the call for the Redeemer (Isaiah 59:20).

Killed by God for his refusal to follow the Laws of Moses, Onan also hampered the constituency of the tribal line of Judah that one day would bring forth Jesus. Eventually the widow Tamar, recognizing that Judah's youngest son, Selah, will not marry her, tricks the elder Judah, her father-in-law, into sleeping with her. Believing Tamar to be a harlot, Judah thus sires Pharez, from whose bloodline Jesus is born 1,700 years later (Matthew 1). But the breaking of ritual purity in marriage left a semitic scar.

Time wiled away idly reduces life to foulness. However, life can be bettered by "redeeming the time, because the days are evil. Wherefore be ye not unwise, but understanding what the Will of the Lord is" (Ephesians 5:16-17).

Hopeful Tamar, because Love covers a multitude of sins (1 Peter 4:8), produces a twin birth. But the

XIX. Addendum C: Destruction of the Human Seed by Behaviors That Destroy Orthodoxy (Essay)

stronger Pharez rushed out of the womb past his brother Zerah, the weaker. The lesser child's descendants will later include the conqueror apostate King Omri of Samaria and his wicked son, Ahab, who took for his wife the even wickeder Jezebel (Genesis 38:27-30; 1 Kings 16-22). But since was a descendent from Pharez, it should be attested that out of human sinfulness, God alone will separate the wheat from the chaff (Jeremiah 23:28; Matthew 3:12).

Modern couples have abortions and use contraceptives because they cynically believe that intimacy will likely propagate excess children—the "useless eaters," with their unwanted "carbon footprints." As if fear of world overpopulation should excuse the wickedness of the "designer-baby" and "transhuman" movement, most people, being very godless, believe that fetal genes should be altered during the zygotic stage, or else childbirth will be a bothersome crapshoot. Modernity has become far more wicked than Onan, who had merely ejaculated his seed onto the floor.

However, sex defined by the Love blessed in Holy Matrimony protects the home, and society by proxy, from that vulgar superstition of fearing situational ambiguities, against which only Love can resolve all negative outcomes. Life, created by God as a miraculous gift, must remain fruitful and devoid of cynicism.

The onus of restraint appears, from a careful analysis of all the biblical texts on the matter, to fall entirely on the male partner, and this is because it is the male who

XIX. Addendum C: Destruction of the Human Seed by Behaviors That Destroy Orthodoxy (Essay)

contains the "seed," the kernel of nation-founding, which any Christian male could at least theoretically be called upon by God to accomplish (Genesis 22:18). He therefore resists adultery, and should Love his wife dearly, listen to her chaste counsel, and she in turn should follow him. (Matthew 5:27-28; 1 Peter 3). This is the orthodox key to societal peace: wisdom stemming from the seed of the home, as surely as Hannah, the loving mother, brought forward Samuel (1 Samuel 1:20).

Love by the Father, the seed-planter, grows strong and shepherds loving, prudent children: "Lo, children are an heritage of the Lord: and the fruit of the womb is His reward. As arrows are in the hand of a mighty man; so are children of the youth. Happy is the man that hath his quiver full of them: they shall not be ashamed, but they shall speak with the enemies in the gate" (Psalm 127:3-5).

Otherwise, children will be left to their idle devices. The Internet, the Android and iPhone, the laptop, and the television, and images of pornography, nihilism, and violence will feed the revolutions aroused by these blind alleys.

Onan is eponymous with the sin of "onanism," a byword for male masturbation and *coitus interruptus*, sins that the Bible signals to be risks to the integrity of bloodlines—a family tree with various moral fruits, of power considered in a spiritual sense, because the practices of masturbation and adultery set examples of

XIX. Addendum C: Destruction of the Human Seed by Behaviors That Destroy Orthodoxy (Essay)

deceit, treachery, and filth, throughout homes, schools, and elsewhere.

These offenses are an affront to God, according to different rationales, by such ancient saints as Jerome, Epiphanius of Salamis, John Cassian, Benedict, Augustine, and Clement of Alexandria. They must be put away, all of them.

Because the devil has been chasing the Church Militant that was borne of Theotokos (i.e., "the remnant of her seed") since the infancy of the Church (1 John 4:3; Revelation 12:17), our constant exigency for Christian spiritual militancy requires us to don the full armor of God (Ephesians 6:12) in the eyes of all. A man, obedient to his wife, who honors his obedient wife, their being of one flesh and mind, has equipped himself with courage to answer anyone who asks him why he eschews evil and does right by God, and willing to suffer for what is right (1 Peter 3; Genesis 2:24; Ephesians 5:31).

A good marriage, to be sure, in God's eyes, has come quite a long way:

A Hebrew husband whose skin became polluted by his seminal fluid, regardless of how it got there, was, for his part, given bathing and isolation rubrics for himself and his wife, so that they may be returned to worshipful strength and ritual purity (Leviticus 15:16-18).

But because neither a tittle nor a jot will be subtracted from the Law until "heaven and earth pass" (Matthew

XIX. Addendum C: Destruction of the Human Seed by Behaviors That Destroy Orthodoxy (Essay)

5:18), it is safe to presume that man's seed remains part of his bodily temple. He must not do as the Gnostics of today and yesterday have always done, to enjoy physical pleasures as if only the spiritual life matters.

A husband's body is the patriarchal temple that sires the "fruit" of the Christian family—and thus the man must therefore restrain himself from the unholy spillage of his seed (as Zechariah 8:12 says, "For the seed shall be prosperous; the vine shall give her fruit"). "Whosoever is born of God doth not commit sin; for his seed remaineth in him: and he cannot sin, because he is born of God" (1 John 3:9).

If one believes that time and matter are relative to one another, then it is all the more evident by similitude that "ejaculating" away precious minutes of time in unaccountable idleness is unwise. We must not weary in well doing (Galatians 6:9).

Says Saint Clement, "Because of its divine institution for the propagation of man, the seed is not to be vainly ejaculated, nor is it to be damaged, nor is it to be wasted" (*Paedagogus*; Saint Clement of Alexandria; Book II; Chapter 10; Lines 91-95; A.D. 191).

Producing a weak society of flaccid men living secret lives is akin to an animal's life in a cave, where the "City of God," according to Saint Augustine of Hippo, cannot be enjoyed: "The same thing which he had before expressed by 'you are animal', you are carnal, he now expresses 'by you are men'; that is, you live according to man, not according to God, for if you

XIX. Addendum C: Destruction of the Human Seed by Behaviors That Destroy Orthodoxy (Essay)

lived according to Him, you should be gods" *(City of God;* Saint Augustine of Hippo; Book XIV; Chapter IV; A.D. 426).

Here, Saint Augustine is referring to Saint Paul's denouncing of the foolishness of the "natural man," whose profane patriarchy while acting like animals can never hope to become the "gods" Christ hopes people to become at their Salvation (1 Corinthians 2:14; John 10:35; Psalm 82:6). So that the Ecclesiastical Polity shall not fail at the unclean hands of licentious parents, Saint Clement holds: "To have coitus other than to procreate children is to do injury to nature" (*ibid. Paedagogus*).

Elevating the creational passions of men into the sublime involves the transcendence of the flesh into godly devotion. The word *semina*, the Latin term for seed, is the root of the word *seminarium,* which can be defined as "breeding ground" and hence was used in reference to plant nurseries in ancient Rome. From *seminarium* we derive the word "seminary," or a school for training men to enter the Priesthood. By tracing the etymology of this word *semina*, a picture develops of the sublimation of the Natural Man, with all his lesser impulses, into the masterwork of Christ (Ephesians 2:10), which is achieved when we are born again. (Note: Derived from the Latin verb *sublimare*, the word "sublimate" means the propagation of man's spirit and body into the godly, the sublime.)

Saint John of Cassian, the founder of men's and women's monasteries in Gaul, devoted his life to the

XIX. Addendum C: Destruction of the Human Seed by Behaviors That Destroy Orthodoxy (Essay)

cenobitic vocation that has this *gratia sublimis* (i.e., great grace) at its heart. Man, as Cassian shall explain below, must exchange carnality for godliness, cashiering all his worldly seminal intentions by resisting the "three forms of fornication"—fornication through sexual intercourse, fornication through masturbation, and fornication through the lust of the eyes: "And just as these three must be avoided by us with equal care, so they one and all shut us out and exclude us equally from the kingdom of Christ" Cassian's explanation is as follows:

> Of fornication there are three sorts: (1) that which is accomplished by sexual intercourse; (2) that which takes place without touching a woman, for which we read that Onan the son of the patriarch Judah was smitten by the Lord; and which is termed by Scripture uncleanness: of which the Apostle says: But I say to the unmarried and to widows, that it is good for them if they abide even as I. But if they do not contain let them marry: for it is better to marry than to burn; 1 Corinthians 7:8-9 (3) that which is conceived in heart and mind, of which the Lord says in the gospel: Whosoever looks on a woman to lust after her has already committed adultery with her in his heart. Matthew 5:28 And these three kinds the blessed Apostle tells us must be stamped out in one and the same way. Mortify, says he, your members which are upon the earth, fornication, uncleanness, lust, etc. Colossians 3:5 And again of two of them he

XIX. Addendum C: Destruction of the Human Seed by Behaviors That Destroy Orthodoxy (Essay)

> says to the Ephesians: Let fornication and uncleanness be not so much as named among you: and once more: But know this that no fornicator or unclean person, or covetous person who is an idolater has inheritance in the kingdom of Christ and of God. Ephesians 5:3-5. (*Conferences*, Saint John Cassian, Chapter 11)

Cassian, echoing his teacher, the dessert monk Evagrius Ponticus, projects the "Praktikos," the Hamartiology, by which he and Ponticus identify a chain of events commencing with any fervently depraved love of the sensual. Cassian uses the term "Principal Faults," as these deadly sins were enumerated in terms of their begetting one unto the other by Abbot Serapion the Wonderworker, in the latter's prayer cell (*ibid. Conferences*):

> "There are eight principal faults which attack mankind; viz., first gastrimargia, which means gluttony, secondly fornication, thirdly philargyria, i.e., avarice or the love of money, fourthly anger, fifthly dejection, sixthly acedia, i.e., listlessness or low spirits, seventhly cenodoxia, i.e., boasting or vain glory; and eighthly pride." (*Conferences*, Chapter 2)

Therefore, resisting these three types of fornication should be practiced in preaching, in pedagogy, and everywhere in life. Certain apostate religious orders could hence initiate their repentance by removing from seminaries heretical writings passed off as "imprimatur," such as expositions on the Enneagram

XIX. Addendum C: Destruction of the Human Seed by Behaviors That Destroy Orthodoxy (Essay)

by Franciscan "Father" Richard Rohr. Rohr's screed employs the teachings of "Fourth Way" guru George Gurdjieff to distort the words of Evagrius, which end up as carnality apologetics offered up to grateful lost seminarians worldwide (*The Enneagram: A Christian Perspective*; Richard Rohr; Crossroad Publishing; Indiana, 2001). Today he has been adopted by, and is a strong promoter of, the Gender Identity movement.

There is also "Father" Donald Georgen, co-founder of the Dominican "Ashram" (an OBGYN-theologian enclave cum assisted-living community, in Kenosha, Wisconsin), whose lewd tome, *The Sexual Celibate*, helps priests reduce their guilt about masturbating and being actively homosexual. This book was a foundational work for the ecclesiastical sexual revolution within institutional Christianity (read: Vatican II Roman Catholicism) that has been a large cause of the desolation from which conservative Christians everywhere are now trying to take refuge for themselves and their families (*The Sexual Celibate*: Donald Goergen; Seabury Press, 1974).

Goergen, a trained Freudian-Adlerian psychoanalyst, uses the term "sexuality" to describe illicitly the human person of Jesus. His introduction employs the following heresy: "A fundamental presupposition of this book is that there is another alternative, that it is possible to be both sexual and spiritual, whether celibate or married, and that this integration is for the greater glory of God" (*ibid. Celibate*, p. 9).

XIX. Addendum C: Destruction of the Human Seed by Behaviors That Destroy Orthodoxy (Essay)

He does not account for the complete purity that defines Christ, but likens Him merely to a person born of Adam. Adam, who in biting the apple became the progenitor of mankind's carnal disposition toward sinfulness (i.e., concupiscence), sired humanity's non-divine corporeal being. Sin concerns ontological agents at whatever level of the *Proslogion* (of Saint Anselm). We know and believe that human depravity characterizes our fallen physicality; angels had sex with women and created Nephilim but are themselves not corporeal; God is neither depraved nor corporeal, except in that God is Jesus and Jesus is God; Jesus, fully man (except for sin) and fully God, is thus pure and does not seek sex in any way. The Holy Ghost, who is consubstantial with the Father and the Son, must purify us or else we become stuck in carnality and face the Second Death (Revelation 21:8). To Goergen, none of this matters so long as one can sound smart.

Again, Jesus does not sin, nor does he procreate: because His proclivity for sex does not exist, He did not include anything false or that was not representative of Himself in the Word, that is, Sacred Scripture. Together with the Psalmist we proclaim, "Thy word is true from the beginning: and every one of thy righteous judgments endureth for ever" (Psalm 119:160).

Goergen had to have his way, however. He says Jesus was "only thirty" at the start of His ministry, adding "But as a Christian and as a secular man, I am dedicated to human growth—human growth through life in Christ." These are odd and telling words coming

XIX. Addendum C: Destruction of the Human Seed by Behaviors That Destroy Orthodoxy (Essay)

from one was nominally an Ordinal Priest, calling himself a "secular man" (*ibid. Celibate*, p .9).

For Goergen, if sexual temptation held sway over Jesus's emotions and character—a speculation all his own without a shred of supporting evidence—then it should be said that He was sexual, even though this would incorrectly imply that Jesus was capable of committing sin. Passing off his sloppy rhetoric as actual theology, Goergen's style earned his sordid 1970s tome bestseller nods. (Note: Goergen wasn't the first one to enter this arena, though. *The Last Temptation of Christ*—that scandalous 1988 movie, directed by Martin Scorsese and based on the original novel written by Nikos Kazantzakis in 1955 and translated into English in 1960—speculated along the same lines, particularly that Jesus struggled in the area of lust. All theological questions appear sloppily "resolved" in the denouement of the plot, but the viewer is still left with a sense of unease in the plot's attack against Faith. Was time really rolled back, and did the Crucifixion actually happen without any stain of sin? Was half the movie but thoughts that were merely running through Christ's mind in the hours when he was left hanging on the Cross? Did Jesus really have lustful feelings toward and want to marry the women who followed Him? And so on.)

Goergen sinfully proclaims, "Sexuality is not sinful and is a dimension of complete humanity," continuing by opining: "One cannot underestimate the importance of John, Lazarus, Martha, and Mary in His life," by which he concludes, "It is in this sense that His sexuality

XIX. Addendum C: Destruction of the Human Seed by Behaviors That Destroy Orthodoxy (Essay)

comes through" (*ibid. Celibate*, p. 27). However, God shall not be mocked (Galatians 6:7).

The term "sexuality" *cannot* apply to Christ, because He does not possess the disposition toward sexuality in any way that we could come close to understanding. Not only does Jesus not have the stain of Original Sin, but He also is homoousian—one substance with the Father, meaning that He is one with the Creator of humankind. Therefore, if Jesus were tempted with sexual desire for His own children, there would be a vast flaw in Him. This of course would be impossible for Jesus, our perfect God, Who is as perfect as the Father and the Holy Spirit. The sexual revolution within the institutional "church" and culture thus projects this mistake as one of its glaring formative godless errors.

In the chapter "Jesus's Sexuality," Goergen writes, "Sexuality is not sinful and is a dimension of complete humanity. It is not possible to accept Jesus's humanity without accepting his sexuality" (*ibid. Celibate*, p. 26). Goergen suggests that Saint Matthew's treatment of the Bethany friendship implies a semantic ambiguity, which he cunningly calls "framework," for accepting Jesus's sexual nature via a "framework of compassion, fidelity, and eschatology," and he upholds his salacious claim by adding, "and there is denial of sensuality" to engender the Son of God with the willpower to resist His alleged sexual urges (*ibid. Celibate*, p. 27).

XIX. Addendum C: Destruction of the Human Seed by Behaviors That Destroy Orthodoxy (Essay)

Later on, positing Samuel-Auguste Tissot, writer of *Thoughts on the Sin of Onan* (1767) as being the party pooper (Tissot had attributed physical ailments to bodily depletions associated with masturbation), Goergen bemoans the jading of all the fun that could have otherwise characterized the Modernist prurient takeover of Christology. "This kind of scientific thinking has given rise to prejudice," and promises, "If we look more carefully at the facts, masturbation is harmless on the physical plane" (*ibid. Celibate*, p. 198).

Goergen promulgates the idea that psychological tumult is actually caused by *avoiding* masturbating. In the chapter titled "The Sexual Life of a Celibate," he warns: "Those who do not practice masturbation or suppress the tendency might equally move in the direction of emotional difficulty" (*ibid. Celibate*, p. 199).

Deviously advising a more "constructive" approach to masturbation, Goergen blazes, "Adolescent masturbation as well as many adult forms of masturbation may be healthy." Bereft of any mention of the story of Onan or the multifarious adulteries in the Bible, "Father" Goergen advises thus: "The masturbatory activity must be integrated into the life of the person in such a way that it is not destructive, whether this means overcoming it or continuing it in a more constructive way" (*ibid. Celibate*, p. 199).

Today, beleaguered Christians look over the devastation of the Church directly caused by rape, molestation, pedophilia, homosexuality, pornography,

XIX. Addendum C: Destruction of the Human Seed by Behaviors That Destroy Orthodoxy (Essay)

and sexual violence, added together with all the sins and sequelae stemming from each of these Mortal Sins. The result, staring back at us, has been destruction of churches and homes. The culprits—the wicked Priests, Bishops, Nuns, and Theologians of these institutional cesspools—have somehow managed to counterbalance their untold monetary losses incurred during ceaseless sexual-molestation lawsuits by altering church doctrine such that a new "emerging market" may provide emergency tithes, all while blaming "modern life" for the mass exodus from the Church. Grateful homosexuals, women seeking the collar, and multifarious deviants and baby-killers seeking the Eucharist without penance, all of them envying the social rewards of church life, become eager to fill church coffers with the coveted cash desired by those filthy, desperate collared culprits. Moreover, the cynic ardently intends that fewer claims of molestation will arise when a disillusioned parent is told to believe that there had been countless opportunities to read the updated doctrine before joining X church, informing her that she had never really cared where she and her children were stepping.

However, neither paradigm shift, artful doctrine, dogmatics, nor survival instincts shall change the Truth of the Bible or anything in it. An Athanasian Christian is he who proclaims: "Let no man add to these, neither let him take ought from these" ("Epistle Number 39: Festal Easter; Saint Athanasius, Part 6; A.D. 367). Even better, in the face all the world's "emperors"—our bosses, our teachers, our neighbors,

XIX. Addendum C: Destruction of the Human Seed by Behaviors That Destroy Orthodoxy (Essay)

even members of our own families—who say to us "the world is against you," an Athanasian Christian will say thus: "Well then, I am against the world!" ("*Athanasius contra mundum.*")

Intellectualizing sin in destructive hopes to clear paths to carnal rewards and other sensual or vainglorious payoffs is the theological and ecclesiastical enemy of orthodoxy and the life given to us by God. "Submit yourselves therefore to God. Resist the devil, and he will flee from you" (James 4:7).

"But if they cannot contain, let them marry, for it is better to marry than to burn" (1 Corinthians 7:9).

XX. ADDENDUM D: History of Traditional Anglican Church of America as of September 2023

Current Overview of the Diocese

Traditional Anglican Church of America (TACA) is an independent ecclesiastical district within the Continuing Anglican church. As of September 2023, its Primate, Abp. Rick Aaron Reid, sits in Newtown, North Carolina.[1][2][3][4][5] Until January 2023, it was a diocese within the Independent Anglican Church, 1934 Canada Synod (IACCS/1934).[6]

TACA has a six-member House of Bishops and two interior dioceses, in both the Eastern and Western United States.[7][8][9] Its formularies include the 1928 Book of Common Prayer and the 1940 Hymnal of the Protestant Episcopal Church in the United States of America, and it professes both the Thirty-Nine Articles of Religion and the Saint Louis Affirmation.[10][11][12] Its American-Southwest grass-roots beginnings in 1973, and its tenure within the IACCS/1934, may characterize TACA as a forerunner to the greater Continuing Anglican Movement.[13][14]

Origins of TACA

TACA started as an informal assembly of conservative Episcopalians in San Antonio, Texas, in 1966.[15][16] At first, an ad hoc mustering called together by Fr. Howard Edwin Caudill, a priest within the Anglican Catholic Church (ACA), a romp fellowship grew within

XX. Addendum D: History of Traditional Anglican Church of America as of September 2023

the ACA's Diocese of the Southwest (DSW).[17][18] In concern over the issuance of four successive "trial-use liturgies" within the Episcopal Church of the United States, increasingly focused assemblages were convoked during the ensuing decades by another priest from the Anglican Episcopal Church in Ventura, California, Rev. Melvin Pickering.[19][20][21] Eventually Pickering would construct a formal district in Las Cruces, New Mexico, as other southwest American traditionalists joined him at St. Mary's Anglican Church at 140 West Taylor Street for worship and traditionalist education.[22][23][24][25] Vexation had progressively arisen against several burgeoning modernist occurrences, which the convocation held were not liturgical: the opening of ordination to women by the U.S. Episcopal General Convention in 1976; the approved revision of the Book of Common Prayer of 1979; and the intention to adopt the "inclusion" aims set forth in the Alternative Service Book of 1980.[26][27][28]

By the 1980s, Caudill had joined Pickering, along with the rest of the Diocese of the Southwest, when the ACA merged into the American Episcopal Church (AEC), into which Caudill was consecrated a Bishop in 1983 by Bp. Robert Condit Harvey.[29] Several months earlier, in 1982, Pickering had been consecrated by Bp. Francis H. Benning.[30][31][32] Convalidating DSW as an AEC diocese, Caudill and his wife (née Padbury) had a three-bedroom house built, at 9022 Wellesley Manor Drive, in San Antonio, in 1984, which would serve as the

XX. Addendum D: History of Traditional Anglican Church of America as of September 2023

Southwest vestry, but consequently, in 1988, withdrew 20 parishes from the AEC over hostile attempts that Caudill alleged had been undertaken by suffragan Bp. Anthony Forbes Morton Clavier, to interfere with affairs of the DSW.[33][34][35] Listing, as property owner, the "Anglican Church in the United States Traditional Episcopal," Caudill also bought a de-sanctified Protestant church at 11919 Orsinger Lane, that he named St. Chad's Church.[36][37][38] In the sanctuary and vestry, Caudill held Prayer and Eucharistic services and organized an adjunct seminary, which he titled St. George's Seminary.[39][40] One of his and Pickering's students was Robert William Baker, a postulant at the Episcopal Theological Seminary of the Southwest in Austin, Texas.[41] Baker would be listed as "Director" of the archdiocese in a non-profit licensure just as his rectorship of his own diocese began, in his native Oregon.[42][43]

Diocese of the Southwest

A growing apostolate, DSW was renamed the Anglican Diocese of the Good Shepherd (ADGS), and expanded to Hill Anglican Cathedral at Las Cruces, New Mexico, with Bp. Pickering realigning the jurisdiction there upon the death of Bp. Caudill in 1998.[44][45][46] The diocese was attracting conservative Christians, who had, by 1989, opposed the first incardination of a woman, by the Anglican Communion, Barbara Harris, as suffragan Bishop of the United States Episcopal Diocese of Massachusetts.[47][48] Moreover, the offering of

XX. Addendum D: History of Traditional Anglican Church of America as of September 2023

ordination to self-professed practicing homosexuals by the Communion, in 2003, had impelled new traditionalist Anglicans to seek out independent conservative churches, such as ADGS, whose religious teachings would offer orthodox catechesis.[49][50][51] To this end, Mavis Anne Caudill, the co-founding Bishop's wife, for years would teach Sunday school and adult religious education at St. Chad's, which also offered a free orthodox seminary.[52][53][54][55] Diverse religious polemics within the Anglican Communion, included arguments as to whether the State was paradoxically manipulating churches by permitting the clergy to retain solely heterosexual marriage licensure.[56][57] Baker, who was now co-consecrated as a traditionalist Anglican Bishop by Pickering and Caudill, had by 1991 moved northward, to his hometown of Klamath Falls, Oregon, at first reserving public rooms at the Shasta Grange Hall community center for prayer services, until he became pastor at St. Mark's Traditional Episcopal Church in 1992.[58][59][60][61][62]

In 2001, Pickering appointed his diocese to be the suffragan jurisdiction for the Anglican Church International Communion (ACIC) and dissolved the seminary, focusing on ethics advocacy within the greater Continuing Anglican Movement.[63][64][65][66][67][68] Presiding over a yearly traditionalist conference of 15 bishops at St. Chad's, Pickering issued the ACIC's statement that the election of openly gay priest Gene Robinson to the U.S.

XX. Addendum D: History of Traditional Anglican Church of America as of September 2023

Episcopal Church in 2003, as the Bishop of New Hampshire, was a heretical elevation, and "by this action they have renounced Biblical teachings," amid widening unrest within the Anglican Communion.[69][70][71][72] Pickering, in semi-retirement, had given his nod to the elevation of Bp. Baker as Senior Bishop, at a Synod at St. Chad's in 2002, during which ADGS was renamed, "Anglican Convocation of the Good Shepherd" (ACGS).[73][74] Pickering, in 2009, acting as emeritus of ADGS, also enlarged St. Mary's church's occupant capacity.[75]

Assumption into a Proto-Continuum Synod and Diocesan Expansion

A decade later, in 2013, upon the archepiscopal adoption of ACGS into the IACCS/1934 historical synod, Bp. Baker became Archbishop of the newly named "Traditional Anglican Church of America."[76][77][78] Chartered within an archbishopric that had been sired by the 1934 Synod of Canada—a writ of ecclesiastical independence that had occurred 44 years prior to the St. Louis Affirmation—the ACGS was now operating in parallel with the Anglican Continuum, but within a much older traditional context than the 1978 greater Anglican "continuation" had been [79][80][81][82][83][84]

TACA was now a sui iuris episcopate, a constituent autonomous diocese within an archprimacy, whose vintage 1934 Synod had theologically anteceded the St.

XX. Addendum D: History of Traditional Anglican Church of America as of September 2023

Louis Congress.[85][86] Abp. Pickering passed away in 2017.[87]

An outrider to the original "Tripartite Synod" (the organizational aim that was promulgated by the 1978 St. Louis Affirmation), TACA, an ecclesiastical polity, existing in its own right, sidestepped all the later identity crises, or any interior aggression, that had gripped the greater Anglican Continuum throughout ensuing decades.[88][89][90][91] While the Anglican Catholic Church suffered bitter coups, and new parishes within the nascent Anglican Church of North America permitted female ordination starting in 2009 (even though it had originally formed as an orthodox reaction against the consecration by the U.S. Episcopal Church of the active openly homosexual Bp. Robinson), TACA carefully organized its hierarchy with comparatively austere Low Church adherence.[92][93][94][95][96]

After his 2010 consecration of the new pro-Cathedral of St. George the Martyr, in Niagara Falls, New York, Archbishop Peter W. Goodrich, expanded the IACCS/1934, archdiocese from Hamilton, Ontario, Canada into the United States, and he adopted five new traditionalist Anglican sub-jurisdictions, whereupon he became Archprimate.[97][98][99] Goodrich also opened St. Matthew's Cathedral College, making combined use of the 1,900 square foot St. George's Church and the adjoining rectory, both built in 1927, and which he purchased in 2010 for $75,000, from the Roman Catholic Diocese of Buffalo, New York.[100] [101][102]

XX. Addendum D: History of Traditional Anglican Church of America as of September 2023

Abp. Baker was thereby elevated to Primate and became the presiding archbishop of TACA, now an independent jurisdiction within an expanded North American See.[103][104]

Expansion of U.S. Polity to Southeast

With the 2013 election of Bp. Dr. Dwight David Irons of Georgia as Diocesan Chancellor, the district's integration of the 1940 U.S. Episcopal Hymnal into daily service now advanced hymnary into liturgical practice, under Irons's musical oversight.[105][106][107] Abp. Baker's appointment of Bp. Louis Chopin Cusachs, a Sorbonne Theoretical Physics scholar, to oversee Louisiana, rounded out TACA's Diocese of the Good Shepherd Southeast.[108][109]

In 2014, upon the emeritus repositioning of Abp. Baker, the Primacy passed to Abp. Irons. Sitting in the Las Cruces church as the pro-Cathedral, Irons was assisted by Canon Rick Aaron Reid, former Right Reverend of the Orthodox Anglican Church, a decorated Gulf War veteran.[110][111] The diocese was advised by Bp. Charles Klughart, the longtime archbishop of Unity Catholic Church in Springfield, Illinois, who became Suffragan in 2018.[112]

House of Bishops as Anglican Patriarchate

Appointments during the next three years would distinguish the greater episcopacy as comprising a de facto Anglican-patriarchate, with the Southeast pulling

XX. Addendum D: History of Traditional Anglican Church of America as of September 2023

into ecclesial predominance.[113] After his elevation as Archbishop on May 1, 2020, Reid appointed Latin/Greek scholar Rt. Rev. Kenneth Walsh as Chancellor. Presiding from the Primate chancery in Newton, North Carolina, Reid would call forward Rev. Paul K. Leeman to be the Diocesan Bishop of the Southwest on June 1 of the same year.[114] On the same day, Reid named, as the co-Suffragan of the Southwest, the Right Rev. David C. Fleming, whom Reid also dubbed as the new Rector of St. Mark's.[115]

With Fleming, who had long been the founding president of a freight transporting company, and with Reid—a decorated First Sergeant in the North Carolina National Guard and Field Manager in the North Carolina Department of Agriculture—the patriarchy of TACA became a customized permanent bi-vocational clergy. Included among these deeply religious Christian leaders, Cusachs was a renowned PhD. chemist and author. Bp. Yasuto Nozawa, an Electrical Engineer, was a founding member of St. George's Seminary and is a Latin scholar. [116][117][118][119][120][121] Abp. Pickering was a commissioned Army Major and professional educator, who had served in both the Korean and Vietnam wars.[122]

By 2015, Klamath Falls Chancery operations were managed by then-Rev. Leeman at St. Mark's.[123] Leeman, who himself was a heavy equipment and excavation company founder, was also the founder of the former St. Paul's Anglican Church in Montague, California.[124][125] Assisted by Coadjutor Ebenezer

XX. Addendum D: History of Traditional Anglican Church of America as of September 2023

Manuagwu of Nigeria, Leeman added oversight from Klamath Falls over the Southwest, issuing a new vestry membership and amending the Articles of the Church; he was consecrated Bishop by Abp. Reid at St. Andrew's Church in Newton, North Carolina, in June, 2020.[126][127][128] Initiated during the 2016 Episcopal Synod at St. Mary's Church at Hill Anglican Cathedral in Las Cruces, New Mexico, the Southwest now comprised the combined bishoprics of Abp. Jorge Martinez of Mexico, Bp. Don Nozawa of Missouri, and Bp. Leeman.[129][130]

While some contemporary Continuing Anglican churches were splintering, TACA was experiencing sudden episcopal attrition not long after Abp. Pickering, the founder, died in 2017.[131][132][133] Upon the momentous deaths, in 2020, of three of its Bishops—Baker, Irons, and Cusachs—the voting in of Bp. Reid as Primate sparked a necessary consolidation of the entire jurisdiction.[134][135][136] The new Archbishop, Reid, had been the four-year Canon and Suffragan for TACA, and had been co-consecrated as Bishop at St. Mary's at Hill Anglican in Las Cruces, New Mexico (by Abp. Baker, Abp. Irons, Abp. Jorge Martinez Zendejas, Bp. Cusachs, and Bp. Walsh) in April 2015.[137][138] Reid, meanwhile, had been holding services at Calvary Baptist Church in Newton, NC, operating there as St. Andrew's Anglican Church.[139][140][141][142] It was in this space, which he now commissioned as the Primary Chancery in 2021, upon his election as Primate, during a vote by

XX. Addendum D: History of Traditional Anglican Church of America as of September 2023

the House of Bishops, that Right Rev. Francis Fontenot was also named by Abp. Reid to be Bishop for Louisiana; Abp. Cusachs had recently retired and moved to Charlotte, NC.[143]

Refining of Diocesan Territories, from East to West

At the time of this writing, in September 2023, Traditional Anglican Church of America is an autocephalous See and a theological constituent of the Independent Anglican Church, Canada Synod 1934.[144] One continuous sui iuris Anglican Diocese, it is comprised internally of two dioceses, the East and the West.[145][146][147] The East houses the Office of the Primate, Abp. Reid, at St. Andrews Anglican Church in Newton, North Carolina.[148][149] The West houses the Diocesan Bishop, Paul K. Leeman, occupying the western church, St. Mark's Church, in Klamath Falls, Oregon.[150][151][152][153]

The House of Bishops consists of Reid, Klughart, Walsh, and Fontenot, in the East; and Leeman, Fleming, Nozawa, Martinez, and Right Rev. Ashley Edward Beckham of Texas, in the West.[154][155]

The Coadjutor of TACA is Fontenot. Suffragan episcopal duties belong to Klughart in the East, and to Fleming in the West. Walsh is the Chancellor of TACA.[156][157][158]

Three parishes compose the diocesan infrastructure: St. Andrew's; St. Mark's; and the new (as of 2021) St. Patrick's Anglican Church in Perkasie, Pennsylvania.

XX. Addendum D: History of Traditional Anglican Church of America as of September 2023

Rev. Gary Mullica assists at St. Mark's. Fr. Michael DellaVecchia is the Rector of St. Patrick's and is the TACA Training Director.[159]. Bp. David Fleming is the Rector of Saint Mark's

Virginia Reid, wife of Abp. Reid, and Lisa DellaVecchia, wife of Fr. Michael DellaVecchia, are appointed Deaconesses. Donna Baker, widow of the Primate co-founder Robert, stands as advisor to the Primate.[160][161]

The Metropolitan for the Independent Mexican Episcopal Church, in *externam unitatis* in Tlalpan, Mexico City, is Abp. Jorge B. Martínez Zendejas.[162][163][164]

Future Provisional Communion Synod

As of July 2023, the permanent provision for Communion with other Traditionalist Anglican churches defines TACA's witness of ongoing shared theological and Eucharistic fellowship. Thus, Communion has been enjoyed with such dioceses as the Reformed Anglican Church, whose pro-Cathedral is in Saint Augustine, Florida. (Although no longer in Communion with TACA, this past Communion is mentioned herein for illustrative purposes.) Moreover, the Emmanuel Communion, whose pro-Cathedral is in Indiantown, Florida, has current Communion with TACA. Additionally, Communion with TACA is also shared with the Traditional Anglican Church of Ecuador, whose Cathedral is in Santo Domingo, Ecuador.

XX. Addendum D: History of Traditional Anglican Church of America as of September 2023

Reflecting the principle of "custom and subsidiarity," whereof material ownership or governance over congregations and missions by a superior prelature of the TACA Archdiocese is permanently nullified, religious bodies of TACA run themselves. A legal fiscal corporation is thus replaced by the convention of each member church owning and self-governing its own property according to its interior Customary. Thus, arch-governance by TACA has been defined by the Constitution and Canons as embodying Archbishopric rule of a broad-based and spiritual nature, according to the traditional Anglican formularies and exemplifying a Christian life of orthodoxy.

Moreover, a future "Communion Synod" which would mediate religious uniformity shared between TACA member bodies and other Traditionalist Anglican jurisdictions, would therefore also be a broad-based fellowship for which, as of September 2023, there remains a permanent provision.

As of January 2023, TACA ceased its Communion and theological subsidiarity with the Independent Anglican Church of Canada 1934 Synod.

XX. Addendum D: History of Traditional Anglican Church of America as of September 2023

REFERENCES

[1] "TACA Clergy Directory: Episcopate & Clergy, Parishes & Ecclesiastical Registry of Traditional Anglican Church of America in Unitate Diocesana sub The Independent Anglican Church Canada Synod, 1934"; File Publ. 01/12/2022; Jeremiad Christian Homesteader Gazette, East Rockhill, Pennsylvania, Vol. 1, Winter 2022, pp. 1-5. https://jeremiadchristianhomesteadersgazette.com/01_taca_article; Retrieved 01/22/2022.

[2] "Traditional Anglican Church of America," January 2022, Newton, NC; https://1928bcp.weebly.com; Retrieved 01/12/2022.

[3] "St. Andrew's Anglican Church," Newton, NC; https://standrewsnewton.weebly.com; Retrieved 01/13/2022.

[4] "St. Andrew's Anglican Church," Church Finder; https://www.churchfinder.com/churches/nc/newton/st-andrews-anglican-church; Retrieved 01/13/2022.

[5] "Parcel Report," Catawba County, NC; https://gis.catawbacountync.gov/nomap/parcel_report.php?key=373016927996&typ=P; Retrieved 01/13/2022.

[6] "Jurisdiction: Traditional Anglican Church of America"; *Independent Anglican Church Canada Synod 1934;* January 2022, Niagara

Falls, NY; http://www.independentanglicanchurch.com/traditional-anglican-church-of-america; Retrieved 01/08/2022.

[7] "House of Bishops, Clergy, and Necrology," Traditional Anglican Church of America, January 2022, Newton, NC; https://1928bcp.weebly.com/house-of-bishops-clergy-and-necrology.html; Retrieved 01/10/2022.

[8] Crumb, Lawrence N. "The Extra-Canonical Ordination of Bishops and the Episcopal Church." *Anglican and Episcopal History*, Vol. 77, No. 4, Historical Society of the Episcopal Church, 2008, pp. 402-13. http://www.jstor.org/stable/42612842.

[9] Anthony F. M. Clavier, *The American Episcopal Church: An Introduction,* Deerfield Beach, FL: St. Peter's American Episcopal Church, 1975 n.d., pp. 4-5, ISBN: OCLC:30630064.

[10] *The Book of Common Prayer and Administration of the Sacraments and Other Rites and Ceremonies of the Church: According to the Use of the Protestant Episcopal Church in the United States of America—Together with The Psalter of David;* Moore, L. M., Ed.; The Church Pension Fund, NY; 1928, Reprinted 1945.

[11] *The Hymnal of the Protestant Episcopal Church in the United States of America: 1940*; Irvine, P.,

Ed., Church Pension Fund, New York, NY, 1940.

[12] "Affirmation of St. Louis," Traditional Anglican Church, 2019; http://traditionalanglicanchurch.com/wp-content/uploads/2016/12/Affirmation-of-St.-Louis.pdf; Retrieved 01/13/2022.

[13] Kersey, John. "Organizational Summary of Groups Descending from Arnold Harris Mathew." Files: Western Orthodox Dot University, July 2020, pp. 1-11; https://westernorthodoxdotuniversity.files.wordpress.com/2020/07/organisational-summary-of-groups-descending-from-arnold-harris-mathew-7.20.pdf; Retrieved 01/13/2022.

[14] Bess, Douglas. *Divided we Stand: A History of the Continuing Anglican Movement*, Chapter 13, Apocryphile Press, Berkeley, California, 2006, pp. 277-281.

[15] Armentrout, Don S. "Episcopal Splinter Groups: Schisms in the Episcopal Church, 1963-1985." *Historical Magazine of the Protestant Episcopal Church*, Vol. 55, No. 4, Historical Society of the Episcopal Church, 1986, pp. 295-320, http://www.jstor.org/stable/42974143.

[16] Anson, Peter Fredrick. *Bishops at Large*, Apocryphile Press, Berkeley, California, 2006, pp. 129-145. ISBN-10: 0977146189.

XX. Addendum D: History of Traditional Anglican Church of America as of September 2023

[17] "The Traditional Anglican Church in the United States, a Traditional Episcopal Body—H. Edwin Caudill, Bob Baker," San Antonio, 1988; Biz Standing; https://bizstanding.com/directory/TX/AN/1405; Retrieved 01/11/2022.

[18] Caudill, Howard E., *An Episcopal Primer: An Introduction to the Church*, Cathedral Publishing, San Antonio, Texas, January 1, 1975, pp. 2-5. ASIN: B000JFUDO4.

[19] "American Episcopal Church Petitions Presiding Bishop," *The Christian Challenge,* January 1984, p. 13; Foundation for Christian Theology, Washington, D.C., Traycik, A. F., Ed.

[20] *The New Liturgy: The Liturgy of the Lord's Supper; The Celebration of Holy Eucharist and Ministry of Holy Communion*, Morehouse Barlow, Co., NY, 1966; http://justus.anglican.org/resources/bcp/new_liturgy1966.htm; Retrieved 01/13/2022.

[21] *The Acts of Convention:* 1973-A102: Amend Canon III.2 and III.3 [Of Candidates for Holy Orders]; https://www.episcopalarchives.org/cgi-bin/acts/acts_resolution.pl?resolution=1973-A102; Retrieved 01/05/2022 [Sec. 1. This Canon shall be interpreted in its plain and literal sense, except that words of male gender shall also imply the female gender.]

[22] "Religion USA," *The Christian Challenge,* August 1983, p. 19. Washington, D.C.; Vol. 22, No. 5,

Foundation for Christian Theology, Traycik, A.F., Ed.

[23] "St. Chad's Anglican Church," *Open Corporates;* https://opencorporates.com/companies/us_tx/0122642401; Retrieved 01/12/2022.

[24] Bess, Douglas. *Divided We Stand: A History of the Continuing Anglican Movement,* Chapter 5. Apocryphile Press, Berkeley, California, 2006, pp. 78-82.

[25] St. Mary's Anglican Church at Hill NM; EIN/Tax I.D.; *IRS Non-Profit Profile,* Melvin Pickering, President; https://eintaxid.com/company/562590225-st-marys-anglican-church-at-hill-nm/; Retrieved 01/17/2022.

[26] *The Alternative Service Book,* 1980. Joint publishers: Oxford/Mowbray. Clowes/SPCK/Cambridge, Hodder & Stoughton. (including psalter).

[27] *Journal of the General Convention of the Episcopal Church,* Denver, 1979 (New York: General Convention, 1980), p. C-8; https://www.episcopalarchives.org/cgi-bin/acts/acts_resolution-complete.pl?resolution=1979-A133; Retrieved 01/13/2022.

[28] Paterson, John. "Review: Alternative Service Book, 1980," *The Furrow,* Vol. 32, No. 2, The Furrow,

1981, pp. 129-32, http://www.jstor.org/stable/27661097.

[29] "Southwest Diocese Votes for Union with American Episcopal Church," *The Christian Challenge,* December, 1983, p. 14, Foundation for Christian Theology, Washington, D.C., Traycik, A.F., Ed.

[30] Ward, Gary L, Bertil Persson, and Alan Bain. *Independent Bishops: An International Directory.* Detroit, Michigan: Apogee Books, 1990, p. 226.

[31] Persson, Bertil. "The Apostolic Successions of the Apostolic Episcopal Church: An outline at the prospect of the 21st Century," St. Ephrem's Institute, Ed.; The Apostolic Episcopal Church Inc; SOLNA, Sweden, 2008, p. 8.

[32] Armentrout, Don S. "Episcopal Splinter Groups: Schisms in the Episcopal Church, 1963-1985." *Historical Magazine of the Protestant Episcopal Church*, Vol. 55, No. 4, Historical Society of the Episcopal Church, 1986, pp. 295-320, http://www.jstor.org/stable/42974143.

[33] Bess, Douglas. *Divided we Stand: A History of the Continuing Anglican Movement*, Apocryphile Press, Berkeley, California, 2006; pp. 92-95.

[34] "The Traditional Anglican Church in the United States, a Traditional Episcopal Body— [Officers:] H. Edwin Caudill, Bob Baker," San Antonio, 1988; Biz Standing;

https://bizstanding.com/directory/TX/AN/1405; Retrieved 01/11/2022.

[35] "The Anglican Diocese of the Southwest," Biz Standing; https://bizstanding.com/report/buy_business_report?org_id=28607863&name=ANGLICAN+CHURCH+IN+UNITED+STATES+TRADITIONAL+EPISCOPAL+BODY&city=San+Antonio&state=TX&zip=78240&street=9022+Wellesley+Manor+Dr; Retrieved 01/13/2022.

[36] Holmes, David L. *A Brief History of the Episcopal Church*, Trinity Press, Valley Forge, PA; 1993, p. 57.

[37] St. George's School of Theology: 210-641-6107; https://www.yelp.com/biz/st-georges-school-of-theology-san-antonio; Retrieved 01/13/2022.

[38] "Anglican Diocese of the Southwest—1986; [Name Change]"; Open Corporates; https://opencorporates.com/companies/us_tx/0101257201; Retrieved 01/14/2022.

[39] "Saint George's Theological College, San Antonio, Texas"; Officer: H. Edwin Caudill, 1987-1989; Open Corporates; https://opencorporates.com/companies/us_tx/0103882401; Retrieved 01/14/2022.

[40] "Saint George's School of Theology—11919 Orsinger Lane," https://www.merchantcircle.com/saint-

georges-school-of-theology1-san-antonio-tx; Retrieved 01/14/2022.

[41] "Obituary of Robert 'Bob' William Baker," O'Hair-Wards Funeral Chapel; https://www.ohairwards.com/obituary/Robert Bob-Baker; Retrieved 01/12/2022.

[42] "The Anglican Church In The United States, A Traditional Episcopal Body," Biz Standing, San Antonio TX; https://bizstanding.com/p/the+anglican+church+in+the+united+states+a+traditional+episcopal+body-28607863; Retrieved 01/14/2022.

[43] "Klamath Falls Reverend Named Archbishop," Herald and News Klamath Falls; Klamath Falls, Oregon; Vol. 1., May 3, 2013, Inside, p. 71.

[44] "Anglican Diocese of the Southwest of the American Episcopal Church—Voluntarily Dissolved," San Antonio, January 6, 1989; Biz Standing; https://opencorporates.com/companies/us_tx/0101257201; Retrieved 01/11/2022.

[45] "Anglican Diocese of the Southwest—1986; [Name Change]"; Open Corporates; https://opencorporates.com/companies/us_tx/0101257201; Retrieved 01/14/2022.

[46] "Inactive—Nonprofit. Filtered by Jurisdiction: New Mexico, Oregon," Open Corporates; https://opencorporates.com/companies?utf8=%E2%9C%93&q=anglican+diocese+of+the+good

XX. Addendum D: History of Traditional Anglican Church of America as of September 2023

+shepherd&commit=Go&jurisdiction_code=&utf8=%E2%9C%93&commit=Go&controller=searches&action=search_companies&order=; Retrieved 01/12/2022.

[47] Maloney, Raymond. "The Ordination of Women," *The Furrow;* Vol. 32, No. 7, 1981, pp. 438-48, http://www.jstor.org/stable/27661178.

[48] "Barbara Harris Elected First Woman Bishop [Suffragan Bishop of Massachusetts]"; *Episcopal News Service;* September 29, 1988 [88201] ["Bishop Graham Leonard of London (Church of England) said the election will cause deep divisions in the Church. 'In common with many other bishops, I would be unable to recognize a woman bishop or the validity of any ordinations or confirmations performed by her.'"]

[49] [Pursuant to Article II, Section 2, and Canon III.22.3 of the Constitution and Canons of the General Convention, the House of Deputies consents to the ordination and consecration of the Rev. Canon V. Gene Robinson as Bishop Coadjutor of the Diocese of New Hampshire]; https://www.episcopalarchives.org/cgi-bin/acts/acts_resolution-complete.pl?resolution=2003-C045; Retrieved 01/14/2022.

[50] "The Continuum and its Problems," Spaulding, Wallace H.; September 2009; https://anglicanrose.files.wordpress.com/201

2/07/continuumproblems.pdf; Retrieved 01/06/2022.

[51] "A 'Historic' Moment For The U.S. Continuing Church," Traycik, Auburn F.; Foundation for Christian Theology, Washington, D.C., *The Christian Challenge* (Washington), October-November 2004, p. 19. https://virtueonline.org/fond-du-lac-historic-moment-us-continuing-church; Retrieved 01/14/2022.

[52] Wilkinson, Philip. "Eyewitness Christianity"; "Timeline [Barbara Harris, First Female U.S. Bishop]"; Photographs: Teague, Steve; Christianity; DK Eyewitness Books [Children's], London, U.K., 2003; p. 67; ISBN 13:9781405316033.

[53] "Saint George's School of Theology—11919 Orsinger Lane," https://www.merchantcircle.com/saint-georges-school-of-theology1-san-antonio-tx; Retrieved 01/14/2022.

[54] "St. Chad's Anglican Church," Open Corporates; https://opencorporates.com/companies/us_tx/0122642401; Retrieved 01/12/2022.

[55] [Listing: Sunday School teacher, Mavis Caudill]; St. Chad's Anglican Church; https://stchadssatx.org/; Retrieved 01/14/2022.

XX. Addendum D: History of Traditional Anglican Church of America as of September 2023

[56] Robinson, Gene. *God Believes in Love: Straight Talk about Gay Marriage.* United States, Knopf, 2012. ISBN-10: 0307957888 ["For the Church, marriage is the joining of one man and one woman in holy matrimony. In some denominations, marriage is considered one of the sacraments (albeit one of the "lesser" sacraments, like confirmation or ordination). As we have seen, however, the Church (at least the Christian Church) came to the "marrying business" somewhat late, that is in the Middle Ages, as a sacrament to be entered into by all church members seeking such a social arrangement. Before that time, marriage was strictly a civil matter. Still, in the minds of most Americans marriage is something that is done in churches and other places of worship. And so, if the government is going to prescribe who can and cannot be married, it would seem that the State is interfering with the internal workings of religious groups, prohibited under the establishment and free exercise clause in the First Amendment." (Pg. 140)] ["The marriage issue has become so confused in this country because, for a very long time now, the State has automatically deputized ordained clergy to act as agents of the State in officiating at weddings." (Pg. 142)] ["Gay marriage advocates are not seeking to change and religious body's theology or practice of marriage. They only seek to add gay or lesbian couples to the list of people eligible to access the civil institution of marriage." (p. 146)]

XX. Addendum D: History of Traditional Anglican Church of America as of September 2023

[57] Higton, Tony. *Our God Reigns*. Hodder and Stoughton, London, U.K., 1988. Print; ISBN-10: 0340426284; https://christianteaching.org.uk/wp-content/uploads/2021/01/OurGodReigns.pdf; ["The Church of England officially accepts the supremacy of biblical authority. Canons A2-4 are at pains to stress that the Thirty-Nine Articles and the doctrine of the Book of Common Prayer are 'agreeable to the Word of God' and that the worship and ordination services are 'not repugnant to the Word of God'. Canon A5 states that 'the doctrine of the Church of England is grounded in the holy Scriptures, and in such teachings of the Ancient Fathers and Councils of the Church as are agreeable to the said Scriptures'. Article 20 of the Thirty-Nine Articles states: The Church hath power to decree Rites or Ceremonies and authority in Controversies of Faith: And yet it is not lawful for the Church to ordain any thing that is contrary to God's Word written, neither may it so expound one place of Scripture, that it be repugnant to another. (Pg. 39)] ["In fact all who break the law are under a curse (Gal. 3:10,13). 'Neither the sexually immoral nor idolaters nor adulterers nor male prostitutes nor homosexual offenders nor thieves nor the greedy nor drunkards nor slanderers nor swindlers will inherit the kingdom of God' (1 Cor. 6:9-10; cf. Eph. 5:5-6; Col. 3:5-6). (Pg.65)] ["The only encouraging signs are in recent statements by a few bishops that they will practise discipline concerning practising

XX. Addendum D: History of Traditional Anglican Church of America as of September 2023

>homosexual clergy and ordinands. Writing in his diocesan letter of December 1986, the Bishop of Southwark says: 'Anyone who resists authority runs the risk of punishment or censure. But in our church there is a long and honourable history of not using the law to stifle dissent, but relying on persuasion and the appeal of the mind of the whole church.' If the bishop is referring to secondary issues such as aspects of ceremonial or details of liturgy, well and good. But sadly this liberal attitude is adopted by the church towards clergymen who deny basic beliefs or live immoral lives. (Pg. 65)]["'We ask that anyone in Holy Orders, who can no longer honestly and unequivocally assent to the basic doctrines of this biblical and credal faith which they were ordained to uphold and teach, be encouraged as a matter of conscience to resign their office and/or Orders without ignominy...'"(Quoting Diocese of Chichester; Pg. 66)]

[58] Bess, Douglas. *Divided We Stand: A History of the Continuing Anglican Movement*, Apocryphile Press, Berkeley, California, 2006; pp. 180-182.

[59] Pruter, Karl. *The Directory of Autocephalous Bishops of the Apostolic Succession*, by 15th Ed., Wildside Press, 2007; ISBN-10: 1434401448.

[60] "Klamath Falls Reverend Named Archbishop," *Herald and News Klamath Falls*, Klamath Falls, Oregon; Vol. 1., May 3, 2013, Inside, p. 71.

[61] Crumb, Lawrence N. "The Extra-Canonical Ordination of Bishops and the Episcopal Church." Anglican and Episcopal History, Vol. 77, No. 4, Historical Society of the Episcopal Church, 2008, pp. 402-13, http://www.jstor.org/stable/42612842

[62] "St. Mark's Anglican Church: Business Entity Data," State of Oregon, Secretary of State; http://egov.sos.state.or.us/br/pkg_web_name_srch_inq.do_name_srch?p_name=&p_regist_nbr=29717881&p_srch=PHASE1&p_print=FALSE&p_entity_status=ACTINA; Retrieved 01/12/2022.

[63] Archived: Anglican Church International Communion; *Northwest Registered Agent,* 2002; https://ininet.org/anglican-church-international-communion.html; Retrieved 01/17/2022.

[64] Archived: Anglican Church International Communion; The Anglican Church: *Casino Database,* 2001; http://www.theanglicanchurch.net/asv.html; Retrieved 01/17/2022.

[65] "American Anglican Convocation"; Saint Louis, Missouri, May 16, 2003; https://bizstanding.com/p/american+anglican+convocation-102764859; Retrieved 01/15/2003.

[66] "St. George's College of Theology," Corporate Filing—*New Mexico Secretary of State;*

https://portal.sos.state.nm.us/BFS/online/CorporationBusinessSearch/CorporationBusinessInformation; Retrieved 01/15/2022.

[67] Revoking of Corporation with New Mexico Secretary of State: "2002—St. George's College of Theology," *Open Corporates;* Las Cruces, New Mexico; https://opencorporates.com/companies/us_nm/2289957; Retrieved 01/15/2022.

[68] Corporate Record, "St. George's College of Theology," *Bizapedia;* https://www.bizapedia.com/nm/saint-george-college-of-theology.html; Retrieved 01/15/2022.

[69] "Becoming a Cult," *Jon Squill Ministries,* Aug. 8, 2003; http://www.jonsquillministries.org/FAQEpiscipalCult.htm; Retrieved 01/13/2022.

[70] Mullin, Robert Bruce. "Trends in the Study of the History of the Episcopal Church," *Anglican and Episcopal History,* Vol. 72, Issue 2, June 2003, pp. 153-165, https://www.jstor.org/stable/42612314.

[71] Leblanc, Douglas; "Dispatch: Darkness in the Afternoon: Openly homosexual Episcopal priest cleared of misconduct, confirmed as bishop"; *Christianity Today;* Carol Stream, Illinois; 1 Aug., Vol. 47, No. 8; https://www.christianitytoday.com/ct/2003/a

ugustweb-only/8-4-31.0.html; Retrieved 01/17/2022.

[72] Siemon-Netto, Uwe; "Are Episcopalians Still a Church?: A Lutheran theologian and journalist examines the Robinson confirmation"; *Christianity Today;* Carol Stream, Illinois; 1 Aug., Vol. 47, No. 8; https://www.christianitytoday.com/ct/2003/augustweb-only/8-4-45.0.html; Retrieved 01/17/2022.

[73] "Klamath Falls Reverend Named Archbishop," *Herald and News Klamath Falls*; Klamath Falls, Oregon; Vol. 1., May 3, 2013, Inside, p. 71; https://www.heraldandnews.com/members/news/inside/klamath-falls-reverend-named-archbishop/article_71adafea-b3ae-11e2-bc37-001a4bcf887a.html; Retrieved 01/12/2022.

[74] "Anglican Convocation of the Good Shepherd"; *Biz Standing;* Saint Louis, Missouri, April 19, 2010; https://bizstanding.com/p/anglican+convocation+of+the+good+shepherd-102828819; Retrieved 01/15/2022.

[75] Zoning Authority Case Analysis: St. Mary's Anglican Church; Community Development Department: Case# V09-005; Dona Ana County, New Mexico; https://donaanacounty.org/sites/default/files/agendas/ETA_2009-11-18_V09-005.pdf; Retrieved 01/17/2022.

XX. Addendum D: History of Traditional Anglican Church of America as of September 2023

[76] Matte, Nick. "A Rebirth for St. George's Church," *Niagara Gazette,* August 6, 2010; https://www.niagara-gazette.com/news/local_news/a-rebirth-for-st-georges-church/article_132b51c5-4237-52b5-91c3-06c527e2d216.html; Retrieved 01/10/2022.

[77] "An Outline of our Church," *Independent Anglican Church Canada Synod, 1934;* http://www.independentanglicanchurch.com/an-outline-of-our-church; Retrieved 01/12/2022.

[78] Robertson, C. K. "The Challenge of Definition: Conflict and Concord in Anglicanism." *Anglican and Episcopal History;* Vol. 78, No. 4, Historical Society of the Episcopal Church, 2009, pp. 373-92, http://www.jstor.org/stable/42612758.

[79] Sumner, David E. "Episcopal Church History From 1940-1980: A Brief Chronology." *Historical Magazine of the Protestant Episcopal Church*, Vol. 54, No. 1, Historical Society of the Episcopal Church, 1985, pp. 83-89, http://www.jstor.org/stable/42974060; Retrieved 01/15/2022.

[80] "Federal Corporation Information," *Government of Canada;* https://www.ic.gc.ca/app/scr/cc/CorporationsCanada/fdrlCrpDtls.html?corpId=0824348; Retrieved 01/06/2022.

XX. Addendum D: History of Traditional Anglican Church of America as of September 2023

[81] "Independent Anglican Church (Canada Synod)," Open Corporates; https://opencorporates.com/officers/109445886; Retrieved 01/15/2022.

[82] Robertson, C. K. "The Challenge of Definition: Conflict and Concord in Anglicanism." *Anglican and Episcopal History,* Vol. 78, No. 4, Historical Society of the Episcopal Church, 2009, pp. 373-92, http://www.jstor.org/stable/42612758.

[83] "An Outline of our Church," *Independent Anglican Church Canada Synod, 1934;* http://www.independentanglicanchurch.com/an-outline-of-our-church; Retrieved 01/12/2022.

[84] "Our Jurisdiction: Traditional Anglican Church of America"; *Independent Anglican Church, Canada Synod, 1934,* January 2022, Niagara Falls, NY; http://www.independentanglicanchurch.com/traditional-anglican-church-of-america; Retrieved 01/08/2022.

[85] Armentrout, Don S. "Episcopal Splinter Groups: Schisms in the Episcopal Church, 1963-1985." *Historical Magazine of the Protestant Episcopal Church,* Vol. 55, No. 4, Historical Society of the Episcopal Church, 1986, pp. 295-320, http://www.jstor.org/stable/42974143.

[86] Bess, Douglas. *Divided We Stand: A History of the Continuing Anglican Movement,* Chapter 13,

Apocryphile Press, Berkeley, California, 2006; pp. 9-200.

[87] "Obituary of Melvin Hugh Pickering," *Cornerstone Funeral Home;* https://memorials.cornerstonehillsboro.com/melvin-pickering/3331924/obituary.php; Retrieved 01/12/2022.

[88] Williams, Rt. Rev. Rowan. "Episcopal Letter, 2004," Archived from the original (PDF) on April 30, 2014. https://web.archive.org/web/20140430055847/ http://www.sc-acn.net/images/61622/6-6-04CCLettertoABC.pdf; Retrieved 04/29/2014.

[89] "Affirmation of St. Louis," *Traditional Anglican Church,* 2019; http://traditionalanglicanchurch.com/wp-content/uploads/2016/12/Affirmation-of-St.-Louis.pdf; Retrieved 01/13/2022.

[90] Spaulding, Wallace H. "The Continuum and its Problems: A Paper Delivered by Wallace Spaulding: To The Fellowship of Concerned Churchmen," Reprint: *The Fellowship of Concerned Churchmen;* September, 2009; https://anglicanrose.files.wordpress.com/2012/07/continuumproblems.pdf; Retrieved 01/06/2022.

[91] Bess, Douglas. *Divided We Stand: A History of the Continuing Anglican Movement,* Chapter 13, Apocryphile Press, Berkeley, California, 2006, pp. 258-265.

XX. Addendum D: History of Traditional Anglican Church of America as of September 2023

[92] "A 'Historic' Moment for the U.S. Continuing Church," Traycik, Auburn F.; Foundation for Christian Theology, Washington, D.C., *The Christian Challenge*, October-November 2004, p. 19.

[93] "Kleppinger vs. Anglican Catholic Church, Inc; Deferred Entry of Judgement."; Decided, April 26, 1998; *Supreme Court of New Jersey: Chancery Division; Case Law*; https://caselaw.findlaw.com/nj-superior-court/1425644.html#:~:text=That%20decision%20was%20eventually%20ratified%20by%20the%20Provincial,Bishops%20at%20Holyrood%20Seminary%20on%20August%204%2C%201997; Retrieved 01/17/2022.

[94] Bess, Douglas. *Divided We Stand: A History of the Continuing Anglican Movement*, Apocryphile Press, Berkeley, California, 2006; Conclusion: The Status and Future of Continuing Anglicanism; pp. 269-280.

[95] Spaulding, Wallace H. "New Province Gets Off Ground with Half its Potential but with an Anti-Priestess Majority," *The Fellowship of Concerned Churchmen*; Spring 2009; https://anglicanchurches.net/fcc-content/The%20Certain%20Trumpet_Spring%202009.pdf; Retrieved 01/06/2022.

[96] Brittain, Christopher. *A Plague on Both their Houses: Liberal vs. Conservative Christians and the Divorce of the Episcopal Church USA*

(London: Bloomsbury T&T Clark, 2015), p. 71. ISBN 978-0567658456.

[97] "2033: St. George the Martyr, Niagara Falls New York, USA," *Ship of Fools: Gadgets for God Magazine,* 2010; http://ship-of-fools.com/mystery/2010/2033.html; Retrieved 01/17/2022.

[98] "Federal Corporation Information," Government of Canada; https://www.ic.gc.ca/app/scr/cc/CorporationsCanada/fdrlCrpDtls.html?corpId=0824348; Retrieved 01/06/2022.

[99] "A Rebirth for St. George's Church," by Matte, Nick; *Niagara Gazette,* August 6, 2010; https://www.niagara-gazette.com/news/local_news/a-rebirth-for-st-georges-church/article_132b51c5-4237-52b5-91c3-06c527e2d216.html; Retrieved 01/10/2022.

[100] "City of Niagara Falls, NY: Property Details," *City of Niagara Falls—Parcel Report;* https://cityofniagarafalls.prosgar.com/PROSParcel/Parcel?id=13910&swis=291100; Retrieved 01/06/2022.

[101] "Independent Anglican Church (Canada Synod)—Incorporation: 1979; Dissolution: 2016"; *Open Corporates;* https://opencorporates.com/companies/ca/0824348; Retrieved 01/09/2022.

XX. Addendum D: History of Traditional Anglican Church of America as of September 2023

[102] "Federal Corporation Information," *Government of Canada;* https://www.ic.gc.ca/app/scr/cc/Corporation sCanada/fdrlCrpDtls.html?corpId=0824348; Retrieved 01/06/2022.

[103] "Parishes and Missions," *Anglican Convocation of the Good Shepherd,* Clifton, Texas, 2011; https://drdirons.wixsite.com/us-anglican-dotgs/events; Retrieved 01/13/2022.

[104] "Klamath Falls Reverend Named Archbishop," *Herald and News Klamath Falls;* Klamath Falls, Oregon; Vol. 1., May 3, 2013, Inside, p. 71; https://www.heraldandnews.com/members/news/inside/klamath-falls-reverend-named-archbishop/article_71adafea-b3ae-11e2-bc37-001a4bcf887a.html; Retrieved 01/12/2022.

[105] *The Hymnal of the Protestant Episcopal Church in the United States of America*; 1940; Irvine, P., Ed., Church Pension Fund, New York, NY, 1940

[106] "House of Bishops, Clergy, and Necrology," *Traditional Anglican Church of America,* January 2022, Newton, NC; https://1928bcp.weebly.com/house-of-bishops-clergy-and-necrology.html; Retrieved 01/10/2022.

[107] "Bishop Dwight David Irons: The Traditional Anglican Church of America (Southeast-Southwest)," *Linkedin;* https://www.linkedin.com/in/bishop-dwight-david-irons-0b60158a; Retrieved 01/06/2022.

XX. Addendum D: History of Traditional Anglican Church of America as of September 2023

[108] "Chopin Cusachs: Bishop at Traditional Anglican Church of America," *LinkedIn;* https://www.linkedin.com/in/chopin-cusachs-0036a119; Retrieved 01/13/2022.

[109] "A Lesson from Two Old Books," *VirtueOnline: The Voice for Global Orthodox Anglicanism,* July 11, 2010; https://virtueonline.org/lesson-two-old-books-louis-chopin-cusachs; Retrieved 01/13/2022.

[110] "Archbishop Rick Reid: Bishop at Traditional Anglican Church of America," *LinkedIn;* https://www.linkedin.com/in/archbishop-rick-reid-9b67862a; Retrieved 01/13/2022.

[111] "General Synod Meeting," *Find Local Business:* Las Cruces, NM, 2016; https://www.findglocal.com/US/Las-Cruces/455857971219700/Saint-Mary%27s-at-Hill-Anglican-Cathedral; Retrieved 01/13/2022.

[112] "Most Rev. Charles Edward Klughart," Current Bishops; *Independent Sacramental Movement Database;* https://www.independentmovement.us/current-listings/current-bishops/name/charles-klughart; Retrieved 01/15/2022.

[113] "Episcopate and Clergy, Parishes and Ecclesiastical Registry," *Episcopal Letter, 12 January 2022,* Traditional Anglican Church of America, Pro-Cathedral Library, Newton, NC; 2022, pp. 1-5.

[114] "Episcopate and Clergy, Parishes and Ecclesiastical Registry," *Episcopal Letter, 12 January 2022*, Traditional Anglican Church of America, Pro-Cathedral Library, Newton, NC; 2022, pp. 1-5.

[115] "Episcopate and Clergy, Parishes and Ecclesiastical Registry," *Episcopal Letter, 12 January 2022*, Traditional Anglican Church of America, Pro-Cathedral Library, Newton, NC; 2022, pp. 1-5.

[116] Listing: David C. Fleming; Business Record: Tower Truck Services. *Bizapedia*. https://www.bizapedia.com/people/oregon/klamath-falls/david-fleming.html; Retrieved 01/17/2022.

[117] "Episcopal Clerical Directory: 2019," *Church Publishing Inc.*, September 2019, ISBN-13: 978-1640651890.

[118] Benson, Jean Scott. "Continuing the Anglican Tradition: *Traditional Anglican Church of America*". jeanscottbenson.wixsite.com; Retrieved 01/12/2022.

[119] "Chopin Cusachs: Bishop at Traditional Anglican Church of America," *LinkedIn*; https://www.linkedin.com/in/chopin-cusachs-0036a119; Retrieved 01/13/2022.

[120] "Louis Chopin Cusachs, Independent Researcher, B.S., Ph.D., D.E.S., Lic. Th., M.Div."; "66 Publications"; *Research Gate*, 2009;

https://www.researchgate.net/profile/Louis-Cusachs-2; Retrieved 01/15/2022.

[121] Cusachs, Louis Chopin: "Non-orthogonal atomic orbitals: Kinetic energy"; *Chemical Physics Letters,* 1975, Vol. 34; Iss. 3; DOI: 10.1016/0009-2614(75)85545-x

[122] "Obituary of Melvin Hugh Pickering," *Cornerstone Funeral Home;* https://memorials.cornerstonehillsboro.com/melvin-pickering/3331924/obituary.php; Retrieved 01/12/2022.

[123] "Updated, St. Mark's Anglican Church: Business Entity Data," *State of Oregon, Secretary of State;* http://egov.sos.state.or.us/br/pkg_web_name_srch_inq.show_detl?p_be_rsn=2001204&p_srce=BR_INQ&p_print=FALSE; Retrieved 01/12/2022.

[124] "Paul K. Leeman Excavating, Inc." *Dunn and Bradstreet: Business Directory;* Camarillo, California, 2002; https://www.dandb.com/businessdirectory/paulkleemanexcavatinginc-camarillo-ca-16454570.html; Retrieved 01/15/2022.

[125] "St. Paul's Anglican Church," *Open Corporates,* 2010; https://opencorporates.com/companies/us_ca/C3305129; Retrieved 01/15/2022.

XX. Addendum D: History of Traditional Anglican Church of America as of September 2023

[126] "Parishes and Missions," *Anglican Convocation of the Good Shepherd*, Clifton, TX, 2011; https://drdirons.wixsite.com/us-anglican-dotgs/events; Retrieved 01/13/2022.

[127] "House of Bishops, Clergy, and Necrology," *Traditional Anglican Church of America, January 2022*, Newton, NC; https://1928bcp.weebly.com/house-of-bishops-clergy-and-necrology.html; Retrieved 01/10/2022.

[128] "Episcopate and Clergy, Parishes and Ecclesiastical Registry," *Episcopal Letter, 12 January 2022*, Traditional Anglican Church of America, Pro-Cathedral Library, Newton, NC; 2022, pp. 1-2.

[129] "Episcopal Clerical Directory 2021," *Church Publishing Inc.*, December 2021, ISBN-13: 978-1640654501.

[130] "General Synod Meeting," *Find Local Business:* Las Cruces, N.M., 2016; https://www.findglocal.com/US/Las-Cruces/455857971219700/Saint-Mary%27s-at-Hill-Anglican-Cathedral; Retrieved 01/13/2022.

[131] Robertson, C. K. "The Challenge of Definition: Conflict and Concord in Anglicanism." *Anglican and Episcopal History,* Vol. 78, No. 4, Historical Society of the Episcopal Church, 2009, pp. 373-92, http://www.jstor.org/stable/42612758.

[132] L'Hommedieu, John. "The Continuing Anglican Metamorphosis: Introducing The Adapted Integrated Model" (2012). *Electronic Theses and Dissertations,* 2004-2019; https://stars.library.ucf.edu/etd/2337; Retrieved 01/11/2022.

[133] "Obituary of Melvin Hugh Pickering," *Cornerstone Funeral Home;* https://memorials.cornerstonehillsboro.com/melvin-pickering/3331924/obituary.php; Retrieved 01/12/2022.

[134] "Obituary of Robert 'Bob' William Baker," *O'Hair-Wards Funeral Chapel;* https://www.ohairwards.com/obituary/Robert Bob-Baker; Retrieved 01/12/2022.

[135] "Obituary of Dwight David Irons," *May and Smith Funeral Home;* https://www.mayandsmithfuneraldirectors.com/obituary/dwight-irons; Retrieved 01/12/2022.

[136] "Obituary of Louis C. Cusachs," *Cremation Society of Charlotte, Inc.;* https://www.tributearchive.com/obituaries/20003310/Louis-C-Cusachs/Charlotte/North-Carolina/Cremation-Society-of-Charlotte-Inc; Retrieved 01/13/2022.

[137] "House of Bishops, Clergy, and Necrology," *Traditional Anglican Church of America,* January, 2022, Newton, NC; https://1928bcp.weebly.com/house-of-

bishops-clergy-and-necrology.html; Retrieved 01/10/2022.

[138] "Obituary of Louis C. Cusachs: Tribute Wall," *Cremation Society of Charlotte, Inc.*; https://www.tributearchive.com/obituaries/20003310/Louis-C-Cusachs/wall; Retrieved 01/13/2022.

[139] "TACA Clergy Directory: Episcopate & Clergy, Parishes & Ecclesiastical Registry of Traditional Anglican Church of America in Unitate Diocesana sub The Independent Anglican Church Canada Synod, 1934"; File Publ. 01/12/2022; Jeremiad Christian Homesteader Gazette, East Rockhill, Pennsylvania, Vol. 1, Winter 2022, pp. 1-5." https://jeremiadchristianhomesteadersgazette.com/01_taca_article; Retrieved: 01/22/2022.

[140] "Jurisdiction: Traditional Anglican Church of America"; *Independent Anglican Church Canada Synod 1934;* January 2022, Niagara Falls, NY; http://www.independentanglicanchurch.com/traditional-anglican-church-of-america; Retrieved 01/08/2022.

[141] "Parcel Report," *Catawba County NC;* https://gis.catawbacountync.gov/nomap/parcel_report.php?key=373016927996&typ=P; Retrieved 01/13/2022.

[142] Record: St. Andrew's Anglican Church; *Join My Church* [Directory], 2022; NC, Newton;

XX. Addendum D: History of Traditional Anglican Church of America as of September 2023

https://www.joinmychurch.com/churches/St-Andrew-s-Anglican-Church-Newton-North-Carolina-United-States/345150; Retrieved 01/15/2022.

[143] "Episcopate and Clergy, Parishes and Ecclesiastical Registry," *Episcopal Letter, 12 January 2022,* Traditional Anglican Church of America, Pro-Cathedral Library, Newton, NC, 2022, pp. 1-2.

[144] "Jurisdiction: Traditional Anglican Church of America"; *Independent Anglican Church Canada Synod 1934;* January 2022, Niagara Falls, NY; http://www.independentanglicanchurch.com/traditional-anglican-church-of-america; Retrieved 01/08/2022.

[145] "House of Bishops, Clergy, and Necrology," *Traditional Anglican Church of America,* January 2022, Newton, NC; https://1928bcp.weebly.com/house-of-bishops-clergy-and-necrology.html; Retrieved 01/10/2022.

[146] "Jurisdiction: Traditional Anglican Church of America"; *Independent Anglican Church Canada Synod 1934;* January 2022, Niagara Falls, NY; http://www.independentanglicanchurch.com/traditional-anglican-church-of-america; Retrieved 01/08/2022.

XX. Addendum D: History of Traditional Anglican Church of America as of September 2023

[147] "General Synod Meeting," *Find Local Business:* Las Cruces, N.M., 2016; https://www.findglocal.com/US/Las-Cruces/455857971219700/Saint-Mary%27s-at-Hill-Anglican-Cathedral; Retrieved 01/13/2022.

[148] [Archbishop Rick Aaron Reid] "Faith Briefs," *Herald and News Klamath Falls,* August 27, 2021; https://www.heraldandnews.com/news/local_news/faith/august-27-klamath-county-faith-briefs/article_4af49a2e-fa83-50e9-b3cf-38a56622e953.html; Retrieved 01/08/2022.

[149] *Not in the Communion*, Munn Obl OSB, Fr. Jonathan; Lulu, Morrisville, NC, October 2020; Fr. Jonathan Munn Obl OSB; ISBN-13: 978-1716485114; Pg. 29.

[150] "TACA Clergy Directory: Episcopate & Clergy, Parishes & Ecclesiastical Registry of Traditional Anglican Church of America in Unitate Diocesana sub The Independent Anglican Church Canada Synod, 1934"; File Publ. 01/12/2022; Jeremiad Christian Homesteader Gazette, East Rockhill, Pennsylvania, Vol. 1, Winter 2022, pp. 1-5." https://jeremiadchristianhomesteadersgazette.com/01_taca_article; Retrieved: 01/22/2022.

[151] [Bishop-elect Fleming; Bishop-elect Leeman] "Faith Briefs," *Herald and News Klamath Falls,* May 15, 2020; https://www.heraldandnews.com/news/local_

news/faith-news-briefs/article_b20256cd-d12d-5816-bdae-f8159bd4628f.html; Retrieved 01/08/2022.

[152] "Updated, St. Mark's Anglican Church: Business Entity Data," *State of Oregon, Secretary of State*; http://egov.sos.state.or.us/br/pkg_web_name_srch_inq.show_detl?p_be_rsn=2001204&p_srce=BR_INQ&p_print=FALSE; Retrieved 01/12/2022.

[153] "Episcopal Clerical Directory 2021," *Church Publishing Inc.*, December 2021, ISBN-13: 978-1640654501.

[154] "House of Bishops, Clergy, and Necrology," *Traditional Anglican Church of America,* January 2022, Newton, NC; https://1928bcp.weebly.com/house-of-bishops-clergy-and-necrology.html; Retrieved 01/10/2022.

[155] "Episcopate and Clergy, Parishes and Ecclesiastical Registry," *Episcopal Letter, 12 January 2022,* Traditional Anglican Church of America, Pro-Cathedral Library, Newton, NC; 2022, pp. 1-2.

[156] *Episcopal Clerical Directory: 2019*, Church Publishing Inc., September 2019, ISBN-13: 978-1640651890

[157] "General Synod Meeting," *Find Local Business: Las Cruces, NM, 2016;*

https://www.findglocal.com/US/Las-Cruces/455857971219700/Saint-Mary%27s-at-Hill-Anglican-Cathedral; Retrieved 01/13/2022.

[158] "Most Rev. Charles Edward Klughart," *Current Bishops; Independent Sacramental Movement Database;* https://www.independentmovement.us/current-listings/current-bishops/name/charles-klughart; Retrieved 01/15/2022.

[159] "Episcopate and Clergy, Parishes and Ecclesiastical Registry," *Episcopal Letter, 12 January 2022,* Traditional Anglican Church of America, Pro-Cathedral Library, Newton, NC; 2022, pp. 1-5.

[160] "Episcopate and Clergy, Parishes and Ecclesiastical Registry," *Episcopal Letter, 12 January 2022,* Traditional Anglican Church of America, Pro-Cathedral Library, Newton, NC; 2022, pp. 1-2.

[161] "TACA Clergy Directory: Episcopate & Clergy, Parishes & Ecclesiastical Registry of Traditional Anglican Church of America in Unitate Diocesana sub The Independent Anglican Church Canada Synod, 1934"; File Publ. 01/12/2022; Jeremiad Christian Homesteader Gazette, East Rockhill, Pennsylvania, Vol. 1, Winter 2022, pp. 1-5." https://jeremiadchristianhomesteadersgazette.com/01_taca_article; Retrieved: 01/22/2022.

XX. Addendum D: History of Traditional Anglican Church of America as of September 2023

[162] "Episcopate and Clergy, Parishes and Ecclesiastical Registry," *Episcopal Letter, 12 January 2022,* Traditional Anglican Church of America, Pro-Cathedral Library, Newton, NC; 2022, pp. 1-2.

[163] Extract: Application for Constitutive Registration of the Independent Mexican Episcopal Church, as a Religious Association, Filing Date: 29 July, 1993; *Secretary of Government Official Journal of the Federation [of Mexico].* Applicant Legal Representative: Jorge B. Martínez Zendejas and Roberto Osnaya Osnaya. Legal Address: Calle 5 de Mayo número 20, Col. San Pedro Mártir, Delegación Tlalpan, México, D.F., C.P. 14650.; http://dof.gob.mx/nota_detalle.php?codigo=4764702&fecha=29/07/1993; Retrieved 01/17/2022.

[164] "TACA Clergy Directory: Episcopate & Clergy, Parishes & Ecclesiastical Registry of Traditional Anglican Church of America in Unitate Diocesana sub The Independent Anglican Church Canada Synod, 1934"; File Publ. 01/12/2022; Jeremiad Christian Homesteader Gazette, East Rockhill, Pennsylvania, Vol. 1, Winter 2022, pp. 1-5." https://jeremiadchristianhomesteadersgazette.com/01_taca_article; Retrieved: 01/22/2022.

XX. Addendum D: History of Traditional Anglican Church of America as of September 2023

ADDITIONS:

Revoked corporation information for Archdiocese of the Good Shepherd, for reference purposes:

https://opencorporates.com/companies/us_or/97213392

https://opencorporates.com/companies/us_nm/2275246

The Canons of Traditional Anglican Church of America

TITLE I: Organization and Administration of the Diocese of TACA

Canon 1: Official List of the Clergy of the Diocese

Section 1—A list of all duly ordained members of the Episcopate, Clergy, Permanent Diaconate, and Honorary/Lay Offices, who are canonically resident or licensed to work in the Diocese shall be maintained by the Ecclesiastical Authority of the TACA Chancery, and kept current by the Registrar, and on file, in the Chancery. The list shall contain the addresses and licensed positions of these offices and shall be made available to the members and their delegates at least 14 days in advance of any meeting or assembly of the council or of a synod—known henceforward as "Formal Meeting."

Section 2—The official list shall be available to any Formal Meeting on the first day of its meeting and shall be the basis for determining a quorum as provided in Article VI. Part A. Section i. of the Constitution.

Section 3—Every member of the Episcopate and Clergy canonically resident or licensed or appointed in the Diocese who is entitled both to vote and to officially address the Diocese shall attend every Formal Meeting, unless excused by the Ecclesiastical Authority.

Section 4—The Archbishop or Primate shall be the prime Ecclesiastical Authority of the Diocese (see Article IV of the Constitution). During any vacancy in the office of Bishop, the Bishop Coadjutor or, if there be none, the Bishop Suffragan shall be the prime Ecclesiastical Authority of the Diocese.

Title I: Organization and Administration of the Diocese of TACA

Section 5—As of September 2023, the Episcopate and Clergy of this Traditional Anglican Church of America (TACA) included the following major religious Bodies, and Office Titles. (Note: The following offices are occupied by the officers, so named below, as of September 2023. Their foundational offices shall be deemed permanent and to be filled by any future incumbents):

The House of Bishops:

Archbishop Most Reverend Doctor Rick Aaron Reid, Primate of TACA, of the Chancery of Saint Andrew's Anglican Church, in the city of Newton, of Catawba County, in midwestern North Carolina.

Diocesan Bishop of the Western Diocese of TACA, Right Reverend Paul Leeman, Presiding at Saint Mark's Anglican Church, in the city of Klamath Falls, of Klamath County, in southwestern Oregon.

Coadjutor Bishop Francis Fontenot, of the Saint Martin's Parish, in the city of Saint Martinsville, in southern Louisiana.

Suffragan Bishop David C. Fleming, of the Western Diocese of TACA, Rector at Saint Mark's Anglican Church, in the city of Klamath Falls, of Klamath County, in southwestern Oregon.

Bishop Right Reverend Ashley Edward Beckham, in the city of McKinney, of Collin County, in northeastern Texas.

Title I: Organization and Administration of the Diocese of TACA

Canon Chancellor Right Reverend Kenneth Walsh, in the city of White Stone, of Lancaster County, in eastern Virginia.

Bishop Right Reverend Donald Nozawa, of the city of Bridgeton, in Saint Louis County, of eastern Missouri.

Diocesan Archbishop Jorge Martinez, of the Cathedral of the Independent Mexican Episcopal Church, of Tlalpan, Mexico.

The Ordained Clergy:

Reverend Gary Mullica, Priest of Saint Mark's Anglican Church, in the city of Klamath Falls, of Klamath County, in southwestern Oregon.

Father Michael DellaVecchia, Rector of Saint Patrick's Anglican Church, in the city of Perkasie, of Bucks County, in southeastern Pennsylvania.

Permanent Diaconate:

Lady Virginia Ann Reid, Appointed Deaconess of the Chancery of TACA, Outreach Coordinator, and Registrar of Saint Andrew's Anglican Church, in the city of Newton, of Catawba County, in midwestern North Carolina.

Lady Lisa DellaVecchia, Appointed Deaconess and Registrar of Saint Patrick's Anglican Church, in the city of Perkasie, of Bucks County, in southeastern Pennsylvania.

Title I: Organization and Administration of the Diocese of TACA

Lay Incumbents—Prebendary, Elder, Precentor, Warden

Prebendary Grace Leeman, Lay Precentor, Registrar, and Elder of Saint Mark's Anglican Church, in the city of Klamath Falls, of Klamath County, in southwestern Oregon. Wife of Western Diocesan Bishop Paul Leeman.

Honorary Canon Donna Baker, Lay Consultant and Elder, in the city of Klamath Falls, of Klamath County, in southwestern Oregon. Wife of TACA co-founder, the late Primate Archbishop Robert Baker.

Elder Sherrill E. Watkins, Senior Warden of the Chancery of TACA, at Saint Andrew's Anglican Church, in the city of Newton, of Catawba County, in midwestern North Carolina.

Virginia Ann Reid, Secretary of the Chancery of TACA, at Saint Andrew's Anglican Church, in the city of Newton, of Catawba County, in midwestern North Carolina.

Charles and Amanda Bartlett, Lay Readers, at Western Diocese.

Title I: Organization and Administration of the Diocese of TACA

Canon 2: Lay Delegates in the Diocese for Voting and Formal Meetings (See also Meetings and Voting, in Constitution, Article V, Parts A, B; Article VI, Parts A-F)

Section 1—A list of all duly appointed Lay delegates of each TACA "Body" (i.e., congregations, ministries, missions, parishes, or any Bodies formally officiating within the Synod of TACA) shall be maintained, compiled, and updated by the Secretary or Registrar of the Chancery or presiding Authority. Each Lay delegate must belong to a TACA parish. The list shall contain the addresses and other appropriate contact information of the Lay delegates and shall be made available to members and their delegates at least two weeks in advance of any Formal Meeting and/or vote of the Diocese. Any Lay delegate whose name is not on the list but wishes to participate as a delegate in the Diocese, shall bring the omission to the attention of the Registrar. Bishops, priests, and deacons, who are licensed or incardinated members of dioceses that are different from TACA may not serve as Lay delegates. Each TACA Body shall select its Lay delegates according to its respective rules, so long as he or she is a member of a TACA Parish.

Section 2—Each Congregation, Parish, and Mission, numbering ten or fewer Lay members may be entitled to the limit of one Lay adult delegate, in any Formal Meeting, for voting or any discussional purpose. If the number of Lay members in said Body is more than ten, this limit may be increased to two. However, each delegate who wishes to vote must be a member of a TACA Parish. His or her inclusion in discussions is at the discretion of Ecclesiastical Authority.

Title I: Organization and Administration of the Diocese of TACA

Section 3—The governing authority of each Parish or Body shall select its delegates according to its respective Customary, with no more than one Alternate Delegate for each Lay delegate so chosen. Any Alternate Delegate must be a member of a TACA Parish.

Section 4—The Chancery shall have opportunity to discuss and affirm the selection of religious delegates to a Bishops' Council, a Regional Synod, or other Formal Meeting. Each Body of the Church (e.g., Parish, Deanery, School, etc.) is allowed no more than eight delegates from the Clergy, Diaconate, Vestry, Faculty, and Episcopate at a Formal Meeting for discursive or voting purposes.

Section 5—*Quorum:* Because the typical size of each religious Body is typically small, the quorum necessary for any purpose of election, balloting, or decisional assembly for a Yearly or Regional Synod, Bishops' Council, or Formal Meeting is equal to half of the number of delegates or official members, voters, or participants expected for that meeting.

Section 6—The Archbishop possesses sole full unilateral authority to ratify or veto a vote; or to abolish, overrule, approve, or nullify the outcome, purpose, election results, conclusion, outcome, or decision of any Yearly or Regional Synod, Bishops' Council, or Formal Meeting.

Section 7—*Override of Archbishop Veto:* Following the Archbishop's veto of a vote, a Referendum Memo must be written, dated, and signed by a two-thirds majority of the House of Bishops to calendar an override vote.

Title I: Organization and Administration of the Diocese of TACA

Section 8—Only the ordained clergy and bishops may vote by a two-thirds majority to override the Archbishop's veto. The vote must occur no less than 24 hours after the veto has occurred.

Section 9—The Archbishop may, at his discretion, ratify or nullify the override conclusion for any reason or purpose.

Canon 3: Confraternal Bodies Subject to Other Jurisdictions

Those Bodies who are in confraternity (having a confraternal relationship) with TACA churches, operating with theological and biblical soundness within the boundaries of this Traditional Anglican Church of America, who are in canonical relationship with this TACA Diocese/Synod, but are under other jurisdictions, will be welcomed into affiliation with this TACA Diocese/Synod, after written permission is given from a TACA Prelate (i.e., the Primate, Archbishop, Bishop, Senior Pastor, Pastor, or Rector, only). Each Confraternal Body may engage in a Formal Meeting(s) and/or Voting, on a case-by-case basis, and, only after an affirmative decision has been made to include that outside-but-confraternal Body and each of its members to participate in any such Meeting(s) or Voting. Approval must be sought only after the submission of a list of written individual names and titles, as well as the expressed intention as to why they are intended to be collaborative with TACA, to the Prelate, who may approve their affiliation. Upon confraternal affiliation, they shall be accorded the degree of participation permitted according to the discretion of that Prelate. The Prelate must, by needs,

Title I: Organization and Administration of the Diocese of TACA

obtain a written participatory approval by the Prelate of that outside jurisdiction, according to that jurisdiction's own ordinances.

Canon 4: Formal Meetings of this TACA Synod (See also Meetings and Voting, in Constitution, Article V, Parts A, B; Article VI, Parts A-F)

Section 1—This TACA Synod shall have annual Formal Meetings and may also have special meetings called for a special purpose. These types of meetings are the Yearly Synod; a Regional Synod; a Bishops' Council; or any diocesan rump or provisional kind of Formal Meeting. They can occur in person or via Internet streaming. They are more elaborately described in the Constitution, Article III.

Section 2—The Archbishop, with the advice and affirmation of the House of Bishops, shall determine the date, time, and place of a Formal Meeting. The Office of the Archbishop, in conjunction with the Secretary or Prebendary of the Diocese, shall prepare the Meeting agenda and all related materials.

Section 3—The Archbishop, with the advice of the Canon, shall propose Rules of Order for adoption by the synod at the outset of each Formal Meeting. The Archbishop shall lead the Yearly TACA Synod. As regards a lesser Formal Meeting, such as a Regional Synod or a Bishops' Council, the presiding Bishop may be the most senior member of the House of Bishops, or any pertinent Bishop from the House, with the Archbishop's affirmation, or may be the Archbishop himself.

Title I: Organization and Administration of the Diocese of TACA

Canon 5: Religious Delegates of the Diocese for a Bishops' Council, Regional Synod, or Other Formal Meeting (See Meetings and Voting, Constitution, Article V, Parts A, B; Article VI, Parts A-F)

Section 1—The Chancery shall have opportunity to discuss and affirm the selection of delegates to a Bishops' Council, a Regional Synod, or other Formal Meeting. Each Body of the Church (e.g., Parish, Deanery, School, etc.) is allowed no more than eight delegates from the Clergy, Diaconate, Vestry, Faculty, and Episcopate at a Formal Meeting for discursive or voting purposes. *Also:*

Section 2—Of that eight, each Congregation or Mission may appoint no more than one Lay member if said Congregation or Body contains less than ten Lay members, or two if it contains more than ten (see TITLE I, Canon 2). *Also:*

Section 3—These limits may change only at the discretion of the Archbishop. They shall be selected by the affirmation of the House of Bishops or merely by the Archbishop, who has ultimate unilateral authority in all formal, executive, ancillary, and any official matters, to approve any list of delegates.

Section 4—The Chancery or House of Bishops shall report the names and contact information of its delegates, and such alternate delegates as it deems prudent to name them, not less than two weeks prior to a Formal Meeting.

Title I: Organization and Administration of the Diocese of TACA

Section 5—All delegates—religious or Lay—must be members of TACA parishes; otherwise, they are not allowed without written approval of the Archbishop.

Section 6—*Quorum:* Because the typical size of each religious Body is typically small, the quorum necessary for any purpose of election, balloting, or decisional assembly for a Yearly or Regional Synod, Bishops' Council, or Formal Meeting equals half of the number of delegates or official members, voters, or participants expected for that meeting.

Section 7—The Archbishop possesses sole, full, unilateral authority to ratify or veto a vote; or to abolish, overrule, approve, or nullify the outcome, purpose, election results, conclusion, outcome, or decision of any Yearly or Regional Synod, Bishops' Council, or Formal Meeting.

Section 8—Override of Archbishop Veto: Following the Archbishop's veto of a vote, a Referendum Memo must be written, dated, and signed by a two-thirds majority of the House of Bishops to calendar an override vote.

Section 9—Only the ordained clergy and bishops may vote by a two-thirds majority to override the Archbishop's veto. The vote must occur no less than 24 hours after the veto has occurred.

Section 10—The Archbishop may, at his discretion, ratify or nullify the override conclusion for any reason or purpose.

Title I: Organization and Administration of the Diocese of TACA

Canon 6: Subdivision of this TACA Diocese Into Regions

Six divisions fall under the authority of the Office of the Archbishop. Named and described in Article X, Part A, Sec. vi, Item d, of the Constitution, they are the Eastern Diocese and Archbishop's Chancery; the Western Diocese; the Southwestern Diocese; and the Northeastern Diocese. These four divisions are based on geographical location. The next two divisions are Prelatures, which are the Canon Prelature and the Coadjutor/Suffragan Prelature.

The Office of the Archbishop shall publish and maintain a customary, on the sectioning of this TACA Diocese into the above Regions and/or its various parishes. It is known as the "TACA Roster." It displays all the year-to-date data, listing names, religious titles, and full contact information of our Jurisdiction's members and of each Body. The TACA Roster is a "rolling" document, not merely because of its personnel's capacity to mutate, but also because of the Confessional-Tabernacle aspect of TACA, which dictates that a bi-vocational Priesthood and Episcopate operating an orthodox and biblical church within a depraved world is subject to poverty, shortages, and relocation. The Confessional-Tabernacle concept is explained in detail in Article X, Part A., Sec. i, of the Constitution. When it shall appear to Ecclesiastical Authority of the Chancery, in consultation with the House of Bishops, that it would advance the mission and ministry of this TACA Diocese, the Ecclesiastical Authority may authorize the organization of additional regions or districts within the Diocese.

Title I: Organization and Administration of the Diocese of TACA

Canon 7: The House of Bishops

This TACA Synod shall have a House of Bishops chosen agreeably by the Archbishop or voted upon (See Article VII, Parts C, D, E, of the Constitution), with such authority as therein provided and such other authority and responsibility as the TACA Synod may determine by the Archbishop in consultation with his Canon or according to his resolution. The bishops of this House shall serve open-ended terms, otherwise limited only according to the needs of their lives and paying careers. The bishops of this House shall be organized according to each role that is appropriately associated with the Regions or Prelatures they serve, as detailed in Article X, Part A, Sec. vi, Item d, of the Constitution. Election of new Bishops may occur by the Archbishop's calling forth of a Formal Meeting by which the TACA Episcopate might thus become incremented. Alternatively, the Archbishop, as is his liberty, may appoint a new Bishop to that Region or Prelature.

Canon 8: The Canon

The Canon of this TACA Synod, appointed by the Bishop, shall be and remain a communicant in good standing. Either a Bishop, Priest, or Appointed Deacon(-ess), he or she is thus a member of the Canon Prelature. He or she shall be learned in the law and licensed to practice in the state in which the Archbishop's Chancery is located and/or incorporated. The Canon shall be responsible for the legal affairs of the Diocese and shall serve as counsel to the Archbishop and the House of Bishops.

Title I: Organization and Administration of the Diocese of TACA

Canon 9: The Secretary

The Secretary of the Diocese, appointed by the Archbishop, serves an open-ended term. He or she shall keep the minutes, journal, and/or imerológio of Formal Meetings and shall submit such reports as the Archbishop may request.

Canon 10: The Treasurer

The Treasurer of this TACA Synod, appointed by the Archbishop, serves an open-ended term. He or she shall be the custodian for all funds of the Diocese, whose name is listed in all public incorporation or informal filings of the Archdiocese. The Treasurer shall be bonded or insured, if needed, in such amount or in such manner as the Chancery shall deem appropriate and shall file an annual report to the Archbishop and the House of Bishops, as needed, on the financial status of this TACA Diocese as well as periodic reports of account for all funds under his or her custody or control, as needed. As of September 2023, there was no Treasurer of TACA. Although the Chancery operates as the religious core of TACA, all fiscal matters are currently under the respective authority of each individual Parish, each with its independent priestly and episcopal leaders (as each Parish operates in ecclesiastical subsidiarity to the Chancery and enjoying legal and fiscal independence from this TACA Diocese outside of the general broad-based religious fellowship identity of this TACA Diocese). Incorporation papers may otherwise include the name of the Treasurer or bookkeeper.

Title I: Organization and Administration of the Diocese of TACA

Canon 11: The Registrar

The Registrar of this TACA Synod, appointed by the Archbishop, serves an open-ended term. He or she shall be the custodian of the official records of this TACA Diocese, and he or she shall issue such certification as may be directed by the Office of Archbishop or requested by the House of Bishops.

Canon 12: Provision for a Finance Team for Entire Diocese

Section 1—If established by our TACA Synod, there shall be a Finance Team of this TACA Diocese, appointed by the Archbishop, who may choose to consult for this purpose with his House of Bishops. The Finance Team shall assist a Chancery Treasurer in preparing an annual budget of this TACA Diocese and shall issue guidelines for audits and investment management. The records and accounts of the Treasurer can be made subject to an independent annual audit. The Finance Team shall issue periodic reports to the Archbishop and the House of Bishops regarding the financial condition of the TACA Diocese as a whole. The formation of a non-profit organization filed as a 501(c) corporation for the TACA Diocese and for any individual Parish or other Body is explained in the Constitution, Articles IX. and XIV. If a Finance Team is not established, its functions shall be performed by the Archbishop's Office with consultation, as needed, by his House of Bishops. A Finance Team may also be regional, temporary, ad hoc, rump, or created provisionally for a given project, program, or movement within the TACA Diocese, by permission of the Archbishop's Office.

Title I: Organization and Administration of the Diocese of TACA

Section 2—With whatever assistance it may require, such a Finance Team at the Archbishopric level, would oversee funds to aid TACA members, such as prospective insurance and benefits programs for members of the Clergy and Episcopate.

Canon 13: Team on Constitution and Canons of the Diocese

Section 1—The House of Bishops may establish a Constitution and Canons Team from the delegates to the Synod, with the Canon, or other qualified overseeing appointee(s), as a member(s). If this Team is not established, its functions shall be performed by the Canon, working with the House of Bishops.

Section 2—The Constitution and Canons may be written, co-authored, updated, and/or edited by any religious member or parishioner, provided that the completion of their writing/editing session or project be wholly reviewed and approved by the Canon and House of Bishops.

Canon 14: Nominations for Bishop or Archbishop

Section 1—An Episcopal Nominations Team may be selected by the House of Bishops. The Team shall have up to eight members from Parishes from anywhere within this TACA Diocese—lay or religious—provided that the Team contain at least two TACA bishops. One of those bishops must be the Chair of the Nominations Team. The Team shall be responsible for recording the names of all nominees for Archbishop, Bishop, Coadjutor, and/or Suffragan. The nomination process may be conducted in person or via Internet streaming.

Title I: Organization and Administration of the Diocese of TACA

Section 2—All nominations must include an acceptance of the nomination in writing by the nominee and support in writing by an authorized member of the religious Body that the nominee is already serving. If one or both of these items is unattainable, written support by the House of Bishops stating that the aspirant is acceptable to be nominated must be obtained.

Section 3—The Nominations Team shall prayerfully review all names placed in nomination and determine whether they meet the criteria established by the Church. Through a prayerful process of discernment, the Team shall reach a consensus decision as to which names shall be offered for consideration by this TACA Synod.

Section 4—If an Episcopal Nominations Team is not established, its functions shall be performed by the House of Bishops.

Canon 15: Uses of High Church and Low Church Traditions

Ecclesiastical Authority of this TACA Diocese shall pay mind to the offering of constant resistance by religious-Body governors to Modernism and all its immoral and amoral distinctions. This TACA Diocese shall therefore set forth a Low Church religious culture that makes orthodox worship project the simplicity that is associated with basic, solemn Apostolic Christian church ritual. A Low Church varietal thus manifests itself via the Confessional way, in that it has a Bible-core approach to executing an elemental but profound interpretation of the Liturgy and Anglican

Title I: Organization and Administration of the Diocese of TACA

formularies, while projecting an unwavering Reformist mindset. This TACA Diocese shall also permit manifestations of the contrasting High Church species, sometimes known as Anglo-Catholic, which strives to serve the same Reformist end, through the use of enhanced ritual and pre-Protestant, non-Trentonian Reformation Christian modalities. The Archbishop shall guide Congregations, Missions, and other religious Bodies that strive to employ the signal High Church offerings of material beauty and ritual purity, resisting Modernism while also participating solidly in our Confessional Reformist distinction.

TITLE II: Organizations and Administration of TACA Religious Bodies/Ministries

Canon 1: Membership in the Diocese, Governing Authority of Religious Bodies

Section 1—The founding Religious Bodies (i.e., parishes and bishoprics) of this TACA Diocese are set forth in the Constitution. Any other group of the faithful may seek to affiliate as a TACA "Body" (i.e., Church Plant, Ministry, Congregation, or Mission), as provided in this Canon. A Congregation normally shall consist of a group of the faithful meeting together in regular worship with an average Sunday attendance of at least twenty (10) members. Any group that meets these minimum specifications may apply to be recognized as a Congregation. Any group not meeting these minimum specifications may apply to the Council of the Diocese to be recognized as a Church Plant, Ministry, or Mission, pending the application, and approval by the House of Bishops, which shall issue a written waiver of these minimum specifications.

Section 2—Any group of the faithful seeking to affiliate as a Congregation or other type of religious Body shall submit a written request to the Archbishop on behalf of his office and the House of Bishops. Upon approval by the House of Bishops and the Archbishop, the Archbishop will receive the individual members of the group into the Church. A religious Body joining or transforming into TACA shall agree in writing to become subject to the Constitution and Canons of this TACA Diocese.

Title II: Organizations and Administration of TACA Religious Bodies/Ministries

Section 3—The governance of each Parish and any other religious Body shall be vested in the Senior Pastor, Rector, or Senior Pastor, and in any duly constituted governing authority of the entity, as established by that Body's bylaws.

Section 4—The Archbishop shall be the governing authority of a religious Body (e.g., Parish, Congregation) that is authorized by this TACA Diocese, except as he may delegate such authority. Regarding governance of lesser Bodies, the governing authority held by the sponsoring Parish or Congregation shall be the governing authority over a subordinate Body (e.g., Mission), which is sponsored by that superior Body, except as the governing authority may delegate such authority. A Ministry, Church Plant, Mission, Deanery, or School may be given a development council to assist in the administration of its affairs. The Vicar, Pastor, or coordinator/leader of a Mission, Church Plant, Deanery, Ministry, or School, appointed as such by the Archbishop or by the sponsoring Parish or Congregation, as applicable, shall be in charge of that subordinate religious Body, while being subject to the authority of the Archbishop or the sponsoring Parish or Congregation, and shall preside over all meetings of that development council.

Section 5—A Parish or Congregation, Mission, or other organized religious Body, which is attached to an outside Anglican or Episcopalian jurisdiction, but wishes to join TACA, may consult with the Archbishop of TACA and/or his House of Bishops, about becoming a member of this TACA Diocese. Any such religious Body shall agree in writing to become subject to the Constitution and Canons of TACA.

Title II: Organizations and Administration of TACA Religious Bodies/Ministries

Section 6—Any organized religious Body whose faithful belong to an outside denomination that is neither Anglican nor Episcopalian, but desiring to become a member of TACA, shall first apply through the Office of the Archbishop. Any such Congregation or other organized group of the faithful of another denomination, which has communicated with the Archbishop's Office and continues to desire to join this TACA Diocese, shall agree in writing to become subject to the Constitution and Canons of TACA.

Canon 2: Clergy, Parish-Level Governance, and Pastoral Guidance

Section 1—The Pastor, Rector, or Senior Pastor of a Congregation may be selected by the Congregation's governing authority (e.g., Vestry, Clergy) or other duly constituted squad assembled by the Congregation for such purpose. The Pastor, Rector, or Senior Pastor shall select all assistant clergy, who shall serve at his pleasure. A prayerful process shall be undertaken in the calling of this official to his Congregation, whereof the Congregation's coordinators shall thus consult with the Archbishop before extending an offer to a candidate. The relationship between the Pastor, Rector, or Senior Pastor and the Congregation is one of affirmed mutual trust and dependence fulfilling the ministerial needs of the religious Body at hand. As the leader of the Congregation, the Pastor, Rector, or Senior Pastor should have the full cooperation and support of the Congregation. That religious Body, in turn, should expect their spiritual leader to model the servant leadership required of all in the basic proclamations and principles of the Constitution of this TACA Diocese (Matthew 10:28). In all circumstances, the Pastor, Rector, or Senior Pastor and the Congregation shall observe the principles of mutual submission called for by the Apostle Paul in Romans 12:10; Ephesians 5:21; Galatians 5:26; and 1 Peter 5:5.

Section 2—The Pastor, Rector, or Senior Pastor and such other members of the Congregation, selected according to the Congregation's bylaws, or appointed by the Archbishop or House of Bishops, shall constitute the Congregation's governing Body.

Section 3—Except for reason of age or disability, a Pastor, Rector, or Senior Pastor may not resign as a Pastor, Rector, or Senior Pastor without giving the remainder of the Congregation's governing Body such notice as it may require. A Pastor, Rector, or Senior Pastor may not be removed against his will except as hereinafter provided or as provided in Canon 3 of this Title of this Canon.

Section 4—Whenever a Pastor, Rector, or Senior Pastor or a majority of the remainder of the Congregation's governing Body believe the pastoral relationship between the Pastor, Rector, or Senior Pastor and the Congregation to be imperiled or hindered by reason of dissension, either or both may present the matter to the Archbishop.

Section 5—Upon notification of such imperilment or hindrance, the Archbishop shall promptly seek reconciliation by whatever means he believes appropriate. The Archbishop, or his appointee for this cause, shall hold conferences with the Pastor, Rector, or Senior Pastor and the remainder of the

Title II: Organizations and Administration of TACA Religious Bodies/Ministries

Congregation's governing Body, who shall participate cooperatively in the process. The Archbishop may issue such interim recommendations appropriate to the cause before issuing a final judgment. Prior to issuing a final judgment, the Archbishop shall consult with the House of Bishops and the Canon of this TACA Diocese. The House of Bishops may hold a Formal Meeting(s) or conference(s) with the Congregation's governing Body before rendering its advice to the Archbishop. At such conferences, the parties may be heard or be represented by a person(s) of their choice.

Section 6—The final judgment shall be made by the Archbishop, after praying over the matter and taking the recommendations of the Congregation's governing Body and of the House of Bishops and the Canon of this TACA Diocese into consideration. The recommendations of the Congregation's governing Body and the Council of this TACA Diocese may include a leave of absence for the Pastor, Rector, or Senior Pastor, a continuation of the pastoral relationship on a provisional basis, or a dissolution of the pastoral relationship.

Section 7—If the relationship is to be dissolved, the terms of judgment may include terms and conditions for compliance by both parties that are just and compassionate. The Pastor, Rector, or Senior Pastor or the remainder of the Congregation's governing Body may petition the Archbishop and House of Bishops of this TACA Diocese for a review and modification of the conditions for compliance of the judgment. The Archbishop shall in all cases render pastoral support to the Pastor, Rector, or Senior Pastor. Upon the Archbishop's judgment of dissolution of the pastoral

Title II: Organizations and Administration of TACA Religious Bodies/Ministries

relationship between the Pastor, Rector, or Senior Pastor and the Congregation, the Archbishop shall direct the Secretary of this TACA Diocese to record the dissolution.

Section 8—If, at the time of a need for episcopal intervention in the relationship between a portion of the Congregation's governing Body and a Pastor, Rector, or Senior Pastor, there be no Archbishop, Coadjutor, or Suffragan, the House of Bishops of this TACA Diocese shall assume Ecclesiastical Authority over this matter and hold a Formal Meeting or Council to decide over this matter, under the provisions of this Canon.

Section 9—If, for any reason, the Pastor, Rector, or Senior Pastor shall refuse to comply with the judgment of the Archbishop (or, as per Section 8, the Ecclesiastical Authority), the Archbishop/Ecclesiastical Authority may suspend the Pastor, Rector, or Senior Pastor from the exercise of ministry within this TACA Diocese until he complies with the judgment. In the case of the Congregation's governing Body refusing to comply with authoritative judgment, the Archbishop/Ecclesiastical Authority may convert the Congregation from a Church or Parish to a Mission, or into another religious Body that is of lesser ecclesiastical standing than a Church or Parish, until the Congregation has complied with the judgment or has conveyed formal written declaration to depart from this TACA Diocese.

Section 10—If the dissolution of the pastoral relationship between the Pastor, Rector, or Senior Pastor and the Congregation concerns and affects the

Title II: Organizations and Administration of TACA Religious Bodies/Ministries

physical occupation by the Congregation of a house of worship (e.g., church, chapel, or other structure formally containing TACA religious services) that is owned by the Pastor, Rector, or Senior Pastor, or by any party whose interests or intentions fall at variance with the rule of the Constitution and Canons, the Archbishop, may freely deign to pay an Episcopal visit to desanctify that property as a TACA Church, Mission, or Parish, while renaming the *sede vacante* jurisdiction for operation in a different or nearby location, or dissolving the Church or Parish as a TACA entity altogether.

Canon 3: Removal of the Pastor, Rector, or Senior Pastor

A Congregation may request the consent of the Archbishop to remove, for cause, the Pastor, Rector, or Senior Pastor from his office, only after showing that sufficient cause for removal exists. If a portion of the Congregation's governing Body desires the Archbishop to remove the Pastor, Rector, or Senior Pastor for cause, it shall give prior notice to the Archbishop and provide an opportunity for him to consult with all or a portion of the Congregation's governing Body prior to any action in the circumstances. As used in this Canon, the term "cause" shall mean the Pastor, Rector, or Senior Pastor has been convicted of a crime or offense involving moral wrongdoing, or the Congregation's governing Body has been presented with evidence that it deems substantial and credible of any of the following: (a) the commission of a crime involving moral wrongdoing; (b) habitual insobriety or drug addiction; (c) dishonest or fraudulent conduct; (d) embezzlement, theft, or intentional destruction of property; or (e) sexual misconduct.

Canon 4: Organization and Business Affairs of a Congregation or Mission

Section 1—Congregations and other religious Bodies shall incorporate under the laws of the jurisdiction where they are located, and each shall be so named according to the name only of itself as that Body. This TACA Diocese, which is the sanctifier of a solely religious bonding with each TACA Body, shall have no entitlement that is titular, nominal, or functionary in relation to or in any part of that incorporation.

Section 2—Every member of the Congregation's governing Body in every Parish and religious Body shall orally pledge their agreement with the Primacy of Scripture in the attainment of Salvation, and express solemn belief that this truth is epitomized by our TACA Diocese and Synod. This pledge may be previously written by that Body, or the following proclamation and covenant may be confessed aloud:

> **Regular Version:**
>
> "I pledge, Almighty Father, to submit myself to the truth, that the Holy Scriptures of the Old and New Testaments are the Word of God, which contains all things necessary for Salvation. I ask of your Grace to place deep within me the Spirit of holiness; that I may henceforth be included in this Traditional Anglican Church of America, as this inclusion comes from You, O God. By the example of the manner of life of Jesus Christ,

and with the power of the Holy Ghost, may You instill in me upright conformity to the Discipline, Doctrine, and Worship of Christ, as this Church has witnessed them. Amen."

Extraordinary Version:

"I faithfully and devotedly believe the Holy Bible to be, without question, the Word of God. I profess at all times that the Holy Scriptures, of the Old and New Testaments, perfectly set forth the unparalleled and loving deposit of Christian Faith. I heartily therefore contend, with unwavering gratitude and lifelong praise to the Triune God, that Sacred Scripture institutes the perfect foundation for Sacred Tradition by which the irresistible gift of God's Grace may show forth abundantly throughout all my works. As I indelibly hold that God's Holy Word contains all things that are necessary for Salvation, I profess my exuberant accord to the unceasing promise of Revelation, and I faithfully assent to follow excellently the example of the life and perfect sacrifice offered by Jesus Christ, my crucified, risen, and ascended Savior, as my lifelong rule. I yield to the discipline, and to the worship, of Jesus Christ, just as this Traditional Anglican Church of America has received them, and as it has accepted its calling to shepherd my vocation to serve, as I seek unblemished fellowship with God, in humble gratitude for the Communion of His Saints. I will loyally and faithfully lead and set out as the Holy Ghost has called me, as a member of this religious Body, always and to the utmost of my ability. Amen."

Title II: Organizations and Administration of TACA Religious Bodies/Ministries

Section 3—The Congregation's governing Body shall be responsible for the management of the Congregation's business affairs, including the following:

a) Aiding the Pastor, Rector, or Senior Pastor and his family, to offset the expenses of running the Church. Such help may include contributions from received tithes and money gifted to his personal retirement plan or pension.

b) A sustainable place for worship as part of the official sanctuary and an appropriate section where Congregation members may access Bibles, prayer books, and hymnals.

c) The programming of music, which shall be under the final authority of the Pastor, Rector, or Senior Pastor.

d) The financial compensation of all hired or stipended affiliates (e.g., janitor, groundskeeper, organist, etc.).

e) An adequate, sensible business plan reflecting sound accounting and record-keeping practices, financial goals, strategic programs, resource budgeting, expense reporting, personnel coordination, a diligent contact-management or database program, member/parishioner data-keeping, form production, time management, software utilization, efficient documentation and filing systems, optimized evangelization strategies, mixed media, Liturgical/diocesan-calendar integration, and attention to regulatory or government status updates.

Title II: Organizations and Administration of TACA Religious Bodies/Ministries

- f) Compliance with the Constitution and Canons of our TACA Diocese and Congregation bylaws.

- g) Establishment of a biblically focused program of financial and in-kind giving by members of the Congregation.

- h) Development of catechesis and Bible instruction and education of Laity.

- i) Support of the Pastor, Rector, or Senior Pastor in all areas of his ministry.

- j) Reasonable approval of and compliance with all contracts and other obligations entered into by the Congregation.

- k) Charitable personal growth, by and large, to lighten one another's burdens, being a good, exemplary, wise, helpful Christian church-family member to one another.

Title III: Administration and Sacramental Worship in Congregations and Other Religious Bodies of This TACA Diocese

TITLE III: Administration and Sacramental Worship in Congregations and Other Religious Bodies of This TACA Diocese

Canon 1: As Regards Translations of the Bible

Public worship shall consist of Lessons that shall be read solely from the King James Version of the Holy Bible and the King James Apocrypha. The reading during public worship of other translations of the Sacred Scripture must be authorized and approved solely by the Archbishop, who shall refuse any translation that does not conform overall, in language and in spirit, with the text of the King James Bible.

Canon 2: As Regards the Book of Common Prayer

Section 1—The Book of Common Prayer as set forth by the United States Episcopal Church in 1928 (BCP/1928). The BCP/1928 shall contain the sections that appear in its Table of Contents, as paraphrased or abbreviated, with original page numbers from that year: the Ratification (iv); the Preface (v); Service of the Church (vii); Psalm and Lessons of the Year (x); the Calendar (xlvi); Tables and Rules for Feasts and Days (l) ; Tables of Precedence (li); Tables for Holy Days (lii); Concerning Service/Original 1928 Book (lix); Lessons/Christian Year (lxiii); Ordinal Morning Prayer (3); Ordinal Evening Prayer (21); Prayers/Thanksgivings (35); the Litany (54); Ordinal Penitential Ash Wednesday (60); Ordinal Holy Communion (67); Collects, Epistles, Gospels (90); Holy Baptism (273); Office of Instruction (283); Ordinal Confirmation (296); Solemnization of Matrimony (300); Thanksgiving Women/Childbirth (305); Ordinal Visitation Sick (308); Ordinal Burial Dead (324); Burial of Child (338); the

Title III: Administration and Sacramental Worship in Congregations and Other Religious Bodies of This TACA Diocese

Psalter (345); Ordination/Consecration Clergy/Bishops (529); Form Consecration Church/Chapel (563); Ordinal/Institution of Minsters at Parishes/Churches (569); Catechism (577); Family Prayer (587); Articles of Religion (603).

Section 2—It is known that there is a diversity of prayer books and Liturgies in the Church. Besides the preexistence of other standard canonical editions of the Book of Common Prayer, i.e., the eight editions preceding and including the 1928 printing, there are many other Liturgies that are still utilized by other orthodox Christian churches (e.g., the Divine Liturgy of Saint John Chrysostom or of Saint Basil). Our TACA Diocese permits the use in public worship of any American and English Anglican/Episcopalian books that were published respectively in the years of 1793, 1822, 1832, 1838, 1845, 1871, 1892, and 1928, all of which shall hereafter be known as TACA-BCP/Versions. No versions published later than 1928 are permitted for use by religious bodies in this TACA Diocese. Use in public worship of different orthodox Anglican/Episcopalian prayer books, such as an American or English Missal of the Anglo-Catholic and High-Church Style (Anglo-H/C books), shall be permitted only by permission of the Archbishop and only if they are exact versions of ably-tried texts that have long reflected the orthodoxy promulgated by the Saint Louis Affirmation of 1978 (O/SLA books). Prayer Books, Liturgies, and Missals different from the TACA-BCP/Versions of any Anglican-Continuum dioceses that are outside of TACA are not permitted for use by religious bodies in this TACA Diocese. Use of sections of Missals, Liturgies, and Prayer Books that are different from TACA-BCP/Versions or the Anglo-H/C books, but which reflect the conservative tone, language, and essence of O/SLA books (e.g., Celtic prayers or Eastern Orthodox Divine Liturgies), may be employed in religious bodies of this TACA Diocese only by permission of the Archbishop.

Canon 3: As Regards Due Celebration of the Lord's Day

All members of all religious bodies of this TACA Diocese are called to celebrate and keep the Lord's Day by regular participation in public worship, by hearing the Word of God read and taught, by partaking of the Sacrament of Holy Communion, and by other acts of devotion and deeds of charity, according to God's holy will and pleasure.

Canon 4: As Regards the Administration of the Gospel Sacraments

Section 1—Considerare Sacramenta Domenicalia, Sacramentum Evangelii, e Sacramentum Religionis:

a) The Sacraments of Holy Communion and Holy Baptism shall be administered by the duly ordained and licensed clergy of this TACA Diocese in accordance with their order of ministry. This provision shall not preclude the administration of Emergency Baptism by any baptized person.

b) Our Sacred Tradition to follow Baptism with Confirmation not only is guided by the ordinals for these offices in our Book of Common Prayer but also shines forth in God's Word in John 14:15-26 and John 20:22. Our Anglican

Title III: Administration and Sacramental Worship in Congregations and Other Religious Bodies of This TACA Diocese

convention is thus to fittingly abide Section 2 of this Canon.

Section 2—As Regards Christian Formation: All Clergy shall take care that all within their Congregations and Missions are instructed in the discipline, sacraments, and doctrine of Jesus Christ, as God has commanded and as they are set forth in the Holy Scriptures, in the 1928 Book of Common Prayer (1928/BCP), with the 1928/BCP Catechism or Office of General Instruction, or in any Catechism that shall specifically be approved only by the Archbishop for use by all members of this TACA Diocese.

Section 3—As regards Holy Communion:

a) Only Bishops and Priests shall preside at the Celebration of the Gospel Sacrament of Holy Communion.

b) All Christians who have been baptized with water (when available), in the name of the Triune God—i.e., in the name of the Father, and of the Son, and of the Holy Ghost—are welcome to receive in this TACA Diocese the Sacrament of Holy Communion as it pertains to a member's oral receipt of the consecrated Eucharistic Bread (or Host) and Wine and his or her rightness and worthiness to receive the Supper of the Lord.

c) *Refusal to Dispense:* Such that the Communicant and Officiant (i.e., the Christian and the Bishop or Priest of Section 3 of this Canon), who shall be collaboratively serving, and eating and drinking this consubstantial Supper of the Lord, intends that he or she is participating in this Gospel Sacrament of Holy Communion as it is a simultaneously spiritual and appetitive Trinitarian Christian act, an Officiant may refuse to dispense both the Bread (Host) and the Wine to the Communicant for the following reasons that would substantiate that the Communicant's obdurate and unrepentant moral turpitude, and/or his or her idolatry, and state of Mortal Sin, shall designate unfitness to receive this Sacrament: a demonstrably fixated disdain for God's omnipotence to redeem him or her; a professed intention to live fatuously in a state of sin; a professed disbelief in God or in the Real Presence; and, failure to be theologically and/or morally commensurate with the Officiant's expectation that any Exhortation spoken during the Liturgy of the Eucharist would be an appropriate prayer to aid the Communicant's seeking of Redemption. In this regard, the Officiant must be willing to state to the Archbishop that he, as the presider over Holy Communion, has employed these criteria to determine that the Communicant has professed or proven via sanely repeated speech, actions, and/or writing that he or she refuses to seek Salvation in general and/or via a sincere demonstration of participation in and receipt of the Sacrament of Holy Communion as it is defined in this Section 3 of Canon 4 of Title III. To be sure, no practitioners or supporters of Abortion, Murder, or any persons remaining unrepentant in a state of Mortal Sin, or who are publicly and fervently supporters of the practice of Mortal Sin, may receive any Gospel,

Domenical (Sunday-given), or Religious Sacrament, or be a member of any part of this TACA Diocese (see Constitution, Title I, Section K, iv-xii) (Revelation 22:15).

d) The admission of baptized young children to the Holy Communion is allowed in this TACA Diocese. It is not first required that they undergo catechesis and Confirmation.

Canon 5: As Regards the Music of the Congregation or Mission

It shall be the obligation of the Pastor, Rector, or Senior Pastor of a Congregation or Mission to appoint Psalms, hymns, and spiritual songs for use, which are appropriate for worship. The Pastor, Rector, or Senior Pastor is the final authority in the Congregation or Mission over all matters concerning music, but may delegate the appointment of Psalms, hymns, and/or spiritual songs to the Choir Director, Music Director, or Cantor, at his discretion.

Canon 6: As Regards Lay Agency

Lay persons may be permitted, as unpaid participants or unpaid appointed agents of a Ministry, to assist the Clergy and other Vestry members in various tasks to further the ministering of the Word and charitable works. Lay helpers may not bear the title of "Minister," but they may be encouraged by our grateful Ecclesiastical Authority of this TACA Diocese to relish the Grace and enhanced Fellowship associated with their aid.

Title III: Administration and Sacramental Worship in Congregations and Other Religious Bodies of This TACA Diocese

Canon 7: As Regards Christian Marriage

Section 1—Because marriage is a lifelong covenant solely transacted between a man and a woman, God affirms that the two shall become one flesh (Matthew 19:5-6). Holy Matrimony is then a natural ordinance of Creation, which is affirmed by God to be both as instinctive as the need for water and sunlight, and—as also commended by Saint Paul the Apostle—a sign of the mystical union between Christ and His Church (Matthew 19:3-9; Ephesians 5:22-32; Deuteronomy 31:35-40). Our TACA Diocese thereby affirms our Lord's teaching that Holy Matrimony is in its nature a union permanent and lifelong solely between one man and one woman, who choose to marry, while others shall remain celibate (Matthew 19:10-11; 1 Corinthians 7:2).

Section 2—Members of the Clergy of this TACA Diocese shall conform to these Canons and Constitution, while abiding the will of Christ that an orthodox Church shall preside at the Solemnization of Holy Matrimony, according to the following constraints:

  a) The two communicants to be married shall be a man and a woman, respectively, who are each currently neither yet married to one another nor to anyone. There shall be made no exceptions.

  b) Both the man and the woman shall have been baptized. Permission to marry a non-baptized person shall be given or refused only by the Archbishop.

Title III: Administration and Sacramental Worship in Congregations and Other Religious Bodies of This TACA Diocese

    c) There shall be given twenty-one (21) days' notice of the intention to marry unless waived for solemn reasons, whereupon the Archbishop shall be notified immediately and in writing.

    d) The Clergy shall provide counsel to both parties on Holy Matrimony with respect to theological and social considerations and responsibilities.

    e) The Clergy shall ascertain that the man and the woman, as parties to the marriage, have a valid unexpired marriage license that is made out in each of their full names.

    f) It shall be within the discretion of any member of the Clergy, to decline to solemnize any marriage. He must be ready to explain his reason, if called forth to explain his reasons to Ecclesiastical Authority, and shall know well how his purposes for refusal reflect well-grounded biblical reasoning and project the best practices and moral strictures defined by these Constitution and Canons.

    g) The time between the end of one marriage (see Section 4 of this Title III) and a remarriage for either or both parties must be no less than one year, unless approved by the Archbishop.

Section 3—The Office of the Archbishop shall develop and maintain a Customary on Marriage, consistent with the teaching of Holy Scripture, the Constitution of this Diocese, and these Constitution and Canons of TACA.

Title III: Administration and Sacramental Worship in Congregations and Other Religious Bodies of This TACA Diocese

Section 4—Circumstances Permitting Dissolution of Matrimony, or Qualifying Permission to Remarry.

a) Adultery on the part of one's previous spouse.

b) Abandonment by the previous spouse or, in the case of effectual abandonment, when the Divorce proceedings were conducted by law in the absence of the abandoning spouse.

c) Homosexuality or bisexuality by one's former spouse, gender reassignment, transgenderism, pedophilia, incest, bestiality, necrophilia, nymphomania or sexual addiction, pornographic addiction, fetishistic disorder, grave marital disruption because of support of social or political attachments to sexually perverse associations or movements, or other serious sexual perversions of the former spouse.

d) Finding, after the fact, that the former spouse was a near blood relation, such as a mother, father, sister, brother, first cousin, aunt, uncle, grandparent, stepsister, stepbrother, stepfather, or stepmother.

e) Use of a false identity by the former spouse to perpetrate fraud against the spouse or legal fraud; or, that legal fraud was found to have been perpetrated by the former spouse, such as in the case of marriage for the purpose of gaining access to financial means, or to attain immigration, fraudulently.

Title III: Administration and Sacramental Worship in Congregations and Other Religious Bodies of This TACA Diocese

f) Criminal activity or conspiracy by the former spouse, or the former spouse's commission of a safety issue or violation against the spouse or children.

g) Sexual impotence or unwillingness to physically consummate by the former spouse, having gone unreported before the marriage.

h) Critical psychological issues, such as insanity or a severe personality disorder characterizing the former spouse, including, but not limited to, psychopathy, sadism, dangerous borderline personality disorder, sexual disorder, narcissism, Machiavellianism, or deliberately untreated bipolar disorder, schizophrenia, or other severe untreated mental and/or emotional disorder.

i) Addiction to drugs, alcohol, or other addictive substances on the part of the former spouse.

j) The former spouse was never baptized and this was discovered after the fact, or the Divorce was filed because marital irreconcilability arose over the former spouse joining another religion besides Christianity after the fact.

k) The person was forced into marriage by the former spouse and/or associates or kin of the former spouse.

l) The person was underage at the time of the marriage and therefore not legally competent to enter into a marriage.

m) As regards rape.

n) Due to human depravity and the mystery of iniquity, there may be other issues not contained within this section that would substantiate a valid, moral, and biblical justification for Divorce that would allow for remarriage. In such cases, an appeal must be made to the Archbishop of this TACA Diocese.

o) Pastoral attention must always pay mindful heed to statutory requirements regarding each State's determination of the legal age for marriage, by which the TACA Congregation or Mission shall always abide.

Section 5—Ecclesiastical Annulment.

The Archbishop of TACA, who is the sole religious grantor of the Annulment of the marital bond, shall determine whether any circumstances in the marriage, as set forth in Section 4, parts a)-n) of this Canon 7, shall prove that a writ of Annulment may be granted for its applicant(s); provided, however, that the applicant(s) for a writ of Annulment by the Archbishop must already have been granted a proper civil Divorce by the appropriate civil authority(-ies).

Section 6—Ecclesiastical Annulment.

An Annulment is hereby deemed a canonical procedure by which the TACA Archbishop voids a marriage and declares it null from its inception. Unlike Divorce, which is a civil dissolution of matrimony that cannot

Title III: Administration and Sacramental Worship in Congregations and Other Religious Bodies of This TACA Diocese

be blessed, the effect of declaring a marriage void is levied retroactively, decreeing that the marriage was void at the time it was entered into.

- a) Basing his authority on the Holy Bible, these Constitution and Canons, and Church Tradition, the Archbishop shall also grant an Ecclesiastical Annulment as regards the dissolution of any thusly voided marriage that permits the remarriage of the Christian whose marriage is to be annulled.

- b) The Archbishop shall employ profound gravity in considering annulling a marital bond. Prayerfully seeking wisdom from God, he must realize that he may not be in possession of the nearly countless facts of any case. He will base his decision upon the guidance he receives from the Holy Bible, these Constitution and Canons, and Church Tradition, while always being grateful for the inspiration of the Holy Ghost through prayer.

- c) Any person who wishes to receive an Annulment in order to remarry, must provide the appropriate documentation showing that he or she has been properly civilly divorced, and that person must explain that he or she has good and sufficient reason for an ecclesiastical Annulment. He or she shall accept that the decision as to whether to grant or deny an Annulment, made solely by the Archbishop, shall be final and cannot be appealed.

d) In applying for an Annulment, the applicant shall provide the Archbishop with a letter stating the history of the previous marriage, reasons for the dissolution of the marital bond, court documents, and other information that the Archbishop shall request.

e) An Annulment shall in no way be granted, nor shall a remarriage be permitted by this TACA Church, on the grounds that the previous marriage was dissolved based upon emotional incompatibility, unless the husband and/or wife had been underage minor children. Inappropriate reasons for declaring incompatibility as the cause for requesting an Annulment may include, but are not necessarily limited to, the following excuses: not getting along, being too young, falling out of love, not being happy, failing to find oneself, yearning to seek one's true soul mate, boredom, adultery on the part of the person requesting the Annulment, or other such excuses.

Section 7—Clergy and Episcopal Divorce and Remarriage.

a) Ordained and Consecrated men must be held to a higher standard than appointed members or members of the Laity. If an Ordained and Consecrated man has been divorced for the following offenses that were perpetrated by him, he shall not be retained in the ministry:

i. Adultery;

ii. Abandonment of his spouse;

iii. Critical psychological issues (as detailed in the Constitution, Article I, Part K, Sec. xv; and Title III, Canon 7, Sec. 3);

iv. Fraud;

v. Rape;

vi. Sexual perversion (as defined in the Constitution, Article I, Part K, Sec. xv; Item i, No. 1;

vii. Any unrepented Mortal Sins and/or Abominable Sins.

b) Ordained and Consecrated men are permitted to remarry after being widowed. They may be allowed to remarry in the case of Divorce if they are the innocent party (as regards a Presentment of Complaint in the civil Divorce).

c) The Archbishop and all bishops shall be very strict but mercifully pastoral in handling cases of Divorce and/or remarriage.

Canon 8: As Regards Standards of Sexual Morality, Gender Reality, and Ethics

Section 1—Members of the Clergy, Episcopate, and Lay leadership of this TACA Diocese are called to be exemplary in all considerations of morality, as a condition of receiving and retaining Ordination, Consecration, or Appointment and Office.

Title III: Administration and Sacramental Worship in Congregations and Other Religious Bodies of This TACA Diocese

Section 2—Sexual intercourse should take place only between a man and a woman, who are married to each other. In view of the teaching of Holy Scripture, this TACA Diocese upholds faithfulness in marriage between a man and a woman in lifelong marriage and believes that abstinence is right for those who are not called to marriage. Therefore, this TACA Diocese cannot legitimize or bless same-sex unions or bless associations that its agents intend to be known as "marriage" (e.g., cohabitation); nor, since Holy Scripture is clear on the consequences of such behavior (1 Corinthians: 9; 1 Timothy 1:10), shall this Diocese ever ordain any person who engages in any sexual activity outside of the boundary of marriage, as described in the Constitution, Article I, Part K, Sec. iv, Part d; Sec. xi.

Section 3—God, and not man, is the creator of human Life. Therefore, consistent with the Constitution, Article I, Part K, Sec. Pref., i, iii, all members and clergy are called to promote and respect the sanctity of human Life, from conception to natural death, knowing unlawful killing of another human being to be murder, and knowing premeditated murder of another adult human being and any Elective Procured infant Abortion of a human infant, to be homicides. This provision, specifically concerning the sanctity of life until natural death, does not, however, preclude the lawfulness of capital punishment, or the God-given right of the State to execute violent criminal offenders.

Title III: Administration and Sacramental Worship in Congregations and Other Religious Bodies of This TACA Diocese

Section 4—Each Congregation and Mission of this TACA Diocese is called upon to show Christlike compassion to those who have fallen into sin, encouraging them to repent and receive forgiveness, and offering counseling and charity to all who suffer emotionally or physically as a result of such sin.

TITLE IV: Ministers, Their Recruitment, Preparation, Ordination, Office, Practice, and Transfer

Canon 1: As Regards Holy Orders and Appointments in this TACA Diocese

Section 1—This TACA Diocese affirms what the ancient Church has always known Ecclesiastical Authority to be, as commonly sensible: namely, the uniformity and sufficiency of the Threefold Office of Prophet, Priest, and King. This ministry of Christ corresponds, for pastoral uses, to the offices of Archbishop/Bishop, Priest, and Deacon ("Ecclesiastical History"; Book I; Ch. 3; Part 8; Eusebius; A.D. 312) Only adult men shall be admitted to the offices of Bishop, Priest, or Ordained Deacon in this TACA Diocese (i.e., minimum age of 35 if a Bishop, and 25 if a Priest or ordained Deacon). These are men who have been called, examined, and ordained or consecrated according to the 1928 Book of Common Prayer. They may also have been ordained or consecrated in a church whose orders are recognized and accepted by this TACA Diocese. Only adult women are to be made Appointed Deaconesses, appointed according to the "Form for the Setting Apart of Deaconesses" in the 1949 Book of Offices: Services for Certain Occasions, or through a Customary or benediction by a Bishop. Appointed Deaconesses may also consist of Deaconesses appointed in a church whose orders are recognized and accepted by this TACA Diocese. Each candidate for ministerial office in this TACA Diocese shall be provided a copy of these Constitution and Canons and shall receive a fair written or oral introduction to this TITLE IV: Canon 2 and the same review to the Constitution, Articles V, VII,

Title IV: Ministers, Their Recruitment, Preparation, Ordination, Office, Practice, and Transfer

X, and XI. Should they wish to continue seeking ordination, consecration, appointment, reception, or incardination, as appropriate, they shall follow the process established by the Archbishop and to whom he delegates such authority, in accordance with these Canons. The process of ordination, consecration, reception, and incardination shall include an independent background check covering the following: the checking of all references and previous employers for the previous ten (10) years, credit reports, records from the Department of Motor Vehicles, and a complete criminal background records check to include the Sexual Predators Directory.

Section 2—No person shall be received as Clergy in this TACA Diocese until they shall have obliged and passed a proper written and oral examination and practicum issued by the Archbishop's Office and Training Officer, and unless they agree to subscribe to the following pledge:

> **Regular Version:**
>
> "I pledge, Almighty Father, to submit myself to the dignity of this Holy Office, believing that the Holy Scriptures of the Old and New Testaments are the Word of God, which contains all things necessary for Salvation. I ask of your Grace to place deep within me the Spirit of holiness; that I may henceforth be included for service in this Traditional Anglican Church of America, as this inclusion comes from You, O God. By the example of the manner of life of Jesus Christ, and with the power of the Holy Ghost, may You instill in me upright conformity to the

Discipline, Doctrine, and Worship of Christ, as this Church has witnessed them. Amen."

Extraordinary Version:

"God, our Almighty Father, I faithfully and devotedly believe the Holy Bible to be, without question, the Word of God. I profess at all times that the Holy Scriptures, of the Old and New Testaments, perfectly set forth the unparalleled and loving deposit of Christian Faith. I heartily therefore contend, with unwavering gratitude and lifelong praise to the Triune God, that Sacred Scripture institutes the perfect foundation for Sacred Tradition by which the irresistible gift of God's Grace may show forth abundantly throughout all my works. As I indelibly hold that God's Holy Word contains all things that are necessary for Salvation, I profess my exuberant accord to the unceasing promise of Revelation and I faithfully assent to follow excellently the example of the life and perfect sacrifice offered by Jesus Christ, my crucified, risen, and ascended Savior, as my lifelong rule. I yield to the discipline, and to the worship of Jesus Christ, just as this Traditional Anglican Church of America has witnessed them, and as it has accepted its calling to shepherd my vocation to serve, as I seek unblemished fellowship with God, in humble gratitude for the Communion of His Saints. I will loyally and faithfully lead and set out as the Holy Ghost has called me, in my life and ministry, and within this religious Body, always and to the utmost of my ability. Amen."

Title IV: Ministers, Their Recruitment, Preparation, Ordination, Office, Practice, and Transfer

Section 3—If the Archbishop has ascertained to his satisfaction that an applicant's qualifications prove soundness in matters theological, ministerial, and academic, and, after ascertaining diligent completion of examination as provided in the relevant Customary for Ordination, Consecration, Incardination, and/or Appointment, may issue the appropriate Reception of that applicant into this TACA Diocese, as provided in this Title IV of these Canons, and in the Constitution, Articles V, VII, X, and XI.

Section 4—If the Archbishop has ascertained to his satisfaction that a Bishop's qualifications prove soundness in matters theological, ministerial, and academic, he may receive Bishops from other jurisdictions outside of this TACA Diocese, after being fully satisfied that their beliefs truly reflect the orthodox Christian values and formularies of Continuing Anglicanism. A Bishop who has been thus received shall devote canonical obedience, in all matters honest and lawful, to the Archbishop of this TACA Diocese.

TITLE V: Ecclesiastical Discipline

Canon 1: Church Discipline

All members of the Clergy (i.e., Priests, Deacons, and Deaconesses) of this TACA Diocese, who shall exercise proper ministry within it shall be subject to the disciplinary principles and definitions of Title IV of these Canons and of the Constitution, Articles IV, V, VII, X, and XI, of this TACA Diocese. Every Lay member of this TACA Diocese shall be subject to the disciplinary customs of the 1928 Book of Common Prayer or any earlier version of this book that is authorized by the Archbishop.

Canon 2: Rule of Subsidiarity Under Ecclesiastical Authority

Discipline and order shall be governed and retained by each Congregation or Mission, each containing its own Customary on rules and procedures as it regards Ecclesiastical Discipline, so long as that Customary is authorized by the House of Bishops, who reasonably affirm that its rubrics abide the orthodoxy that is associated with these Constitution and Canons. (The House of Bishops may also be called, at any and all times, any of the other following appellations: Tribunal, Ecclesiastical Authority, Council, Trial Court).

Title V: Ecclesiastical Discipline

Canon 3: Affirming of Accordance with the Constitution and Canons

In conducting a review of any matter, perchance a Trial, or conference of entitlement or removal thereof, or any other action, Ecclesiastical Authority shall comply with all applicable provisions of these Constitutions and Canons.

TITLE VI: Adopting, Amending, and Revoking Canons

Canon 1: Power and Authority Over Amendments

Section 1—The Canons of this TACA Diocese or part(s) thereof may be amended or revoked by any Yearly or Regional Synod, or during any Formal Meeting called for that purpose, as allowed by the Archbishop, who has the sole authority to employ his authority and power to amend and/or revoke Canonical legislation. Advance notice of at least two weeks prior to the Formal Meeting must be issued before the occurrence of that meeting. No amendment shall be adopted until it has been reviewed by the Committee or the Ministry that has been commissioned by the Archbishop's Office to author and edit the Constitution and Canons of this TACA Diocese. In advance of any adoption, the final draft of that amendment or recommendations regarding it, must be issued to the House of Bishops and to all delegates of that Synod or Formal Meeting.

Section 2—The Constitution and Canons or part(s) thereof may only be amended or revoked by a two-thirds majority of the delegates present at a Yearly Synod or Regional Synod or Formal Meeting called to its purpose, provided it is allowed by the Archbishop, who has the sole authority to employ his authority and power to amend and revoke canonical legislation. It shall also be abided, thereto:

Section 3—The Archbishop shares or stays the sharing of his amending and decisional power. No party other than the Archbishop of TACA, as *Archiepiscopi Unilateralis*, may allow a vote or decision to amend or revoke a written entry to take place in these Constitution and Canons. Neither an individual member, nor members of a religious Body, nor a cross-section of TACA, nor the House of Bishops of TACA may have the authority or power to amend or revoke part(s) of the Constitution and Canons of this TACA Diocese, unless they have received the Archbishop's written permission. The Archbishop thus may deign to lend to said Formal Meeting or Synod the authority and power to amend and adopt or revoke, via its meeting and voting, the Constitution and Canons of this TACA Diocese. Alternatively:

Section 4—It is thus also by the Grace and pleasure of the Archbishop to share his power and authority (to write, edit, amend, and adopt or revoke part(s) of the Constitution and Canons of TACA) instead with only the House of Bishops. It would thus be his alternative unilateral choice to lend this dominion to a ballot given only to the House of Bishops. After voting to adopt or repeal said amendment, the Archbishop may ratify or veto the results of the vote.

Section 5—The Archbishop may ratify or veto any vote attained by any religious Body within TACA as regards amending or revoking any part(s) of these Constitution and Canons.

Section 6—Formal Meetings and voting as regards amending, writing, or changing the Constitution and Canons of this TACA Diocese shall follow the guidelines of the Constitution, Article XVI, of this TACA Diocese.

TITLE VII: Benefit and Usage of Customaries

Canon 1: A Customary, Defined and Usage Explained

Section 1—As described in these Constitution and Canons, a Customary is a set of standards, procedures, and guidelines employed to establish governance and Subsidiarity within religious bodies within the Diocese. Consistent with Holy Scripture, it affirms the Constitution and Canons of this TACA Diocese as regards any religious Body and any given circumstance hereof.

Section 2—The guidance of Customaries, instead of Canon Law, to ensure alignment with the mission and ministry of this TACA Diocese allows for the formalizing of certain processes of governance that are judged necessary by the Office of the Archbishop, without the need for Canonical amendment or revocation to adjust those processes that no longer best serve the interests of the mission and ministry of this TACA Diocese. This Subsidiarity allows for a more natural and relational approach to the normative governance of this Church. As regards the governance of this TACA Diocese, the Archbishop, the House of Bishops, the Clergy, the Laity—as one autonomous constituent Synod in theological Communion with other churches, such as the Emmanuel Communion of Indiantown, Florida—functions to advise and enjoy fellowship throughout this TACA Synod and shall operate under the authority of Holy Scripture, and within the discipline of these Constitution and Canons.

TITLE VIII: Public, Legal, Fiscal Identities

Section 1—Traditional Anglican Church of America, or TACA, when it is defined as a legal or fiscal entity is solely a broad-based or grassroots spiritual fellowship that is enjoyed by various churches and other religious Bodies knowing themselves to be "Traditionalist Anglican."

Section 2—All fiscal doings, public filings, and legal incorporations are solely conducted by and for the respective authority of each religious fellowship church or religious Body, such as a Parish or Congregation, each operating under its own independent pastoral leadership conducting its own independent affairs.

Section 3—Said entity calling itself Traditional Anglican Church of America, or TACA, has no—and shall have no—legal or fiscal responsibility or liability toward any other entity within said fellowship or elsewhere, nor any expectation as regards legal, political, employment (e.g., hiring or firing), payment, compensation, or indemnification of any kind.

Section 4—Each religious Body operates with complete legal and fiscal independence from Ecclesiastical Authority within this TACA Diocese. The use of the word "subsidiarity" or "subsidiary" refers solely to the broad-based fellowship that defines this TACA Diocese that is entirely spiritual in its relationships and theological or religious in its shared communications.

Section 5—The name "Traditional Anglican Church of America" or "TACA" shall not be used except to refer to

Title VIII: Public, Legal, Fiscal, Identities

the grassroots and broad-based spiritual fellowship identity of this TACA Diocese. Name usage is limited to common verbal usage of a nature that is referential, social, religious, or theological. Name usage may not be written or spoken for purposes of profit or non-profit ventures, personal or enterprise endorsement, political endeavors, online or electronic identification and domains, promotions of concrete/abstract property, public or monetary filings of a nature that is legal, corporate, business, or advertising or marketing, or any other such nature or kind, and as regards any domain, property, or possession.

Section 6—Definitions and principles regarding name usage, legal and corporate filings, permissions, entity identity, and the fiscal and legal autonomy of each religious Body within this TACA Diocese, which is a grassroots and broad-based spiritual fellowship, are located in the Constitution, Articles IX, XII, XIII, and XIV, of this TACA Diocese.

Certification

CERTIFICATION:

It is Hereby Certified: That at a Formal Meeting of the House of Bishops held on the date of September 19, 2023, as officiated by His Excellency, the Archbishop Most Reverend Doctor Rick Aaron Reid, who, as being honorably served by the Religious and Lay adult communicants held in good standing as qualified Electors and Delegates, it has been thus decided to adopt and ratify these __1__ (-st/-nd/-rd/-th) Constitution and Canons to be our written rules and practices, which govern the diocesan policy, structure, and procedure of this Traditional Anglican Church of America.

_____
Archbishop of Traditional Anglican Church of America

_____
Secretary and/or Registrar of Traditional Anglican Church of America

www.ingramcontent.com/pod-product-compliance
Lightning Source LLC
Chambersburg PA
CBHW050325010526
44119CB00003B/111